TRAVELS

WITH

HENRY

TRAVELS WITH HENRY

Richard Valeriani

Illustrated with Cartoons
and Photographs

BOSTON

HOUGHTON MIFFLIN COMPANY   1979

Library of Congress Cataloging in Publication Data
Valeriani, Richard.
  Travels with Henry.
  1. Kissinger, Henry Alfred—Journeys.   2. Statesmen
—United States—Biography.   3. United States—
Foreign relations—1969-1974.   4. United States—
Foreign relations—1974-1977.   5. Valeriani, Richard.
I. Title.
E840.8.K58V34   973.924′092′4 [B]   78-31577
ISBN 0-395-27091-X

Printed in the United States of America

V 10 9 8 7 6 5 4 3 2 1

This book probably
should have been dedicated
to the boys on the plane.
But for reasons they will
all understand, it is dedicated
instead — with love — to
Kathie Berlin, my joy
and inspiration.

ACKNOWLEDGMENTS

Many people contributed their recollections to this book, and I'm grateful to them.

I have trusted the accuracy of their retrospection, mindful, however, of Dean Acheson's observation that he never saw a memorandum of conversation in which the author lost the argument.

I particularly want to acknowledge the contribution of Bruce van Voorst in helping to research and prepare this manuscript. As an experienced Kissinger-watcher himself, who traveled a third of a million miles as the able diplomatic correspondent for *Newsweek* magazine, van Voorst was uniquely equipped to make this contribution.

CONTENTS

8 pages of photographs follow page 180

TRAVELS
WITH
HENRY

The Vit and Visdom
of Henry Kissinger

Two tourists were standing outside the Sheraton Hotel in the resort town of Macuto, Venezuela, as I was walking in.

"Look," said one of them. "There's Richard Valeriani."

"Oh," said the other one. "Kissinger must be here."

More than 500,000 miles of travel went into helping produce that anecdote, which, as the former Secretary of State himself might say, has "the added virtue of being true."

I was one of the Kissinger 14 — one of the correspondents who traveled in the back of Henry Kissinger's plane on most of his frequent overseas missions.

Kissinger was a complex and fascinating personality. He was brilliant, witty, and charming. He could also be overbearing and thoughtless. He had the touch of genius. At times he also had a touch of slob.

When he walked up to the solitary microphone in the Great Hall of the People in Peking and delivered an eloquent and incisive after-dinner toast, you could be proud that this short, fat, German immigrant represented the United States. When you saw him on his plane, stuffing candies or pretzels or nuts or potato chips into his mouth,

drooling from the lips, or standing in the aisle chatting with correspondents with the fly of his baggy pants open, you wondered if this
was the same man who overpowered presidents and prime ministers
and kings with his intellect and disarmed them with his charm and
wit.

This man who had written about Metternich, Castlereagh, and
Talleyrand, this international celebrity who ran the State Department from his airborne office — this was the same man who badgered members of the Air Force crew for the copies of *Playboy* and
Penthouse they had brought on board.

For three years, Kissinger played a kind of diplomatic mating
game with members of the press. He tried to seduce us into writing
it his way. We tried to resist; we usually succeeded. But sometimes
so did he.

Curiously, despite all his careful nurturing of the press during his
years in Washington, he did not learn about some of the fundamentals of press reporting until 1975, when he had already been Secretary
of State for eighteen months, following more than four years as
National Security Affairs adviser at the White House.

The realization hit me during the second Israeli-Egyptian Shuttle.
The negotiations had not been going well. The lack of significant
progress was apparent in Kissinger's testiness as well as in the atmosphere in Aswan and Jerusalem.

Kissinger and Egyptian President Sadat had called newsmen in for
a picture-taking session following one of their evening meetings, and
as usual, the session turned into an impromptu news conference. The
American reporters pressed Sadat on a number of touchy subjects:
What about joint Egyptian-Israeli patrols? "Out of the question."
What about direct trade with Israel? "Absurd," snapped Sadat. It
was that kind of session, and Kissinger sat there looking more and
more pained, if not downright embarrassed.

The next morning, we were seated in the back of the plane waiting
to take off when he came storming back, complaining about our lack
of restraint and challenging us about "our responsibility on these
trips," wondering out loud "if it's really a good idea to take the press

along on every trip." He ranted at some length and finally suggested that we have a thorough discussion of the subject during the traditional off-the-record champagne session he always held with the traveling press on the flight back to Washington at the end of every mission.

As soon as we were airborne, I suggested to Kissinger's press spokesman, Ambassador Robert Anderson, that a group discussion would inevitably turn into a gang-bang — a confrontation between Kissinger and the traveling press — and that if he were serious about having a useful discussion of the matter, it would be better to do it on an individual basis.

Just a few minutes later, Anderson came to the back of the plane and said Kissinger wanted to see me before we landed. He was sitting in his cabin, facing forward across a small table next to his bunk, and I sat in a chair facing him. The anger was gone, but the anguish was not.

He explained that Sadat was "from a different culture" and didn't understand — could not understand — the ways of the American press, especially the way we acted. Why couldn't we show a little restraint? I tried to explain that it was Sadat's decision — and his — whether to invite us in, knowing full well that we would ask questions.

"Mr. Secretary," I said, "there's an axiom in our business that there is no such thing as a bad question. There are only bad answers. Once a news conference is under way," I told him, "you can't expect us to ask only the questions you would like asked. If you're worried about the questions, then you shouldn't have us in. It's as simple as that."

Kissinger suggested that perhaps he was briefing us too much. He was worried about how the stories out of Alexandria would look, what kind of signals would be sent to the Israelis. Perhaps it would be better if he didn't see us quite so often.

"That's up to you," I said. "We all know that you're in control of the flow of information. We try to find out as much as we can on the ground, but everybody recognizes that you set the tone for the reporting in your briefings. And," I reminded him, "if *you* don't brief frequently — if you leave an information void — it will be filled by others." I pointed out to him that the wire services (Associated Press, United Press International, and Reuters) have to file at least twice a day. They have a cycle for morning papers and a cycle for afternoon papers, and once they come on a trip like this, they have to write at least one story for each cycle. We television people do not have to send a report by satellite every night, I explained, only when there's significant news. But it's different with the wires.

Kissinger reflected for a moment, and then said, "Frankly, I can't really complain. The reporting has really been pretty good on this trip, pretty accurate." I thought to myself, He couldn't really object to that reporting, since he had been the source of much of it. And then he said a startling thing: "I know all of you are back there rooting for me to succeed."

"Mr. Secretary," I said immediately, "I don't want to sound harsh about this, but there's something I ought to explain. As American citizens, we may be sitting back there rooting for you to succeed. But as professional journalists, we don't care whether you succeed or fail!" It came out a little more blunt than I had intended.

Kissinger looked as though I had just told him the plane was landing in Albania.

"You can't be that objective," he argued.

"Mr. Secretary, that's our job as professionals," I said. "And even if we can't always be objective, we always try to be fair."

By then we were descending into Damascus. It was extremely bumpy. We fastened our seat belts, and Kissinger looked out the window, signaling, I guessed, that that was all he wanted to say on the subject. I got up to leave, but before I went, I threw in a quick question about the current negotiations.

Kissinger looked grim. "It's very painful," he said, using a word that was one of his favorites — and significantly so. "There's some progress," he said, "but it's moving too slowly, too painfully."

"Do you still think you'll get an agreement?"

"I don't know, there's still a chance." But the tone was heavily pessimistic, a foreshadowing of the eventual outcome of the mission and an extremely useful guide for me in my subsequent reporting, which was downbeat — in contrast to the reporting of some of my colleagues.

There are two footnotes to this incident:

I was telling one of my colleagues about my conversation with Kissinger, and I said I thought I had been rather blunt when I told him that we didn't care whether he succeeded or failed. My colleague said, "Actually, it's a better story if he fails."

And, about two days later, I noted that Kissinger had absorbed his brief lesson in Wire Service Reporting I. Barry Schweid of the AP asked him an offbeat question, and Kissinger looked at him with a smile that bordered on the triumphant. He pointed at him and said with obvious exaggeration, "I know why you're asking that. You have to file for the afternoon cycle. You have to file twice a day." It was like watching a young geometry student go rushing out to square the hypotenuse of a triangle.

I was a Kissinger-watcher during the entire eight years that Henry Kissinger survived, prospered, and survived in Washington. I watched him first as a White House correspondent, then as a State Department–diplomatic correspondent. I listened to him philosophize and analyze and occasionally sermonize for hours. I listened to him expound the current diplomatic history of the United States in speeches and news conferences all over this country and in every major capital of the world. I ate meals with him, saw sights with him, fell asleep at the opera in Peking with him. His monochromatic, rumbling baritone with the Cherman accent became as familiar to me as my own voice. So I have some observations about what made Henry run, or, more to the point, what made Henry win.

Henry Kissinger was the smartest man I have ever met. And he was witty, charming, clever, shrewd, cunning, astute, hard-working, articulate, profound, debonair, gregarious, and a little boy. Those characteristics all contributed to his success. He was also devious, secretive, volcanic, tempestuous, impatient, loquacious, tyrannical, and insecure. Those traits ultimately diminished his success. He was also the first Secretary of State since World War II who did not part his hair. And he was the only Secretary of State in the postwar era besides General George Marshall who was not a lawyer. (Considering what happened during Watergate, that was undoubtedly a blessing.)

But whenever you talk about Henry Kissinger, you have to start with his intelligence. His intellect is overpowering, and he has a great facility for communicating what is on his mind. Unlike his immediate predecessors at the White House, McGeorge Bundy and Walt Rostow, he was not arrogant about his intellect — at least not with the press.

He once told us about an exchange with Premier Chou En-lai, one of the few world leaders with a brilliance to match Kissinger's. Following their first conversation, Chou remarked, "You're a very intelligent man, Dr. Kissinger." Kissinger replied, "That means, Mr. Prime Minister, that from a Chinese point of view I'm of mediocre intelligence." Chou did not dispute him on that, Kissinger told us, with a malevolent chuckling sound that indicated that he was amused.

Kissinger's analytical prowess was celebrated even by those who didn't necessarily like him. One career Foreign Service officer who was not an admirer acknowledged that he was "uncannily effective at going to the vitals of an issue. He could identify a problem with tremendous speed and accuracy."

Kissinger was a conceptual thinker, and his brilliance lay in his capacity to analyze several layers of a problem at a time. His mind was at ease with the long-term view. And he was a connoisseur of nuance.

The former Chancellor of West Germany, Konrad Adenauer, claimed that Kissinger had "the most compelling intellect" of any man he had ever met. Adenauer went so far as to say that he thought Kissinger, although a Jew, could one day have become Chancellor of his native land — after Der Alte, of course. (When a somewhat less prominent German politician said the same thing, more or less, to humorist Art Buchwald during a Kissinger visit to Bonn, Buchwald did a double-take and replied, "You've got to be kidding!")

An Israeli official who frequently sat in on late-night sessions with Kissinger said it was "awesome" to hear him summarize and analyze lengthy, highly complicated Arab negotiating positions down to the minutest detail without referring to notes. Kissinger's mind gobbled up whole pages of reading material in seconds. An interviewer once wrote: "On the phone he reads while the other person talks, handling both at once, and puts aside the reading only when he responds." I once gave him a three-page paper in his office. He took off his glasses, held the papers about four inches from his eyes, and zipped through them without ever missing a beat of my conversation. He responded to what I was saying and then went on to discuss the contents of the paper. Beyond that, as Bill Moyers once pointed out, "Henry Kissinger is still learning, he is still open."

What I'm about to write here will sound facetious, but it's probably true: When Kissinger first arrived in Washington, the members of the White House and State Department press corps recognized that he was even smarter than they — a rare admission.

Kissinger's intelligence was leavened with an irrepressible wit. He had the timing and the quickness of a good stand-up comedian. He used his wit to charm, to disarm, and to relieve tension. On the day after he was nominated as Secretary of State, he held an open-air news conference at San Clemente. The answers were all very serious. This was not the Kissinger I knew, so as it ended I asked for one more question of a "technical nature": "Do you prefer being called 'Mr. Secretary' or 'Dr. Secretary'?"

"I don't stand on protocol," he replied. "If you will just call me 'Excellency,' it will be okay." All the television people knew before the laughter subsided how their reports would end on the air that night.

A reporter on his plane once prefaced a question by saying he'd like to have "an extremely candid answer." But before he could ask it, Kissinger cracked, "What do you want me to do, make history?"

During one of the Mideast shuttles, at the height of a tense negotiating session with the Israelis well after midnight when tempers were rising and hopes for progress were fading, Kissinger finally burst out to Israel's foreign minister: "For Christ's sake, Yigal . . . not that that means anything to you . . ." Allon snapped back, "Let me remind you, Henry, that Christ was a Jew." The tension was relieved, the debate subsided, and the two sides quickly resolved their dispute.

At a Washington cocktail party given to celebrate the publication of Marvin and Bernard Kalb's *Kissinger,* a New York publisher rushed up to the Secretary, gushed compliments, and asked if he had read the book. "No," he replied, "but I like the title."

A quip was never far from his lips, even in his most somber moments. Much of his wit was self-deprecating, a calculated antidote to his megalomania. Since he was not going to try to change his faults, he tried to mitigate them with humor. When he appeared at the exclusive Bohemian Grove north of San Francisco, he was introduced with such flattery that he started his speech by saying, "After that introduction, there is nothing left for me to do but walk on water."

He enjoyed barbs directed at himself, as long as they were reasonably clever. He indulged in a kind of intellectual locker room humor, a cerebral bantering comparable in style if not content to the kind of joshing that goes on in locker rooms after an athletic event.

After a reported kidnaping threat, Kissinger couldn't wait to tell us that he had asked Walter Bothe, one of his favorite Secret Service agents, what could happen if somebody tried to kidnap him. And Walter had replied, "Don't worry, Mr. Secretary, we won't let them take you alive." Kissinger once told a White House reporter: "Everything is going ahead on schedule — right over the cliff."

Occasionally his bon mots took a bad bounce. He jokingly referred to "sex-starved nuns" in connection with an alleged kidnaping plot against him in 1970, and he got angry letters from all over the country. He not only replied to every letter, but he also called two cardinals to apologize. When the Jefferson Room was first opened on the eighth floor of the State Department, Kissinger unveiled a statue before a crowd of influential donors who had underwritten the refurbishing, and he quipped, "Oh, I thought it would be me." The contributors did not seem amused.

But he made humor a tool of diplomacy. His banter inspired banter in others and usually led to a more relaxed atmosphere in the private, formal discussions or negotiations with world leaders. The humor opened the door to more frankness and less ritualized recitations as well. In that regard, Kissinger lightened the whole heavy international diplomatic scene.

His wit also served to convert routine swearing-in ceremonies at the State Department into popular attractions. Newsmen attended in greater numbers in search of a Kissinger quote for a story. And bureaucrats attended in greater numbers for the sheer enjoyment of the occasion. As Kissinger sowed, so did he reap.

For example, when Bill Rogers, a well-to-do Washington lawyer — and a prominent Democrat — was sworn in as the undersecretary for economic affairs, the number four job at the State Department, he said his wife had trouble understanding why he stayed in government, considering the big pay cut, and he gave this explanation: "Foreign policy is something like pornographic movies. It's a lot more fun doing it than watching others doing it." It was not the sort of line heard before or since on the eighth floor of the State Department.

In addition to his intelligence and wit, Kissinger had a masterful command of English, an acquired tongue that he had acquired uncommonly well. His voice rumbled and droned, and his sentences plodded, but he was lucid and precise and frequently eloquent, although ponderously so. His formal speeches recalled a phrase by a British writer who reviewed one of Kissinger's books: "I don't know if Mr. Kissinger is a great writer, but anyone finishing his book is a great reader."

It was in his role as a White House briefer that he first began to dazzle the Washington press. The seeds of his later media glories were first planted at "background" briefings. Whenever President Nixon made a major speech on foreign policy (and the White House billed every Nixon speech as "major"), Kissinger met beforehand with reporters to try to make sure they got the point the White House wanted them to get. According to the ground rules, however, Kissinger, who was then the President's adviser for national security affairs, spoke "on background." That meant he could not be quoted by name. One reason for anonymity was to ensure that he would not be quoted instead of the President. Another reason was to enable him to explain some things a little more candidly.

Kissinger was a briefer par excellence. He was articulate, direct, and intellectually impressive. Not even his accent got in the way; in fact, it soon became a conversation piece. Henry's "ve" and "vant" were not reflected in the speech of his brother, Walter, a millionaire industrialist on Long Island. Walter spoke English without an accent. His explanation: "I'm the brother who listens."

The subject once came up in the Oval Office when Nixon received Israeli Prime Minister Golda Meir. The President made the customary small talk as the photographers and cameramen were called in to snap their pictures and roll their film. Here's how it went:

NIXON: You know, Madame Prime Minister, we have something in common.
GOLDA (going along with the gag): What's that, Mr. President?
NIXON (archly): We both have Jewish foreign ministers.
GOLDA: Yes, but mine speaks English without an accent [Abba Eban].

Kissinger's accent once led to some curious scheduling. Kissinger told a staff aide he wanted to see "Vinston at two-thirty the following afternoon." He meant Winston Lord. But the staff aide thought the Secretary was referring to his tailor, Mr. Vincent, who lives in New York. So the aide dutifully called Mr. Vincent and asked him to appear in the Secretary's office the next day at two-thirty, which Mr. Vincent did. "Not Vincent," Kissinger bellowed when he saw the tailor. "Vinston!" And he used to crack up members of his staff every time he talked about the negotiations at the Law of the Seas Conference. It came out sounding like Law of Disease.*

*Interestingly, everybody who ever recounted a Kissinger anecdote to me did his own imitation of the Kissinger voice and accent, which are obviously impossible to reproduce in print.

Some Kissinger skeptics believe he deliberately avoided losing all of his accent in order to retain a certain "foreign charm." Those who have heard him speak other languages, however, challenge such skepticism. When Kissinger went to Munich in September 1972 to meet with Chancellor Willy Brandt, he pointed out, "I had occasion to make a brief statement on television, and I thought I might watch myself speak in one language correctly. Now I find I speak German with a Swedish accent." He concluded there was no language he spoke without an accent. His intellectual breadth did not extend to linguistics.

Kissinger himself joked not only about his accent, he also joked about his syntax. Somebody tried to ask him at a press conference, "If the short answer, then, is that there aren't going to be any trade concessions — " Kissinger interrupted the questioner to say, "There are no short answers in my press conferences."

When Kissinger went from an anonymous White House briefer to an on-the-record Secretary of State, his eloquence did not suffer. In December 1975, he held a news conference at the State Department, and in a major tour de force, he extemporized a forty-five-minute response to critics of the 1972 arms control agreement with the Russians. In a sardonic epilogue, however, he noted that if it took you forty-five minutes to answer your critics' one-liners, then people automatically thought you were guilty of something.

Before a trip to the Middle East, a reporter good-naturedly asked the needling question: "Mr. Secretary, would you say that peace is at hand in the Middle East?"

Kissinger: "I haven't used that line for four years."

Question: "Where are you going, exactly?"

Kissinger: "Wait a minute. You don't think I am finished with a thirty-second answer. I haven't even placed my verb yet."

At the 1973 Summit in San Clemente, a reporter challenged Kissinger "to enumerate as briefly as possible the total package of benefits that will accrue to the United States as a result of the past few days' activities." Kissinger fended off the challenge: "I can see this is not somebody who has attended previous briefings, or he wouldn't have made a demand for brevity."

Accent or no accent, Henry Kissinger can be an extremely charming and engaging man — when he wants to be. And he wants to be whenever it can do him some good. In one of the most perceptive lines ever uttered about Kissinger, one of his secretaries said, "He saves his charm for those who think he's charming."

He saved most of his charm for women. He had a weakness for female reporters. And when his male aides had to give him some memo or a schedule they knew might cause an explosion, they asked a female secretary to take it in to defuse a blowup. The tactic usually worked.

Kissinger also saved much of his charm for members of the press and Congress. For the most part, he acted as his own press spokesman, carefully determining the flow of information. Almost every Washington newsman was a potential target for Kissinger's personal public relations campaign. When Lars-Erik Nelson was a Reuters correspondent (he later moved to *Newsweek*) covering the State Department, he waged a long campaign to overcome the prohibition of reporters working for non-American news organizations from flying on the Secretary's plane. To that end, he tried to get as close to Kissinger as he could, hoping to put in a word for his cause.

One afternoon, Nelson drove out to Dulles Airport, about twenty-five miles from Washington, for the arrival of Foreign Minister Abdel Halim Khaddam of Syria. He knew Kissinger would be there to greet Khaddam. The Secretary arrived early and was chatting with some Arab ambassadors when he spotted Nelson — the only reporter there — behind a red velvet rope. Kissinger immediately went over to Nelson and chatted with him inconsequentially. As Nelson recalls, "I thought to myself, as I desperately tried to conceive questions to exploit the opportunity, 'Doesn't this man have better things to do than talk to me?' But I was an unknown to him, an uncaught soul, an uncaptured mind and heart. It was apparently worth his while to try to win me, and in some ways I suppose he succeeded." In one way Nelson also succeeded. He got Reuters on the plane.

Kissinger did try to manipulate newsmen as well as the news, as most public figures do. He realized that if he had a good press it helped his image, and if he had a good image it helped his diplomacy. And while, as a historian, he understood that the history books of tomorrow would be more meaningful in the long run than the newspaper columns of today, he also understood that the newspaper columns of today would provide some of the raw material for the history books of tomorrow, and he wanted to make sure that his version got into print.

Kissinger's cultivation of the press defied the attitude of the rest of the White House crowd, who took orders from a press-hating President. He swam against the tide, and he was the only upstream survivor. While others at the White House railed at the press in private, Kissinger won points with his needling wit in public. "As you know," he told one gathering, "the White House press has moved into the swimming pool area. There was some heated debate between the President and the Vice President [Agnew] before that occurred. The President prevailed, and we drained the pool before we put the press in it." And he told a White House backgrounder, "The other day, when I was asked to do one of these briefings in which I understand that my job is to communicate with you, I thought of a story of a Christian who was thrown into the arena with the lions. He thought he had better start with a prayer before that ordeal. When he did this, he found that the lion was also adopting a rather reverential pose. He said, 'Well, thank God, at least I am communicating with you.' The lion said, 'I don't know about you, but I'm saying grace.' "

When it came to press and congressional relations, Kissinger was his own best agent; he had a flair for self-promotion. As a former high-ranking State Department official described it, "Henry was able to project his personality in a favorable light to a wide spectrum of observers."

The stroking of the press and the Congress played a major role in Kissinger's rise to superstardom; he understood that they were keys to a successful career in Washington; originally they were his principal constituencies, although he didn't really take the House of Repre-

sentatives too seriously in dealing with foreign policy. He also understood the need for mastering the bureaucratic techniques that are
baffling to outsiders. He was a skilled bureaucratic in-fighter, first at
the White House, later at the State Department. As he once explained to someone who taunted him about his fanatic concern about
access to the Oval Office, "You don't understand. If I'm not in there
talking to the President, then someone else is."

Whatever someone else was doing, Kissinger was usually doing
more. An extraordinary stamina matched his singular drive. In a city
full of workaholics, he still managed to set an indefatigable pace. He
needed only four to five hours of sleep and could get by indefinitely
on three to four hours' sleep a night. Sixteen-hour days were commonplace on the road, and exhaustion was in plentiful supply among
staff and press during a trip. One of his aides literally fell asleep in
the middle of a sentence while talking to the South Vietnamese in
Paris. When a reporter complained half-jokingly about the long
hours, Kissinger replied half-jokingly, "*You* don't have to sit in on
the meetings."

State Department officials making their first trip with him would
come back shaking their heads over his endurance. One who went
to China with him noted, "He was still mentally fit when the rest of
us were shot. No one was his match." Another marveled, "He has
an incredible psychological capability of not being bothered by space
and time change."

Former Israeli Prime Minister Yitzhak Rabin told me that sheer
stamina was one of Kissinger's best negotiating tools. He simply
outlasted everybody else at the table — sometimes the entire Israeli
negotiating team. Kissinger once said he knew where he was going
and would work harder than anybody else to get there.

He had an iron constitution and, some said, a rear end to match.
Yet, a masseur in San Clemente once observed that Kissinger "did
not have a muscle in his body." Paradoxically, Kissinger's girth grew
in direct ratio to the workload. It's amusing to look back on the
pictures of the slender Henry Kissinger who first came to Washington in early 1969. He explained that when he negotiated, he got

nervous, and when he got nervous, he ate, and since he was always negotiating, he was always eating.

I recall waiting for Kissinger to come down from his suite in the Excelsior Hotel in Rome at the peak of his fame. A big crowd waited in the lobby and outside on the street, where dozens of motorcycle cops were lined up. Finally, the elevator doors opened and out strode Kissinger, waving, smiling, surrounded by Secret Service agents. He walked briskly to the front door as the crowd in the lobby applauded and cheered. Two American women were standing in front of me. One turned to the other and said, "He's just a short, fat guy!"

So how had this short, fat guy — once described as looking like "a prosperous delicatessen owner from the Bronx" — been transmogrified into the playboy of the West Wing? It was almost pure accident. Plus circumstance. On the otherwise dull gray canvas of the Nixon administration, Henry Kissinger and Martha Mitchell provided the only splashes of color. If it hadn't been for them, the society pages of the Washington papers could have been filled with want ads.

As an *éminence grise* of the Nixon White House, Kissinger became much more *éminence* than *grise,* although he risked the hostility of the White House squares by socializing among the Georgetown set that Richard Nixon despised. And if it boggles the mind to think of Henry Kissinger as a "secret swinger," you've got to remember that what passed for sex symbols in the Washington of that time were Wilbur Mills and Strom Thurmond.

Just as nature abhors a vacuum, so do the Washington social pages abhor a vacuous administration. The vacuum was partially filled one night in the fall of 1969; a cocktail party given by Washington hostess Barbara Howar for Gloria Steinem provided the setting. Kissinger was photographed at the party with Ms. Steinem and Senator George McGovern. All three of them were destined to go on to greater fame, but it was not the kind of Georgetown tableau that caused joy in Nixonville.

Sally Quinn, who writes for the Style section of the Washington *Post,* asked Kissinger, "You really are a swinger underneath it all, aren't you?" History was in the making as shy, modest Henry replied, "Well, you couldn't call me a swinger because of my job. Why don't you just assume I'm a secret swinger?" The quote appeared in print the next morning, and a quip became a myth.

The party set off a chain reaction of gossipy fission. When Nixon asked at a Cabinet meeting who Gloria Steinem was, Secretary of State Rogers replied, "That's Henry's girlfriend." When Ms. Steinem heard that, she retorted, "I never have been and never will be Henry Kissinger's girlfriend." Kissinger had the last word, as far as is known, at a Washington dinner: "That doesn't mean that if nominated, she wouldn't run, and if elected, that she wouldn't serve."

In a lighter moment, Kissinger explained his glamorous image as a swinger: "Power is the ultimate aphrodisiac." In a more serious moment, he analyzed it: "I am no fool. I realize the game. I am their celebrity of the hour, the new man in town. I don't kid myself."

He didn't kid his son, either. His son, David, once said to his Uncle Walter, "Now that Dad has left the table, I'd like to ask you a question. Do you think Dad is a secret swinger? That's what they're saying at school." Uncle Walter slipped his arm around his nephew's shoulder. "David," he said, "when your dad comes back to the table, you take a good look at him, then tell me if he looks like a secret swinger." A few moments later, Kissinger returned to the table. David looked at his father, smiled at his uncle, and quickly shook his head from side to side.

And if *you* think Henry Kissinger was a swinger, then you believe in Santa Claus, the Easter Bunny, and the Tooth Fairy. But as we say in the news biz, it was good copy.

After he got married in the spring of 1974, a news conference questioner wanted to know if "marriage has in any way affected your outlook toward life in general or foreign policy in particular?"

Kissinger replied, "I don't have to give the answer that Ziegler [White House Press Secretary Ron Ziegler] recommends for this particular thing."

Reporter: "What does he recommend?"

Kissinger: "Well, he recommends that I say it hasn't affected mine, but it has affected my wife's."

Washington columnist Tom Braden, who socialized with Kissinger off duty, attributed a measure of the Secretary's success to his "boyishness." He wrote: "There is a certain boyish quality about our Secretary of State, which makes him intensely likable and also makes one wonder whether boyishness is not a necessary ingredient in the personalities of really first-rate men."

There was one other reason why I think the Kissinger story sold well: It was a classic case of "only in America." Kissinger was — is — an outstanding tribute to the American system. He came to this country as an immigrant boy of fifteen, a refugee from Nazi Germany, and, in a kind of ethnic Horatio Alger fashion, he rose through the academic ranks to become the first Jewish Secretary of State in American history and the first naturalized American to hold the job.

On the day Kissinger was sworn in by Chief Justice Warren Burger, Nixon presided over a moving ceremony in the East Room of the White House. The new Secretary of State spoke with feeling about the occasion. "There is no country in the world," he said, "where it is conceivable that a man of my origin could be standing here next to the President of the United States." In the words of Congressman Jack Brooks, Henry Kissinger had become "the American dream with a German accent." But some of the people who worked for him — and a lot of others who didn't — hardly considered him "dreamy."

Kissinger was no candidate for canonization, his own egocentric view notwithstanding. He acquired a long list of critics with a long list of complaints, starting with the disdainful observation of an old State Department pro, who noted that "Henry picks his nose." He also chewed his fingernails to the nub, but none of us ever saw him in the act. It was apparently a touchy point. Bob McCloskey once mentioned this nervous habit to a correspondent but called later to put the information off the record.

When Kissinger moved to the seventh floor of the State Department in September 1973 — "I never knew the Secretary of State was such an exalted personage," he said upon showing the huge office to a visitor — he took with him a hard-earned reputation for virtuoso solo performances. But, he told his colleagues, the time for one-man-band diplomacy and diplomatic spectaculars was over; it was time to institutionalize foreign policy. Instead, Kissinger became the institution. Samuel Lewis, now Ambassador to Israel, said jokingly that what Kissinger really meant was that people who worked for him for a while were ready to be "institutionalized."

Kissinger the Secretary of State continued to play it close to the vest, and he had a rather ample vest area. Even though Kissinger the Harvard historian had once written: "The statesman is suspicious of those who personalize foreign policy, for history teaches him the fragility of structures dependent upon individuals," seldom has foreign policy been so personalized as during the Kissinger era, which is one reason the criticism of foreign policy became so personalized. Yet one of the country's most respected columnists, James Reston of the New York *Times,* wrote that "State is not a one-man flying band, but probably the youngest and most talented foreign office in the world."

From his new vantage point, Kissinger might also have taken note of the suspicions of those who acquire too much power in foreign policy. When he took over the State Department, he did not give up his job as assistant to the President for national security affairs. The two jobs combined gave him a virtual stranglehold on the making of policy. A White House photographer once needled Kissinger in a good-natured way as he was coming out of the Oval Office, "How do you like being close to the seat of power?" Kissinger shot back, "What do you mean, close?"

By keeping the White House job, Kissinger made sure — for a while — that nobody got between him and the President. It also meant he held on to the chairmanship of most of the administration's key intelligence committees. After he lost the National Security Council position in the so-called Sunday "Hallowe'en" massacre, he was asked at a news conference how much influence he thought the President's assistant for national security affairs should have in the making of foreign policy? His wry response was: "Well, at this moment I am very much opposed to the assistant for national security having *any* influence." In a more serious vein, Kissinger once told us on the plane that no NSC adviser should ever again have as much power at the White House as he had.

At a subsequent news conference, a reporter asked solemnly, "Mr. Secretary, do you expect to last out President Ford's term?" Kissinger came back, "Well, I don't answer my telephone on Sunday."

The dual White House–State Department role also satisfied Kissinger's penchant for secrecy, for he was excessively secretive. He understood that information was power, and he hoarded it, cutting out as many people as feasible. He had an obsessive aversion to news leaks except for those he perpetrated himself. He wanted full control. Kissinger's attitude toward secrecy was well developed before he reached the White House. In 1968 he had written: "The only way secrecy can be kept is to exclude from the making of the decision all those who are theoretically charged with carrying it out." His style, to quote one State Department official, was "secret diplomacy, secretly arrived at."

Whenever the secrecy issue arose, Kissinger used to say over and over again, "If I proclaimed state secrets from the top of the Washington Monument, they'd still say I was too secretive." But I never saw him at the top of the Washington Monument. And when a State Department official suggested sending CIA Director William Colby before a congressional committee to present the administration's case for military aid for Turkey, Kissinger responded sarcastically, "No, we can't do that. Every time Colby goes up to the Hill, he feels he has to confess to some terrible crime."

During the 1976 presidential campaign, after Jimmy Carter had criticized Kissinger's Lone Ranger style and promised an administration that would be more open and have less secrets, Kissinger observed, "Everyone is for more openness and an end to secrecy." After a pause, he added, "Until they're elected." Yet in dealing with the traveling press, he was more open in talking about the directions of American foreign policy than any other official in recent times.

Some of his critics in Congress and in the press said that Kissinger lied. I heard him "lie" only once — about a list of Israeli POWs. His justification then was that lives were at stake. I heard him shade the truth more than once. I heard him exaggerate the truth. And I know he emphasized different things to different people. To get the right answer from Henry Kissinger you had to ask precisely the right question. For example, if you asked him, as we once did on the plane, "Are you going to see Soviet Foreign Minister Andrei Gromyko in Damascus tomorrow?" he could truthfully answer, "No" — because he was going to see Gromyko in Cyprus the next day.

Israeli Foreign Minister Abba Eban explained Kissinger's verbal slipperiness in his autobiography. "I felt that if he wanted to sell us a car with a wheel missing," Eban wrote, "he would achieve his purpose by an eloquent and cogent eulogy of the three wheels that remained."

One Foreign Service officer who worked very closely with Kissinger on a daily basis insisted that "Henry didn't lie on important issues. In a negotiation, he was meticulous in reporting to one side what the other side had said. But in little things, he delighted in misleading people . . . He could rewrite a situation so completely from one description to another, and I'm sure he'll rewrite history just as much in his book."

A former top State Department official described as "authentic genius" Kissinger's "ability to keep so many balls in the air at one time — to tell a hundred people a hundred different versions of the same event and yet not slip up in what he had said." This official added, "Henry's concept of the truth is what helps him accomplish what he considers to be legitimate objectives." This characteristic was complicated by his impatience with people who didn't comprehend quickly what he was saying. Nahum Goldmann, the former president of the World Jewish Congress, said of Kissinger, "If he were ten percent less intelligent and ten percent more honest, he would be a great man."

Kissinger was not a great man to many who worked under him; he was an administrative terror who bullied and abused his staff. On a flight from London to Washington, Ambassador Anne Armstrong watched Kissinger chew out Roy Atherton, the extremely able but quiet assistant secretary of state for Near Eastern affairs. She later told another Kissinger aide that she had never seen such a performance and could not understand how another adult could take such abuse. One of the department's most senior officers, George Vest, another able but quiet man, decided after six months as Kissinger's press spokesman that he could not take it, and he asked out. Not long after Kissinger became Secretary, an old riddle began making the rounds at the department: Why is working for Henry Kissinger like being a mushroom? Answer: Because you're kept in the dark all the time, because you get a lot of shit dumped all over you, and in the end, you get canned. Another Foreign Service officer came up with a more original line. "Think of Henry Kissinger as a corkscrew," he advised a colleague, "and think of yourself as the cork." Former Brazilian Foreign Minister Antonio Silveira perceived that domineering quality in Kissinger's personality. "He's a carnivore," Silveira said. "He has to bite."

He also had to roar. It was part of his personality. In some ways it was helpful — to him. After he had blown his stack following a tough session with the Russians in Moscow on the issue of Jewish emigration, his doctor told a reporter, "Kissinger's ability to do that keeps him from being a cardiac case."

At times his roaring seemed irrational, and his acid tongue flapped out of control as he dumped vituperation on those whom he felt had crossed him. At other times he was play-acting. One of his secretaries said the key was to know the degree of his anger, which was not always reflected in how he was behaving. "I've seen him sound absolutely livid in handling somebody," she said, "and then turn around and smile."

While Kissinger inspired fear and loathing among some officers, he commanded great loyalty from others. One of them was his personal aide, Jock Covey. Once, when Nancy was away and Kissinger had to go out of town suddenly on a weekend, there was no one to take care of Tyler, his golden Labrador retriever. Covey volunteered for the job and showed up at Kissinger's Georgetown house at seven the next morning. Kissinger greeted him in his pajamas.

"Where are you taking my dog?" Kissinger wanted to know with mock seriousness.

"To Virginia," Jock said. "I'm going to spend the day with some friends."

"What are you going to do there?" Kissinger asked.

"Skydive," answered Covey. "I'm a skydiver."

Without hesitation, Kissinger followed up, asking, "How will my dog get home if something happens to you?" He did not smile.

Covey did smile. "Don't worry," he said. "My friends will make sure your dog is well taken care of and brought home."

When Kissinger left office, Covey took a leave of absence from the Foreign Service to continue working for him.

Another of Kissinger's loyal aides, Winston Lord, gave him a poster of a fierce-looking gorilla with the caption: "When I want your opinion, I'll beat it out of you." Kissinger hung it in his spacious office among the works of art on loan from the Museum of Modern Art. But the first time a visiting foreign minister came to call, the front office staff took it down as too indecorous. Kissinger had it put back up.

Washington *Star* reporter Jerry O'Leary once interviewed Kissinger on Kissinger and noted, "You are said to be a reasonably demanding taskmaster."

Kissinger: "*Extremely* demanding. But, first of all, I don't demand anything of my associates that I don't do to myself. Secondly, I have high standards. I believe that it is the task of people in charge of an organization to discover qualities in their subordinates they didn't know they had, and therefore I have found very often that people who work for me do things they have never done in other jobs. Do I lose my temper? Yes. Usually I lose my temper more on trivial things than on big things."

O'Leary: "They say you throw ashtrays and kick wastebaskets . . ."

Kissinger: "That is not true. I don't throw objects. I become very impatient when what I consider trivial obstacles get in the way of things that I need, believe me, to be done."

Some of his blowups over trivial and not-so-trivial matters were legendary. And he may not have thrown "objects," but he was known to throw other things. Once, on a flight from Washington to Vail, Colorado, Kissinger discovered that a topographical map he wanted for a briefing for the President on a Mideast negotiation had not been put on the plane. The Kissinger volcano spewed lava; briefing books went flying all over the plane while Nancy and the two Kissinger children tried to stay out of his way. Somebody working in the State Department Operations Center remembers getting a message that day from Kissinger's Jetstar, saying, "We've just had a nuclear explosion aboard the plane." Kissinger was so angry he even had his aide call the department from the plane on an open line — something he never did because of concern about Russian monitoring in Washington. He ordered that the map be sent to Vail forthwith. Another plane was not immediately available, however, so the map was sent in pieces over a telephone reproduction device, which obviously could not reproduce the topographical features. The presidential staff in Vail had a lot of trouble trying to match the pieces of the map. They spread it out on the floor like a giant jigsaw puzzle and got down on their hands and knees to try to line up the grids and coordinates properly. They never did, and Kissinger finally decided to brief the President without the map that somebody had spent so much time constructing.

Some of his reputation was based on sheer insensitivity. In the fall of 1974, Kissinger delivered a major address to the World Food Conference in Rome. One of his speechwriters, Robie Palmer, had traveled through South Asia with the Secretary en route to Rome in order to keep working on the text, which as usual went through several drafts. The long hours and the bug Palmer had picked up in India had wiped him out, and he was exhausted. As the plane was leaving Rome, Kissinger came out of his airborne office, looked at Palmer drifting off to sleep, and said, "You better get busy on that Chicago speech."

But most of Kissinger's reputation was based on some irrepressible urge to bully people who didn't stand up to him, such as Deputy Secretary of State Robert Ingersoll, supposedly the number two man in the department hierarchy. Kissinger asked Ingersoll at a staff meeting what he had to report. Ingersoll said, "Nothing." With heavy sarcasm, Kissinger muttered, "That's about what I would expect." The remark was not untypical.

Kissinger once pointed out with some pride to an interviewer that "one of my associates has said that the highest praise they can get from me is the absence of abuse."

As Kissinger was leaving office, Malcolm Toon, then the Ambassador to Israel, told him that he had been a great Secretary of State, but "a son of a bitch to work for." Toon said Kissinger seemed more pleased by the second part. One of Kissinger's personal aides later conceded that despite all the pressure and discomfort, "there was a tremendous sense of excitement, a sense of sitting in on history, in working for him."

Kissinger claimed the pressure was two-way. Speaking of the hard-working undersecretary of state for political affairs, Joe Sisco, Kissinger said, "If anything, Sisco drives me, I don't drive him." And Sisco agreed, sort of: "Well, we have a private joke . . . After we've put in fourteen or sixteen hours, the private joke is we've gotten a good day's work out of him. But I think he does reasonably well with us."

At a small farewell party arranged in his office by his closest associates, Kissinger typically turned to humor to acknowledge his administrative tyranny. "Since English is my second language," he deadpanned, "I didn't know that 'maniac' and 'fool' were not terms of endearment."

In addition to acquiring a reputation for abusing his staff, Kissinger was also accused of neglecting the bureaucracy he headed. He already had a visceral disdain for the foreign policy bureaucracy when he arrived in Washington, and it was reinforced by his boss, Richard Nixon. Kissinger's pregovernment writings were peppered with criticism about the lack of originality within the bureaucracy.

As Washington *Post* writer Murrey Marder pointed out: "Kissinger arrived at the White House with his own long-standing antipathy toward bureaucracies, but for different reasons. Bureaucracies, to him, were grossly overstaffed, slow-witted, initiative-stifling, press-leaking, foot-dragging, responsibility-shirking institutions. They needed to be circumvented until they could be slashed to the bone, drastically reoriented and made responsive to the will of the White House."

Despite his titular leadership of the Foreign Service, he was forever deprecating it in public, usually with cutting humor. His management aide at State, Dean Brown, accused Kissinger of indulging in a kind of "intellectual McCarthyism" against the Foreign Service and warned him that he was crippling morale, even though, as Secretary, he had put the State Department back into the center of the foreign policy action.

Kissinger was too intelligent not to recognize and appreciate what a talented group the Foreign Service was, by and large, and in his final days, he went out of his way to praise the gifted men and women with whom he had worked. His favorite device was to claim that "with respect to my qualifications for Secretary of State, you have to remember that I am surrounded by individuals in the Foreign Service who hold the view that the only way I could ever have participated in the foreign policy–making of the United States was by what they call lateral entry — by getting in at my present position — that I probably would not have been qualified to be a Foreign Service officer." The skeptics said he ended up praising the Foreign Service just for the record. But his supporters said he really meant it. And I think he did.

Kissinger's view of the bureaucracy was undoubtedly filtered through his own ego, and he was a card-carrying egomaniac. He often joked about it: "I have been called indispensable and a miracle worker. I know, because I remember every word I say." The Washington press corps joked about it: "When Henry Kissinger gets up in the morning and looks in the mirror, he says, 'There but for the grace of God goes God.'" A prominent Nixon Cabinet member was serious about it. Attorney General John Mitchell described Kissinger as "an egotistical maniac." Kissinger responded, "At Harvard, it took me ten years to develop a relationship of total hostility to my environment. I want you to know I have done it here in eighteen months."

Kissinger's stratospheric estimate of himself was not new to Washington. Back in the days when he was working for Nelson Rockefeller, he found out that one of his speeches had been rewritten. "When Nelson buys a Picasso," Kissinger groused, "he does not hire four house painters to improve it."

To paraphrase Winston Churchill, Kissinger had a lot to be megalomaniacal about. His megalomania was almost matched by his paranoia, which he claimed blossomed at Harvard and matured in Washington. "Actually," he once said, "I suffer from a persecution complex, and the good thing about [my] job in the government is that my enemies here really exist." He never stopped looking over his shoulder, and if the State Department had been a saloon, he would never have sat with his back to the swinging doors.

Throughout his career, Kissinger tended to show impatience with the working of the democratic system. This trait once provoked Congressman John Brademas (D-Indiana) to charge that "Kissinger is known to dissemble. He is not at home in a constitutional democracy with a separation-of-powers system. He doesn't know how to deal with separated institutions that share power." Brademas, pro-Greece and an outspoken critic of Kissinger's policy on Cyprus, was not a fervent admirer of the Secretary of State.

Surprisingly, one of Kissinger's closest and most loyal aides, Larry Eagleburger, agreed in some respects with Brademas's criticism. He acknowledged that Kissinger found the American system cumbersome and would probably have been more comfortable with a parliamentary system, where the executive must have a legislative majority in order to be the executive. Kissinger also felt strongly that while Congress should be consulted on the strategy of foreign policy, it was simply not equipped to be involved in the day-to-day tactics.

In a related area, Kissinger was frequently accused of cultivating adversary nations while taking friends for granted. His answer: "Our initial negotiations were directed to authoritarian governments because that was where we faced the danger of war. Negotiations with allies are more complex in this phase of the development of Western democracies, but in the long run more important."

His critics also charged that he was more comfortable dealing with totalitarian regimes than with democracies because of his own authoritanian instincts. It was true that the leaders of nondemocratic countries could make decisions faster and so speed up the negotiating process at hand. The most pertinent examples came during the Middle East shuttles. Kissinger was almost always much more frustrated when dealing with the Israelis than with the Arabs — or with some of the Arabs. In Egypt, for example, he had to convince only Sadat. In Israel, he had to convince the entire cabinet, usually a messy exercise. When Kissinger commented on one particularly raucous session with the Israeli cabinet, Prime Minister Golda Meir twitted him, "What are you complaining about? You only have to go through it every once in a while. I have to go through it every day."

At the policy level, Kissinger was decidedly Big Power oriented; he tended to see the entire world through the prism of American-Soviet relations. This view led him to ignore the developing world except as the underdeveloped countries related to the Big Power picture. The oil embargo in 1973 jolted him into a new appreciation of the growing economic power of the Third World. And when his efforts to organize the oil consumers into an effective bloc to confront the oil producers were frustrated, he began paying more attention to the so-called North-South dialogue between the world's haves and have-nots, emphasizing conciliation rather than confrontation.

International economics was by no means his long suit, but he insisted on playing it. One of his former aides, Fred Bergsten, said at the time Kissinger became Secretary that his record on economics was "dismal." Yet he waged a never-ending bureaucratic battle for State Department control over international economic policy, even though he would joke on the plane that "anybody who discusses international economics with me is in a lot of trouble." On his frequent trips to the Middle East during the oil embargo, he never took along an oil expert — possibly in order to maintain the fiction that oil policy was kept separate from Middle East diplomacy.

The struggle between the State Department and the Treasury Department was not always as good-natured as Kissinger made it seem at a news conference in Chicago: "I have a treaty on nonaggression with [Treasury] Secretary Simon, because he holds the view that my knowledge of economics is an argument against universal suffrage. And the agreement is that if I will not speak about economic matters, he will take over foreign policy only slowly."

Kissinger camouflaged his defensiveness about his knowledge of international economics — or lack of it — with humor. He concluded a news conference in Vladivostok following the Ford-Brezhnev meeting by replying to a reporter, "I didn't hear the question, but it dealt with economics, so I don't want to answer it." But he grew more confident as he learned that economics was not an exact science. He told a Cincinnati news conference: "It used to be said that my knowledge of economics was an argument against universal suffrage . . . And I tended to believe that until I started dealing with the economists."

The basic concern at Treasury was that Kissinger would sacrifice economic principles for political ends, that he might be too willing to relax American free market standards in making worldwide commodity agreements under pressure from Third World forums. Yet once Kissinger really got interested in international economics, even his critics conceded that he energized the government's economic bureaucracy and prodded it to expand its horizons and deal with the so-called big issues, such as energy and other raw materials, world food prices, and the role of multinational corporations.

One of the most persistent criticisms leveled at Kissinger was that he sacrificed morality in American foreign policy on the altar of pragmatism. He did view foreign policy as essentially amoral, and he would probably agree with the thesis that a nation has no friends, only interests. His answer to the charge came in a speech during the presidential campaign. "We must give up the illusion that foreign policy can choose between morality and pragmatism," he said. "America cannot be true to itself unless it upholds humane values and the dignity of the individual. But equally, it cannot realize its values unless it is secure. No nation has a monopoly of justice or virtue, and none has the capacity to enforce its own conceptions globally."

Kissinger argued that our principles are not shared by much of the rest of the world, and it's one thing for an outsider to indulge in rhetoric advancing lofty moral precepts, but it's quite another for the policy-maker to try to get things done in a pragmatic way without sacrificing moral values. He also argued that keeping peace and preventing nuclear war represented the highest morality of all. And Kissinger, the pragmatic historian, felt that history would be the ultimate judge of morality.

These rhetorical efforts to balance morality and pragmatism were undercut by his attitude toward Chile. He believed the United States had some kind of right to intervene in the internal affairs of Chile because Chile might have become a threat to other countries in the hemisphere and so affect our interests. (However, he never seemed to take Latin America as a whole too seriously; he once joked that "Latin America is a dagger pointed right at the heart of Antarctica.")

It was perhaps a more precise criticism that Kissinger did not relate politics to people. He was extremely sensitive on that point. When he was quoted in *Newsweek* as saying after the *Mayaguez* rescue that the twenty-eight dead "don't matter," he was furious. He complained vociferously, but *Newsweek* stuck to its quote.

The one issue on which Kissinger was most vulnerable was wiretapping. His role in the tapping of several reporters and White House aides, including members of his own staff, was shabby at best, although the complete story is still buried in White House and Senate files. Ironically, while the White House wiretapping almost did him in, leading as it did to his threat to resign in Salzburg, in June 1974, it was another case of wiretapping that made him Secretary of State in the first place. That moving scene in the East Room of the White

House might never have taken place had it not been for what the White House called a "third-rate burglary" at the headquarters of the Democratic National Committee in a hitherto obscure office building named Watergate.

By the end of President Nixon's first term in office, Kissinger had not made it to the White House "enemies' list," but he was no longer the fair-haired boy, either. The President didn't like the way his national security affairs adviser hogged the limelight. He was also displeased with the "peace is at hand" statement in October 1972 and with the subsequent convolutions in the Vietnam negotiations. And he didn't take kindly to Kissinger's whispering to Washington columnists that he was a secret dove on the Christmas bombings and other controversial actions during the Vietnam War.

Kissinger knew he was in trouble and once confided to a friend afterward: "Haldeman almost got me" (H. R. "Bob" Haldeman, Nixon's chief of staff).

After the 1972 election, Nixon had planned to name an old friend, Deputy Secretary of Defense Kenneth Rush, as Secretary of State, replacing William Rogers, and he had so told Rush. Kissinger also reportedly knew of this intention. And he was planning to leave the administration once Vietnam was cleaned up following the signing of the Peace Accords in January 1973. But Rush's would-be nomination was delayed because Bill Rogers, who had been humiliated by Kissinger's White House wheeling and dealing, did not want to go until Kissinger went. He did not want to give the appearance of having lost the battle altogether.

Rush fully expected to be named by the end of February, but by then the White House was pulling up the drawbridges to defend itself against the Watergators, and Nixon, who was spending more and more time trying to save himself, was not prepared to let his number-one foreign policy adviser leave in the midst of the domestic turmoil. So Kissinger stayed and Rogers stayed. Rush became deputy secretary of state instead of Secretary.

People who knew both men say Kissinger never really thought highly of Rush, but cultivated him because he was so close to the

President. One of Kissinger's first moves after his nomination as Secretary was to have breakfast with Rush. He talked of a partnership, told Rush he wanted him to stay on. But immediately afterward he told another close aide, "We've got to get rid of him somehow" — meaning Rush.

Against this backdrop, Kissinger's behavior in December 1973, when he was Secretary of State and Rush was deputy secretary, seemed curious. Al Haig, the White House Chief of Staff, called Rush and said the President wanted to appoint him as a special counselor on Watergate and wanted to announce it right away. Kissinger was at that time on a trip to the Middle East and China, and Rush said any changes should wait until Kissinger got back. He then went to the White House to read transcripts of the White House tapes. He found them quite different from the published version. Haig called again. Again Rush put him off. "Wait until Henry gets back," he urged. "Kissinger would blame me if there were a change while he was gone." When Kissinger did return, he and Rush talked about the White House job. Kissinger asked Rush if he wanted it. Rush said no, but the President was pressing. Kissinger was upset.

Just before Christmas, Haig called Rush again, suggesting an announcement be made. Rush, now resigned to being dragooned to the White House, asked Haig to wait until Wednesday, the day after Christmas, to make the announcement. On Wednesday morning, Rush told his staff at State he was going to the White House. But the announcement never came. Instead, Rush got another call from Haig, explaining that Kissinger had gone to the President and told him that as Secretary of State, he could not continue vital negotiations unless Rush were around to run the State Department. The President acquiesced, Haig told Rush, "in the interest of the country." Afterward, Rush could conclude only that the Secretary of State did not want him at the White House, in close daily contact with the President. So Kissinger not only survived Watergate, he prospered because of it.

He got word from the President about his nomination to the Cabinet while in a swimming pool, of all places. It was August 1973,

and President Nixon was taking his annual summer break at what
was called the Western White House in San Clemente. Julie Nixon
Eisenhower had called Kissinger on the phone and invited him and
his children to cool off at the Nixon pool at La Casa Pacifica. Kissinger and the kids were taking a dip when the President showed up
and eased into the water. "Why don't you and I go down to the other
end?" he said to Kissinger. At the shallow end of the pool, with
Kissinger sitting on the steps, the President made his pitch. "If you
will let me," he said, "I would like to nominate you for Secretary of
State tomorrow." Henry let him. Henry also let Nixon keep him as
the national security affairs adviser.

Only two weeks after he was sworn in as Secretary, Kissinger was
jolted by a major and almost totally unexpected crisis — the outbreak of a new Middle East war. About a week later, he was asked
at a news conference how the State Department had handled the
diplomatic aspects of the war. The Secretary of State, still a presidential aide, replied, "We at the White House are very impressed by the
leadership that the State Department has received." The rest of the
world soon became impressed by the leadership the U.S. State Department was receiving, and after Kissinger put "shuttle diplomacy"
into the history books and arranged disengagement agreements between Israel and Egypt and Israel and Syria, the accolades really
piled up. The wordsmiths searched for new adjectives and catch-
words, and the encomia included: "Henry the K . . . Henry the Kiss
. . . the Metternich from Yonkers . . . Super-Kraut . . . diplomatic
superstar . . . Mr. Fix-it . . . Super-Kissinger . . . a diplomatic
Kohoutek . . . Super-K . . . Prime Minister Kissinger . . . Super-
Secretary . . . diplomatic Houdini . . . the most important American
import of this past century . . . the name that made foreign policy
famous . . . an American hero in an age starved for heroes . . . the
diplomatic Lone Ranger — bold, secretive, supremely confident
. . . most successful diplomat and negotiator in American history
. . . a unique national institution . . . the only Toscanini in town
. . . the most intriguing American statesman to appear since
Franklin Roosevelt . . . the most important number-two man in
history . . ."

Critic Richard Holbrooke wrote: "His *persona* has transcended his achievements." Friend and columnist James Reston wrote: "Henry Kissinger has got beyond the news . . . He is going to be left to the psychological novelists." ABC commentator Howard K. Smith intoned: "Henry Kissinger is a true phenomenon. Transformed from an immigrant who had trouble with the language to a little-known professor . . . into a national resource like Alaskan oil . . . from a writer of turgid academic prose into a genuine star that tourists gather to get a glimpse of as they would Elizabeth Taylor."*

Congressman Jonathan Bingham proposed an amendment to the Constitution allowing foreign-born citizens to become President of the United States. Kissinger was named the Most Admired American in the popularity polls. The contestants in the Miss Universe contest voted him "the greatest person in the world today." He became the most popular political figure in Madame Tussaud's wax museum in London.

A new twist on an old joke made the rounds in Washington. It noted that Nixon was just a heartbeat away from the presidency; if anything happened to Kissinger, Nixon would indeed become President.

Kissinger was a Secretary of State who was treated like a head of state. When he traveled, he dealt with number one: Chairman Mao Tse-tung, Premier Chou En-lai, Communist Party Chief Leonid Brezhnev, presidents and prime ministers and kings. Communiqués were issued in the presidential manner following a Kissinger visit to a foreign capital. Governments greeted him with military honors. Kissinger became, in effect, a deputy President for foreign affairs.

He also became a global status symbol, and countries clamored for a visit. They felt neglected if he did not drop in. Henry Kissinger, described by *Time* magazine as "unpropertied, unelegant and unimposing" at the time of his nomination, became one of the most celebrated international figures of his time. Almost anything he did

---

*But to his Secret Service agents, Kissinger was always just "Woodcutter," their code name for him on the intercom. Former Nixon aide John Ehrlichman, another of Kissinger's nonadmirers at the White House, got in his digs at Henry when he wrote a novel and had the Secret Service code-name him "Wiener schnitzel."

Kissinger makes the cover of Newsweek *as Superman.*

or said, anyplace he went or anyplace he might vaguely be considering visiting — all of this made headlines. He joined an exclusive league whose other members were Jackie Onassis, Frank Sinatra, and the Beatles. Automatic news. Big box office. A *National Enquirer* reporter even went through his garbage.

In the spring of 1974, he appeared on the cover of *Newsweek* in a Superman costume. And indeed it did seem that he was traveling as fast as a speeding jet, able to leap diplomatic hurdles in a single bound, stopping oncoming crises with his bare hands. And over the skies of Cairo and Jerusalem and Moscow and Paris, it wasn't a bird, it wasn't a plane, it was Super-K!

In the midst of the adulation, however, columnist William White wrote prophetically: "Secretary of State Kissinger has reached that most dangerous of all high plateaus in a democratic society. He is becoming something close to the indispensable man in a political structure that resents and ultimately rejects indispensable men."

Kissinger eventually did become a victim of his own prestige. He could not go on topping himself. As one aide noted ruefully, "If he belches, it becomes an international incident." In addition, his environment turned hostile. Washington had once been described by Adlai Stevenson as a city of "protocol, alcohol and Geritol." In the post-Vietnam, Watergate era, a fourth component had been added to the mix: vitriol. There was blood in the water, and all the goldfish had become piranha.

Columnist Meg Greenfield observed in *Newsweek*: "Kissinger is paying a personal price for personal success achieved in a very personal way. He has bested too many adversaries in government and these have become enemies. And he is under attack for those very idiosyncrasies and habits of mind and ways of doing things that Washington honored *and encouraged* over the years. His exaltation and decline tell us as much about ourselves as they do about him."

The fleetingness of fame was trenchantly — and amusingly — underlined when the Secretary of State traveled to Atlanta and was introduced by Georgia's Governor George Busbee as "Harry Kissinger." Kissinger himself reflected an awareness of the new atmosphere in the nation's capital when he told a State Department reception: "Foreign visitors have often looked upon this town with a jaundiced eye. Nearly a century ago, James Bryce, once British Ambassador to Washington, called it a 'city without commerce or manufacture, where political intrigue and semi-political intrigue is the only gainful occupation.' He had seen nothing."

When Kissinger returned from his exhausting but successful thirty-three-day Syrian-Israeli shuttle and held a news conference at the State Department, he was shocked out of his diplomatic euphoria by a series of jarring questions. His testimony on his knowledge of the White House "plumbers" was challenged, and after one reporter asked him five questions in a row about his role in the wiretapping, Kissinger snapped, "I think that this is a press conference and not a cross-examination."

Ironically, one of the questions that shook him up the most came from a young Washington gadfly whom nobody in the press corps took at all seriously. His name was Peter Peckarsky, and he got his press credentials as the Washington representative for the student newspaper at MIT. Peckarsky was known chiefly for shouting out largely irrelevant or nitpicking questions at the daily White House briefings. But Kissinger didn't have any idea who Peckarsky was when he stood up and challenged Kissinger's testimony about a Watergate matter and then said, "I wonder if you could . . . tell us whether or not the Special Prosecutor or any other prosecutor or agency of the U.S. government has contacted you with reference to a perjury investigation of [your] statements and . . . whether or not you have consulted and retained counsel in preparation for a defense against a possible perjury indictment?" Kissinger was outraged. "I have not retained counsel, and I am not conducting my office as if it were a conspiracy," he said. "I stand on the statements that I have made and I will answer no further questions on this topic." But the questions persisted.

During his thirty-three days out of Washington, Kissinger had become deconditioned to the intense pressure of the Watergate atmosphere. Following the news conference, a spate of stories and editorials appeared, questioning his real role in the wiretapping of White House aides in 1969. Kissinger saw himself becoming entangled in Watergate and worried about the consequences of the attacks. He sulked. One of his closest aides, Larry Eagleburger, urged him to lance the boil. Kissinger brooded, consulted with friends in Washington, and finally decided he had to do something. He did it in Salzburg, Austria, a would-be "rest" stop en route to the Middle East with President Nixon. Kissinger dramatically threatened to resign unless his name were cleared of all wiretap wrongdoing by the Senate Foreign Relations Committee.

It was an animated performance. But when I talked to him immediately afterward, he was calm and reasoned. He explained that he felt the gush of leaks and half-truths feeding the stream of the articles and editorials in the New York *Times,* the Washington *Post,* *Newsweek* ("A blot on Mr. Clean?"), and the Baltimore *Sun* had to be stopped; otherwise, they would begin feeding on themselves, and he would be irrevocably tagged as a Watergate figure because of his tenure in the Nixon White House. He also felt that on the eve of a trip to the Middle East, no serious diplomacy could be carried out if the credibility and survivability of the Secretary of State were suspect at precisely the same time the President of the United States was facing impeachment proceedings.

Kissinger did not mention his own hurt feelings, his battered ego. He had once told an academic colleague, "I know I have a first-rate mind, but that's no source of pride to me. Intelligent people are a dime a dozen. But I am proud of having character." And he felt his character was now being impugned by nameless, cowardly attackers.

The dramatic tactic worked — in the short term. The immediate crisis passed. The Senate cleared him again. The flow of Watergate stories slowed to a trickle. But the process left the Superman costume in shreds and Kissinger was off the "high plateau" of indispensability. A restless, assertive Congress, led by a latent-blooming Greek lobby, crucified him for his policy on Cyprus following the Greek-led coup on the island, the overthrow of Archbishop Makarios, and the Turkish invasion that followed.

And then a terrible thing happened to Henry Kissinger. Richard M. Nixon resigned as President.

The central authority of the United States was resuscitated as Gerald Ford became President. Ford, a novice at foreign affairs despite his twenty-five years in Congress, was one of Kissinger's biggest fans, and his basic approach to foreign policy as President was "leave it to Henry." Even before he was sworn in, Ford announced he would keep Kissinger as Secretary of State. But the disappearance of Nixon removed Kissinger's lightning rod. All the critical thunderbolts were now directed at him. The pent-up reluctance by an opposition Congress to pillory the Secretary of State while the President was going under burst forth. Chile. Vietnam. Secrecy. CIA operations. The Republican right wing tore at his policy of détente with the Russians. The arms control negotiations slowed down.

At that time, I noted a bumper sticker:

SELL KISSINGER, NOT WHEAT.

Vietnam fell. The third Kissinger shuttle in the spring of 1975 failed. Angola seethed with civil war. The Secretary learned that minorities punish, but majorities do not protect. Ten months after the Superman cover, Kissinger was back on the cover of *Newsweek,* this time as Gulliver being tied down by Washington Lilliputians. Kissinger was deeply hurt and brooded again about getting out, but the wit still flashed. He analyzed his difficulty: "In the past, I had excessive praise. Now I'm getting excessive criticism. But I tend to regard any criticism as excessive." Besides, he would say, "Anyone who criticizes me cannot be in good faith."

At a news conference in October 1974, a questioner asked, "Do you feel that the criticism that has been leveled against you in the past month on a whole variety of issues is fair, and do you believe that the criticism has to any degree affected your capacity to run foreign policy?"

"Well," Kissinger responded, "I think it is fair to say that my own estimate of myself may be at variance with that of some of the critics.

But then I can't expect my critics to be right a hundred percent of the time." When the laughter subsided, Kissinger went on: "I think the fact of criticism is certainly fair and was certainly inevitable. I think that there may have been a period, as I pointed out, in which there may have been excessive restraint, and this may be counter-balanced now by finding the more critical aspects. I assume that it will even out over a period of time. I don't think it has affected my effectiveness."

He had been bemused for some time by the fact that he, Henry Kissinger, a deeply conservative man, had come under attack from the right. He noted that he was first exposed to right-wing extremists at the time of President Nixon's visit to China in 1972. "They sound very much like left-wing extremists," he said, "only their vocabulary is not as good."

At the height of the criticism, William Macomber, the U.S. Ambassador to Turkey, urged Kissinger to seek solace from the career of Lord Castlereagh, the nineteenth-century British statesman about whom Kissinger had written as a historian. "He accomplished a great deal," Macomber pointed out, "and yet he was vilified even more than you. He did much in the service of his country." "Good God," replied Kissinger. "Castlereagh committed suicide."

Throughout, Ford never wavered in backing him. The President even went to Andrews Air Force Base one night with several members of the Cabinet, all in their tuxedos following a formal dinner at the White House, to see Kissinger off on a mission and to declare his strong support. On board the plane, newsmen teased Kissinger about the White House endorsements by reminding him of the usual fate of a manager of a losing baseball team who has just been backed by the team's owner. The Secretary acknowledged he might be in a lot of trouble: "I'm the only guy in town who has had two presidential statements of support in a single week."

But Kissinger was a survivor. As columnist Mark Childs once pointed out, "Kissinger's survival for five years in the Byzantine intrigues of the Nixon White House is in itself a small miracle. The atmosphere was a cross between Kafka and Little Orphan Annie with a pious facade out of J. Walter Thompson and the blessing of Billy Graham. In surviving, Kissinger's footwork then must have been agile." As Kissinger said of himself in the context of his soccer-playing days in Germany, "I wasn't fast, but I was tricky."

The Nixonites resented Kissinger as the lone survivor of the Nixon White House, and they never gave up trying to get him, providing frequent headlines. They weren't the only ones. At times, it seemed as though the press had declared open season on him. The Washington *Post* published a story on its front page, beginning: "Secretary of State Henry A. Kissinger forced the Office of Education to hire his brother-in-law, David Maginnes, even though there was no work for him to do, the Civil Service Commission said in a report released yesterday."

The commission's report said no such thing, and it turned out that David Maginnes was hired sixteen months before Kissinger married his sister. It was another example of the goldfish-turned-piranha tasting the blood in the water.

Kissinger's decline and near-fall, however, were largely a Washington phenomenon. Beyond the banks of the Potomac, he retained his number one standing in the Most Admired polls. And overseas he was still an authentic American hero in most places, even if Athens was not one of them. He humorously acknowledged his decline in his own country at a luncheon given by the Public Broadcasting Service. "I understand," he said, "that you are now exporting more programs than you are importing. So, one could argue that you are appreciated more abroad than at home. This is a feeling with which I sympathize."

In the summer of 1976, Kissinger exported himself to Latin America for the second time. His trip was scheduled around a meeting of the Organization of American States in Santiago, Chile, and one of the preliminary stops was Santa Cruz, a small city of nineteenth-century charm in the lowlands of Bolivia. Kissinger arrived at night, and the next morning he met with Bolivia's President, General Hugo Banzer. Banzer was a plain, gruff, rough-edged soldier, a straightforward man who ignored his briefing papers for the Kissinger meeting and launched instead into a long discourse on his country's overriding passion of the moment, an outlet to the sea. After about forty minutes, the subject was exhausted. Banzer leaned back and started talking about something else. "You know, Dr. Kissinger," he said, "perhaps I have failed in my elementary duties of welcoming you to Bolivia.

"I know you were welcomed properly last night because I sent my foreign minister to the airport to greet you, and he reported to me this morning that he had done so."

Banzer went on, "It would have been improper for *me* to greet you at the airport as the President of Bolivia because of protocol. But power is temporary and citizenship is permanent, and as a citizen of Bolivia, I did not want to miss your arrival. And so I was there with my wife and my two children in the crowd that greeted you at the airport." It was said with simplicity and directness.

For once, Kissinger was speechless. He finally said, "Mr. President, I'm very touched by that," and then he said it again. For all his egomania, Kissinger never recounted that story to newsmen.

With the press, he remained his wisecracking self. On one trip, a reporter asked, "Are you going to Washington soon?" Kissinger smiled and said, "Why should I? I only visit friendly capitals."

And visit them he did. He kept on traveling throughout 1975 and 1976. In the summer of '75, he arranged another Israeli-Egyptian agreement, and late in 1976, he pulled one more rabbit out of the diplomatic hat: a Rhodesian commitment to black majority rule.

But on November 2, the voters elected Jimmy Carter to replace Gerald Ford in the White House, and the ugly duckling who became a swan at the State Department was turned into a lame duck. His wings were clipped, but not his humor. At a reception at the Soviet Embassy right after the election, Kissinger said he was under consideration for a new job — chief of protocol. Later, he told a reporter, "I'm looking for a job with the CAB" (Civil Aeronautics Board).

At the State Department, officials began speculating about his successor with the certain knowledge that Kissinger would be missed. One of his former personal aides summed up the Department's general attitude toward Kissinger in this perceptive way: "Everybody had strong, mixed feelings about him." And one official who had asked for a transfer to get away from him described him as an "artichoke." Like an artichoke, he explained, Kissinger was multilayered and combined a tart bitterness with a hidden but tender heart. Kissinger, the official added, was an acquired taste.

Mike Peters, with permission from *Dayton Daily News*

T W O

On the Road

In one of the most gracious introductions I ever heard — and wanted to believe — NBC anchorman John Chancellor once presented me to a luncheon audience in New York by saying, "When Dick Valeriani was sent to cover the State Department after having covered the White House, Henry Kissinger had the good sense to follow."

Henry Kissinger followed me to the State Department in September 1973. I remember saying at the time, "Well, at least I won't be traveling as much." That prediction turned out to rank right up there with the *Literary Digest*'s forecast of an Alf Landon victory in 1936. Kissinger was more prescient. Soon after he was nominated as Secretary of State, he said of his new employees: "My advice to them will be to get to know their wives very well before my confirmation, because afterward they may not see as much of them." I thought he was kidding. But 667,732 miles and 59 countries later, I knew he wasn't.

Much of the travel as a White House correspondent had involved commuting between Washington and the presidential playgrounds: Key Biscayne, Florida, and San Clemente, California. That proved to be kid stuff once I started trailing Kissinger.

A few days after moving into the State Department, the new Secretary addressed the employees in the courtyard. "In convincing me of the wisdom of doing this," he told them, "my new colleagues pointed out that Secretary Dulles met a similar group. They forgot to mention that this was the last time anybody in the department saw Secretary Dulles." During the next three years, three months, and twenty-eight days, Secretary Kissinger spent approximately four hundred nights away from Washington on official visits, not counting routine trips to California or Colorado to consult with President Nixon or President Ford. Somebody pointed out that Deputy Secretary of State Kenneth Rush spent more time as Acting Secretary than some people had actually spent as Secretary. Kissinger was away so much that he once began remarks to a group of visiting Europeans at the State Department by saying, "I want to tell you how delighted I am that my visit to Washington coincided with yours."

Kissinger's travel record became obvious grist for columnist Art Buchwald's humor mill. "We're having tremendous excitement in the nation's capital this week," Buchwald wrote. "There is a rumor going around that Secretary of State Henry Kissinger may visit Washington, D.C. Officially, State Department spokesmen are denying it. But despite the denials, preparations are going ahead for the Secretary of State's visit."

At the end of one of the trips, the traveling newsmen wrote an arrival statement for the Secretary to read at Andrews Air Force Base. It began: "I'm delighted to be a guest in your country for the next forty-eight hours. I look forward to constructive talks with your President."

Most of the foreign trips were brutal — a string of one-night stands and day-long schedules. In late 1973, we hit thirteen countries in fifteen days. A year later, we zipped through seventeen countries in eighteen days, covering 26,880 miles. Washington *Post* diplomatic correspondent Murrey Marder, a veteran of many years' reporting from the State Department, described the latter trip as a case of "jet-set lunacy."

On one of those trips, Jerry O'Leary of the Washington *Star* came aboard the plane in a state of fatigued stupefaction and muttered in his gravelly voice, "I feel like one of the Visigoths, wandering all over the world and never knowing where I am." Whereupon Barry Schweid of the AP cracked, "Yeah, but at least they got to rape and pillage. All we get is briefed."

Kissinger himself cracked up his staff on one of his extended whirlwind swings through the Middle East by turning around as he was about to leave the airplane and asking with mock seriousness, "What country is this?" During one of the longer trips, one of my radio broadcasts began: "It's another three-country day for Kissinger — breakfast in Rumania, lunch in Yugoslavia, dinner in Rome."

Kissinger did conduct a considerable amount of diplomacy across a meal table. On another trip, he had breakfast with British officials in London, lunch with the Shah of Iran in Zurich, and dinner with French officials in Paris. (In an unusual display of gastronomic diplomacy, Kissinger once had all three meals in Washington with Israeli Prime Minister Yitzhak Rabin.) The *Wall Street Journal* dubbed Kissinger "the Galloping Gourmet of diplomacy."

What made Henry fly? The superficial answer came from UPI's Helen Thomas, who knew him at the White House: "Henry goes on sheer love of himself. It's the conquering hero. His momentum is built on his own sense of self-fulfillment." Ego gratification did play a part. But more important, Kissinger was a strong believer in personal diplomacy. Especially when his persona was involved.

By the time he became Secretary of State, he had already racked up a remarkable record of achievement to reinforce that belief, much of it compiled during personal diplomatic excursions to China, Moscow, and to Paris. His White House office contained a globe with a penciled note on it: FRAGILE — DO NOT TOUCH. But Kissinger felt a compulsion to touch the fragile world out there, and he did so whenever he thought he had to.

As one of his biographers has noted, Kissinger was concerned principally "with those who exercised authority . . . States, for Kis-

singer, were real entities. Their leaders were no less real." In addition, a lot of their leaders were already known to him. They had been
students at the Harvard International Seminar he ran during sum-
mers in Cambridge. Participants had come from the middle ranks of
government, politics, economics, and journalism, and now they were
prime ministers, foreign ministers, and other high-ranking government officials all over the world.

Watergate and Vietnam and recent American history also fueled
Henry's diplomatic wanderlust. Within a period of only eleven years,
a President had been assassinated, a major presidential candidate had
been assassinated, a President had been hounded out of office because
of an unpopular war, and another President was paralyzed by scan-
dal. That kind of history hardly projected a picture of strength and
stability to a world hungry for leadership.

As Nixon's troubles deepened, Kissinger was concerned that other
countries, primarily the Soviet Union, would begin looking for tar-
gets of opportunity if they perceived the United States to be weak in
an exploitable way. During this period, he frequently worried out
loud about the erosion of "central authority" in the United States.
A besieged President could not go out and give speeches and make
commitments that were meaningful. So Kissinger felt he was the one
who had to give the speeches and make the commitments. As a
nonelected official, he felt he could not do it so much from his base
in Washington. He felt much more comfortable filling the power
vacuum on the scene, on the battlefield, as it were. Kissinger traveled, not as a messenger, but as a general in the field.

And Henry Kissinger came to symbolize and represent and em-
body to the rest of the world the continuity and constancy of American foreign policy at a time of severe constitutional crisis. His reputation preceded him, and the very fact of his previous diplomatic
success helped to produce new diplomatic successes. As one of his
aides astutely observed, "The better he did, the better he did."

The timing was also right. London *Times* foreign editor Louis
Heren noted that "much of the world, East as well as West, hankers
for Superman. The role was thrust upon him, although presumably
he did not have to be persuaded."

Later, looking back on his government career, Kissinger felt his greatest achievement had been holding American foreign policy together during the lengthy Watergate period and through the presidential transition. But long before Watergate, Kissinger had folded his personal flamboyance into diplomatic practice.

As a Harvard historian, he had written: "The art of statesmanship is to understand the nature of the world and the trend of history." And he tried to tailor not only policy but also style to the nature of the world and the trend of history as he saw it. Another quotation from his Harvard days was even more pertinent to his mode of operation. In *A World Restored,* Kissinger wrote: "The key to success in diplomacy is freedom of action, not formal relationships."

As a White House aide, Kissinger elaborated on that maxim in fulsome fashion in a colorful interview with Italian journalist Oriana Fallaci. Speaking of his success as a secret presidential agent, Kissinger was quoted as saying: "The main point stems from the fact that I've always acted alone. Americans admire that enormously. Americans admire the cowboy leading the caravan alone astride his horse, the cowboy entering a village or city alone on his horse. Without even a pistol, maybe, because he doesn't go in for shooting. He acts, that's all: aiming at the right spot at the right time. A Wild West tale, if you like . . . The cowboy doesn't need courage. It's enough that he be alone, that he show others how he enters the village alone and does everything on his own. This romantic, surprising character suits me, because being alone has always been part of my style, or of my technique, if you prefer. Independence, too." When the interview first appeared, Kissinger instructed his aides to deny it. But they talked him out of a denial, and he later lamented, "Why I agreed to it, I'll never know."

Instead of "leading the caravan alone astride his horse," however, Kissinger saddled up a trusty four-engine jet to take him to his *High Noon* showdowns around the world.

Ironically, for a man who spent so much time in an airplane, Kissinger didn't like to fly. His uneasiness was intensified during rough flying weather. I remember once sitting in his airborne office during a briefing when the plane suddenly shuddered. A look of terror flashed across his face as he grabbed the edge of the table with both hands. He thought that rough weather was somehow the pilot's fault. During another briefing session when the plane hit a bad spot, Kissinger remarked sarcastically, "My ears are popping. Is that madman in a dive?" Once he was talking to CBS correspondent Marvin Kalb when the plane suddenly went into a fairly steep descent. The seat-belt sign flashed on, and Kalb hurriedly got up to return to the rear section. "No, you don't," Kissinger said jokingly as he grabbed Kalb's arm. "You sit down. If I'm going, I'm not going alone." He especially disliked flying in helicopters, but he steeled himself to accept it.

Beyond the policy and philosophical reasons for Kissinger's compulsive wandering lay simple personal tastes. As a top department official put it, "Henry had an insane love for the prerogatives of office." He reveled in the "perks of power." When Kissinger traveled, he traveled in style, and he was treated with style. He had the best room in the best hotel in town if he was not staying at a presidential palace or guest house or U.S. Embassy residence. Virtually every whim was satisfied.

Sometimes his aides could be holier than the Pope. One of them was overheard screaming into a mouthpiece in Jerusalem, "I don't care about anything else. You just stay there and be always ready to greet Henry Kissinger." An American Embassy employee in London who was involved in setting up the Kissinger visits there put it simply: "He loved Class — with a capital C." He especially liked the style and service at Claridge's, and London was invariably included in his itinerary whenever he flew east.

Although a reporter once estimated the cost of Kissinger's travel to the government at about $20,000 a day, it was impossible to come up with a precise accounting. And nobody ever did. Kissinger himself never paid any attention at all to that kind of detail. One of the occupational hazards of government officials is a callous attitude toward public funds. When they start tossing around budgets involving billions of dollars, they tend to become casual about smaller sums.

When Kissinger first became Secretary of State, he was the host at an elegant dinner at the Metropolitan Museum in New York for the heads of the UN delegations. Nelson Rockefeller, Kissinger's principal patron in pregovernment life, picked up most of the tab, but a bill for $35,000 for security and other items went to the State Department. The bill was leaked to a columnist, who called the press office for confirmation of the amount, which included $7000 for flowers. Kissinger was furious when he was asked about it by the press officer. Why, he wanted to know, were people nitpicking him on this chicken-shit sort of thing? And why did the department have to put out the figures? Because, he was told, we were asked.

During his battle with Congress on how to respond to Soviet and Cuban intervention in Angola, Kissinger lamented during the on-plane briefings about America's failure to act when "only trivial sums" were involved — by which he meant tens of millions of dollars.

The cost of any Kissinger trip was multiplied by the heavy security requirements. An Air Force C-141 usually preceded him to whatever foreign capital he was visiting. It carried Secret Service agents and a specially armored Fleetwood Cadillac limousine that Kissinger used on most of his overseas visits (but not in police states like the Soviet Union and China, where security was not high on the list of concerns). Each car weighed four and a half tons and had its own self-contained ventilation system to change the air if a gas bomb were thrown into the interior. In the words of one of the agents, "It could take a bazooka head on."

The Secretary himself flew in a big, gleaming, blue and white Boeing 707 from the presidential fleet at Andrews Air Force Base. His plane, tail number 86970, was formerly used by Lyndon B. Johnson as Vice President.

During a period when Kissinger seemed to be in decline, we arrived at Andrews Air Force Base for a late night departure to find a different, less well appointed plane waiting. When the Secretary came on board, he explained, "The other one is in the shop. It will be ready soon." "That's what they always say," taunted a reporter.

Kissinger shot back in jest, "You just wait until you get on a god-damned plane that has no windows."

His regular plane was divided into five sections. The front section housed a back-up flight crew and a solid wall of communications equipment that kept the Secretary in instant touch with the White House and the rest of the world. (The communications technicians also kept the traveling party in touch with such vital matters as pro football scores.)

Just behind this front section was a compartment that served as private quarters for Kissinger and for members of his family when they traveled with him. This compartment had two beds, a small desk, and a private bathroom. The seal of the Secretary of State hung on the door.

On the other side of the private quarters, in the middle of the plane, was a compartment that Kissinger used as an office. It had a curved, L-shaped table that could be raised and lowered by pushing a button — thanks to LBJ's love of gadgetry. A bank of seats lined each side of the compartment, with a large easy chair at the corner of the L. This is where he usually briefed the press in flight.

The fourth compartment served as a kind of State Department flying office. It had a table between the seats on each side of the aisle, filing cabinets, and a cramped space for a typist, who was kept busy throughout every flight. The seats were occupied by senior aides.

This compartment also housed an indispensable copying machine, a temperamental device that seemed to suffer frequently from altitude sickness. It simply would not reproduce unless the plane was absolutely level. This meant that the time available for copying on the flights between Israel and Egypt or Israel and Syria was limited. But the Kissinger party usually needed to have certain key documents reproduced and in hand as soon as we hit the ground, so the staff would frequently advise the pilot to taxi for as long as possible after landing to provide time for the necessary documents to be copied for the next round of talks. In the back of the plane, we newsmen would be making bad jokes about how we were "driving" to Aswan or Tel Aviv, or how the pilot was a frustrated bus driver.

But as we were rolling along on the ground at airports throughout the Middle East, the machine was copying away in the interests of peace.

Behind the office was the largest section of the plane. It held the traveling correspondents, the Secret Service detail (normally eight agents on board), secretaries, communications specialists, a State Department doctor who always accompanied the Secretary, and some staff personnel. The seating was two abreast, but the seats were not as wide as those in the first-class section of a commercial plane. The correspondents were all charged first-class round-trip fare to the farthest point from Washington, plus one dollar, to prevent any complaints from commercial carriers that the government was undercutting them.

Even though a White House aide does not ordinarily get Secret Service protection, these bodyguards had been a constant feature of Kissinger's life ever since an alleged plot to kidnap him was discovered in 1970. When he became Secretary of State and had to decide whether to keep the Secret Service agents or switch to State Department security, he told one of his favorite agents, Walter Bothe, with tongue in cheek, "Walter, I'd rather have incompetents I know rather than ones I don't know."

At least two assassination plots were reported against him as Secretary, but when the issue came up at a formal State Department news conference, he pointed out with something less than overwhelming concern, "The administration has taken a very strong stand against any attacks on me . . ." Even in the absence of assassination plots, the travel security for Kissinger was always tight, and all our hand luggage was subjected to a rigid search to make sure that no explosives had been slipped in without our knowledge.

At the rear of the plane was the galley, where the Air Force stewards struggled to make the flights as palatable as possible. One of the rules of a traveling correspondent is to eat whenever a meal is available, since you never know when the next meal will be. This rule was deliberately breached when possible during Kissinger trips. It's not that the stewards didn't try hard. Once they turned out

McDonald's hamburgers. (It was one of the better meals, and Kissinger, in a weak moment, even allowed himself to be photographed in a McDonald's cap.) Another time, they showed up with Shakey's pizza. But most of the time, the London broil tasted like filet of sole (as in shoe), the chicken Kiev fought back, and the lasagna would have tasted as bad by any other name. However, the prime rib roast traditionally served on the return flight to Washington usually provided a prime meal — when it wasn't overdone.

In spite of his difficult personality, the stewards generally liked traveling with Kissinger because of his sense of humor. Once, right after being served dinner, he hit the call button. When the steward arrived at his cabin, Kissinger was sitting there with a plate broken in two and a steak in his lap. "The next time," he droned, "either bring me a sharp knife or a better plate." Thereafter, he had a knife he could shave with.

One of the stewards, Carl Resnick, learned to do a good imitation of Kissinger. He used to sneak up behind one of Kissinger's closest aides, Larry Eagleburger, and make him jump by saying something outrageous in his Kissinger voice. As Resnick neared retirement, he was prevailed upon to do his imitation for the real Henry. After hearing Resnick's number, Kissinger fixed him with a stare and said, "You're going to like it in Alaska." When Resnick left, he opened a bar-restaurant in Accident, Maryland, called Little Henry's. An autographed picture of Henry Kissinger hangs over the bar.

Whenever new stewards were assigned to an overseas flight, they would be given a copy of Kissinger's diet, prepared by a State Department nutritionist, but they soon learned to ignore it. And they would invariably ask if the Secretary required kosher food. The answer: "Hell no." (In fact, a local Washington synagogue, trying to put together a book of recipes favored by prominent Jewish Washingtonians, asked Kissinger for one of his favorite dishes. He sent back a recipe for a Basque omelet, which contains ham. The synagogue discreetly published the recipe without the ham.)

On the plane, Kissinger generally ate what everybody else ate, although his front-section galley was always stocked with special foods so that he could have a steak or scrambled eggs whenever he wanted them. The stewards remember Kissinger as a good eater. Once, after finishing a steak in his own compartment, he wandered back to the press section, where he saw meat loaf being served. He went back to his compartment, hit the buzzer, and asked the steward for a meat loaf sandwich. Before the stewards had finished serving, Kissinger had downed three meat loaf sandwiches, and the cook was slicing the stuff a little more thinly.

While the press contingent on a Kissinger trip usually numbered fourteen, no single reporter made all of the trips. But I made more than any other reporter — over 500,000 miles abroad. When it became apparent how much traveling he — and we — were actually going to do, I had buttons made up that read: FREE THE KISSINGER 14.

When Kissinger traveled, he did not leave the State Department behind. He took it with him. There was no problem about who was going to mind the store. Kissinger *was* the store. He didn't deputize. He traumatized. (It was not surprising that when he was asked during a three-hour NBC special on foreign affairs if anybody "really knew how foreign policy was made," he replied with a wry smile, "I do.") His blue and white 707 became a flying State Department. Unlike his immediate predecessors, Kissinger insisted on running the department from wherever he was. As Washington *Post* reporter Murrey Marder once said, "Dr. Kissinger may well be the biggest permanent floating foreign policy establishment in our history — in the air or on the ground." (For those readers who have led a sheltered life, the adjectives "biggest, permanent, floating" used in that order usually apply to a crap game. But Marder will have to speak for himself.)

All of Kissinger's trips originated and ended at Andrews Air Force Base, about ten miles outside Washington. Whenever Kissinger left or returned, the entire State Department hierarchy would show up to see him off or welcome him back. I was never sure whether it was a command performance or simply a way to accumulate brownie points.

For Kissinger, returning from those trips when Nancy had trav-

eled with him, the most welcome sight at the airport was four-legged
— Tyler, his bumptious yellow Labrador retriever. It had been
Nancy's idea to get a dog. Kissinger himself had not been enthusias-
tic about the idea since, he explained, "I was afraid I'd get too
attached to him." He spoke from experience. During World War II,
Kissinger had picked up a cocker spaniel at a pet shop in Paris and
carted him all over Europe in a knapsack. Canine history repeated

Dwane Powell, *The Cincinnati Enquirer*

itself, and he became emotionally tied to Tyler as well. So did Nancy. Near the end of his tenure, the Secretary of State was asked if he might go to Oxford or Cambridge University to teach once he left office. "No," he said. "Tyler would have to go into quarantine, and Nancy would move into the kennel."

However, Kissinger managed to evade the quarantine for dogs when he went to Jamaica, a former British colony, which shared the Motherland's fanatical concern about rabies. But it wasn't easy. The Kissingers had arranged to take a vacation at a private estate near Ocho Rios, and Henry wanted to take Tyler along. The Jamaicans said Tyler would have to be quarantined, but the Secretary of State said, in effect, Have me, have my dog. Cables flew back and forth between Washington and Jamaica to the point of causing some strain in diplomatic relations. The Jamaicans finally relented, and the Kissinger party, including Tyler, flew to Jamaica in a government Jetstar. When they landed, the Secretary of State walked over to the waiting press while an aide sneaked Tyler off the Jetstar and onto the plane that would fly all of them to Ocho Rios. The second plane, as the aide recalls, "was a funny-looking trimotor plane which resembled a World War I Fokker. If it got overloaded in the back, it would tilt back on its tail. So we loaded Henry first — up front. As we took off, the Jetstar pilots lined up outside their plane and stood at attention with their hands over their hearts."

Right after buying the dog, Mrs. Kissinger asked the reporters on the plane to suggest names. In a burst of collective imagination, they came up with Rover and Spot. Nancy decided to name him Tyler. "He just looked like a Tyler," she explained. Kissinger, however, attributed the name to his "WASP wife's revenge."

While still a puppy, Tyler made the newspapers. The Secret Service responded to an alarm in the Kissingers' home in Georgetown and found it had been set off by Tyler; he had chewed up an intercom terminal. Normally, he chewed Kissinger's shoes. Tyler was also a frequent visitor to the Secretary's seventh-floor office at the State Department, where, in fun-loving fashion, he occasionally snatched secret cables off the desk and romped around.

Tyler's popularity among staff aides was tempered by the fact that they were occasionally pressed into walking-the-dog duty. The Secret Service agents flatly refused to walk the dog, but they did, of course, go along when Nancy and Henry walked Tyler in Georgetown. One of the walks turned out to be embarrassingly eventful. The Kissingers lived in an area of Georgetown heavily populated by homosexuals. One evening while being walked, Tyler disappeared down an alley and didn't come back. Finally, a Secret Service agent accompanying Nancy Kissinger went looking for him and found him sitting in the alley, watching a gay couple *in flagrante*.

While Tyler never followed his master overseas, he did occasionally go to New York when the Secretary visited the UN. Very undiplomatic sources reported that one morning Tyler didn't make it out of the Kissingers' Waldorf Towers suite to Park Avenue in time, and there is said to be a Tyler Kissinger Memorial Spot outside the elevator on the thirty-fifth floor.

While American embassies never had to worry about making arrangements for Kissinger's dog, they had their hands full with plenty of other matters. In advance of any Kissinger trip, six four-page cables would go out from the Secretariat — the support office for the Secretary of State — giving the embassies detailed instructions on the logistical requirements of their leader. In addition, an advance team — a member of the Secretariat and a secretary — would also visit the cities on Kissinger's itinerary to make sure the arrangements were handled correctly. Its chief function was to ensure that the Secretary's party could get off the plane and go immediately to work in the six or seven offices that had been set up in the headquarters hotel. The visits to London and Paris became so frequent that the local Embassy administrative officer eventually learned the procedure by rote so that an advance team was no longer required. A Secret Service team also went to the locations on the itinerary in advance to check on security arrangements.

The members of the Secretariat were responsible for keeping Kissinger on top of everything happening around the world, while his personal staff had the impossible task of keeping him up to date with his briefing books and arranging his personal schedule. It was impossible because Kissinger simply would not pay attention to his schedule.

When he first became prominent as a White House aide and became quotable, one of his most quoted lines was delivered to a personal assistant. "I'm not a dentist," he groused in complaining about appointments scheduled for him every fifteen minutes. Yet, after ranting and raving about being overscheduled, he would usually end up by asking them to squeeze in somebody else he had promised to see. At the State Department, his frustrated staff once devised a sure-fire scheme for making him look at his proposed schedule. Playing on his ego and his paranoia, they drew up four special folders and placed his schedules inside, knowing he would look at those folders first. The covering labels read: ADULATORY CABLES, OFFERS OF AWARDS, CONVERSATIONS BETWEEN THE PRESIDENT AND GEN. BRENT SCOWCROFT (Kissinger's NSC aide at the White House), and a fourth, simply SONNENFELDT.

Helmut ("Hal") Sonnenfeldt was the counselor of the State Department and Kissinger's chief adviser on Soviet affairs. He was sometimes referred to as Kissinger's Kissinger. The two men had known each other a long time and enjoyed a love-hate relationship. Like Kissinger, Sonnenfeldt was a German-born Jew. Like Kissinger, he was brilliant, with a good sense of humor and a prickly personality. He had an amazing facility for driving Henry wild. For instance, he would sit in during the on-plane briefings that Kissinger would give about Soviet affairs and wince or roll his eyes whenever the Secretary said something Sonnenfeldt might disagree with. Sonnenfeldt also always knew where the cameras were, and he always tried to slip into the picture — which also drove Kissinger up the wall.

The relationship between the two men was reflected in their remarks during Sonnenfeldt's swearing-in ceremony. "One of the first things Sonnenfeldt wanted to know about at the National Security Council was mess privileges and parking space," Kissinger joshed. "For the record, I want to say Hal has access to the public cafeteria on the first floor . . . We have been friends for a long time . . . The friendship is sometimes skewered by the severity of his criticism. Sonnenfeldt is a perfectionist. As he said to me after the first Moscow Summit, 'I got pretty good work out of you on this occasion.' "

Sonnenfeldt rejoined, "I didn't have a good line on your remarks here, and since I didn't write them myself on this occasion, I'm not exactly sure how to respond. Another rumor, that I always move my lips when the Secretary speaks, is not true either."

It was against the backdrop of this relationship that the Kissinger staff once decided to have some fun with their boss. In arranging his schedule, the staff had deliberately avoided a purely social occasion, a White House luncheon honoring Notre Dame's president, Father Theodore Hesburgh. The staff went through the State Department hierarchy trying to find a substitute for the Secretary; they found the other top officials busy, and they didn't come to rest until they got down to the counselor. Sonnenfeldt accepted. Aides Larry Eagleburger and David Gompert knew the Secretary would flip out if he thought Sonnenfeldt had been invited to the White House instead of him, so they wrote a memo to Sonnenfeldt entitled, "Your Luncheon with the President." Then, while Sonnenfeldt was in a meeting presided over by Kissinger, Eagleburger marched in and presented the counselor with the memo, saying, "Here's the paper you've been waiting for." Kissinger, as was his wont, immediately snatched the memo out of Sonnenfeldt's hands. "It was like opening the door a crack and rolling a hand grenade into the room," one eyewitness put it.

After the smoke had cleared, the staff was faced with two alternatives: Cancel the White House luncheon or rearrange Kissinger's schedule so he could attend. Cancellation of the luncheon was obviously impossible, so the schedule was rearranged. The Secretary of State ended up going to a White House luncheon as a sit-in for his counselor.

And that's one of the ways the Kissinger staff kept its sanity. The gag with the four file folders was a one-day wonder. Kissinger laughed about it, promised to pay more attention to his schedule in the future, and then promptly went back to his old habits.

Despite some public criticism of Kissinger's constant travel and his insistence on running the department from thirty-five thousand feet in the air, a lot of his underlings in Washington claimed the department functioned more efficiently when the Secretary was traveling because they could get him to concentrate and decide quickly on important matters by sending him a cable, which he had to answer. In Washington, he was always being distracted by telephone calls, staff meetings, and personal visits.

Kissinger's plane was amply supplied with research material on any subject that might come up in the course of his travels. This material included every public statement the Secretary had ever made on any subject. Before Kissinger left on a trip, the department would send a cable to the various American embassies along the way, advising them that "the party's classified material, which must be moved between aircraft and hotels at each stop, consists of six large footlockers, two large steamer trunks and thirty or so bulky briefcases." Some staffers joked that the cable sounded like a description of Nancy's luggage.

While Kissinger was on the road, between one and two hundred cables went between his plane and the State Department every day. The volume was so heavy that area missions were ordered on a "minimize" procedure, which restricted all but the most essential traffic and required senior Embassy officials to certify that a cable was necessary. The plane's cable traffic covered every conceivable matter, since Kissinger wanted to know about everything going on at the department down to the most trivial detail.

The trivia traveled both ways. The most urgent form of communication — a "flash" cable — was once sent from the plane to the Embassy in Rome, requesting appointments for Henry and Nancy at a barber shop and a beauty salon, respectively.

Kissinger's punctilious attention to detail even got him involved in menus. During one of his African trips, a State Department protocol officer had put together a rather exotic menu for a dinner the Secretary was giving in Nairobi. The main course was to be impala. One of Kissinger's aides sent the protocol officer the following cable:

"You should find suitable substitute for impala. Secretary is not a fan of venison at all and finds the prospect of eating impala saddening." The cable was classified "Limited Official Use."

When Kissinger came back from a trip, he hit the ground running, and at the last stop before Washington, his aides always sent a cable like this one:

SUBJECT: WELCOME HOME

1. WOULD APPRECIATE YOUR ARRANGING TO HAVE FOLLOWING ITEMS AVAILABLE AT PLANESIDE UPON ARRIVAL ANDREWS:

2. SUNDAY TIMES AND POST.

3. UP-TO-DATE SET OF RABIN BRIEFING BOOKS (A SECOND SET FOR THE SECRETARY, AS WELL AS A BACK-UP SET, SHOULD BE AVAILABLE IN THE DEPARTMENT BY 0800 MONDAY).

4. A MODEST SELECTION OF CHITTED CABLES AND TICKERS (PLEASE COORDINATE WITH S/S-O TO ENSURE THAT THE SELECTION IS FRESH).

5. PLEASE TRY TO AVOID BRINGING ACTION ITEMS TO PLANESIDE. IF SOMETHING TRULY URGENT COMES UP, HOWEVER, AND IT IS NOT POSSIBLE TO CABLE IT, PLEASE ALERT US.

6. PLEASE BRING THE MATERIALS DIRECTLY TO THE RAMP SO WE CAN GET A QUICK LOOK AT IT BEFORE PUTTING IT INTO THE LIMOUSINE.

KISSINGER

LIMITED OFFICIAL USE

The support staff on the plane included three secretaries, two personal aides, and two members of the State Department Secretariat. In addition, several senior aides always traveled with the Secretary. The aide who made the most trips was Peter Rodman, a staffer from the National Security Council at the White House. One of his principal jobs was to take notes during the Secretary's conversations with world leaders.

Kissinger seldom knew the people from the Secretariat. In fact, his managerial style at the department was to deal essentially with the assistant secretaries of state, who headed the various regional bureaus, and he left the managing of the bureaus to them.

On one trip, he walked into the plane's office and saw a new face, which belonged to Russ Lamantia of the Secretariat. Kissinger, in his intimidating way, did not ask Lamantia directly who he was. Instead, with something close to disdain in his voice, he asked another staffer, "Who is that?" Lamantia piped up, "I'm Valeriani's staff assistant." Kissinger did a double-take, then chuckled, and remembered Lamantia after that.

The secretaries worked in shifts and were always busy; they seldom got out of their hotels to do any sightseeing or shopping. "Without the ability to sleep in a motorcade," one secretary said, "we'd never survive."

The workload was especially heavy when Kissinger was writing a speech that required some consultation with other agencies in Washington. During the Middle East shuttle that produced a second disengagement agreement between Israel and Egypt in September 1975, Kissinger was working on a mammoth speech to be delivered to a special session of the United Nations. He was intensely meticulous about speeches. Each one had to be handcrafted as though it were chipped in stone. Some of them went through as many as twenty drafts. Aide Winston Lord produced one of the best known and most quoted of the early Kissinger stories by describing what it was like writing a speech for the Secretary. "He'll ask for a paper, and after he gets it he'll call the writer in and say, 'Is this the best you can do on this?' The guy says, 'Well, I'll try again.' A couple of days later, the writer returns with another draft. The same ritual is repeated. After about five or six times, the writer, weary and frustrated, takes in another draft, and when Kissinger asks again, 'Is this the best you can do?' the writer finally replies, 'Yes, damnit.' 'Good,' says Kissinger, 'now I'll read it.' "

The speech for the UN special session included a lot of technical economic material, so it had to be checked out frequently with Washington. When it was finished, it filled 117 triple-spaced pages. The whole thing had to be cabled back to Washington. Six typists were kept busy full time in Egypt and Israel. Since Kissinger was obsessed about leaks, the speech was sent NODIS — No Distribution — which means it had to be coded. And once the coded speech reached Washington, it had to be hand-delivered rather than sent through chutes since it was NODIS.

Kissinger never even got to deliver the speech in person. The Israeli-Egyptian negotiations dragged on longer than anticipated, and Kissinger stayed to wrap up the agreement. The speech was delivered for him by Ambassador Daniel P. ("Pat") Moynihan, who sent him a cable, which read: "Your speech was major success, and you had added advantage of not having to sit and listen to it for one hour and forty-five minutes."

In addition to keeping Kissinger abreast of his schedule or finding one of the three pairs of eyeglasses he was always misplacing, the staff faced a number of other major problems on the road. One of them was breakfast. Kissinger was a fanatic about his breakfast: orange juice, two four-minute boiled eggs, and coffee. It had to be prepared just right, and it had to be delivered right on time. He was fastidious about starting his day a certain way. And if it started badly, his staffers knew it would be a long day. Some of the aides who got to know him best concluded that a crisis over breakfast was unavoidable. It would either arrive too early or too late; the eggs would be overdone or underdone; the juice would be too sour, the coffee too tepid. Larry Eagleburger once told other aides, "You'll never get it right. Just try." The crisis was frequently avoided when Kissinger stayed in places like Claridge's in London. But elsewhere . . .

In Algeria, Kissinger stayed at a government guest house. The staff had ordered breakfast for him at seven. But after Kissinger was awakened, he immediately called to complain that his breakfast wasn't there. It has to be, a staffer said; they called from the kitchen fifteen minutes ago and said it was on the way. But it wasn't. The staff called for another breakfast from a kitchen that didn't know the meaning of the words "short order." Half an hour later, the kitchen reported breakfast was again on the way. But a few minutes later Kissinger, by then furious, called again to ask where the hell his breakfast was. The staff, baffled, ordered a third one.

This time, when the kitchen called back to say the breakfast was en route, Dave Gompert, one of the Secretary's personal aides, went outside to wait for it. He saw the Algerian waiter go up the steps, down a long passageway, and disappear into the Secret Service control room. Gompert raced to save a third breakfast from vanishing. Nobody had explained to the Secret Service agents what was going on, so when the breakfasts appeared, they ate them. For the Kissinger staffers, that was a very long day.

Accommodations could also cause problems. Whenever the President traveled, Kissinger insisted on having the room closest to him, but when President Ford went to China in 1975, a White House aide rather than the Secretary of State had the room nearest him at the government guest house. Kissinger grumbled about it to Ambassador George Bush so much that Bush finally told him, "Henry, I don't do rooms." But the Secretary of State made sure that a cable went out from Peking to Jakarta, the next stop on the trip, improving his proximity to the President.

Several of Kissinger's close associates pointed out that he was outstanding in coping with the major complications of his job. He was superb in his approach to negotiations, in plotting strategy and executing tactics. But, as a personal aide pointed out, trivial things drove him "around the bend, such as not having the right tuxedo shirt or not having his shoes polished." While Kissinger was coping with the big things, his staff learned to cope with his tantrums over the little things, for they knew that if something went wrong, they would have to take the heat.

An American Ambassador in Europe watched the fuse burn down quickly one night in the Secretary's suite at the Hilton Hotel in Brussels. It was late, and Kissinger was scheduled to give a speech the next morning. He went through some folders on a table, looking in vain for the final, retyped draft of the speech. Kissinger blew. He buzzed the intercom, and aide Jerry Bremer came running. Bypassing the verbal buzzsaw, Bremer walked calmly over to the table, pushed the top folder aside, and picked up a second folder containing the draft of the speech.

Kissinger, more wolfishly than sheepishly, said, "I guess it was there all the time, and you're suggesting I didn't see it." Bremer, a bright, long-suffering, Kennedyesque-looking young Foreign Service officer replied matter-of-factly, "Oh no, sir. Obviously I just put it there." Then he added without sarcasm, "If I ever get the better of you, you'll fire me." Another crisis passed congenially.

Kissinger understood his own temperament as well as those around him. When he first moved into the Secretary of State's spacious quarters on the seventh floor of the State Department, a White House staffer asked him how he liked his new office. "It's too big," groused Kissinger. "At the White House, when I come storming out of my office in a rage, there are people to scream at. But my State Department office is so big that by the time I get to the door, I've cooled off."

One of the few certainties of Kissinger travel was its uncertainty. The Secretary's itinerary was frequently juggled after he was on the road, and "mystery stops" were often added to the original schedule. That "the mystery stop on this trip is Washington" soon became a stale joke. His constant rejiggering of the schedule was a nightmare for television, which had to provide film crews for coverage on short notice. And no one ever dared leave Kissinger uncovered. In that respect, he was like the President. Where he went, the cameras went. As Richard Reston of the Los Angeles *Times* once wrote: "Traveling the world with Henry Kissinger is a little like going to the theater with a movie star. Everything is a show, a production."

During one of his African trips in 1976, his staff aides had the navigator do thirty different flight plans over a ten-day period, covering all sorts of contingencies. The navigator was frequently awakened in the middle of the night to do a new flight plan on his calculator. Once the schedule was changed, an advance team had to be sent to the area, and the Embassy had to make all the necessary preparations on short notice. "Controlled pandemonium," one Embassy official called it. The possibility of sudden changes in the itinerary was enhanced because, at any given time, Kissinger had a standing invitation to visit more than fifty countries.

In late 1974, a planned visit to Turkey suddenly had to be scrubbed when the government fell. Tunisia was substituted. Kissinger arrived the night of the local Marine ball — which quickly had to be rescheduled. It was no wonder that Embassy employees sighed a collective sigh of relief when Kissinger left their area for good. And the only way they knew he had left for good was when they heard he was back in Washington.

The surprise visit to Tunisia provided a graphic illustration of Kissinger's virtual autonomy in the conduct of diplomacy. In the final days of the Nixon administration, Kissinger seldom mentioned the name of the President while traveling. He denied that this was deliberate, but it was clear that Nixon's name did not evoke an image of great authority in 1974. But after Gerald Ford moved into the Oval Office, Kissinger carefully included his name in afterdinner toasts and airport arrival statements. Often we were told that Kissinger had delivered a letter from the new President to the leader of the country he was visiting. So, soon after we arrived in Tunis, we were told that Kissinger had given President Habib Bourguiba a letter from President Ford. But since Tunis had been added to the itinerary on Thursday, and it was now Friday, some of us wondered aloud how the Secretary of State had received a letter from the White House to be delivered to Bourguiba so quickly. "Very easy," explained a Kissinger aide. "It arrived as fast as it took me to write it."

Not long afterward, Washington columnist Russell Baker observed that President Ford "often speaks for Kissinger on foreign policy."

While Kissinger sometimes seemed to be acting like a President, his hosts frequently treated him as if he actually were one. He was often greeted at airports with the military honors usually accorded a visiting head of government. Pakistani Prime Minister Aly Bhutto once explained to a national television audience that since he had to provide honors for every "moron" who happened to be a head of government, he decided he might as well do it for Kissinger, who "deserved" it, even if protocol did not require it.

On the road, much of the time-consuming trivia of travel was taken care of by officers of a special section of the department's Executive Secretariat. Before leaving on a trip, we turned in our passports and visa applications to the press office, and we didn't see them again until we got back. When we arrived with Kissinger at his destination, we had press buses or, occasionally, cars to take us to the headquarters hotel. At each stop, the baggage was delivered to our rooms, in which we had been preregistered, and then was picked up outside the rooms the next morning. The local Embassy would set up a control room at the hotel where we could change money and buy sundries such as toothpaste, shaving cream, or peanuts, as well as booze at duty-free prices or cold beer.

The only place that didn't permit convenient traveling was Japan. The Japanese insisted that all the reporters go through immigration and customs like all other tourists. (They were — and still are — much more difficult about facilitating other American imports.)

The travel accommodations were as much a necessity as a convenience. The pace of traveling with Kissinger was frenetic enough, and the work hours long enough, without having to go through the bureaucratic red tape that entangles travel in most countries. When Kissinger got off the plane, for example, we had to race to hear his arrival statement, since that would provide a film clip for television or an on-the-record comment for print journalists; it would then be used as the framework for weaving in his nonattributable comments on the plane.

Kissinger generally tried to make his arrival statements meaningful, in the sense that he wanted to communicate some message to the host government or to put some particular spin on a forthcoming negotiating session. But that was not always the case. When a reporter once asked him if he were going to say something at the airport, he replied, "I will, but if it's significant, it will be accidental."

A special place in the Valhalla of travel has to be reserved for baggage calls. Kissinger always began his day early, which often meant an early takeoff from one country for the flight to the next stop. An early departure meant a very early baggage call, so we frequently had to have our baggage ready at 4:00 or 5:00 A.M. To avoid getting up and dressed that early, most of us simply took out what we needed for the next day along with a toilet kit and put our bags outside our door the night before, when we went to sleep. This operation was often performed at the end of an eighteen- or twenty-hour day, when we weren't at our sharpest.

On one of the early trips, Murrey Marder of the Washington *Post* showed up in the morning with a rather strange-looking shirt. We hadn't traveled much as a group, and we didn't know Marder's tastes all that well, but the shirt was indeed strange. It turned out to be his pajama top. He had forgotten to leave out a shirt the night before. *Newsweek*'s Bruce van Voorst showed up for the reopening of the U.S. Embassy in Cairo wearing a suit, a raincoat, and little else. He had forgotten to leave out a shirt, socks, and shorts.

I once put my shoes outside my door at the hotel in Damascus, thinking the floor boy would polish them. Instead, the baggage handler threw them into my suitcase, which was also outside my door for an early call. Luckily, I had a pair of sneakers in an overnight bag. When Kissinger's plane landed in Tel Aviv, an Israeli photographer spotted my sneakers and took a picture, and I became a front-page item in one of Israel's afternoon newspapers.

Nancy Kissinger narrowly escaped a more serious oversight during a visit to Isfahan in Iran. While she was in the bathroom, her husband called from the bedroom to ask what she was wearing. "The red dress," she replied. "What red dress?" asked Kissinger. "The red dress on the bed," she said. "There is no red dress on the bed," exclaimed Kissinger. They managed to get the red dress retrieved from a suitcase down the hall just before it was carted off to the airport.

The fatigue of Kissinger travel produced another occupational hazard, a by-product of the affluent society. It was not all that difficult when you got up in the morning — with the world outside a blur, your body clock all out of whack, and with time running out to check out of the hotel to catch your plane — it was not all that difficult to grab the wrong aerosol can. It was not all that difficult to try to spray your underarms with shaving cream. Or to put deodorant on your face. One reporter got up one morning and splashed hot comb lotion instead of shaving cream all over his face.

He thought he was blinded. Another reporter put Nupercainol, an antihemorrhoidal medicine, on his toothbrush instead of toothpaste. He threw away the toothbrush. Barry Schweid of the AP noted that while the Nupercainol man didn't have to worry about blinding himself, he did have to be concerned about shrinking his teeth.

One of the other advantages of traveling with Henry was tourism. We got to see Luxor, the Temple at Philae, the Forbidden City, the Great Wall, the Taj Mahal, the Dead Sea Scrolls, Petra (in Jordan), Masada, Persepolis, and a variety of mosques and musuems — always with a guide who was one of the leading authorities on the art or architecture of the particular country. Moscow was the only place where Kissinger did not go sightseeing. It was mostly business with the Russians.

In spite of all the VIP arrangements, Kissinger's celebrity still managed to intrude at times. When he visited the Prado in Madrid, he was surrounded by a throng of cameramen, photographers, and reporters, who swept along with him from picture to picture as the guide lectured on the works of Goya and other great artists. Finally, with some exasperation in his voice, Kissinger noted, "There must be a more reflective way of viewing art." There was, but not as long as he was Secretary of State.

Host governments frequently tried to cram Kissinger's schedule with more sightseeing than he wanted — or was able — to do, and he personally decided what he would see rather than leaving it to his staff or the U.S. Embassy. But even that practice didn't always protect him. After viewing the splendor of Victoria Falls in Zambia, he was treated to an exhibition of tribal dancing, and Kissinger watched stoically as one of the performers, dressed in a wild monkey suit, poured dirt into his open eye.

Stoicism escaped him, however, when he went to visit Iran's principal caviar-processing plant in Bandar Pahlevi on the Caspian Sea. The Shah had personally requested that he see the plant, and Kissinger agreed to go only after being assured by Ambassador Helms that no fish would be slit open in front of him. Helms explained that it was the wrong time of the year for that — the temperature had hit

100 degrees — and besides, Helms himself had visited the plant previously without seeing any eviscerations. What the Ambassador didn't know was that the Iranians had saved two large sturgeon especially for Kissinger, and by the time the Secretary arrived — late, as usual — the workers had removed the fish from their tanks and had whacked them over the head with a two-by-four.

Kissinger, who had once quipped that there wasn't anything he would not do to get caviar, now found out that there was: He couldn't watch it emerging straight from the fish's belly. His face paled and he refused to look down; his eyes locked on the Iranian expert, who was producing a steady stream of commentary. The evisceration hardly affected his appetite, however; the Secretary recovered quickly enough to go into the dining room and partake copiously of a caviar brunch laid out by his hosts. Not surprisingly, so did the rest of us. Inspired by all the fresh caviar — including some of the Shah's special "golden" caviar — Ken Freed of the AP wrote afterward: "Two Caspian Sea sturgeon died today for Henry Kissinger." (In addition to learning a lot about caviar production, we also found out that the Shah himself is allergic to fish and never eats his country's most famous product.)

Like any good, devoted tourist, Kissinger often sent postcards from the exotic places he visited. Before he remarried, he sent a postcard from Peking to one of his "dates," actress Marlo Thomas, a critic of the war in Vietnam. "I still think of you with affection," he scribbled, "even though you're working to put me out of a job." And like any good, would-be "swinger," Kissinger continued to cultivate his romantic image, even after he remarried, in the exotic places he visited. On the road, he found time to meet Elizabeth Taylor in Germany, Liv Ullmann in Norway, Gina Lollobrigida in Italy, and in Venezuela and Brazil, Raquel Welch, who was on tour. In fact, he once told us that the "most important thing I did on my trip to Latin America was to introduce the foreign minister of Venezuela to Raquel Welch."

Those tête-à-têtes all represented ego-tripping. The "secret swinger" became the public husband when he married long-time companion Nancy Maginnes in Arlington, Virginia, on March 30, 1974, in a simple ceremony before Judge Francis E. Thomas, Jr. Only a few close friends attended the wedding, which was artfully shielded from the press.

The marriage took place shortly after the Secretary's return from a mission to Moscow. On the return flight to Washington, reporters aboard the plane asked him if he were getting married. "Absolutely," he replied. Everybody thought he was joking. He also said he would give newsmen four or five hours' advance notice. But his penchant for secrecy prevailed over his promise. He was married on a Saturday afternoon with no advance notice and no reporters present. That morning, he held extensive talks with Israeli Defense Minister Moshe Dayan in his State Department office. A secretary interrupted to remind him that he had to end the talks in order not to be late for the "meeting" he had arranged — with Nancy and the judge. Dayan found out about the wedding in the morning newspapers.

Kissinger's second wife was thirty-nine, eleven years younger than he. Later, when the American Ambassador to Portugal, Frank Carlucci, married a woman fifteen years his junior, the Secretary of State sent him a congratulatory cable saying: "Pleased to hear you married a younger woman. Imitation is the highest form of flattery."

Like his wedding, his very first trip abroad as Secretary of State also went uncovered by the press — by his choice. That first trip was made with the same secrecy that surrounded his earlier mystery journeys as the President's — and the country's — number one secret diplomatic agent.

After he had been nominated as Secretary, Kissinger met with the newsmen who regularly covered the State Department to discuss ways to "improve" the dissemination of information. The newsmen urged him to follow the practice adopted by Secretary of State William Rogers, who took reporters on the plane with him when he traveled abroad, unlike *his* immediate predecessors, Dean Rusk, Christian Herter, Jr., and John Foster Dulles. Kissinger agreed. But his first trip abroad was not announced in advance. What had been announced was Kissinger's first *scheduled* trip abroad, a four-day visit to Peking in November 1973.

Two weeks before that trip, the Chinese threw a dinner for Kissinger, including members of his staff and of the press who would accompany him to China. It was held at the Mayflower Hotel in Washington, since the mainland Chinese did not yet have their own building. Several senior congressional figures were also invited, including Senate Majority Leader Mike Mansfield and Senate Minority Leader Hugh Scott. Watergate and the Middle East War dominated the headlines at that point, and the correspondents were more interested in finding out what the Senate was doing about Watergate and what was going on in the Middle East than what Kissinger was doing about China.

As we left the hotel after dinner, around eleven o'clock, a Baltimore *Sun* reporter, Jim Keat, asked the Secretary if there was "anything new" in the Middle East. Not particularly, said Kissinger as he got into his limo. But most of us received calls from our offices later in the night, telling us that Kissinger had just left for Moscow to try to work out a cease-fire in the Middle East with the Russians. We were particularly surprised — and annoyed.

Kissinger had informed his Chinese hosts beforehand that he would have to leave early in order to fly to Moscow. It was an especially touchy position for him, considering the Chinese attitude toward the Americans' growing coziness with their archenemies. But not a single word leaked in advance. His aides explained that there wasn't enough time to arrange for the press to go along. But the dramatic midnight flight to Moscow was the last time Kissinger left America on official business without newsmen accompanying him.

Once Kissinger began traveling regularly, we, the Kissinger 14, had frequent access to him in his Boeing bailiwick. He spoke as "a senior American official" rather than as himself. The eventually transparent guise of "senior official" enabled him to keep the press reasonably well informed and/or to send signals through them to foreign governments in a way that would not require foreign officials to react to his remarks, since they were not attributed to the Secretary of State.

From our vantage point in the rear of the plane, we sometimes caught a glimpse of Kissinger in unguarded moments. If the doors between the compartments were left open, the Secretary could occasionally be seen raging at his staff, and we knew he would be irascible at the coming briefing. During one such session, the radio-telephone began ringing in his office. He ignored it at first, but when it continued ringing without being answered, he shouted in an exasperated voice, "Can't someone answer that phone? I know you can't get on this plane if your IQ is more than fifty!"

He was exposed in another unguarded moment during one of his early trips to Saudi Arabia to confer with King Faisal and Foreign Minister Omar Saqqaf. When he came to the rear of the plane to chat, he was wearing corduroy trousers and a baggy sweater, and his fly was wide open. I was sitting on one side of the aisle where he stood. Marilyn Berger of the Washington *Post* was sitting on the other side. It seemed to me that somebody should let him know, even if his best aides wouldn't, so I penned a note to his press spokesman, saying: "I suggest you tell HAK that if he doesn't zip up his pants, when he gets to Riyadh, Omar may want to do more than just kiss and hold hands."

The spokesman, Bob Anderson, decided that discretion was not the better part of Valeriani, and he simply handed Kissinger the note after the briefing was over. The next time Kissinger wandered back, his fly was not open. He pointed to me and said with mock exaggerated seriousness, "And listen, Valeriani, I don't need any more technical assistance from you."

On the last leg of overseas trips, Kissinger almost always invited us to his office for a glass of champagne and an off-the-record session, which meant we couldn't use tape recorders or even take notes, since he wasn't to be quoted at all. Some of the sessions recalled a story Kissinger told to a gathering of congressional wives at the State Department. After receiving a glowing introduction, Kissinger said he felt "as I did once in Hawaii on the way to China, when I was sitting on the beach and a young lady came up to me and said, 'I understand you're a fascinating man, Dr. Kissinger . . . Fascinate me.' "

Many of the sessions *were* fascinating, as we sat for an hour or more over drinks, watching one of the most celebrated figures of his time stuff himself with peanuts, pretzels, potato chips, and hot hors d'oeuvres, listening to him pour out profundities and analyses about history and current events. Some of it was just fun. If he were in a playful mood, he would start out by saying things like: "Never have I known so many secrets. Never have I had such influence on world events. Yet no one has tried to seduce me with beautiful women." Then, following a dramatic pause: "It kills me."

This repartee was recorded for posterity coming out of Peking in November 1973, following a whirlwind tour of the Middle East:

Q: Is next Thursday really Thanksgiving?

K: If it's Thanksgiving, it must be Damascus.

Q: Have we been to Damascus on this trip?

K: Sure, Damascus is the place where the foreign minister held my hand.

Q: We were beginning to wonder about you.

K: I was beginning to wonder about myself. Once, Brezhnev kissed me on the mouth and now the foreign minister holds my hand . . .

Q: If this is on background, do we write that "A high U.S. official said Brezhnev once kissed him on the mouth"?

Humorist Art Buchwald decided to make one of the European trips. He was not only an old chess-playing buddy of Kissinger's, he was also in search of material for his thrice-weekly column. Kissinger was flying to Bonn from Geneva, where he had just met with Gromyko on arms control negotiations. Much of Kissinger's on-plane briefing focused on the complicated negotiations with the Russians on SALT and on banning underground nuclear explosions. Following a long discussion of the negotiations on the "threshold" for peaceful nuclear explosions, this exchange took place:

KISSINGER: Yeah, so we are talking about peaceful nuclear explosions. It has nothing to do with SALT, but peaceful nuclear explosions that are either off the test site or are of a magnitude — [Kissinger suddenly looked up at Buchwald.] Goddamn it, I know you're not taking this down.

BUCHWALD: This is the only part I *am* taking down.

KISSINGER: I'm going to be a goddamned parody. This guy, he can print
it straight and it will be funny.
REPORTER: Ask him about the threshold.
KISSINGER: What's a threshold, Art?
BUCHWALD: You got it. The people are going to love it.

Buchwald did print it straight, and it was so arcane it did sound
hilarious.

Remarkably, for all of Kissinger's openness on the plane —
and he would frequently speak quite frankly, although not for attribution, even in front of tape recorders — he never got burned by an
airborne briefing. The conversations in his flying office could range
over almost any topic, and did: His relations with Nixon, his approach to negotiations, his philosophy, his heroes.

We had one session with him right after President Nixon had held
a news conference in Washington. John Wallach of the Hearst Newspapers quoted something the President had said the night before and
then asked Kissinger, "Is that accurate?" One of the reporters rolled
his eyes skyward in a gesture of disbelief, and as they came level
again, he noticed that Kissinger was watching him. It was all Kissinger needed. "No," he exploded with mock exasperation. "No, the
President of the United States doesn't know what the hell he's talking
about. Jesus Christ, I thought you'd never ask."

Kissinger generally refused to discuss his relationship with Nixon,
although bits and pieces would occasionally slip out. Back in 1968,
when he was supporting Nelson Rockefeller for the Republican nomination, he had said Nixon was "not fit" to be President. But Kissinger was not an ideologue, and when Nixon offered him the job of
national security affairs adviser, he grabbed it. He frequently used to
point out to us that Nixon had named him to two of the most
important jobs in the country, NSC adviser and Secretary of State,
and he owed Nixon something for that. He did refer to Nixon as an
"oddball," and he once told us that Nixon secluded himself for three
days to prepare for a news conference and one day to recover from
it. We heard from other officials that Kissinger would say such things
as, "I've got to keep this guy calm, or he'll go off like a bomb." But
he never said things like that to the traveling press.

Much of the time he defended Nixon. Chicago *Tribune* correspondent John Maclean recalls "an intense Kissinger, punching his fists like a fighter in a clinch, exploding after still another question about Watergate. 'Damnit, Richard Nixon was capable of any irresponsibility in domestic affairs, but never in foreign policy. Never! Look at the record.' "

Nixon was the principal subject of conversation on the one occasion Kissinger did get burned by speaking bluntly into a microphone. But he didn't know the mike was open. It happened in Ottawa. The Secretary of State was on an official visit in October 1975 in response to Canada's criticism that he had neglected it, despite its being one of America's two closest neighbors and America's largest trading partner. Throughout a dinner in his honor, the microphones set up for the postprandial toasts were live, and his entire conversation, barely heard over the clatter of plates and silverware, was piped into the press room nearby. But only Bruce Garvey of the Toronto *Star* was there to hear it. All the other reporters were at the Press Club, watching the Cincinnati Reds defeat the Boston Red Sox, 6–5, in ten innings, in the third game of the classic 1975 World Series. We didn't return to the press room until it was time for the toasts. By then, Garvey had a story we didn't. (But through a misunderstanding, his own paper didn't get it first. Garvey also filed it for the Washington *Post,* which did not send a reporter to Canada, and the *Post* printed the story — on page 1 — before it appeared in the Toronto *Star.*)

The story about the overheard conversation reported that Kissinger had described'Nixon as "odd, artificial, and unpleasant." But he still defended his former boss as "one of our better presidents . . . He was very decisive in his own way. He went to the heart of the problem." After the story appeared, Kissinger complained about the lack of journalistic ethics, and he called Nixon to apologize.

Not long afterward, when the Secretary spoke at the swearing-in ceremony for a new American Ambassador to Canada, Tom Enders, he said good-humoredly, "I would like to give him a few pieces of advice in this new [job] — not to trust backgrounders with the press, and above all, stay away from microphones."

When Kissinger was speaking into microphones he knew were

open, he was always careful to protect the image of his subordination to the President, even when it became apparent that Nixon was only a figurehead. "The Secretary of State has to be the agent of the President," Kissinger told a San Clemente news conference, "or he represents nothing."

After Nixon's resignation in August 1974, Kissinger said he thought the former President had been ineffectual since around January. Yet, Kissinger staunchly defended Nixon's overseas ventures that year — to the Middle East and to Moscow — from a foreign policy point of view. The Secretary said he was never worried about a military threat against the United States during Watergate, but he was concerned about the impact on foreign policy. He said he supported the pardon but not necessarily its timing, and he said he had no role in it. A trial, he said, would have been disastrous, and Nixon would have probably cracked up.

He refused to give out any details about Nixon's final days in office, except to say he talked several times by telephone with Nixon two nights before the resignation and had a long meeting with the President the day before. He said he had written it all up for history. When a reporter asked him if it were true, as reported in *The Final Days,* that he had kneeled down and prayed with the outgoing President, Kissinger danced away with a humorous jab: "I am not exactly the praying type, you know." But the story was true.

Soon after Ford took office, Kissinger told us on the plane that his "relations with the new President are superb . . . better than with the former President. It's much easier, infinitely easier on human grounds. There's no problem whatsoever between the President and me." But he wouldn't comment for the record. When he was asked at a news conference if he had a freer hand in conducting foreign policy under Ford or under Nixon, he again reverted to humor: "No matter how I answer that question I will ruin myself." He then turned serious to give a gracious answer: "As for my own relationship with them, I had a relationship of confidence with both, and I had the backing of both, and I had the guidance of both in the conduct of foreign policy." His audience applauded.

A follow-up questioner pointed out that "former President Nixon has indicated that he was the primary idea man behind the Kissinger policies. What is your comment?" "My comment," evaded Kissinger, "is that I'll write my book after he completes his."

On the plane, Kissinger occasionally recounted amusing anecdotes about himself and the President. He once boasted about "one of my great faux pas. The first time I was at Camp David, I didn't know they had a bowling alley up there. Nixon and Rebozo were out, and I was waiting for Nixon. He came in. He said, 'I just scored one twenty.' And I said, 'I didn't know they had a golf course up here.' "

He once told us about slipping out of a private meeting between the President and Emperor Haile Selassie of Ethiopia, leaving Nixon, to his annoyance, to listen to the familiar litany from the Flowering Lion of Judah. "If you guys want to know what goes on in those private meetings," he said, "it's a fifty-minute monologue which Haile Selassie then repeated word for word at the state dinner that night."

One of Kissinger's all-time favorite stories involved Nixon's visit to the Vatican and the Sixth Fleet in 1971. He used to laugh uproariously when he told it, and he told it with zest. When President Nixon went to see Pope Paul during a show-the-flag visit to the Sixth Fleet in the Mediterranean, he flew by military helicopter. The Vatican was upset that Nixon would arrive in St. Peter's Square in a military vehicle, straight from a warship, to see a man of peace. So the Vatican asked, and the White House agreed, that the Secretary of Defense not accompany the President.

But Melvin Laird was the Secretary of Defense at the time, and it was not for nothing that he had earned a reputation as an operator. So when Nixon and Kissinger and their party reached the Vatican, who was already waiting for them? Indeed. Laird said that he had to check out the helicopters — you know what I mean? Not only was he there, he was smoking one of the big, long cigars he liked. It was explained to him, however, that one didn't smoke in the presence of His Holiness (nothing religious, the Pope just didn't like smoking). Laird, having just started on his cigar, was reluctant to throw it away, so he just flicked it out and stuck the long stub in his coat pocket.

Nixon, Kissinger, and Laird went in to see the Pope. While they were talking, they smelled smoke. They turned toward Laird. His coat pocket was on fire. Laird started slapping it furiously with his hand to put it out. The cardinals standing in the back of the audience room heard the sound of Laird's slapping. They thought the Pope had said something worthy of applause, and so they started clapping. It was the Keystone Kops at the Vatican.

By this time in the story, Kissinger would be slapping his side in imitation of Laird and collapsing with laughter himself.

The story had an intriguing follow-up that Kissinger did not tell us about. The White House image-makers produced a big crowd for Nixon in Rome. The traffic jam created by the crowd defeated the purpose of the helicopters, and Nixon got delayed in the Eternal City while others in his party flew to a Sixth Fleet aircraft carrier in the Mediterranean. While waiting for Nixon, Kissinger, Laird, and Secretary of State Rogers were watching a movie aboard the carrier. A Navy messenger came in with a wire service bulletin reporting that Egyptian President Gamal Abdel Nasser had just died. He gave it to Rogers, who looked at it and dismissed it, noting, "We would know about it if it were true." But after a few minutes Kissinger got nervous. He went out and had a message sent to the American diplomatic office in Cairo. The United States did not have formal diplomatic relations with Egypt then, but it did maintain an "interests section" in Cairo. Back came a classic bureaucratic reply: "We cannot confirm nor deny report of Nasser's death. However, we can report that as of 2 P.M. today, all programming on Cairo Radio went off the air, and they've been playing funeral music ever since. We regard this as unusual." Kissinger then decided — on his own — to cancel the big display of firepower by the Sixth Fleet. When Nixon got back and found out about the cancellation, he was, in the words of a White House aide, "really pissed off. He loved the boom-boom." He was so mad that the next time the opportunity arose, he would not let Kissinger ride on the presidential helicopter. And in the Nixon White House, that was a serious matter.

During his briefings, Kissinger also used to give us short personality sketches and insights into the make-up of the world figures he was dealing with. He always accentuated the positive, although his only praise for Brezhnev was as a "survivor." We became so accustomed to his phrases that when he first went to Africa, we drew up a series of cue cards with the expected words on them. When he came to the press section of the plane to chat, we asked him about the various leaders, and every time he used a familiar phrase, we would flash the card behind him: "He is very bright, very sophisticated, he has a good sense of humor . . ." Et cetera. When the Secretary caught on to what we were doing, he stopped and said, "Come on, you guys, I'm serious." Then he laughed and uttered an earthy profanity.

If he couldn't praise, he was usually careful not to criticize. In that sense, his private meetings with world leaders did not turn into Kissinger-and-tell sessions afterward. However, after a visit to Chicago that included a session with Mayor Richard Daley, Kissinger joked, "Let me tell you someday about when I briefed Mayor Daley about foreign policy. Somehow I got the impression it was not at the center of his concerns." And he chuckled heartily.

After Rhodesian Premier Ian Smith committed his white minority regime to the principle of black majority rule within two years at a meeting with the Secretary in South Africa, Kissinger said that Smith and his cohorts "behaved with great dignity through what must have been the most painful experience of their lives." One of Kissinger's aides later told a reporter that Smith's palms had been exceptionally sweaty when he had shaken hands with the Secretary, and the reporter then asked Kissinger about it. "The person who told you that should be strung up," he snapped.

When Kissinger conferred with Prime Minister John Vorster of South Africa for the first time, he emphasized that the meeting was not an endorsement of South Africa's racial policies, which he condemned. But he never criticized Vorster himself, a man who subsequently became a vital link in Kissinger's African mediation.

At the picture-taking session with Vorster, the Secretary demonstrated his distance from the South African by forgoing his usual banter with the press. Inside the conference room, however, it was the jowly Afrikaner who cracked a joke or two — to no one's surprise, at the expense of black Africans. His favorite joke was about Idi Amin. Vorster suggested that the name of the country should be changed from Uganda to Idi since, he explained, the people who live on Cyprus are called Cypriots.

Kissinger often used the sessions to explain — and defend — his negotiating techniques. And he would occasionally give us insights into the psychology he applied in different situations. When dealing with the Chinese, he explained, "If they are serious, they rarely raise an issue in a way that it can be turned down and thus be embarrassing. So they come at you peripherally. When we negotiate, they ask us to produce the first draft of a communiqué, and then they modify it. And then their negotiating technique is quite different from others. Basically, they tell you their real position and don't move. My experience is that basically, they have no trouble accepting ninety-nine percent of what you put forward. To give the Russians your minimum position is suicide. They need to haggle to show what they've got. The Chinese don't have that hang-up." Most of the Russians, he said, were "sleazy traders" in negotiations, so he set outrageous initial positions from which he could then back off.

The lend-lease negotiations in 1972, Kissinger said, were a case in point. "We had to give them something to go back to the Politburo with, so I jacked up what we'd really settle for outrageously — and then when I came down ten million dollars every ten minutes, Gromyko went away a happy man. But I ended up thirty-five million dollars above my bottom position."

Kissinger always insisted in these sessions that allegations that he said different things to different people when he was mediating or negotiating were simply wrong. "It's extremely important never to say anything that can't be realized," he told us. "You can't make fake promises. It's absurd to try. In the conduct of foreign policy, the reality of power and the continuity of U.S. policy have to be of paramount concern. Three years is nothing in the history of a people. You must try to do something that others will want to carry on. Otherwise, it will be just a comment."

He was fond of saying that the successful conclusion of any negotiation would leave both sides dissatisfied. And he had no aversion to seeking refuge in ambiguity. Discussing a session in Damascus, he said, "There's no attempt to fool the Syrians. Sometimes, the art of diplomacy is to keep the obvious obscured."

In Africa, he discovered a special problem: "The reluctance of anybody to admit that negotiations are possible before they know that negotiations will succeed."

He also knew when not to negotiate. When Cambodia and Vietnam were going under in 1975, he made no effort to negotiate with the North Vietnamese, whom he used to refer to in private as "shits" and "bastards." "Listen," he said, "I met Le Duc Tho once when they were winning. That's not something I want to repeat. What are the chips on our side? . . . There's nothing that can be done now. What can anybody do in Washington? It has always been a knee-jerk reaction — 'Now you have to negotiate.' If I'm an expert on anything, it's on Vietnamese negotiations. The time to negotiate is not when you are getting your brains beaten in."

In public, he resorted to quips rather than philosophy to explain his negotiating success. After Kissinger had persuaded Prime Minister Ian Smith to accept black majority rule, a British newsman asked the Secretary how he had done it. "Personal charm," said Kissinger. And when a questioner in Cincinnati stood up and said, "Dr. Kissinger, obviously you endure as one of the most successful negotiators of the century. I sincerely mean that. To which personal attribute do you most attribute this?" Kissinger replied, "The morale of my staff requires frequent absences from the country."

He also discussed his heroes with us. As he once told Jerry O'Leary in an interview, "Metternich is not one of my heroes. I think Metternich was an extremely skilled diplomat, but not very creative." He explained that he focused on Metternich as a means of getting to Bismarck, but he only completed half a dozen chapters on his book on Bismarck before abandoning it. Maybe one day in the future, he said. (But obviously not until he completes the memoirs of Otto von Kissinger.)

Yet Kissinger himself contributed to the misconception that he admired Metternich. He facetiously told a press gathering at Georgetown University, "Let me say that I categorically reject your frequent assertions that I celebrate Metternich's birthday as a religious observance. Lighting a few small candles on May fifteenth is hardly religious; it is no more than respectful."

Who, then, were Kissinger's heroes?

Israeli Prime Minister Yitzhak Rabin told me, "He had no heroes. All his heroes died one to two hundred years ago." And Rabin added, "I don't think he saw anybody in this world who was a match for him." Of contemporary figures, Kissinger probably respected the two principal leaders of the People's Republic of China, Chairman Mao Tse-tung and Premier Chou En-lai, more than any others. He defined great figures as those who achieved something that "made a qualitative difference in the life of their people and without whom it would be difficult to imagine that the history of their people would have been the same." In that category he put Franklin D. Roosevelt, Charles de Gaulle, Mao Tse-tung, Winston Churchill, and to some extent, Konrad Adenauer.

As for his own role, he once told ABC News, "Now I would like to think that what keeps me going is not the consciousness of success, but the sense of history and the sense that after I've left, people will look at some permanent achievement." He conceded that "some failures are inevitable because when you conduct the foreign policy of a major country, you're up against people of equal ability in a lot of places and there are many events that are outside your control, and, in addition, you're bound to make a mistake — sometime."

Did Kissinger make any mistakes? "I have been known to be wrong," he once quipped, "but I cannot offhand give you any examples."

And if Henry Kissinger were not Henry Kissinger, who would he like to be? "I have often wondered," he once said, "what it would be like to come to meetings of the National Security Council in dark glasses and tennis shoes, and I have been tempted to hold all my

briefings over the long-distance telephone. But it is only a dream."
(It was really only a joke. Howard Hughes's reclusiveness was certainly not Kissinger's style.)

While he was still an academician, Kissinger wrote: "Men become myths, not by what they know, or even by what they achieve, but by the task they set for themselves." The task he set for himself was the establishment of a new world order, whose organizing principle would be international stability, where ideology would not be so important as playing by the rules of the game. But he became mythic by what he knew and what he achieved.

Yet there were times when he was gloomy, and at those times his gloom pervaded the briefings. At the height of the criticism against him in 1975, he said he was tempted to quit and turn it over to someone else, but, he said, his successor would not have an easier time of it, would face the same problems — and would lack Kissinger's global authority. When his style came under fire, he reverted to his professorial status and argued that the value of American foreign policy would ultimately be judged on substance, not style.

One of his constant themes was that we in the United States could no longer overwhelm our problems with unlimited resources, as we did following World War II. We now had to conduct our foreign policy like everybody else did, with skill and dexterity. One journalist felt that Kissinger had been profoundly affected by the holocaust and by Hiroshima and was determined that neither tragedy should ever be allowed to occur again.

The gloom was rare, however, and throughout most of his missions his spirits were as high as his stamina was extraordinary. The adrenalin almost always seemed to be pumping. When we asked him how he did it, he likened himself to a tightrope walker, who can't afford to relax until he reaches his destination. The comparison was apt. Kissinger was frequently engaged in a diplomatic high-wire act. Ironically, when a mission was over, when he had chalked up another diplomatic victory, was when the adrenalin stopped flowing, and he often seemed depressed precisely at the moment of triumph. But most of the time he was still bouncing while the rest of us were dragging. He even used routine refueling stops for substantive discussions with foreign ministers.

On some of the longer trips, it seemed at times as though we collectively passed through phases — from weariness to fatigue to exhaustion. On one ten-day Middle East excursion, I calculated for the *NBC Newsletter* that I had averaged 3.8 hours of sleep a night. Long afterward, I found out that one of Kissinger's favorite secretaries, Chris Vick, had managed only twenty hours of sleep during the trip. "If you couldn't go around the clock," she said, "you couldn't make the team."

Murrey Marder of the Washington *Post* wrote after returning from a typical whirlwind journey abroad: "Veterans of presidential and Cabinet-level travel rated the twelve-day trip with Dr. Kissinger the most physically demanding one in memory. Two to three hours' sleep during some nights of the journey showed a toll on everyone except the extraordinarily durable fifty-year-old Kissinger."

After returning from a two-week, twenty-six-thousand-mile jet trek through Africa, the Secretary paused long enough to make an arrival statement at Andrews Air Force Base, then left immediately by helicopter for Hot Springs, West Virginia, to address the prestigious Businessmen's Council. In summing up that trip, Mike Kaufman wondered in the New York *Times* if Kissinger's African journey had been "a diplomatic mission or an endurance test."

The travel in Africa produced a unique experience for Kissinger. It was the only time in all of his travels that he got sick enough to have to cancel his schedule. A catchy wire service lead out of Kinshasa said the Secretary of State canceled his day's activities after waking up with a stomachache following a dinner of wild boar and leaves of manioc plants. It went on to say that Kissinger, who had eaten all kinds of exotic foods on his numerous trips abroad without missing an appointment, had a mild case of gastroenteritis. However, the Secretary's iron stomach had not been corroded by either the wild boar or the manioc leaves. It was the cream icing on the cake at the dinner the night before that laid him low. The dinner had been served by candlelight, since the power was out in part of the Zairian capital, and the cake was presented with sparklers. Despite medical admonitions against eating cream icings in that part of the world, where the heat is fierce and the refrigeration suspect, Kissinger was apparently unable to resist a cake with sparklers. Unfortunately for him, his traveling doctor, Martin Wolfe, was seated beyond eye contact. Aide Peter Rodman did catch Wolfe's eye, and he remembers being waved off the cake.

The traveling press received word of Kissinger's indisposition with some skepticism. Visions of Henry's Delhi belly in Pakistan danced in our typewriters. We remembered that it was under the cover of gastroenteritis that Kissinger had slipped secretly into China in 1971, and we now wondered if he were off in the bush meeting with Ian Smith or one of the guerrilla leaders still fighting in Angola against the Cubans. Or whether he had gone to Luanda itself.

Several of us rode out to the sumptuous guest house where Kissinger was staying to double-check, but none of us saw him. Press spokesman Bob Funseth was in the lobby, insisting the Secretary was upstairs and was indeed sick, and yes, Funseth said, he had just seen him. Other aides also swore to us that they, too, had seen the stricken Secretary in his room. But they all did it with just enough of a deliberately bemused air to keep our doubts alive. Murrey Marder called Dr. Wolfe to tell him that he was also suffering from an intestinal disorder and would like to get "the same medicine the Secretary is getting." But Marder wasn't probing: he had eaten the same icing.

It turned out that Dr. Wolfe was treating Kissinger not only with wonder drugs; he was also prescribing chicken soup. "Dr. Wolfe," Kissinger told him, "you practice medicine like a Jewish momma. And I know, because I have one." Wolfe replied, "I know. I have one too." (The doctor has a picture hanging in his office with the inscription: "To Dr. Martin Wolfe, who practices medicine like a Jewish mother. With High Regard, Henry A. Kissinger.")

At one point during the Secretary's bedridden stint, aide Winston Lord entered his room and said, "Your staff has voted six to one that you remain ill for another day so they can get some rest." Wolfe looked up and asked, "Who is the one?"

When Kissinger did not feel better as soon as he would have liked, he teased Wolfe, saying, "You're a wonderful human being, but a lousy doctor." When he did recover, he felt bad about that crack and made sure the doctor knew he had said it in jest and that he did appreciate the doctor's ministrations. One sign that he was recovering was another jibe at Wolfe. "I think," he said, "my staff must be paying you to keep me this way."

Kissinger got back on his feet when it was time to leave for the next stop, Liberia, but he still wasn't a hundred percent. "I feel pregnant," he told an aide. "I have morning sickness." Almost everybody in the Kissinger party went through a similar experience at least once.

But however tiring the travel was, it was seldom tiresome. As Marilyn Berger of the Washington *Post* once wrote, in conformity with the Reporter's Creed: "There is only one thing worse than going on a Kissinger trip. It's not going on a Kissinger trip."

THREE

China

The first time Henry Kissinger went to China, he slipped in surreptitiously in the middle of the night, held unpublicized talks, then slipped out again carrying an invitation for Richard Nixon to visit Peking. It was all a super secret until Nixon announced it on nationwide television in a grand *coup de théâtre* in July of 1971.

The first time I went to China it was different. I arrived with the Secretary of State in November 1973 by way of Rabat, Tunisia, Cairo, Amman, Riyadh, and Lahore. I had a touch of sinusitis (to go with my touch of Sinology). When I talked, I sounded like Andy Devine's voice coach. The punishing travel through the Middle East had left me exhausted, and I stumbled off the plane like one of the walking wounded. But I was excited.

China. Exotic China. Forbidden Fruit. Forbidden City. Mysterious Middle Kingdom. The Chinese charm began exerting itself on us almost at once. Nothing so gross as a press bus here. We had cars — Shanghai's resembled a 1950 Plymouth as much as anything else — each fully equipped with one well-conditioned, thoroughly indoctrinated, Foreign Ministry official escort. Kissinger climbed into a Red Flag limousine, and the motorcade took off at high speed for

Peking — Kissinger to a government guest house, the rest of us to the Min Tzu (Nationalities) Hotel, a big square box built and furnished by the Russians in the days when they and their Chinese comrades weren't screaming at each other.

I raced to my room, picked up an ancient cradle telephone, and placed a collect call to New York, eager to make my first broadcast with the signoff: "This is Richard Valeriani, NBC News, in Peking." We only had half an hour from the time we reached the hotel until we were to leave for our first banquet, in the Great Hall of the People. The Chinese operator sounded as though she were reading her questions from a card. No matter what you said, she went right on with her ritual of getting information for the call. Seven minutes before we had to leave for the banquet, the telephone rang.

I leaped at it, tape recorder at the ready, primed to transmit my recorded radio broadcasts to New York. "Sorry," said the little Chinese voice, "New York says very, very busy, please call back." "Call *back?* For God's sake, don't they know this is Peking? Like they get a call from China every morning? Call them back, miss, and tell them they are *not* too busy and to take this call immediately." Talk about letdowns. The operator did call back, and the New York radio desk did take in my recorded spots. But by now it seemed anticlimactic, and my exhilaration had flagged by the time I left to eat a nine-course meal, flavored with toasts to the new American-Chinese friendship, and to listen to the People's Liberation Army Band play "Home on the Range."

I subsequently found out that Kissinger's clandestine journey had its own contretemps. He had bought three new shirts specifically for his visit to China. Henry had never been a candidate for anybody's ten best-dressed list, especially in his days as NSC adviser at the White House, but he wanted to look particularly well attired for his first meeting with the meticulous Chinese. During the supersecret preparations for the hush-hush departure from Pakistan at 3:00 A.M., an NSC aide, David Halperin, forgot to pack the shirts. He didn't remember them until the Pakistan Airlines plane carrying Kissinger was already winging its way across the Himalayas and Halperin was on his way back to the airport. Did he panic? He threw up.

When Kissinger found out, he blew up. There he was, on one of the most exciting diplomatic missions of all time, and he was fretting about his missing shirts. Only one other member of the party had a neck size as large as Kissinger's (16 ½), John Holdridge. He is 6' 3"; Kissinger is 5'7". So the first time Henry Kissinger met Premier Chou En-lai in Peking, he was wearing one of John Holdridge's shirts, with the sleeves held up by rubber bands in the style of an old Mississippi riverboat gambler. Somebody who was there said, "Henry looked like a penguin."

That's not all. When the shirts came back from being laundered by the Chinese, someone noticed the label: Made in Taiwan. Had Chou En-lai known — and he probably did, because the Chinese generally come to know everything about their guests — he probably would have been amused. In his candid way, Chou once told a foreign diplomat that China had a long way to go in developing its economic and commercial relations. "We've got to learn from Japan and Taiwan," he said, and he pulled out a piece of the long johns he wore under his tunic to show to his guest. "Every time this gets washed," he said, "it gets an inch longer. I have to keep cutting it off. We can't expect to export if we have this kind of quality."

Somehow, the American-Chinese initiative survived Kissinger's short-shirtedness and became history.

One of the unsung figures who helped make the history was the American Ambassador in Pakistan, Joseph Farland, a one-time FBI agent turned diplomat and a high-powered intelligence operative. In April 1971, Farland's reading of the diplomatic traffic and his instincts told him something was up. He quietly made plans to have his wife return to the States on "family matters." In early May, he got a supersecret message, through a back-channel communications system operated by the U.S. Navy, which directed him to go immediately to California to meet with presidential aide Henry Kissinger. Traveling under the cover of "urgent" private business, Farland left his Embassy in Islamabad even before receiving State Department travel orders.

Two days after getting the message, he showed up in Los Angeles, where he went "undercover" at the airport, transferred by prearrangement to a private plane, and flew to a secret rendezvous with Kissinger. The State Department had absolutely no idea where its Ambassador to Pakistan was. Neither did anybody in the Embassy in Pakistan.

"Henry," a travel-weary Farland said when he saw Kissinger, "what the hell is this all about?" The answer left even an old pro like Farland with his mouth wide open: "I want you to put me into China." Those were virtually all the instructions Farland received. Kissinger explained the secret contacts with Peking leading up to his request, and he said he needed about two and a half days in China. The details of the "hiding place" were left up to the Ambassador. Kissinger cautioned — superfluously — against leaks, and Farland returned to Pakistan to begin a carefully calculated campaign of artful deception, coordinated, of course, with President Yahya Kahn and eventually a handful of others. But *not* with the Chinese Ambassador in Pakistan; any contact with him would have aroused suspicions.

The first problem was communicating with Washington. Farland was based in Islamabad. The secret, back-channel communications system terminated in Karachi. The Ambassador suddenly developed a craving for lobsters, which had to be flown in from Karachi, with surprising frequency. Farland was worried that his number two man might find out what was going on, so he pushed, prodded, and cajoled him into taking a vacation. He also persuaded his principal press officer to take off. And he sent the Embassy doctor on a mission to East Pakistan, since he had decided Kissinger would have to get "sick" in order to disappear for a while, and the Embassy doctor would obviously insist on seeing him — unless the doctor were a thousand miles away. During the final stages, Farland did cut in his local CIA station chief. They talked in the Embassy "bubble," a specially constructed enclosure suspended in one of the Embassy's rooms so that it could not be penetrated by listening devices.

Meanwhile, Farland became a practitioner of the Diplomatic

Method School of Acting. He had arguments with the Foreign Office about Kissinger's schedule, he had arguments with Kissinger's own advance agents about changes in the schedule, and he even laid on an "argument" with President Yahya Kahn at dinner the night Kissinger arrived (July 8). The President insisted that Kissinger extend his stay — he just had to see the sun rise over the Himalayas. "No, no," said the U.S. Ambassador respectfully, "Dr. Kissinger must keep to his schedule, and I object strenuously to any deviations." Kissinger was not surprised when Farland weakened and agreed to take him to the American rest house at Muree, about ten thousand feet up in the mountains. Nor was Kissinger surprised when President Kahn then suggested he stay at a Pakistani rest house at Nathiagali, about fifteen miles beyond Muree. It was so agreed.

But Kissinger never made it to Nathiagali. He went to Peking instead at three o'clock the next morning on a Pakistan International Airlines plane flown by Chinese pilots who had earlier made a test run, since they were not flying the usual commercial route. One of Kissinger's aides thought it was a marvelous tribute to the discipline of the Secret Service agents that when they boarded the plane and saw the Chinese, they didn't turn around and get right off.

The next day, a Pakistan Government announcement disclosed that Dr. Kissinger was suffering from a "slight indisposition" and would have to remain at Nathiagali. To anybody familiar with that part of the world, a "slight indisposition" translated into a case of Delhi belly, diarrhea, which is certainly common enough. Even so, a lot of reporters were suspicious. But an elaborate charade of official visitors to Nathiagali, including a Pakistani doctor, served to allay the suspicions.

The doctor actually had someone to treat, a Secret Service agent who discovered to his sorrow that boiling water at an altitude of ten thousand feet does not necessarily sterilize it. Ironically, Kissinger himself had suffered a mild case of Delhi belly two days earlier.

That night, at a cocktail party in Islamabad, AP reporter Arnie Zietlin was chatting with the Embassy political officer, Dennis Kux, who was also the control officer for the Kissinger visit. Zietlin said something like, "Aw, c'mon, Dennis, where is Kissinger for real?" And Kux replied nonchalantly, "I wouldn't doubt but that he's in China." Everybody howled, including Kux. If the young political officer had nurtured any such suspicion, he had discarded it when he sent a cable to Washington, signed by the Ambassador, informing the White House of Kissinger's "slight indisposition." Kux had even stopped at a pharmacy to get Kissinger some medication.

Despite the elaborate cover operation, the Pakistani foreign minister, Sultan Mohammed Khan, one of the principal players, was nervous. He was worried that the one road to Nathiagali would be closed by a rock slide — a common occurrence — and there would be no way to explain how Kissinger would get back.

The rocks didn't slide, but Kissinger's schedule in Peking did. He returned to a remote section of the military base at Islamabad an hour and forty-five minutes late and still had to be taken to the government guest house as though he had just been driven in from Nathiagali. But Ambassador Farland had already shown up at the guest house in Rawalpindi, expecting that he and Kissinger would converge as planned. So he had to concoct still another story to explain why Kissinger wasn't there yet. He said that on the way back from the mountain retreat, Kissinger had suddenly decided that he wanted to stop at the bazaar in Muree so he could do some shopping. When it was all over, members of Farland's staff told him he deserved an Oscar.

From Pakistan, Kissinger flew directly to California to report to President Nixon. Kux left Pakistan two days later for reassignment, and on the way back to Washington, he stopped to visit relatives in Switzerland. His aunt woke him up in the morning to tell him that Kissinger had just been to China. Kux thought he was still asleep, dreaming. When Kux returned to Washington, he ran into Kissinger at the White House. Henry asked him gleefully, "Did I really fool you?" He really had — along with just about everybody else.

I was in a Washington television studio the night Nixon announced he was going to China. And, like the rest of the world, I was flabbergasted, even though I had not believed the cover story of Kissinger's illness in Pakistan. NBC anchorman John Chancellor had talked with me about it on the phone, and he hadn't believed the story either. We thought Kissinger was up to something with the North Vietnamese, that he might have slipped secretly into Hanoi. We were not at all prepared for the China bomb.

When Chancellor came back on the air following Nixon's announcement, he was so astounded that he couldn't talk without chuckling, almost giggling. He asked me about it, and my response just popped out: "I don't want to suggest that I knew what was coming, John, but I would like to point out that I had dinner tonight at the Peking Restaurant in Washington." And I had. It seemed like a good idea at the time. A number of people went out of their way afterward to tell me they thought it was quite appropriate for the occasion. But I later heard from my bureau chief that "they" — the brass in New York — had not appreciated it at all.

Some four years later, the Peking Restaurant once again figured in a China story. My best friend and cousin-in-law, Air Force Colonel Philip Gehring, called to tell me he was coming to Washington on business, and he suggested we have dinner. "Okay," I said, "let's go to the Peking," which we both liked. At four o'clock the next morning I was awakened by a phone call from my assignment desk: Mao Tse-tung had just died. I got up and went to the studio to do a spot for the *Today* program. I did not mention where I had eaten dinner.

Later that day, I saw Barrie Dunsmore of ABC at the State Department. He also had been called at four in the morning. I told him about having eaten at the Peking the night before. "That's funny," he said. "I had a yen for Chinese food last night and went to the Yenching Palace." On a hunch, I checked to see where Marvin Kalb of CBS had eaten dinner the night before. Naturally, Kalb had also felt in a Chinese mood and had gone to the North China in Bethesda. It's one of the least-known coincidences of all time that on the night Mao Tse-tung died, the three network correspondents who cover the State Department all had Chinese meals. But, then, coincidences are not uncommon to Chinese affairs. Following the dramatic Kissinger breakthrough in Peking, the first three American correspondents allowed into China in more than twenty years were John Rich of NBC, Jack Reynolds of NBC, and John Roderick of AP. All three have the same initials: JR. The significance of that escapes me.

So much for the serious stuff.

During his eight years at the White House and the State Department, Kissinger visited China nine times. A clause in the Shanghai Communiqué stipulated that "from time to time, there shall be periodic visits by high-ranking officials." Kissinger was the high-ranking official who made the visits most periodically. (The Shanghai Communiqué, signed by President Nixon and Premier Chou in 1972, provided the guidelines for American-Chinese relations.)

Kissinger had a great sense of discovery about China. As one official put it, "It's his baby, and nobody else even gets to change the diapers." The secret trip was, for those who took it, a kind of diplomatic Long March. When Kissinger walked in on some elaborate State Department setup on the road, he would invariably ask, "Who are all these people?" And then he would point out with some disdain, "I opened up China with five people."

When he arrived as Secretary of State, the Chinese assembled all the people connected with the visit at the Great Hall of the People for what the locals called the "bleachers shot." Everybody was lined up on a row of bleachers — something like the picture of a high school class on a visit to Washington — and when everybody was in place, Chou brought Kissinger in to be photographed with the assembled multitude. The members of the plane crews, the stewards from the plane, the secretaries — everybody was in the picture. As usual, Kissinger wanted to know who all those people were, and he later demanded that the number be reduced on subsequent trips. It wasn't.

Kissinger's fascination with China transcended the sense of discovery. Chairman Mao Tse-tung and Premier Chou En-lai were among the few world leaders who could rival Kissinger himself for intellect, dynamism, celebrity, and a record of achievement to match. And it was apparent to anyone who traveled with Kissinger that

Chou was the one international figure he respected more than any other he dealt with — and he dealt with everybody in his time. For him, none of the others had the dazzling combination of intelligence, charm, sophistication, wit, and — to revive a once-popular word — charisma that Chou possessed. Or, as an American secretary in Peking put it, "Chou was really sexy for an old man." He talked philosophically and acted pragmatically. And he had been involved in achieving something monumental in his time. Like Kissinger, he was an intellectual who had power and knew how to use it. And like Kissinger, he was a man whose sense of nuance was highly developed. This personal chemistry created a bond between them, a bond that was strengthened by the fact that Kissinger thought of Chou and himself as partners in some great enterprise — the opening of the American-Chinese connection after a twenty-year lapse.

When Kissinger first arrived in Peking in 1971, he obviously couldn't be sure what he would find. He didn't like one of the first things he found. The Chinese had left an English-language magazine in the bedroom of each member of the American party. Not so accidentally, the magazines were opened at a page featuring an article that was highly anti-American. Kissinger had an aide round up the magazines and present them to a Chinese official with the explanation that there must have been some mistake. Not only did it not happen again, but on the way out of Peking, a protocol officer pointed out to him a billboard where an anti-American slogan had been replaced by something more inspiring, such as "Increase Productivity."

Before they met, Kissinger knew almost everything there was to know about Chou and vice versa. The Chinese leader lived up to his reputation. He appeared at the guest house shortly after Kissinger arrived, and the chemistry was instantaneous. Their first conversation began on an almost metaphysical level as they talked about the nature of mystery. But Chou later indicated that Kissinger might have outdone him in one area. He told a group of visiting American editors, "I could learn from that Dr. Kissinger. He can talk for half an hour without giving one substantive answer."

The two men also shared a disdain for bureaucracy. Soon after

they talked for the first time, Kissinger asked Chou if he minded
being called Mr. Prime Minister, since he had some difficulty in
pronouncing the word "Premier." Chou said he didn't mind at all.
In fact, he explained, had it not been for a lousy translator at the
Geneva conference in 1947, he would now be referred to as Mr. Prime
Minister. He went on to note: "And that translator is now a high
official in our Foreign Ministry."

Kissinger appreciated the kind of intellectual gamesmanship Chou
practiced. The Secretary and his aides assumed that their guest house
was bugged — there was no way to conduct a security sweep in
advance, as in other countries — and when they wanted to talk
privately, they went outside and talked while walking around the
compound. The area had several guest villas and lagoons, with
bridges connecting them. On his first visit, he found that whenever
he approached one of the bridges on his walks, a People's Liberation
Army guard always materialized from the side of the road to stop
him. After a while, he told Chou he felt like the plumber in Kafka's
Castle, who was called to the castle but couldn't get in. He spent all
his life trying to get in and eventually forgot why he had been called
there in the first place. Two trips later, after one of their postmid-
night sessions at Chou's villa, the Chinese Premier said his final
good-night to Kissinger, then suddenly said, "Wait a minute," and
began walking his guest back to the guest house with his car trailing
slowly behind, its lights dimmed. Along the way, as they talked, they
crossed three or four bridges, including the one leading to Kissinger's
villa. At which point Chou turned to Kissinger and asked, "Why did
you want to cross the bridge?" He then got into his car and drove
off.

Kissinger and everybody else who sat in on his meetings with
Chou always remarked on how frank they were in their discussions.
They held nothing back. For example, the Americans were frequently amused to hear the Chinese dismiss the Communist parties
of Europe with scornful ridicule.

Kissinger claimed that the best tactic with the Chinese was to give
them his real position and to make sure it was sensible. He recalled

negotiating with Chou on the Shanghai Communiqué. The original Chinese draft had two sentences that were offensive to the United States, and even though they were prefaced by the phrase "The Chinese side maintains," it was still a document that had to be signed by the President of the United States.

Kissinger said to Chou, "You take out these two sentences and I'll give you two." Chou replied, in effect, If you want to give two sentences to anybody, give them to your President. I don't want them. If you want those two sentences out, you tell me why, and if I agree, I'll take them out. Kissinger said the two sentences were eventually taken out and the Chinese asked nothing in return. But, he later noted, the Chinese are frugal in such matters. The two phrases that were dropped eventually showed up verbatim in a speech delivered by a Chinese official at the United Nations.

Kissinger also explained that dealing with the Chinese is totally unlike dealing with the Russians. If you say to the Russians, "Take out the comma," they say, "Okay, we want a semicolon." Kissinger also made the point that the Chinese "always keep their end of a bargain." Then he added meaningfully, "And that's more than you can say about some other nations I know."

He especially appreciated the historical perspective of the Chinese. Their leaders, in his view, demonstrated a wide scope of interests and were capable of taking a long-range look at world affairs. "The Chinese," he once said, "talk about things in terms of three to five years. Most prime ministers I know can't get beyond two to three months."

Kissinger talked at length about Chou to British journalist Henry Brandon, who later wrote:

> Kissinger was impressed with the depth of Chou's psychological insights, his objectivity, candour and subtlety, and his long-range outlook on history. Kissinger explained to me, 'Chou En-lai would suggest, It can't be settled now, but such is the possible evolution. De Gaulle could think that way, but no other leader today can.' The intellectual approach, the gentle humor, the thoughtfulness and human quality of the Chinese prime minister all made a deep impression on him.

Chou was the man of subtle intellect, with a shrewd, astute mind. He asserted himself not by his physical presence but by his dextrous mental mobility and his electric charm. He was the clever negotiator and diplomatic practitioner — the super-manager. But he was also thoughtful and contemplative. He was deeply concerned about human values, about life in chastened China which somehow lacks the vitality it used to have.

Chou and Kissinger had something else in common. For all their charm and intellect and cleverness, they were not numero uno. In China, Chairman Mao was clearly the boss — his Buddha-like face beamed down from gigantic portraits all over the city — and Chou, the astute mandarin, was always deferential in the presence of the shrewd peasant-poet leader.

Kissinger was impressed by Mao as a leader, not only by the scope of his mind, but perhaps even more so by his overpowering physical presence. As the Secretary once described Mao, "He had the quality of being at the center wherever he stood. It moved with him wherever he moved." Looking back on his first meeting with Mao, during the Nixon visit, Kissinger marveled that the Chinese leader had outlined what came to be the Shanghai Communiqué in his conversation, which was mostly indirect, allegorical, and marked by the Socratic manner: He asked questions to make a point. "Mao's remarks are like an overture to a Wagnerian opera," Kissinger later lyricized. All the themes were sounded and then developed afterward.

The ability of both Mao and Chou to talk about highly complex subjects at great length without recourse to notes impressed Kissinger enormously. Chou spent about twenty hours talking to Kissinger during the secret visit in 1971, and the Chinese Premier never once used a note. Kissinger himself has the same ability, which is one reason he's so impressed when he finds it in others.

For all his love of permanent revolution and proletarian protocol, Chairman Mao retained some of the customs of imperial China — at least in its imperiousness. The Chinese historically regarded their country as the Middle Kingdom, to which the "barbarians" came to pay homage and tribute, and they still tended to regard foreign visitors as supplicants, more or less, although they were usually not arrogant about it. And they played a maddening game with a Mao meeting. In the first place, they considered a session with the Chairman to be an audience with the Pope, an utterance from the Delphic Oracle, and a compliment from Charles de Gaulle, all rolled into one. It was the diplomatic equivalent of an orgasm, and no foreign visit reached a climax without it. The honored guest not only did not know in advance *if* he would see Mao, he also never knew when. The meetings always came on short notice. Nixon received his invitation within minutes after reaching his villa, a highly unusual circumstance.

When Kissinger returned to China for the first time as Secretary of State, in November 1973, he was not told he would see Mao, but he felt he should. And he did. Kissinger was flattered to receive the invitation, not only for himself, but also for the resident Ambassador, even though the United States and the People's Republic did not have formal diplomatic relations. In a rare departure from Chinese practice, the venerable David K. E. Bruce was also invited. It was his first and only meeting with Mao.

Winston Lord, one of Kissinger's top aides on China, was also invited. But this was not *his* first meeting with Mao. Unbeknownst to anybody but Nixon and Kissinger, and of course the Chinese, Lord had gone along when the President saw the Chairman in 1972. He had been invited as a special favor to Kissinger, who had requested it both as a favor to Lord, who had a Chinese wife, and also as a favor to himself, since Lord took the notes during the conversations with Mao, and therefore Kissinger himself didn't have to.

But Kissinger also baffled the Chinese back in 1972 by asking them not to publicize Lord's presence at the Nixon-Mao meeting. William Rogers, the Secretary of State, had not been invited, and that was humiliating enough without the further knowledge that one of Kissinger's lowly NSC aides was allowed to bask in the presence of the great man. So the pictures flashed around the world in 1972 were, in a sense, a fake. The Chinese had duly cropped Lord out of all the photographs of the Nixon-Mao meeting they distributed for public release. But they gave Lord himself a picture that showed him there.

In 1973 they assumed that since Kissinger was going to see Mao, he would undoubtedly want Lord to go along, and so they invited him this time without any prompting.

Kissinger's sixth visit was different from his previous five as a White House aide in a number of respects, apart from the fact he arrived there following a diplomatic blitzkrieg through the Middle East. He left from the same airport in Pakistan from which he had departed secretly in the night on his first mission. This time, however, it was daytime, and he got a big sendoff, with troops passing in review and bands playing. When he landed in Peking, he was met by the Chinese Minister for Foreign Affairs, Chi Peng-yi, not a flunky from the Protocol Office. And he was also the head of the U.S. Foreign Service, which meant that he was the boss of the people who worked at the U.S. Liaison Office in Peking. The Liaison Office was an embassy in everything but name, and Kissinger had set it up with the Chinese the previous spring, before he was elevated to his Cabinet position.

USLO, which was referred to in the vernacular as Yoos-low, had an ambassador, a building that looked exactly like the Greek Embassy next door, and Marine guards, but it was not an embassy as such because the People's Republic refused to establish full and formal diplomatic relations with the United States as long as the Republic of China on Taiwan had an embassy in Washington. USLO was an effort to square the circle. It enabled each country to have an ambassador in the other's capital without having formal diplomatic relations. Kissinger was more interested in substance than form.

The establishment of the PRC Liaison Office in Washington had led to a quick mini-crisis in American-Chinese relations. One of the Chinese officials who went to Washington from Ottawa to help set it up died rather suddenly. The Chinese were convinced he had been poisoned. And they refused to permit an autopsy to be performed on the dead man's body. General Alexander Haig, Kissinger's deputy at the NSC, had to go talk to the Chinese Ambassador at the United Nations more than once before Chinese suspicions were overcome sufficiently to permit an autopsy. It showed he had died as a result of eating some herbs he had bought in Washington's Chinatown.

To show the importance they attached to their Washington connection, the Chinese sent Huang Chen, a veteran of the Long March, to head their Liaison Office. Huang was a chubby, jovial man with a good sense of humor. He was once asked how China felt about liberalizing its emigration policies in order to qualify for favorable trade treatment from the United States, in accordance with legislation sponsored by Senator Henry Jackson of Washington. Huang replied, "Any time Senator Jackson wants ten million Chinese in the state of Washington, all he has to do is let me know."

The opening of the American Liaison Office in Peking had none of the drama of its Washington counterpart, just some bureaucratic overkill. Kissinger had wanted his NSC man, John Holdridge of shirts fame, to head the mission. But the State Department pushed for an old China hand, Alfred Jenkins, who had been among the last American diplomats to leave. A compromise solution sent them both to Peking as coequal heads of a mission that didn't have all that much work for even one chief since Kissinger himself handled all the serious business with the Chinese. The arrival of the respected diplomatic sage, Ambassador Bruce, established primacy.

USLO had a small staff, which included Elizabeth Gaston, who had been a secretary in Saigon with a remote connection to Kissinger. During one of Kissinger's visits to Vietnam, the *Stars and Stripes* had run a composite picture of him taken from the *Harvard Lampoon.* It showed Kissinger's head superimposed on the body of a naked man, lying on a rug and smoking a cigar. Elizabeth clipped the picture, thinking it would be a super idea to get Henry to autograph it. She invited some of his secretaries home for lunch and asked them about getting it signed. They told her he was a little miffed that the caption in *Stars and Stripes* had not explained that the picture was a composite, but that if she wanted him to autograph it, it would be better for her to ask directly.

So one night in Saigon, she waited for him to come out of Ellsworth Bunker's office, and she asked him to autograph the picture of Henry Kissinger's head on the body of a naked man. He was indeed charming. He signed it, pointing out, "This is a composite, you know." Elizabeth wanted to say, "Yes, sir, it's somebody else's head." But she didn't have the nerve. She had the picture framed, and when she was transferred to Peking, she hung it over her desk. Just before the Secretary of State arrived in Peking in November 1973, however, her superiors made her take it down. Not decorous, you know, to have that kind of picture of the Secretary of State hanging in the U.S. Liaison Office, even though he himself had autographed it. The bureaucratic mind at work.

When she came back to the United States, she hung it over her desk in Washington — with a gold-foil seal of the Secretary of State strategically placed where a fig leaf might have been. Then she got a color version of the picture, and on Kissinger's last day in office, Elizabeth Gaston Andros (now married) stood in the long line of people to say good-bye. When she reached Kissinger, she asked him to autograph the color picture. Again, he was charming. He signed it and told her this time, "When my father saw the picture, he knew it wasn't me because he knows I don't smoke."

During his 1973 visit, Kissinger spent an inordinate amount of time talking to Ambassador Bruce. But he was not talking about Chinese affairs. He was talking mostly about American affairs. Kissinger was worried about Watergate and about the potential erosion of American authority around the world. He wanted to hear from Bruce what one of America's most respected diplomats thought he should do personally and professionally. Kissinger's concern about Watergate became dramatically apparent before the visit was over.

It began routinely enough. The easy relationship between Kissinger and Chou was immediately apparent as we watched them drink tea against the backdrop of a silk screen with a poem by Mao in one of the dozens of rooms in the Great Hall of the People. Chou noted with headline-catching acuity that following Kissinger's sweep through Rabat, Tunis, Cairo, et al., the Secretary would now be known as "The Mideast Cyclone." Then Chou said, "I can't read all the papers put before me, but you, Dr. Kissinger, are so young and vigorous, you can do it." Replied young Dr. Kissinger, "One more Mideast swing like this and I'll be aged."

All of the conversation was carried on through a Chinese interpreter, usually Nancy Tang, from Brooklyn. Kissinger always relied on the Chinese for the interpreting, perhaps out of simple deference, an indication of his confidence in the relationship. One of his aides explained that the Chinese interpreters were far better than their American counterparts. And besides, the Kissinger party always included somebody who spoke Chinese so he could be sure the translations were not going astray. Yet it always seemed curious to me that a man whose ear was so finely tuned to nuances would not want to have his own translator present for important substantive talks. And the "deference" argument lost weight because he operated the same way in the Soviet Union. The absence of an American interpreter may be more easily explained by Kissinger's penchant for secrecy: An "outsider" who did not belong to the inner circle did not have to be brought into the talks. One less person knew the secrets.

In his toast at the arrival night banquet, Kissinger harked back to his diplomatic Long March. Looking down at Chou, he said, "None of us who took the trip can ever forget the sense of excitement on entering China for the first time, and we thought it was a mysterious country until the Prime Minister pointed out it was more out of our ignorance than China's mystery." He was referring to their first discussion.

The next day, Kissinger and Chou held their first delegation-to-delegation meeting in the Great Hall. And we reporters got some insight into the proletarian nature of this fragile mandarin with the agile mind and electric charm. When Chou came in, he shook hands with the photographers and the cameramen, but not with the reporters. Afterward, one of the photographers wondered aloud about this to his escort officer, who told him, "You are the working people, who have to carry the equipment." Chou also went out of his way to learn the names of the Secretary's secretaries and the Secret Service agents.

Throughout a Kissinger visit, the Chinese always arranged plenty of sightseeing for the one-time professor of history, although many of their sights predated his specialty, the nineteenth century, by several hundred years. On each visit, Kissinger saw a different part of what is popularly known as the Forbidden City — the imperial palaces of the Ming and Ch'ing dynasties. Work began on them in 1406. The Forbidden City included three big halls — the Hall of Supreme Harmony, the Hall of Middle Harmony, and the Hall of Preserving Harmony — and those names came to symbolize Kissinger's gradually declining relationship with the Chinese. Other parts of the complex were the Palace of Heavenly Purity, the Hall of Union, the Hall of Mental Cultivation, the Palace of Earthly Tranquility, the Six East and West Palaces, and the Imperial Garden.

On this trip, Kissinger was also taken on a pilgrimage required of all distinguished foreign visitors: a visit to the Nan Yuan commune on the outskirts of Peking. It was a field day for the photographers. First, they snapped the marvelous craggy faces of old people in the Home for the Respect to the Aged, and then there was Kissinger among the flapping, quacking ducks, walking around the pens where the birds are force-fed before they end up on the table as the famed Peking duck. For once, the Kissinger wit failed to flash. He managed to watch workers plunge a rubber food tube into the duck's gullet without relating the exercise to briefing State Department reporters. He later acknowledged that he had "missed a cue."

Kissinger also managed some pre-Revolutionary sightseeing. He was taken to the Hall of Prayers and Altar of Prayers, where Chinese emperors traditionally prayed for good crops. The reporters were already standing on the sunbathed pavilion when Kissinger's Red Flag arrived behind schedule. Out of the crowd came a voice saying, "Here comes the Emperor again."

Just before you get to the hall, there's a circular walled compound, about eighty yards across, with a large building in the middle that features remarkable acoustics. A word whispered into the stone on one side is easily heard all the way around on the other side. "Looks to me like a reasonable way to carry on negotiations," cracked Kissinger. At the other end of the pavilion, there's another acoustical marvel. You stand on a marble stone and speak, and your voice seems amplified several times over. The vice foreign minister and the UN Ambassador, Chiao Kuan-kua, trying to match Kissinger's one-liner, said, "I sure could use that in New York."

Some of the Sinologists thought one reason the Chinese scheduled so much sightseeing for Kissinger was to give themselves time to update their negotiating position or prepare responses to his suggestions.

Another "sight" turned out to be a subtle form of Chinese torture, in which they used dancing instead of water. It was known as Revolutionary Ballet.

China's policy on the literary and performing arts derived, like almost everything else, from a quotation from the Chairman: "There is, in fact, no such thing as art for art's sake, art that is detached from or independent of politics . . . Literature and art operate as powerful weapons for uniting and educating the people and for attacking and destroying the enemy." Ars gratia propaganda. Mao's wife, Chiang Ching, had taken over the arts and carried out his dictum with great revolutionary vigor, not to say vengeance. One of the products was an interminably long treatise set to dance and music and called *The White-Haired Girl.* The plot was the same as all plots in China: Landlord oppresses girl. Girl joins Red Army. Enlightened girl helps Red Army overcome wicked landlord. (The subtlety and sophistication so often attributed to the Chinese by Kissinger did not extend to their operas. The one he saw in 1975, *Azalea Mountain,* features the "landlord tyrants" led by Poisonous Snake.) The female dancers all wore slacks. All women in China wear slacks, for that matter. I have spent nine nights in China, and if Chinese women have legs, you couldn't prove it by me.

Kissinger undiplomatically fell asleep at the ballet, and UPI's Helen Thomas was undiplomatic enough to report it. If the truth be known, he wasn't the only one in the party who was seen checking his eyelids for holes.

During the sightseeing, the American reporters were taken to a "sight" Kissinger did not see, an underground air-raid shelter. We were told that it and others had been built to counter the threat from "enemies to the north." The Soviet Union lies north. There seemed to be a lot of symbolism involved. The Chinese appeared to be saying to us, We're dealing with the Americans (erstwhile Running Dogs of imperialism) because we're worried about the Russians. But we're not that worried, since the shelters aren't all that deep nor are they stocked with large amounts of food and water.

On the third afternoon of the visit, while the two full delegations were meeting, one of the American participants noted that Chou En-lai engaged in what was "an obvious delaying maneuver. He was reworking the ground a bit too thoroughly." An aide entered the room, whispered to Chou, who then told Kissinger that Mao wanted to see him that evening. The visit was now an official success.

The meeting lasted two hours and forty-five minutes, one of the longest Mao ever had with a foreign visitor. The Chinese described it as having taken place "in a friendly atmosphere," which was not the usual friendly thing they did. And Mao even reportedly spoke some English, asking the Secretary to convey his regards to President Nixon. During the meeting, Chairman Mao exhibited some of his renowned "earthiness" — a euphemistic way of saying he talked like Lyndon B. Johnson in private. He wondered why the American people were "farting" so much about Watergate. It was a somewhat more colorful way of referring to the problem than Ron Ziegler's "third-rate burglary," but I never used the quote on the air.

Mao's earthiness also produced a memorable remark about his radical wife, Chiang Ching. Speaking to some Communist cadre about one of his wife's political errors, Mao explained that "she shit wide of the mark." Or at least that's what the CIA said he said. And the CIA doesn't use words like that lightly.

The timing of Mao's summons ensured that the American press would find out about it right away. Ambassador Bruce had scheduled a reception at USLO, with Kissinger as the star attraction, at the cocktail hour. When both principals failed to show up, however, it did not take us long to figure out why.

The Mao meeting turned into a nightmare for Don Anderson,

USLO's "barbarian watcher" — the press liaison officer for the trip. The Liaison Office was not big enough, nor did it have enough customers, to warrant a full-time press officer. During a Kissinger visit, the political officer who drew the short straw was assigned to us. (The imperial Chinese used to assign "barbarian handlers" to deal with foreign visitors, all of whom were considered to be barbarians primarily because they were not Chinese. It's not really all that different in contemporary China. And USLO playfully adopted the term for the ad hoc press officer.) One of Don Anderson's duties was to distribute the film and still photographs of the Mao-Kissinger meeting, which were provided by the Chinese. No American photographers were allowed to enter the most inner socialist sanctum.

From a strictly pictorial point of view, the Mao-Kissinger picture may not have been all that flashy, but it was probably the newsiest of the trip. Almost immediately after the Foreign Ministry had delivered the photos to Anderson's suite in the Min Tzu (he was allowed to lodge there, close to his barbarians), the UPI photographer happened to walk in. He asked innocently if he could have his copy of the picture. He could. About twenty minutes later the AP photographer, Harvey Georges, showed up. And when he found out what had happened, he went off like a Chinese firecracker. His opposition had a twenty-minute head start. He ranted, raved, threatened to have Anderson censured by the White House Photographers Association (now *that* will make a diplomat tremble), and said he would make sure a formal protest was filed at the State Department. By the end of the trip, however, he had calmed down enough to leave Anderson a bottle of brandy and a typewriter. The gift of the typewriter was not all that altruistic. The machine was broken. And Georges knew from previous experience that it was virtually impossible to leave anything behind in China. Whatever you left in your room, the Chinese would pack up and bring to you at the airport.

Diane Sawyer, a lovely blond assistant to Ron Ziegler at the White House, had learned this with embarrassing clarity during the presidential visit in 1972. The departure ceremonies were already under way at the airport when a Foreign Ministry official appeared on the windy tarmac carrying a pair of pantyhose, which waved in the breeze like a banner. They belonged to Diane Sawyer. They were torn, so she had left them in her room. When she saw the Chinese official, she knew immediately what was happening but tried to pay no attention. She failed, and the torn pantyhose were brought back to the United States.

Kissinger once told us that during one of his presecretarial trips to Peking, his return flight was stopped just as it was about to take off from the airport. Kissinger felt a sudden concern. What had gone wrong? A Chinese military vehicle roared out to the plane, and a polite official delivered a collection of wire coat hangers that had been left behind by a member of the party.

On the final night of the 1973 visit, it was Kissinger's turn to be the host at a banquet. He had asked his staff to come up with an appropriate proverb for the occasion. They produced: "When among friends, a thousand cups are not enough." And he used it, adding an epilogue: "We've been practicing this at the head table tonight." A later quote from the toast set off a thousand alarm bells among the journalists present. Perhaps inspired by Mao's observations about Watergate, Kissinger said that the American opening toward China was a constant feature of U.S. foreign policy, "whatever administration is in power." This was November 1973, and a besieged Nixon was gathering the wagons in a circle around the White House. His words had "Watergate" written all over them.

The accompanying newsmen made a big run at Bob McCloskey, the official spokesman, as we filed out of the Great Hall. McCloskey's instincts were good, especially when it came to protecting his boss. He denied there was any Watergate implication in what Kissinger had said, but he figured the best move at this point was to let Kissinger himself fend us off.

The Secretary and Chou were walking down the majestic stairway covered with red plush carpet in the Great Hall. At the foot of the stairs, Kissinger was forced into an impromptu news conference. His host/guest, Chou, stood back and observed, bemused, for about five minutes, then went off to a private room to wait for Kissinger and more talks. The Secretary tried to fend us off by saying that he was simply trying to make the point that the new approach to China was bipartisan and would not be changed even if the Democrats won the White House in 1976 — three years later!

Everybody wrote a Watergate story. Kissinger had obviously felt the need to give the Chinese some reassurance in public that the new U.S. policy toward China would survive Nixon. Later, on the flight leaving Peking, Kissinger insisted to us that the Chinese had been very much interested in our *long-range* policy. There was some concern about Watergate, he said, but "there's nothing we [Kissinger and the Chinese] can do about it." The Chinese wanted to know if our policy was for real or an "accident of Nixon and myself," he told us. "They want to know if the Democrats are isolationists."

Interestingly enough, there is no public record of Kissinger's "Watergate" toast. The toasts he made in China in 1974 and 1975, as well as virtually every other word he ever uttered in public as Secretary of State, were all published as routine State Department press releases. But not the exchange of toasts in Peking in 1973.

Whenever Kissinger or his aides talked about visiting China, they always emphasized that everything was carefully orchestrated and meticulously carried out. The Secretary claimed that from the moment he stepped off his plane in Peking, the schematics of the visit became steadily apparent. He felt no Chinese official ever said anything to him that was not a part of a general plan. "You can assume," he once told us, "that anything any Chinese tells you, no matter how spontaneous it seems, or off the cuff, has been carefully rehearsed." He said he could get the drift of what the discussion would be like as soon as the first protocol officer spoke to him. And, he pointed out, the Chinese always kept each other fully briefed; they knew who had said what to whom. Kissinger was so impressed that he even ordered the State Department to make a study of the Chinese protocol office. One thing he learned was how the Chinese maintained his schedule so scrupulously, even the sightseeing schedule, when the hosts couldn't possibly be sure in advance what would interest their guest most. The Chinese broke the schedule down into eight-minute segments. If they lost a minute or two in one segment, they rearranged a later segment. One major exception to this rigidity was conversation with Chou, which sometimes lasted until three in the morning.

On his trips to China, Kissinger always deferred to his hosts to make all the physical arrangements. He used their cars rather than bringing one of his bulletproof limousines. And his Secret Service agents gave up their walkie-talkies. They could pack sidearms, but they had to check their radios at the door. The Chinese felt Kissinger did not need *that* much security in their country. China was the only place in the world where the agents didn't run around talking into their sleeves (where the small microphones were), looking like a convention of the deaf, with all those earplugs and wires. One of the agents, Charlie Potts of Georgia, made a rare contribution to bridging the culture gap. When he was off duty, he sat in his hotel room and played a tape cassette of *Johnny Cash at Folsom Prison* while he drank beer and whooped to the music. Chinese hotel workers gathered in the hallway in front of his door, chattering and giggling as they listened to the strange sounds coming from within.

Given the Chinese passion for orchestration, it was not surprising that the press was handled with great precision. Suggestions that we "drop in" to visit a school with laughing children or some other paradigm of the workers' paradise always sounded impromptu. But as Kissinger used to reflect, the Chinese had raised to an art form the process of making the totally planned seem spontaneous.

The first time a reporter goes to China, he may not be immediately aware of how totally controlled everything really is because of the Chinese style of doing things with charm and grace. We were all much more familiar with the heavy-handedness of the Russians. That explains in part why much of the reporting from China during Nixon's presidential trip had a certain "gee whiz" quality.

It was virtually impossible to crack through the official veneer to get to the people. Whatever you heard, you heard from your official escort. There were no peasant-in-the-street interviews. Bob Keatley of the *Wall Street Journal* and some others tried to get a feel for the life of the common people by going to a restaurant where workers ate. It was terribly crowded, but after a short while, the locals all moved away from the table where the newsmen were eating, leaving the Americans just as isolated as if they had gone to a private dining room, where foreigners usually eat. AP photographer Harvey Georges had a more telling experience. Boredom got the better of him late one night in his hotel, and he decided to go for a walk. He left the hotel and aimlessly wandered through the streets of Peking. Several blocks away, he paused and simply watched the sparse traffic passing. He heard a voice say, "Hello, Mr. Harvey." It was his escort officer, Mr. Yang.

Using the press to emphasize the bilateral aspect of relations with the United States, the Chinese excluded all resident foreign correspondents from Kissinger functions. They even barred them from our hotel until USLO intervened with the Foreign Ministry. Any American reporter covering the event had to arrive on Kissinger's plane. So rigid were these restrictions that Pierre Salinger, the American in Paris who works for *L'Express,* had to get accreditation from *New Times* magazine in order to cover a presidential visit.

Since American reporters rarely got to Peking, I wanted to do as many sidebar stories as time permitted. It didn't permit many. One of the big problems was simply getting around in Peking. We were all assigned a car and a driver, which took us where the Chinese wanted us to go. The lack of taxicabs at our hotel provided another clue to the Chinese concept of control. The cabs all had "disappeared" two days before Kissinger arrived. One way to get around was to use the cars of the resident French and British correspondents. The tradeoff was information from us on the American briefings or bits of color from the meetings or quotes from the banquet toasts.

One of the stories I did was on the *People's Daily,* the world's largest newspaper, with a circulation of about three and one half million and with no advertising. Its news, which always cleaves strictly to the party line, is carefully selected. Premier Chou En-lai used to edit the front page personally for important stories. (Nixon was once heard to remark that he'd like to have the same privilege.) This news, such as it is, is also posted on bulletin boards outside the printing plant. Not a single word ever appeared there about Watergate. Unofficially, however, millions of Chinese were informed about Watergate through a confidential publication called *Reference News Bulletin.* It's distributed to more than seven million people in responsible positions, but it's not for sale at any newsstand, nor is it available to foreigners, not even diplomats. It contains verbatim reprints of articles and editorials appearing in Western newspapers and magazines, including those highly critical of Nixon. So, in typical Chinese fashion, the word about Watergate got around without ever being attributed to official outlets.

I also did the first filming of the U.S. Liaison Office, which is undoubtedly the only American mission in this computerized world where the local employees use an abacus.

During the Nixon visit, live television pictures were beamed directly back to the United States. During subsequent Kissinger visits, the ground station was still in place — a gift from American television — but daily satellites were no longer possible because the Chinese didn't have the proper equipment. But they did know how to transmit via satellite. The American technicians on the advance team for the Nixon visit came away with a story about how diligently the Chinese had worked to learn how to operate the totally unfamiliar equipment. They even learned the jargon — or most of it. At the end of the training period, the "responsible person" on the Chinese side told the head of the technical advance team that he understood "video" and "audio" and "IFB" (feedback) and the like, but after listening to the American technicians, there was still something he didn't understand: What was "fucking video"?

In addition to its journalistic and touristic allures, China offered one other special attraction — its food, especially after the gastronomic wasteland of the Middle East. The first-night banquet was full of promise, but not all nine courses were impressive. Some of my colleagues were repulsed by the sea slugs. We approached lunch the next day with great anticipation. The Chinese news agency, Hsinhua, had invited us to the International Club, a huge complex that looks so antiseptic it could be mistaken for a ward for contagious diseases.

It's financed by the Foreign Ministry and features two indoor tennis courts for Western diplomats.

We had more than nine courses. They included fried chicken, baked ham, macaroni and cheese, coleslaw, spaghetti and meatballs, baked beans, potato chips, and a variety of other "typically Chinese" dishes. Our hosts loved it. They went back for seconds and thirds. (I couldn't help recalling when I was a child and a finicky aunt used to visit and tell me, when I hadn't cleaned my plate, to think of all those starving people in China. But it was hard to do, since she also used to tell me that if I talked while I was eating, the angels would come down and choke me.) For dessert, we had apple pie — without fortunes. My only satisfaction at lunch was to explain to a baffled Chinese official that Marco Polo had shown the Chinese how to make noodles.

By the time Kissinger returned to China for the seventh time in November 1974, Chou En-lai was in a hospital, slowly dying of cancer, and Richard Nixon was in exile in San Clemente. Chairman Mao was still running the revolutionary show, but Kissinger never got to see him, never found out why, and was not at all pleased about it. The Secretary had to contend with a new cast of characters as Mao's subordinates. Just before he arrived, the Chinese UN Ambassador, Chiao Kuan-kua, was elevated to foreign minister, replacing Chi Peng-yi. Chiao was a Chou protégé, an intelligent man with a quick laugh and good sense of humor who enjoyed needling Kissinger. He spoke German as well as some Russian and Japanese and had studied philosophy in Germany in the mid-thirties. Chiao had been a vice foreign minister when Kissinger first went to China, and for some reason, Kissinger had trouble remembering his name. At times in the formal discussions Kissinger's mind blocked on Chiao, and he would cop out by saying, "As the vice foreign minister has said . . ." So Chiao took to referring to himself as "Mr. X" when he was with Kissinger.

During Kissinger's second trip to Peking, his NSC aide Dick Solomon was with him. Solomon arrived on his thirty-fifth birthday, excited beyond measure — as though life would all be downhill fol-

lowing this exalted experience. When Chou En-lai showed up, he
took special note of Solomon. "This is the first time you've been in
China," Chou said. "We want to thank you for escorting our Ping-
Pong delegation around the United States . . . And I understand you
speak Chinese well. Where did you learn it?" The situation seemed
to call for a reply in Chinese, and Solomon did not miss his cue. He
answered in Chinese, "Your Ping-Pong players taught me." Kissinger's head snapped around when he heard Solomon talking Chinese. "I see we will need a translator for one of our staff," he said.
The next day, as Kissinger was leaving the guest house, he spotted
Solomon and told Chiao jokingly, "I forbid Mr. Solomon to talk
Chinese in my presence." Whereupon Chiao immediately turned to
Solomon and began talking to him in Chinese.

Chiao was a meticulous host. The Chinese knew Kissinger liked
Peking duck, so Chiao arranged a dinner for him at a private restaurant that specialized in the dish. Two of the more junior members
of the American party arrived early and were then afraid Kissinger
would raise hell about their getting there before he did. As they were
talking over what they should do, the door to the kitchen opened,
and out walked Foreign Minister Chiao Kuan-kua, who had been
personally inspecting the night's menu to make sure everything was
all right. Can you imagine Kissinger testing the soup and checking
the salad dressing?

Chiao was also the host for the arrival night banquet. This time
Kissinger had brought along his wife, Nancy, and his two children,
David and Elizabeth. Nancy had made a striking entrance into the
People's Republic, descending from the plane wearing a full-length
mink coat into a sea of proletarian blue uniforms at the airport.
(Kissinger once said to a newsman who commented on the coat,
"That was before me.")

Chiao's toast was full of Mao-like quotes. "The current international situation is characterized by great disorder under heaven. In
our view, the entire world is amidst intense turbulence and unrest.
This reflects the sharpening of various contradictions and is something independent of man's will. This history of mankind always

moves forward amidst turmoil. In our view, such turmoil is a good thing, and not a bad thing." Although Nixon was gone, he was not forgotten. The Chinese showed him more reverence than they did their own leaders who had fallen from grace. "Here," Chiao said at one point, "we ought to mention the pioneering role Mr. Richard Nixon played" in developing friendly relations between the American and Chinese peoples.

Kissinger then picked up on Chiao. "We live in a period of great change and a period that is characterized by much upheaval. We believe that this change must lead to a new and better order for all of the people of the world, and it is to this goal that American foreign policy is dedicated." Kissinger was subtly one-upping Chiao.

Kissinger had come to Peking less than twenty-four hours after leaving the USSR, where President Ford and Soviet leader Leonid Brezhnev had reached a new agreement in principle on limiting nuclear weapons. The Chinese were not only edgy about the Ford-Brezhnev Summit and détente, they were also unhappy about the meeting place, Vladivostok, which they claimed the Russians had stolen from them. Kissinger's 1974 mission was thus primarily aimed at reassuring the skeptical Chinese that President Ford had done nothing to affect them adversely and to reaffirm that their relations with America were not being subverted by détente.

When Kissinger talked about détente with the Chinese in private, he frequently referred to "your friends, the Russians." The Chinese always laughed. They, in turn, cracked themselves up by referring to the Soviet Union as "the polar bear," and the Secretary emulated them when he felt a light moment was needed. The Chinese also amused themselves by referring to their propaganda broadsides as "firing cannons," and the metaphor came to be a constant part of the banter on both sides.

A lot of Kissinger's spur-of-the-moment quips were untranslatable, but the Chinese translators always tried, and his Chinese hosts always managed an amused smile if not a laugh.

During his 1974 visit, the Secretary of State also wanted to reassure the Chinese government that Watergate had not destroyed the central authority of the United States, which had changed its leaders without dropping its leadership role.

These themes tended to be articulated obliquely rather than openly. Without a major focal point for reporting, the press drifted toward the issue of Taiwan, especially since we were hearing about it constantly from the Chinese officials who dealt with us. Full diplomatic relations with Peking — and a concomitant break in relations with Taiwan — would represent the next Big Leap Forward in American-Chinese relations. But the pace of normalization had slowed to mini-steps, and the Chinese appeared to be getting impatient. No progress had been made on reconciling differing points of view on Taiwan. Chou En-lai had told visitors during the previous year that there was a need to "cut off the tail" of the Shanghai Communiqué. Chou meant they had to clear up the ambiguities on Taiwan, but Kissinger insisted the Chinese never pressed him on that point.

During a briefing on another trip, Kissinger had once said, in connection with an Arab-Israeli negotiation, "If I had asked Chou in 1971 — or any time — that for five years he make no claim on Formosa, he would have thrown me out of the room because nobody [among the Communist] Chinese can do that. But in fact, that's what he did . . ." I became convinced after hearing that statement that Kissinger had an actual understanding with the Chinese that they would not force the Taiwan issue until the second Nixon administration ended in 1977 (sic).

During the 1974 visit, Chiao was not the major interlocutor on the Chinese side. With Chou in the hospital, many of his functions were taken over by Teng Hsiao-peng, a small, squat, seventyish official who had made a political comeback in China as remarkable as Nixon's in the United States. Teng had fallen into disgrace during the Cultural Revolution and had dropped out of sight. But when Chou got sick enough to know the end was coming, he maneuvered the return of Teng, a pragmatist and effective administrator. Kissinger had dealt with him at the United Nations earlier in the year, and was startled to note that during a conversation lasting more than three hours, Teng never once mentioned the name of Chou. So

Kissinger was somewhat apprehensive about what he might find within the Chinese leadership in 1974. The Americans also found Teng to be rather diffident and lacking self-confidence. That lack diminished as his power grew. Kissinger later came to appreciate, if not admire, Teng's "instinct for the jugular."

It was clear early on that Chou En-lai's elegance was missing from the meetings. One of Kissinger's aides recalls looking up from making notes at one point during the delegation-to-delegation talks after he heard a loud *splat*. Teng had virtually disappeared from view. He was leaning way over to one side in order to spit into a big brass spittoon placed strategically nearby. He seemed to take special delight in spitting right in the middle of some profound Kissinger disquisition, and the *Wall Street Journal* reported later that Kissinger had referred to Teng in private as a "nasty little man."

After the sightseeing and a visit to Premier Chou in the hospital, Kissinger went into the regular formal discussions with the Chinese. At the first session, he allowed himself to be overheard telling his hosts that he hoped talks like these would soon be held in Washington. The Chinese replied politely that while they would like to go to Washington, they had to refuse. But they omitted the usual propaganda. The lack of polemics was apparently no accident. Chiao used the first picture-taking session to make a nonpolemical point. He said he did not believe reports that American-Chinese relations had cooled since Kissinger's last visit to Peking more than a year before. But almost everything that happened during the next few days seemed to contradict Chiao's analysis. Kissinger did not meet Mao; the toasts at the banquet were brief; the communiqué was only nine lines long, and it made no mention of progress toward normalization.

The visit did end with an announcement that President Ford would visit China, and the ho-hum reaction among the press befuddled Kissinger. "Less than four years ago," he said over and over again, "the announcement that the President of the United States would visit Peking would have been regarded as mind-boggling and astounding. Now," he marveled, "it's treated as some kind of defeat."

For his part, Chiao Kuan-kua pointed out that the two sides had reviewed developments "in a candid spirit." The use of the word "candid" signaled disagreement. That's what nuances are all about.

If the banquet was not remarkable for prolix toasts, it was memorable for the timing. It fell on Thanksgiving Day. Thanksgiving is one of the few holidays in America that escaped being shifted to a Monday for the sake of a three-day weekend. But since Kissinger happened to be in Peking on Thanksgiving, all the Americans at USLO had to work, so Ambassador George Bush decreed that the following Monday would be Thanksgiving for them. (Actually, the day of giving thanks for most embassy employees was the day Kissinger left town, so it worked out about the same.)

The Kissingers did have a kind of traditional Thanksgiving at the Embassy residence. On very short notice — like twenty minutes — the Bushes found out the Secretary and his family would be there for lunch. They served chicken and everybody pretended it was turkey. The only food resembling Thanksgiving fare at the banquet that night in the Great Hall was the yams. And they were served as dessert. Otherwise, we had stuffed bean curd soup, abalone, fried prawns, braised duck, exotic vegetables, and Mongolian hot pot with cucumbers. The background music was appropriate: "Turkey in the Straw." Pure coincidence.

Obviously it was not the food that made this an American banquet, but the designation. The Chinese foreign minister was the host at the arrival banquet, and Kissinger was the host at the departure banquet. That meant that at the departure banquet the Americans paid for the food and Kissinger got to give the first toast.

The "home and home" series placed some protocol requirements on us, the other members of the "delegation," as well. During the arrival banquet, the "most responsible person" (Chinese) at the table distributes the food to the guests, plucking it from serving bowls with his chopsticks and placing it on the plates. At Kissinger's banquet, the visiting Americans reciprocated, although we didn't get too involved in who was the "most responsible" among us as we served the Chinese. At all times there were table toasts, apart from the toasts of the principals. We clinked glasses, shouted "Gambei" (the Chinese equivalent of "Bottoms up"), and drank mao tai. But if you really bottomed up, you didn't make it through all nine courses. And a half-hour later, you certainly didn't feel like you needed more mao tai. At this banquet, we also spent much of our time trying to explain Thanksgiving to the Chinese. But ideologically, they were with the Indians.

We all left the banquet wondering whether Kissinger would be diverted from his flight to the resort city of Suchow the next day to see Mao. He wasn't.

Suchow was on the itinerary because Kissinger had twice visited Hangchow, another southern Chinese resort town, and he asked to go someplace else on this trip. The Chinese supplied the transportation — British-made Tridents — while the Secretary's Air Force 707 flew to Shanghai to await us. The 707 was Kissinger's link to the world, and to the White House in particular. He used to boast that his communications system was so good that he could be swimming in the Mediterranean on some isolated beach, and if the White House called, he could be in touch in less than two minutes. That's what he thought.

The Chinese had promised to set up a communications link between the 707 parked on a ramp at the Shanghai airport and a guest house where Kissinger was having lunch in Suchow. Aide Peter Rodman and the USLO barbarian-handler for that trip, Lynn Pascoe, went to check out the line. They found an old hand-crank field phone and a woman operator. Pascoe, who spoke Chinese, asked for a check of the line. They reached military installations all over China, but they never got through to the plane. Pascoe finally made a commercial long-distance call to the White House and was patched through to the plane. He was assured nothing was going on.

The installations at the 707's end were no less primitive — a long wire stretched to a lonely old-fashioned telephone that hung on a short pole on the tarmac near the plane. But the doors of the plane were closed, and the people on board could not have heard the phone ring anyway. A political officer from USLO spent most of his time cranking the phone, trying to get through to Suchow. When he did get through, he spoke to a maid who didn't know from Henry Kissinger. Or else she didn't understand the officer's accent. Kissinger never knew how far out of touch he was.

In Suchow, the tourist attractions included the famed walled Garden of Humble Politics, an elegant smattering of rock and flower gardens scattered among small lakes. Kissinger and Chiao strolled in the gardens and were photographed, and finally the two hardly humble politicians crossed intellects on how best to describe the significance of the classical Chinese garden in the fewest possible words.

Chiao took the ideological route: "I believe, Mr. Secretary, you will find the significance of the Chinese garden is its utilization, through the teachings of Chairman Mao and Marx, Engels, Lenin and Stalin, in instructing the broad mass of the proletariat in the wicked pre-Revolutionary bourgeois period."

Kissinger naturally disagreed. "No," he said, "the significance of the classical Chinese garden is its concentration of so much intelligence in so small an area." As Chiao made a mock grimace of defeat, Kissinger turned to the accompanying newsmen and said, "And don't give me any more of your stupid jokes about this Peking trip being David's bar mitzvah present. I'm saving that for Saudi Arabia."

Suchow had been the scene of considerable political agitation not long before the Americans arrived, so the Chinese security people had been out in force. Fresh whitewash obliterated the proliferation of political slogans and posters on the walls. The people of Suchow had been instructed to be nonchalant. Even so, they were southern and therefore more hospitable than the Pekinese. They were also more naturally demonstrative, and some even waved. The Suchowese were different from their northern neighbors in one other noticeable respect: They wore brighter clothes, even patchwork jackets or brightly colored pants, not just the uniform blue of Peking. We found out much later that many of those people casually strolling along the streets or wandering the country roads in their going-to-a-party-meeting clothes were actually militiamen masquerading as the regular folks of Suchow, contributing to the Chinese version of a Ptomkin village.

A similar Ptomkinesque incident had occurred during the Nixon visit in 1972. When the President went to the Great Wall (which, as he said, really was a Great Wall), he saw children playing with toys and transistor radios. After Nixon left, the toys and radios were rounded up and the kids sent packing. Some of the television people who stayed behind to break down the equipment noticed this, and it was duly reported. Premier Chou En-lai later apologized informally to some American correspondents about the incident, explaining that the Chinese were trying to make a good impression on their American guests.

While the southern sights of Suchow amazed and delighted the eye, the southern-style cooking of Suchow boggled the palate. The luncheon feast bordered on the spectacular. The honey-coated ham outdid anything we had eaten in Peking. A colorful bird-of-paradise hovered over the table; it was made of bits of twenty-three fresh vegetables. Dozens of elaborately worked marzipan animals were scattered around for those who had room for dessert.

We ate late in the afternoon and then flew to Shanghai, where the local Communist Party had laid on another super banquet featuring Shanghai-style food in a dining room at the airport. It was our fourth meal of the day, and the sun hadn't set. During this dinner, ABC correspondent Herb Kaplow was overheard saying, "I just ate my towel." (It looked like an egg roll.) Kissinger later approached him and said, "I hear you didn't like the food."

Within a matter of days, Kaplow's quip had been transformed into "reality," and Kissinger staffers were recounting the experience of a newsman who had mistakenly plucked his rolled-up towel with his chopsticks, thinking it was an eggroll, and had taken a bite. Such is the stuff of legends. Kissinger himself eventually used the line in a conversation with Foreign Minister Chiao. It went over like a lead won ton. Kissinger later told Kaplow, "That's the last one-liner I'm going to steal from you."

For all its charm, Suchow did not have the same impact as its resort twin, Hangchow, for some visiting Americans. The members of the White House team who had surveyed Hangchow for Nixon's 1972 visit all came down with a rash on their butt. A doctor in the group discovered that the Chinese, in sprucing up the guest houses, had relacquered all of the toilet seats that might be used by the Americans with a lacquer containing sumac, which caused the rashes. On the first anniversary of Nixon's visit, newsmen who had made the trip and various White House types threw a commemorative party. Nixon, who was sinking into Watergate by then, had no intention of attending, so staffers from the NSC prepared a funny telegram for him to send instead. The telegram celebrated the Red Rumps of Hangchow, done in the classical style of a Chinese ode. But Nixon, who despised the press, declined to send it. In the words of one of the staffers, it remains an "unpublished masterpiece."

In October 1975, Kissinger returned to China for the eighth time, but on this visit he was acting essentially as a senior advance man for President Ford, who would be there later in the year. Even before arriving, he betrayed some apprehension about the outcome. "I hope we can get through one China trip," he said to the reporters on his plane, "in which you fellows don't set goals and then accuse *us* of not fulfilling *your* goals. In general, China trips are designed to review the international situation and see where there is common perception, and where this is lacking, to understand the ramifications of that," he went on. "That's the essence of our trip.

"Inevitably, there will be some discusison of Taiwan," he said. "Do me a favor, though, and don't go to the Chinese and say, 'Kissinger says you are not interested in Taiwan.' They are interested. Sure, they have to bring it up, they cannot not bring it up, but it is not central."

A reporter wanted to know if Kissinger expected the issue of Tibet to be brought up. "I wouldn't be astonished," he said, adding, "Having said that, if they bring it up when you're all around, I'll say I'm astonished."

From the very beginning, the 1975 visit did not go well, although Kissinger put on the best possible face. Soon after his arrival, UPI's

Dick Growald filed a story saying there were no flag-waving children anywhere along the route of the Secretary's motorcade into Peking. Spokesman Bob Funseth pointed out that there were never any flag-waving children on a Kissinger trip to China. Growald replied that he had simply reported that there were no flag-waving children, and indeed, there were not. Whenever there were flag-waving children, or flag-wavers of any kind, on subsequent Kissinger trips, the Secretary would look around and ask, "Where's Growald?" But Growald's initial observations may well have captured the mood of the entire trip before it even began.

The opening night banquet toast by Foreign Minister Chiao Kuan-kua was much sharper than anybody had expected. He began with the usual revolutionary references: "The current international situation is characterized by great disorder under heaven, and the situation is excellent . . . The factors for both revolution and war are increasing. The stark reality is not that détente has developed to a new stage, but that the danger of a new world war is mounting. We do not believe there is any lasting peace. Things develop according to objective laws independently of man's will. The only way to deal with hegemonism is to wage a tit-for-tat struggle against it. To base oneself on illusions, to mistake hopes or wishes for reality and act accordingly, will only abet the ambitions of expansionism and lead to grave consequences." He quoted Mao: "Dig tunnels deep, store grain everywhere, and never seek hegemony." Hegemony was a code word for Soviet expansionism, and Chiao was welcoming Kissinger to China with a public lecture on the evils of détente and the wrong-headedness of American policy.

Kissinger ad-libbed a tart response: "Each country must pursue a policy suitable to its own circumstances. The United States will resist hegemony as we have already stated in the Shanghai Communiqué. But the United States will also make every effort to avoid needless confrontation when it can do so without threatening the security of third countries. In this policy, we will be guided by actions and realities and not rhetoric." The bloom was off the American-Chinese rose.

The Kissinger toast was noteworthy in one other respect: For the first time in eight visits, the Secretary ventured into the risky waters of the Chinese language, despite the efforts of some of his entourage to dissuade him. "On this, my eighth trip to China," he said, "I have finally found the courage to say something in Chinese. I ask your indulgence to listen carefully while I say it: *Pan chiu jung yi, ch'ing k'o nan,* which for those of you who think I spoke Cantonese means, 'It is easy to prepare a banquet, but it is hard to be a good host.' " The quality of the Chinese pronunciation was unmentionable. The aptness of the quotation, supplied by Winston Lord's Chinese-born wife, Bette, became the subject of considerable debate among American Sinologists for at least the next twenty-four hours. Some felt it insulted the Chinese since it suggested they were not good hosts, that it was a toast Kissinger should have given when he was the host.

This conversation took place at one of the tables immediately afterward:

REPORTER: What did you think of his toast in Chinese?
CHINESE OFFICIAL: Interesting.
REPORTER: How was his accent?
C.O.: Unique.
REPORTER: What did he say?
C.O.: I don't know. I didn't understand a word of it.

Kissinger later observed, "Don't blame me. It was my American accent."

Afterward, a reporter told the Secretary, "One Chinese at our table said you had a very nice voice. Another one said you did your best." Kissinger replied, "Who was it who said I was out of practice? That I liked."

The prickly tone set by Chiao's toast carried over into the head-to-head discussions. In the first meeting, Teng Hsiao-peng, now more secure in his position and more self-confident, unloaded another broadside against détente. Kissinger was taken aback. He called a recess, held a rump session with his team in the Great Hall, then went back to respond.

In his reply, Kissinger eloquently marshaled all aspects of U.S.

relations with the Soviet Union, then reminded the Chinese that it was Nixon who had implemented the policy of détente as well as the opening to China, and he emphasized that the disappearance of Nixon did not mean the China policy would also disappear. One Sinologist, who was not a devoted Kissinger fan, said it was the best diplomatic performance he ever saw.

The overall Chinese attitude left Kissinger concerned about how President Ford might be treated. He pushed for, and finally obtained, assurances not only that Ford would be well received, but that he would definitely have a meeting with Mao. It was a rare break with Chinese custom to guarantee such a meeting beforehand.

Kissinger himself got to see Mao on this trip, although the timing was curious. The meeting took place while Ambassador George Bush was holding a reception for foreign diplomats at the International Club, with Kissinger to be the star attraction. But as the diplomats lined up for the receiving line, Kissinger was off in the Forbidden City, in Mao's study, chewing the fat with the Chairman rather than shaking diplomats' hands.

When Kissinger had received word of the meeting with Mao, he was told he could take along whomever he wanted, including his wife. But Nancy was shopping in the porcelain section of the Friendship duty-free shop when the summons went forth. The Chinese knew exactly where she was, of course, and her shopping was rudely interrupted when Chinese officials appeared at the store, told her brusquely she must leave at once, and whisked her off without explaining why. This was the first time Mao had seen Henry and Nancy together. The Chairman, aging and palsied, looked up at her and down at him with an exaggerated gesture, playing the comic as he noted the big difference in their heights. Nancy left, however, before the substantive conversation began.

Mao's speech had become so slurred that two Chinese interpreters were present: one to translate from his Hunanese dialect, the other to translate into English. Despite Mao's obvious physical degeneration, his mind was still apparently working well. Kissinger and other American officials said that when they looked over the typed transcript of the talks, they found Mao's performance — on paper —

to have been as masterful as usual. Kissinger later marveled, "It's always extraordinary to me how much Mao is on top of things. For example, he knew the entire content of the talk I had had the previous night with Teng in great detail. There's no way they could have done this orally. He had to have read it. So, you know, he's still very much there."

As Kissinger was explaining to us on the plane, "As Mao said to me," he was brought up short by Bernie Kalb. "How do you know?" Kalb interrupted. Kissinger looked puzzled and asked what he meant. Kalb persisted, "How do you know? The Chairman grunts something unintelligible, and the interpreter says anything she wants. You wouldn't know." Kissinger looked stunned. It was the kind of exchange that should have appeared in "Doonesbury." And it eventually did.

Before he left Peking, Kissinger went to see some of the sights he had missed on previous trips. He had high-level company this time — Teng Hsiao-peng. During a tour of a museum, they spent some time looking over an old compass, an arrangement of a cart and fingers that always pointed south. Kissinger pointed out that the arrangement must make the North Vietnamese nervous. Teng either missed its import or simply let it pass. Kissinger also turned in a repeat performance at a Chinese opera: He fell asleep. He took the chiding that followed good-naturedly: "It was one of the most merciful sleeps I ever had."

The 1975 visit included, for the first time, a trek into the Western Hills on the outskirts of the capital for a "picnic." USLO officials were somewhat concerned about the scheduling, since the Western Hills were indeed hilly and the Secretary was booked for about an hour of hiking. In their deft way, however, the Chinese drove Kissinger by car to the top of one of the hills, and the hiking was all downhill. The "picnic" turned out to be a full-dress banquet in a Western Hills restaurant. During a return visit to the Temple of Heaven pavilion, which featured an echo chamber, Kissinger clapped his hands but got no echo. Aide Winston Lord showed him how. Kissinger told his Chinese escort, "That's a member of my terrified staff." The Secretary then tried again, and again he failed. Then he informed the Chinese, "I mean, a former member of my terrified staff." And that's the way it was, sightseeing with Henry.

Kissinger did not get to see Chou En-lai on this trip. The Premier was in the hospital, too ill to receive visitors, so the Secretary sent him flowers. (Two months later, Chou was dead.)

At the farewell banquet, Chiao's toast put a frosting on the chilly atmosphere. "Our two sides had a frank exchange of views on the current international situation," he said. It was obvious by then that they had not seen eye to eye.

Not only the political atmosphere had cooled. Even the economic climate was less accommodating. The people on the 1972 and 1973 trips came away raving about the shopping bargains in China. They had done most of their shopping at the Friendship Store, a three-story department store reserved for foreigners, where only foreign currency is accepted. The salespeople, perhaps aware of China's trade deficit with the West, knew how to hustle. One of them told Bernie Gwertzman of the New York *Times,* "See this piece of jade. Officially, we have to tell you it is no more than eighty years old, but take my word for it, it is more than one hundred years old. And at its price, it is a very good bargain." By 1975, however, most of the bargains were gone. The Communist Chinese had discovered the capitalist Americans and the capitalist Japanese. A jade bracelet that cost $30 in 1973 cost $90 two years later. And that's a controlled economy?

Kissinger was angry throughout the 1975 visit, but he managed to conceal it well. He had already become a kind of political football back home, and now even the Chinese — who had collaborated in one of his greatest diplomatic triumphs — seemed to be enjoying his discomfort. One of his aides recalled that Kissinger's "ego was bruised. He was taking it personally." The aide further explained, "The Chinese could never let down enough to relate to you as a human being. It was always manipulative, always calculating . . . Personal contacts were used only for their own political ends." The aide noted poignantly, "Kissinger fell in love with the Chou En-lai China. When Chou went, it changed."

After leaving Peking, on the flight to Tokyo, Kissinger told a reporter, "They're not mad at us because of détente. They are trying to position themselves. They find us less impressive than a few years ago. I have said for years," he explained, "that foreign policy requires authority. That's not new. Every country is going to give us passing or not-passing grades. That's the nature of foreign policy. You can't fake it. You can't talk it up. You can't pretend it. So you get graded every day. The Chinese are a little more cold-blooded than others, and their analysis of the world situation is a little more subtle. Therefore, their grades are more important."

It was clear Kissinger had not received a good grade in Chinese Perceptions 1975, and he came away deeply disappointed by the trip. When he got back, he recommended that the President shorten his planned visit to China from six to four days and to go to some other countries as well to fold China into an Asian context. He denied he was doing it out of "pique." Ford acquiesced, and Indonesia and the Philippines were added to the presidential itinerary.

Soon after, Kissinger used wit rather than pique to put his visit into perspective. A news conference questioner in Pittsburgh wanted to know, since Kissinger had recently been there, why did "President Ford have to go to China instead of remaining here attending to our current problems?" The question was greeted with applause. Kissinger replied, "There is a school of thought that holds that he has to go there to clean up after me." The answer also drew applause as well as laughter. On a more serious note, he added, "No American President has talked to Chinese leaders since 1972. There has been a change in the presidency here and a change in the operating responsibilities in China. We therefore consider it of considerable importance that an opportunity exist for the President to exchange personally his understanding of the international situation with the Chinese leaders to prevent any misunderstanding or misconceptions from developing."

Someone in the audience followed up by asking, "Mr. Secretary, what effects will the disappearance of the present Chinese leaders have in U.S.-Chinese relations?" Kissinger sidestepped with humor. "Well," he said, "three weeks before going to a country, I do not know how diplomatic it will be to speculate on the disappearance of their leadership." However, he did speculate on the outcome of the trip. He advised a group of European writers beforehand not to expect too much from the Ford visit to Peking. "It is very important that we don't have to have spectacular results. The only really spectacular result would be to turn over Taiwan — and we have exhausted our quota of giving up countries lately." That last part, referring to Vietnam, Cambodia, and Angola, was said with some bitterness.

The Ford visit did indeed live down to its expectations. In connection with the visit, USLO distributed background information papers for the press. The section on the Chinese language noted that the names of foreigners were put into Chinese characters that approximated their sound. Since all Chinese characters had meaning, the names often took on an exotic significance in Chinese. Supposedly, the translation of the name of a British diplomat, Lord Napier, into Mandarin came out as "laboriously vile" and contributed to the outbreak of the first Sino-British war. Ford had no such problem. His name came out as "happiness/special." Kissinger transcribes as "foundation/acrid/style." Make of that what you will.

As an advance man for the Ford visit in November 1975, Kissinger had done his work well. The American President was well received, with all the courtesy and correctness of the Nixon reception and then some: Foreign diplomats were invited to the airport for the arrival. But the Chinese were unyielding on one point. They would not allow any more American newsmen to cover Ford than had covered Nixon. But the technology had changed during the three-year interval, and so had the manpower requirements. A compromise was struck. The same number of "reporters" would be admitted, but the number of "technicians" would be increased. So a number of network executives, producers, and directors went with President Ford as "technicians."

One of the most exciting moments during the Ford visit came early one morning between 4:00 and 5:00 A.M. Kissinger and members of his party were awakened by the sound of gunfire off in the distance. It was still dark outside. Later in the day, one of the staffers asked the Secretary if he had heard the gunfire. "Yes," he said. "What were they doing, shooting counterrevolutionaries?" Nobody ever found out.

The President did have his meeting with Chairman Mao, but the Chinese did not bend their imperial manners further. They did not give any advance notice. When the meeting took place, the lusty old Chairman briefly overcame his dotage, and his face lighted up as he greeted young, blond, blue-eyed Susan Ford.

Kissinger sensed this might be his final trip to China as Secretary of State — at least this time around — and he grew somewhat sentimental about it. In one respect, he was a different man in China. He had a great sense of discovery about it somewhat akin to the person who finds a terrific, small, out-of-the-way restaurant and can't wait to tout it to his friends. China was the one place where he encouraged everybody who traveled with him to go out and see the sights rather than slave away in the old Secretariat.

The 1975 trip *was* his last visit. By 1976, China policy was par-

alyzed by the presidential election campaign, and Kissinger didn't want to schedule a trip to Peking until the election was over. He knew for certain that if Ford lost, the Chinese would not want to deal with a lame duck. There was nothing sentimental about them. As Kissinger used to say matter-of-factly in private conversations, without rancor, they were simply "cold-blooded bastards."

The Chinese invitation to Nixon a few months later hardly fell into the category of sentimentality. The Chinese were clearly using Nixon, the presidential pioneer in opening relations with Peking, to demonstrate once again their displeasure with what they considered American appeasement of the Russians. Since their own relations with the Russians were strained, they could not play off Washington against Moscow as effectively as the United States was playing Peking off against Moscow. So they found another dramatic way to make their point. Whether the invitation was timed to the New Hampshire primary or not, only the Chinese know for sure. For Nixon, the invitation was a chance to escape his lonely West Coast exile and return again, albeit briefly, to the limelight. The China-watchers in Washington thought it outrageous of the People's Republic to invite Nixon — and just as outrageous of Nixon to go.

The subject of the former President's private trip to China came up soon after at an Atlanta news conference, where Kissinger was asked: "If Mr. Nixon had asked you beforehand whether he should go or not, what would have been your advice?" Kissinger, who by then was feeling hot political breath on his own neck, dodged nimbly. "Well," he said, "I have my hands full advising President Ford."

The political heat on Kissinger was coming from the Republican right wing. Meanwhile, back at T'ien-an Men Square, one of his old antagonists, Teng Hsiao-peng, was under attack from the Chinese left wing. Kissinger took note of their simultaneous problems when he was asked in New York about "the effect of the current succession problems in China on U.S.-China relations." "I must say that I have some sympathy for what Teng Hsiao-peng has been going through," he joked. "I am in the 'wall poster' stage myself." At that same session, somebody asked if Nixon had been in violation of federal law in going to China. Kissinger replied, "It is not a violation of federal law to speak about foreign policy in foreign countries — although there have been occasions in recent years when perhaps I wished it had been."

When Nixon returned home, he sent the White House a report that was never made public. Kissinger's comments about the report were not meant to be made public, either, but Bob Keatley of the *Wall Street Journal* came across some transcripts of Kissinger's telephone conversations:

NIXON: How are you?

KISSINGER: Okay. I wanted you to know I have read the report and I find it very fascinating.

NIXON: As I said, there are a lot of things that are repetitive.

KISSINGER: But that too is interesting. The fact there is repetition is interesting.

NIXON: There are some nuances as you can well see that are new, and some of them are potentially troublesome . . . I'm not sure that maybe some of your other people saw it, but you could see the subtlety of the analysis I was making on these points.

KISSINGER: I thought you were very, very clever.

Then comes a brief discussion of when and if the United States could recognize the Peking government and drop its diplomatic relations with Taiwan.

NIXON: I said, before the elections, it just absolutely would raise hell and afterwards I said it might have the same kind of consequences, and I said you would have to measure whether you consider Taiwan more important.

KISSINGER: I though you were very, very good on this.

NIXON: I think too we made some pretty good talks on the SALT talks. After all, they walked right into that by coming out with that conventional weapons thing.

KISSINGER: I thought that was very clever . . . Did you do all that alone?

NIXON: I was alone all the time. [A Nixon aide] went in on one of the two meetings and made a few notes but I did it all. I have a fairly good memory and did it the same day. The notes are fairly accurate. I went into each meeting alone, without notes.

KISSINGER: It is fascinating.

Soon after, Kissinger and Vice President Nelson Rockefeller talked about the Nixon report.

KISSINGER: I have read the Nixon report on his trip now. He is such an egomaniac. All he wrote was his —

ROCKEFELLER: His memoirs.

KISSINGER: Just what *he* said. Nothing that the Chinese said. Practically nothing. A fascinating account of himself.

FOUR

The Soviet Union

Fittingly, Moscow was the first foreign capital Henry Kissinger visited as Secretary of State. It was fitting because Kissinger viewed the rest of the world through the prism of the relationship between Moscow and Washington. "The peace of the world depends on stability with the Soviet Union," he said, "and that should be our first order of business." It was also fitting because the purpose of Kissinger's mission was to arrange a cease-fire in the Middle East, where he would come to spend so much of his time and creative energy.

The Moscow trip had some of the flavor of Kissinger's presecretarial days as the nation's number-one secret diplomatic agent. He slipped out of Washington after midnight. Only a handful of aides accompanied him. There was no advance announcement. He took no press. He flew to Moscow at the urgent request of the Russians, who suddenly saw the immediate need for a cease-fire when their guys, the Arabs, started getting clobbered by our guys, the Israelis.

When Kissinger went to the Soviet capital, he dealt with the number one man, Soviet Party Chief Leonid Brezhnev, and it was no different this time. Kissinger doesn't like to negotiate immediately following a long plane ride, but he knew Brezhnev would insist on a meeting right away, so he was prepared. He told staff aides before-hand, "I'm making no decisions tonight. I'll filibuster." And that's what he did, "beautifully," recalled one aide, "while the rest of us were propping our eyes open. The Russians were overanxious and wanted a cease-fire agreement that night because their boys were on the run. Kissinger knew when the power was on his side. The Israelis were turning the tables, and he was going to play that one out for a while."

After that one had been played out for a while, Brezhnev sprang a surprise. "I've got a little dinner for all of us," he said. Everybody trooped off to the Soviet leader's private dining room and had a five-course meal. An aide said later, "There was vodka going by the bucketful until 2:00 A.M., by which time we were all dead on our feet and Brezhnev was getting a little sloshed. But Kissinger did what he had planned to do — nothing until the next morning."

Before going to bed, around three in the morning Moscow time, Kissinger called the White House. He had trouble getting through to Chief of Staff Al Haig, and he complained to his NSC aide, General Brent Scowcroft, that the White House people were letting a lot of Mickey Mouse political stuff interfere with foreign policy. "That's typical of your sense of priorities," he shouted at Scowcroft, who couldn't tell Kissinger what was going on because he didn't know. Kissinger recalled that when he finally did get through to Haig "there was some shouting, and I said loudly to him, 'Don't you yell at me. What the hell have you got to do around the White House on a Saturday night?' "

What Haig had to do around the White House on a Saturday night October 20, 1973, came to be known as the Saturday Night Massacre, when President Nixon fired Archibald Cox as the special Watergate prosecutor and Attorney General Elliot Richardson and his deputy, William Ruckelshaus, both resigned.

Kissinger, who was wrapped up in the cease-fire negotiations, did not become aware of the full impact of the Massacre until he reached London the following Monday morning and saw the headlines in the British newspapers. His reaction: "Oh, my God."

It had not been so long before, only eighteen months, that Richard Nixon himself was in Moscow, creating headlines of a different kind as he celebrated one of the major triumphs of his first term: the first visit to the Soviet Union by an American President and the signing of a historic agreement on limiting nuclear weapons. It was Kissinger who had laid the groundwork for that 1972 Summit. He had done most of the negotiating and made most of the arrangements, slipping into Moscow for four days in the spring with such secrecy that even U.S. Ambassador Jacob Beam didn't know he was there.

En route to that Summit of '72, President Nixon had stopped overnight in the picture-postcard city of Salzburg, in neutral Austria. As usual, one of Kissinger's jobs was to brief the press — anonymously. His pre-Summit arranging had produced a number of new American-Soviet agreements to be signed by Nixon and the Soviet leaders. Max Frankel of the New York *Times,* aware of the timing of the imminent agreements, asked what he described as a procedural question: "Do you plan to dribble out announcements through the week, or is there going to be one big orgy of agreements?" The question drew laughter, as did the answer: "I see that Max, with the dispassionate nature that we associate with his newspaper, has given us a choice between an orgy and dribbling it out, so that whatever we do, we are doing very badly." Kissinger paused, then added, "Our plan is to dribble out an orgy of announcements."

Whenever the President went to Moscow, he stayed in the Kremlin, and that courtesy was extended to Kissinger and his NSC aides. When Kissinger went alone, he usually stayed in House 40, a sprawling official residence behind Florentine yellow walls up in the Lenin Hills overlooking Moscow. In either place, the Americans assumed automatically that their rooms were bugged. If they had something private to say, they went outside and talked while walking around, or they made a lot of noise in their rooms and tried to talk above it. An open telephone line in Moscow was considered about as secure as a hand-delivered note to the KGB (the secret police). One staffer got a blunt reminder of this when he said something on the phone that Kissinger thought was sensitive. "Goddamn it," bellowed the

Secretary, "you're going to get the Order of Lenin from the KGB if you keep that up."

Kissinger frequently joked with some of his hosts about the bugging. Surprisingly, they joked back. During one session of the arms control negotiations in 1972, Kissinger held a document up in the air toward the chandelier and said, "Can I have two copies of this delivered to my suite?" Foreign Minister Andrei Gromyko, who had a sense of humor, told him no, he couldn't. The hidden cameras had been installed in the Kremlin during the time of Ivan the Terrible, deadpanned Gromyko, and their lenses were not good enough to pick up the print of documents.

Kissinger remembered the line, and at another session, when everybody was sweltering in one of the most elegant rooms in Saint Catherine's Hall, he pointed to the beautifully ornate chandelier and cracked a line about the camera put there by Ivan the Terrible. Once again, Gromyko demurred. In this room, he said, Ivan the Terrible had designed the air conditioning. There was fruit on the table, and Kissinger asked Gromyko if he should speak into the apple or the orange. Gromyko pointed to the breast of a carved woman's figure above them and indicated Kissinger should talk in that direction.

Kissinger also joked once with Brezhnev about bugging, but Brezhnev was not amused and Kissinger did not persist. However, Kissinger didn't mind joking about bugging in Brezhnev's bathroom. During a toilet break in the talks that were being held in Brezhnev's study, the members of the American delegation all went into an elegant Kremlin bathroom with paneled walls. Kissinger shouted out to his aides from one of the stalls, "It's really been modernized. It's got a bug built into the seat."

Winston Lord sank to even lower depths. Peter Rodman imagined there was a plaque on the wall reading: "This urinal was used by Ivan the Terrible from 1422 to 1431." Lord quickly punned, "It would be more appropriate if it were Peter the Great." It was not their only bathroom joke. During the 1972 Summit, when American officials were roaming around the Kremlin for the first time, Rodman and Lord laughed about finding a good spot in one of the men's rooms to tell Barry Goldwater about.* End of bathroom humor.

The bugging wasn't all bad. At the Lenin Hills guest house, if the Americans wanted some fresh fruit, they would say out loud, "Gee, I sure wish we could get some fresh fruit." And the next day they had fresh fruit. Kissinger aide Carl Maw remembers a time when the Russians botched up the breakfast eggs. So he and another staffer went back to their rooms and had a loud conversation about how eggs should be properly fried. Sure enough, the Russians straightened up and fried right.

So concerned were Kissinger's aides about bugging that they didn't even risk using electric typewriters. The intelligence people told them the Russians could record electric typewriters and decipher from the sounds what was being written. So manual typewriters were used. The secretaries, who were all accustomed to electric machines, made lots of mistakes. The security precautions also extended to copying machines. The Americans insisted on taking their own photocopiers with them, but when the machines broke down, nobody knew how to fix them.

The working conditions in the Kremlin were not all that good for other reasons as well. During the 1972 Summit, the NSC staffers had no office space as such, so they worked out of their bedrooms, with typewriters and other office paraphernalia scattered around the ornate eighteenth-century furniture. But while the White House staff was struggling to keep the paper flowing within the Kremlin walls, a large State Department operation was languishing in the nearby Hotel Rossiya. (The hotel had a top-floor dining room dubbed the Top o' the Marx.) Just as the American Ambassador had been cut out of Kissinger's secret trip to Moscow earlier in the year, the State Department in general was cut out of the big-ticket items in American-Soviet relations. So most of the workload fell on the NSC staff.

Not all of the 1972 Summit negotiations were conducted in the Kremlin. The talks on Vietnam — which were loud and theatrical — were held in a dacha outside Moscow, perhaps to symbolize Viet-

---

*Goldwater had once suggested lobbing a bomb "into the men's room of the Kremlin" to make the Russians show a little respect.

nam as an issue apart that should not interfere with the main business of the Summit. When the motorcade carrying the American delegation left the Kremlin, the two NSC staffers who specialized in Vietnamese affairs, Winston Lord and John Negroponte, were not in it. They had been given the wrong departure time. But when they tried to find out where Nixon and Brezhnev were, the KGB wouldn't tell them. In a panic, Lord and Negroponte called another NSC staffer, Bill Hyland, a specialist in Soviet affairs. Hyland put them on to the head of the KGB, General Yuri Andropov, who was less uptight than his flunkies. Andropov arranged for them to be taken to the dacha in time for the talks.

As head of the KGB, Andropov was a powerful man. And he ran a powerful agency. In Moscow, the KGB made all the arrangements for a Summit, and they thought the Secret Service did the same for the Americans. When the American advance teams first showed up in Moscow, the KGB wanted to negotiate with the Secret Service, not with the White House or State Department types. The KGB officials were perplexed and even somewhat miffed when the Secret Service refused to talk about anything except security. One Secret Service agent remembers that trying to get the KGB to cooperate was like trying to resurrect Lenin. He recalls making a number of requests of a KGB official and being told, each time, "No problem." When the agent finished making his requests, the KGB official summed up by saying, "No problem. All impossible."

The KGB also apparently miscalculated the Secret Service in another way. When the Americans traveled, they were always doubled up in rooms to cut down on expenses. The KGB thought they roomed together because they liked one another, and so the American agents would occasionally get soliciting calls in their rooms — from men. During one Kissinger trip to Moscow, a number of traveling newsmen also got calls in their hotel rooms, but these were from women with honey in their voices and who-knew-what on their minds. If the newsmen were suspicious — and they were — they had a right to be. First of all, it was not that easy to call a visiting American in the Intourist Hotel since there is no central switchboard. Each room has a telephone with an individual number. Second, the calls came in just after midnight. And third, in each case the sweet-talking voice started out in Russian and then switched to whatever language happened to be common to caller and callee.

If the newsmen were curious, only one of them did anything about it. Jerry O'Leary of the Washington *Star* made a date for the next day with a woman who identified herself as Olga and who spoke Spanish. As O'Leary later wrote: "I, being securely married and fiftyish, felt I owed it to the profession — mine, not Olga's — to see if all the stories I have heard about spy ladies in the USSR were true." What O'Leary got to see was a rather dumpy Russian woman who wanted to know, during the course of a dinner bought by the Washington *Star,* if her new American friend had two cars and a swimming pool. He didn't have a pool, and he lied about the cars. He said he only had one. But let O'Leary tell it: "Unless my perception for such things is diminished drastically," he wrote, "there was no attempt made to seduce me." So much for Mata Hari and the American press.

At the official level, the availability of female companionship was signaled quite clearly to the Americans by Andropov, who used to boast to Kissinger and others about "his girls." One staffer remembers that the KGB chief even tried, "in a crude way, to get us all involved with his girls during our early trips." When he saw a pretty girl on the street, Andropov would nudge Kissinger or one of the other Americans and say, "She's one of mine." Kissinger would reply, "I don't need your girls. I have Hollywood girls." But Andropov wasn't impressed. "Try my girls," he'd say. "They're better."

The chief of the secret police and the Americans also used to josh each other about their secret agents. At a luncheon for the visiting Americans, Andropov told Hyland, "All these waiters work for me." Hyland wanted to know how they got promoted — by getting information or by being good waiters? Andropov just laughed.

For all the joking, the members of the American party were constantly aware of the surveillance, which led to a comment by Kissinger that became retrospectively memorable for its heavy but unintentional irony. During one of his early visits, Kissinger was negotiating with Brezhnev in his study in the Kremlin. The Secretary decided he needed a break to confer with his staff, so he simply gathered everybody in a corner of the room to talk confidentially, noting, "This is probably the only place in the whole Kremlin that's safe. He wouldn't bug *himself.*" By the time Nixon returned to Moscow — and Brezhnev's study — for the 1974 Summit, it was well known that Nixon had been bugging *himself* — to the point of impeachment.

Nixon made it clear to the Russians that he needed their help, and they made it just as clear that they were keeping their distance. As Kissinger had observed about the Russians on a pre-Summit visit, "Excessive gentleness is not one of their basic traits." But, he always claimed, Watergate never really interfered with the SALT negotiations. (Corroboration of that must await the publication of *Brezhnev Remembers.*) In any event, the Soviets were certainly wary about Nixon's status at the '74 Summit.

The first night, the President said in a speech at a Kremlin dinner that previous agreements between the United States and the Soviet Union had been made possible because of the "personal relationship" established between Brezhnev and himself. Nixon was clearly basing the last line of his Watergate defense on his expertise and experience as a manager of foreign policy. But it wasn't selling well, not even to the Russians. The word "personal" was dropped from the official Russian translation of the speech. The White House Press Office spent most of the day trying to minimize the omission in Moscow.

Nixon's comments in public were reflected by his behavior in private. Nixon pointed out to Brezhnev that he was not in good shape with an impeachment-minded Congress, and pushing the "personal relationship," he virtually pleaded with the Soviet leader to cooperate more on certain issues so as to improve his position on Capitol Hill. Moreover, unlike in 1972, Nixon wandered from his briefing papers and "often didn't know what he was talking about," according to one of the participants. At one point, Brezhnev told him his SALT figures were wrong. And they were. (One of Nixon's closest aides told me the President spent much of his time in Moscow in 1974 listening to White House tapes.)

Kissinger was distraught about the President's behavior, and he let out his frustration to his staff, making comments that bordered on open contempt. During one Kremlin meeting, he even passed notes with sarcastic remarks like "Our strong leader!" to staffers. But Nixon was oblivious to the note-passing.

On a lighter note, Kissinger and Gromyko were putting the finishing touches on a minor agreement that required some last-minute haggling. They were meeting just before Nixon was going on Soviet television to make a nationwide speech emphasizing American-Soviet friendship and their joint efforts on behalf of peace. Kissinger and Gromyko were working in the room next to the one in which Nixon was speaking. The Secretary of State turned to the Soviet foreign minister and said, "We could really make history if the President's speech started, and we yelled, 'Never, never, never!' " But they didn't.

The 1974 meeting was a movable Summit. Following the Moscow talks, Brezhnev took Nixon to Oreanda, in the Crimea. Oreanda was a part of Greater Yalta, but the White House deemphasized the connection because in the theology of the conservatives, Yalta connoted the sellout of Eastern Europe to the Soviet Union after World War II.

While Brezhnev was showing Nixon the Soviet version of San Clemente, Helen Thomas of UPI asked Kissinger what was going on. "Don't ask me," Kissinger joked. "I just walk ten feet behind Nixon and Brezhnev." Thomas took the remark seriously and reported it that way. When Kissinger briefed the press at the end of the Summit, he began by saying, "Mr. Ziegler said I should entitle this briefing, 'The View from Ten Feet Behind.' " But that line did indeed reflect Kissinger's uneasiness throughout the Summit. He was especially nervous when Nixon talked with Brezhnev alone for almost three hours in the Soviet leader's "grotto" office. I myself always imagined that whatever Nixon was saying to Brezhnev, the Soviet leader was telling him, "No problem."

In addition to visiting the Crimea, Nixon also flew to Minsk before returning to Moscow. On one of these flights, with Nixon, Brezhnev, Gromyko, Premier Alexei Kosygin, and President Nicolai Podgorny all aboard, one of the Soviet plane's engines wouldn't start. It was an embarrassing moment for the Russians. Kissinger, who was sitting next to Podgorny, commented about the perverseness of objects. "For example," he said, "when you drop a piece of buttered bread, it always falls butter side down." Podgorny looked puzzled. "You know," persisted Kissinger, "when you drop a coin, it always rolls away from you." Podgorny said that when he dropped a coin, it didn't always roll away from him. One man's perverseness is another man's obtuseness. Kissinger didn't have to deal much with Podgorny anyway.

Every time I saw Kosygin, I thought of Secretary of State William Rogers's story about a Nixon dinner with Canadian Prime Minister Pierre Trudeau. Rogers was seated next to the Prime Minister's lovely young wife, Margaret, who was not yet widely known in the United States for her outspokenness and her free-spiriting. Brezhnev and Kosygin had just visited Canada, and Madame Trudeau was talking to Rogers about them. She said she found Brezhnev to be personable and likable, but "Kosygin," she said, "he's a real shit!" Rogers said he almost dropped his fork.

During the 1974 Summit, the press naturally covered the meetings in Oreanda Yalta. When we arrived, the Russians, in their usual heavy-handed way, made things as unpleasant as possible. It was very hot, but as we got off our planes, a Russian official held everybody up on the tarmac instead of letting us go to the bleachers to set up for the arrival of Nixon and Brezhnev. He would not explain the delay. After a few minutes, some of us television people decided to hell with it, and we ignored the Russian official and started walking toward the bleachers. Several bulky Russian security men came running out and physically blocked our way. I was standing next to CBS cameraman Cal Marlin, a veteran of some of the same civil rights battles in the South that I had covered. As soon as the Russians stopped us, he looked at me, I looked at him, he put down his

camera, and we broke into song: "We shall overcome . . ." Other
reporters joined in. The Russians didn't have the foggiest idea of
what was going on. But at that point we didn't care. It was a cherished moment.

The unexplained delay on the tarmac epitomized the difficult
working conditions journalists faced in the Soviet Union. And while
we visitors thought conditions were bad, our colleagues stationed
there told us they never had it so good as when a Summit was taking
place.

I got some personal insight into the nature of dealing with the
Russians during the 1972 Summit. President Nixon and most of the
White House party and press had gone to Leningrad on what was
essentially a sightseeing trip. I stayed behind to try to find out what
was going on in the negotiations. From a resident correspondent, I
had learned a few words in Russian so I could order a special
breakfast: a fresh orange, a caviar omelet, and coffee. Since most of
the Americans had left before dawn, the breakfast room was virtually
deserted when I came down. I sat at a table and waited. And waited
and waited. First mistake. In typical Russian fashion, half a dozen
waiters with absolutely nothing to do stood to one side of the room
and managed to pay no attention whatsoever to me and my waving.
Finally, I got up and walked over to the waiters and asked one of
them to take my order. He even came to my table.

I told him in my recently learned Russian that I wanted a fresh
orange, a caviar omelet, and coffee. I went two for three. The waiter
haughtily told me, in Russian, caviar omelet, *nyet.* Armed with the
knowledge that one of my colleagues had eaten a caviar omelet the
day before in that very dining room, I fired back, caviar omelet, *da.*
The waiter said again, caviar omelet, *nyet.* I said again, caviar omelet, *da.* This colloquy went on for longer than the rational mind can
imagine, each of us repeating our position over and over again. If
anybody was watching, he must have thought one or both of us were
crazy. But I was too determined at that point to feel silly. Finally,
the waiter cracked. Caviar omelet, *da,* he agreed, and he eventually
even brought it — scrambled eggs with caviar. It was one of the best
breakfasts I have ever eaten.

On the final day of the 1972 Summit, I decided to learn a little more Russian. For the first three days I had entered the elevator and pointed to my floor — 15 — for the operator. Belatedly, I thought it would be a good idea, at the very least, to learn how to say the number. So when I got on the elevator the last day, I put my finger on 15, leaned over and looked at the operator, and said to her in a very deliberate way (as though talking slowly would make her understand), "How . . . do . . . you . . . say . . . that?" I turned my head toward the button. A woman's voice with a very British accent piped up from the back of the elevator: "Why, that's fifteen!" John Chancellor was so amused, he used the story on the *NBC News* broadcast from Moscow that night.

I was not the only one who did not go to Leningrad in 1972. Henry Kissinger didn't go either. He stayed in Moscow to continue negotiating. In fact, for all the times Kissinger went to the Soviet Union, he never did go to Leningrad, although a trip was scheduled for him almost every time. He used to tease the Russians about it, saying, "There is no Leningrad."

In October 1974, Nancy Kissinger accompanied her husband to the Soviet Union, and the Russians arranged to take her to see Leningrad. The day before she went, Gromyko brought up the subject at a luncheon he gave for Kissinger: "As I see it," he said, "you still have certain doubts as to the existence of Leningrad, but we hope that after Mrs. Kissinger's trip, she will succeed in confirming to you that Leningrad does exist." Kissinger, in the best tradition of diplomacy, replied, "I have been asked, as usual, a very direct question by the foreign minister, which is to affirm the existence of Leningrad. All I can say is that we are in the preliminary stage of our negotiations. It is too early to draw a final conclusion, but we have talked in a constructive and positive manner, and I think with good will on both sides we may achieve a reasonable conclusion. We cannot expect to make a unilateral concession on so grave a question that must be on a mutual basis." When Nancy got back, Brezhnev told Kissinger, "Your wife can now testify to the fact that Leningrad does exist." "Yes," quipped Kissinger, "but you just built it."

Not only did Kissinger never go to Leningrad. He never did any of the sightseeing he did in other countries. He did take in the Bolshoi Ballet (we joked that he needed the sleep). And he once went to the famed Moscow Circus. But for the most part, it was all business.

And with the Russians, it was never easy business. Although they had an overwhelming compulsion to have a written schedule for a Kissinger visit, the scheduling itself was "whimsical, arbitrary, and capricious," in the words of one Kissinger sidekick, and the Russians seldom kept to the schedule they wrote down. When an 11:00 A.M. meeting was suddenly postponed to 2:00 P.M. during one visit, Kissinger shouted into the air in his presumably bugged suite, "I didn't come ten thousand miles to Moscow to go sightseeing in Lenin Hills."

Ambassador Gerard Smith, the former chief American delegate to the first SALT negotiations in Geneva, had an explanation for the Soviet behavior. He recalled that during the 1972 Summit, Kissinger cabled him from Moscow that "he never knew from hour to hour with whom he was to meet or what the topic would be." Smith concluded, "The Soviets have a way of bending local arrangements to their advantage."

Negotiations on nuclear arms control or making arrangements for a presidential Summit were the customary reasons for a Kissinger mission to Moscow. At the 1972 Summit, it took some tough last-minute bargaining to produce a SALT I agreement limiting antiballistic missile systems and freezing the levels of offensive nuclear weapons. The '72 agreement led to one of the most egregious puns of our time. Back in 1970, Kissinger reportedly had second thoughts about the American "incursion" into Cambodia. When he fretted about it, Nixon told him, "Henry, never look back; remember what happened to Lot's wife." "And indeed," wrote presidential wordsmith Bill Safire, "at the 1972 Summit, Kissinger did indeed turn into a pillar of SALT."

Kissinger regarded the problem of strategic arms control as "one of the central issues of our time." The complexity of the problem also provided a stimulating intellectual challenge, which Kissinger accepted. For the next four years, he argued and agonized — with his own colleagues in the U.S. government as well as with the Russians — over how to go about solving the problem, but a follow-up treaty eluded him. The complex issues involved, plus the complex internal situation in both countries, proved to be too formidable to overcome.

In March 1974, encouraged by optimistic reporting from Soviet Ambassador Anatoly Dobrynin, Kissinger set out to achieve what he termed "a conceptual breakthrough" in the SALT talks in Moscow. (The "concept" involved limiting the deployment of missiles with multiple warheads, known as MIRVs.) He began the trip with a personnel breakthrough, taking Dobrynin aboard his plane to Moscow. And he also took along his children, Elizabeth, fourteen, and David, twelve, who were on spring vacation.

Moscow in March is as changeable as Brezhnev's negotiating tactics. Brisk spring winds sweep a succession of varying climes across the gray and somber rooftops. A flurry of wet snow may suddenly blot out a burst of sunshine. Moscow's March climate was perilously symbolic for Kissinger's sixth visit to the Soviet capital. The weather was typically variable as Kissinger was driven at high speed — usual in a Moscow motorcade — from the Lenin Hills through a narrow Kremlin gate to the rather pedestrian Council of Ministers Building. The correspondents had been taken to the second-floor office meeting place ahead of Kissinger, and they found Brezhnev waiting there, standing next to a large T-shaped desk covered with green felt, ready for another round of high-stakes negotiating. Pictures of Lenin and Marx stared down from the walls with Communist resoluteness to contrast with the mood of Brezhnev, who clowned a bit for his American journalistic audience. He showed off his cigarette box with the time lock that can be set to open only after a specified period. It was designed to help him cut down on smoking, but he always bummed cigarettes from Kosygin and Podgorny anyway. They somehow never refused him. Brezhnev let the smoke curl mysteriously in front of his face, noting, "This is a shot our photographers particularly like." The photographers dutifully clicked away.

Brezhnev, who was wearing his customary Hero of the Soviet

Union medals on his ample chest, turned more serious when he talked about the arms control negotiations. "The other alternative," he concluded bluntly, "is war — there is no other alternative." And he took a swipe at some of his critics in America: "Opponents of détente are introducing many petty matters that have no bearing on détente."

When Kissinger entered the room, Brezhnev gave him a big hello and a friendly needle. "I had a long discussion with your Ambassador the other day," Brezhnev said, nodding toward Ambassador Walter J. Stoessel, Jr. "Good," said Kissinger. "And we both hurled arrows at you." Brezhnev laughed. "I knew that about Ambassador Stoessel," Kissinger shot back, "but Mr. General Secretary, I'm surprised at you."

Brezhnev then turned to his stone-faced foreign minister and joked, "Let me introduce Gromyko." Kissinger cracked, "The face looks familiar."

The Secretary also put in a plug for Dobrynin. "Your Ambassador

'YES, A SMALL CONCESSION PERHAPS, BUT I DOUBT IF ANYBODY WILL REALLY MISS NEW JERSEY...'

knows more senators than I do," he said, perhaps with some accuracy.

Brezhnev next turned his attention to Hal Sonnenfeldt, the State Department counselor and expert on Soviet affairs. "Sonnenfeldt looks younger every time," said Brezhnev. "That's because he drinks Pepsi-Cola," explained Kissinger. Brezhnev said, "We'll all be drinking a lot of Pepsi-Cola soon. Then we can export more vodka to you." "I think," smiled Kissinger, "we're getting the better part of the bargain."

Brezhnev had been making a political point about the soft drink business. A Pepsi-Cola bottling factory was due to open in a couple of months — another tangible sign of improved relations between Moscow and Washington. It may also have been a sign of the friendship between Pepsi-Cola's president, Donald Kendall, and Richard Nixon.

After the reporters had written down all the wisecracks, they were invited to leave, and the serious talks began.

To the discerning eye, the Russians provided a clue to their positive outlook. When the Soviet Journalists' Association held a reception for their visiting American counterparts, the caviar was in plentiful supply. If the mood was downbeat or relations strained, the caviar stayed in the tins.

Also in plentiful supply at the reception was a lot of curiosity and serious questioning about Watergate and the fate of Nixon, in spite of the casual quality of the official party line on the subject as expressed by official party members. During the flight over, Ambassador Dobrynin had told newsmen on the plane, "Even if he is impeached, they can do business. If he's President, he can sign. We don't worry." Georgy Arbatov, a leading Soviet specialist on U.S. affairs, told one American newsman, "If our countries restricted visits only to periods of no problems, we'd never get together." And Mikhail Ameyanin, the chief editor of the Communist Party newspaper, *Pravda,* said rather wickedly, "The President is the President. Nixon is not our favorite candidate for President — Gus Hall [the head of the Communist Party in America] is — but so long as

Nixon's in office, it is a cornerstone of our noninterference concept that we don't make judgments."

Despite the heaps of caviar, despite Brezhnev's joviality, and despite Dobrynin's optimistic reporting, the Russians hit Kissinger in the private talks with a counterproposal that surprised him (based primarily on the number of warheads on each side). They also embarrassed him in one of the sessions. Brezhnev blustered about some test the United States had conducted in the South Pacific, contrary to an agreement with the Russians. He cited the time and place. Kissinger and his aides looked at one another in bafflement. Nothing in the briefing books reflected Brezhnev's charge. Kissinger said he knew nothing about the test but would find out. Immediately after the meeting, he got in touch with Washington. Back came a message acknowledging that the U.S. Navy had indeed tested something when and where Brezhnev had said. At the next session in the Kremlin, Kissinger expressed his regrets to the Soviet leader, conceding that "your intelligence is apparently better than mine." It was not the kind of situation that Kissinger thrived on.

By the end of the talks, it was clear that the "conceptual breakthrough" had gone the way of "peace is at hand," and Kissinger left Moscow in a morose mood. The reporters naturally looked to the Watergate cloud hanging over the talks. But Kissinger insisted on the flight that "Watergate doesn't get the same attention in Moscow that it does in Washington." He added solemnly, however, "The Russians are obviously looking at us, at our relationship, wondering what they get out of it."

Later, in the rear section of the plane, he sounded a theme that he would return to frequently in the future. "Leaving me out of this thing personally," he said, "it strikes me that historians will wonder why Americans took to bad-mouthing détente . . . The critics expect so much more from it than it was ever designed to achieve . . . I think it is regularly achieving much of its original intent." If he thought détente was being "badmouthed" then, he hadn't seen nothing yet. In less than two years, a new American President would be banning "détente" from the diplomatic lexicon.

The failure to achieve the conceptual breakthrough in March meant there would be no new SALT agreement in July. And there was none. But there was another Moscow Summit, part of the home-and-home series Nixon and Brezhnev had arranged. However, a Summit without SALT was like a day without sunshine, as one wine-drinking diplomat joked. En route to the '74 Summit a reporter asked Kissinger if the President and Brezhnev, in the absence of an agreement, would be going for a "conceptual breakthrough." The Secretary of State smiled at the maliciousness of the question. "I generally try," he said, "to avoid making the same mistake twice."

While the diplomats were having SALT problems, the television correspondents were having technical problems of their own. The Soviet authorities, angered by reports by the traveling journalists about Russian dissidents, ordered the technicians at the Moscow television center to pull the plug while we were sending our stories to the U.S. by satellite. Subtle they were not.

Afterward, during a Kissinger briefing at the Intourist Hotel, a reporter wanted to know if the new American-Soviet agreement on limiting the size of peaceful nuclear explosions would prevent the Russians from doing anything "we know they had planned to do." Kissinger replied mischeviously that "to tell you what we know about what the Soviets are planning to do would present a major problem of hospitality." Before the laughter died down, the reporter muttered aloud, "We have had some already." "You are supposed to *laugh* at my jokes," Kissinger shot back, "not *top* them."

The U.S. and the USSR also agreed in the summer of '74 that a new treaty, when it was completed, should run until 1985. Why then? "Because," Kissinger explained with a straight face, "we couldn't pick 1984."

The briefing took place in the Starry Sky, the ground-floor dining room–nightclub of the hotel. It was considerably less dramatic than the briefing he had given in 1972 just before dawn, following a desperate night of diplomatic haggling over SALT. Then he had stood before a microphone in front of an empty bandstand, with rotating, winking ceiling lights above him, with a blinking colored-glass mosaic of a prone woman behind him, with the rest of the darkened room filled with American reporters. And he talked about instruments of monumental destruction and the first superpower agreement that attempted to get them under control. The mixture of the doomsday subject with the discotheque atmosphere memorialized the briefing with an unforgettable sense of eeriness.

Before the briefing, General Al Haig, then Kissinger's deputy at the NSC, had been up all night working on the briefing papers. When Kissinger showed up, however, he told Haig he had changed his whole approach, so the papers would have to be redone. At that point Haig gathered up the papers and hurled them at Kissinger. "If you want the papers redone," Haig yelled, "you can redo them yourself!" When Haig returned to Moscow in 1974, he had moved into Bob Haldeman's slot as the powerful White House Chief of Staff, dealing with a President who had become an impeachable source. And Kissinger, of course, had become Secretary of State.

Within two months of Nixon's resignation, Kissinger was back in Moscow. He would have returned in October for more SALT talks even if Nixon had not resigned, but the change in the presidency made the trip all the more necessary. He wanted to find out if the spirit of détente was alive and well and still living in Moscow. And he wanted to assure the Russians of the continuity of basic American policy. As we left Washington, a reporter, recalling the March trip, needled, "Why didn't you bring Dobrynin?" Kissinger, also recalling the March trip, feigned indignation. "He might have given you guys a briefing," he said. "The S.O.B. even misled me . . . I figure if he talked to the press that way, he had to know something he hadn't told me."

We all knew beforehand that Kissinger would achieve a nonconceptual breakthrough on the October trip; he and the Russians would announce a meeting between President Ford and Brezhnev in Vladivostok the following month. When a reporter asked him about the meeting, he gave us some insight into the meaning of the change of President as it pertained to style: "With the preceding President," he said, "this [leak] would have been a sure prescription for suicide."

En route to the Soviet capital, Kissinger stopped off in Copenhagen. For the traveling newsmen, Denmark turned out to be rotten. First of all, *Time* correspondent Strobe Talbott was notified that he had to leave the plane; the Russians would not give him a visa. Talbott, a Soviet scholar and one-time Moscow correspondent, had been involved in the translation of the memoirs *Khrushchev Remembers,* and his name was apparently on a list somewhere. Kissinger knew before he left Washington that the Russians wanted to bar Talbott. But the State Department press office and Ambassador Robert McCloskey, the former department spokesman, had advised him to allow Talbott to get on the plane at Andrews in hopes the Russians would cave on the issue. But the Russians didn't cave. In fact, Gromyko raised hell with Kissinger about Talbott, which meant that Kissinger had to raise hell with somebody. That somebody was McCloskey.

When Talbott got bounced in Copenhagen, the rest of the newsmen on the plane wrote a statement of protest. Since the rest of the newsmen included the reporters from the two major wire services, AP and UPI, the statement was distributed worldwide. Before we left Copenhagen, Kissinger talked with a group of Danish journalists. But the traveling press had already been taken to the plane, and Kissinger's inept press spokesman of the moment, Bob Anderson, made no move to protect us. When we reached Moscow, most of us had messages waiting for us from our home offices, telling us what Kissinger had said in Copenhagen and asking, in their polite, snotty, cable language: "Where you please?"

We also found the Russians in a prickly mood. They arbitrarily limited to ten the number of traveling correspondents who would be permitted to watch the Brezhnev-Kissinger greeting. For us, it was not a glimpse of the traditional Kremlin tableau that was important; it was the access to the Soviet boss and the chance to ask him a question or two. Since there were fourteen of us, we objected strenuously to any limits. The Russians argued the room wasn't big enough to accommodate us all. Actually, the room was big enough to accommodate everybody on board Kissinger's plane, including the crew.

Plus the Red Army Band. The argument was still going on when the meeting got under way. And none of us was inside. The head of the Foreign Ministry's Press Division, Vsevolod Sofinsky, then showed up and told us, "The meeting has already begun. Excuse me, but the press was not invited. The General Secretary did not want it." Barry Schweid of the AP cracked, "Another Soviet public relations coup!"

Kissinger himself got some unaccustomed treatment. *Pravda* did not follow its practice of printing his picture and arrival story on page 1. The mystery of this curious diplomatic snub remained unsolved, although we explained it privately in terms of the typical Soviet charm and grace in reacting to the correspondents' protest against the exclusion of Strobe Talbott. It goes without saying that there was no caviar at the Soviet journalists' reception this time.

Whatever setbacks we were suffering on the political side, we had achieved some progress on the economic side going in. In March, the Russians had charged each newsman $104 a day for a third-rate hotel with fourth-rate food and service. (I am taking a risk here that some of my colleagues will accuse me of upgrading.) The daily rate was supposed to include a car and driver, an interpreter, and a guide, among other benefits, but the chance of getting all those things was roughly equivalent to the chance of getting a dancing bear with your breakfast.

I raised the issue of hotel prices with Kissinger following the visits to Moscow by French President Giscard d'Estaing and West German Chancellor Helmut Schmidt. The French journalists had simply refused to pay the Intourist rate, so the Russians had lowered it to $65. The Germans had refused to pay even the $65, so the Russians, under pressure, had lowered it to $35. One more notch and they would have been on the money.

When Kissinger heard our complaints and learned about the successful bargaining of the Germans and the French, he got the undersecretary of state for political affairs, Joseph Sisco, to take up the issue with the Russians. Our offices supposedly did get rebates for this one trip. But the price went right back up on the next visit. We were always convinced that our problems with the Russians over hotel bills or coverage arrangements in Moscow were related to the negotiations themselves. The Russians tended to regard any concession to us as a concession to the U.S. government, and, therefore, they expected something from the government in return.

We felt the State Department did not want to expend any of its negotiating capital on our behalf. However, Kissinger did expend some wit on our behalf. When a Soviet official made a snidely jocular remark about the behavior of the American reporters, Kissinger needled, "You have the press under better control than we do."

Apart from press problems, Kissinger had a full supply of trouble with the Russians, ranging from SALT to the Jackson Amendment. The Jackson Amendment required a foreign nation to permit free emigration in order to qualify for American trade benefits. The amendment aimed at the Soviet restrictions on the emigration of Jews was sponsored by Senator Henry Jackson of Washington, a relic of the Cold War who was planning to run for President. Jackson made an announcement about Soviet concessions on the emigration issue from a podium at the White House. The Soviets had been prepared to live with the terms of the amendment itself, but the handling of the announcement made it appear as though they had knuckled under to one of their prime antagonists, and they were furious. When the subject came up in Kissinger's talks with Brezhnev, the Soviet leader's reaction was described as "violent." The Russians followed up by sending Kissinger an extremely brusque note on the subject written in Russian. Normally, such a note was translated into English as a diplomatic courtesy, but on this subject they had no time for courtesy.

Prior to the Jackson announcement at the White House, Kissinger had been warning consistently that if the Russians were pushed too far in public on the touchy issue of Jewish emigration, they would eventually decide the game was not worth the candle. He made the point that the Russians did not want to look as if they were caving in to pressure. He also argued that no aspect of American foreign policy — including the normalization of trade — should depend on trying to force the Russians to make internal changes.

For Kissinger, the Jewish emigration issue was especially sensitive. It touched on the whole policy of détente, it touched on relations with Israel, and it touched on the criticism that Kissinger's approach to foreign policy ignored human rights. "Whether we like it or not," Kissinger once told me, "the Jewish problem is an internal domestic matter."

During the 1972 Summit, the issue was highlighted by humor. Exit permits were hard to come by, and the joke of the moment concerned a man who applied for permission to emigrate to Israel while insisting to the Soviet authorities that he, personally, really wanted to stay. However, he explained, his wife was demanding to go, his son was demanding to go, and his mother-in-law was demanding to go. "In that case, Comrade," he was asked, "why don't you stay and let them go?" "Because," he replied, "I'm the only one who's Jewish."

Kissinger's preference for dealing with the issue quietly was underscored in a briefing on the plane following one of his meetings with Gromyko in Europe. Marilyn Berger of the Washington *Post* pressed Kissinger on the subject: "Did you actually raise the emigration issue?"

Kissinger: Marilyn, I've been trying to explain to you that I will not go into that in detail.

Marilyn: So you discussed it? [Silence.] It will be hard to write.

Kissinger: I want it hard to write.

The Secretary's most detailed defense of his position on the issue came in a speech to the Synagogue Council of America. "Through quiet diplomacy," Kissinger said,

> this administration has brought about the release or parole of hundreds of prisoners throughout the world and mitigated represssive conditions in numerous countries. But we have seldom publicized specific successes.
>
> The most striking example has been the case of Jewish emigration from the Soviet Union. The number of Soviet Jews who were permitted to emigrate in 1968 was four hundred; by 1973 that number had risen to thirty-five thousand.
>
> The reason for this quantum leap lies largely in persistent but private approaches to the Soviet government and the parallel overall improve-

ment in U.S.-Soviet relations. Hundreds of hardship cases were dealt with in quiet personal discussions by the President or his senior officials.

No public announcement or confrontation ever took place. But the results were there for all to see.

When even greater advances were sought by confrontation and legislation, the result was tragic.

Today Jewish emigration from the Soviet Union has dropped to approximately ten thousand a year.

I stress this not to score debating points against men whose seriousness of purpose and dedication to Jewish emigration I greatly respect. Rather, it is to indicate that moral ends are often not enough in themselves. The means used also have a moral quality and moral consequences.

Despite Brezhnev's "violent" reaction to the aftermath of the Jackson Amendment, the general atmosphere for Kissinger's talks in October 1974 was described as "very cordial." Ambassador Dobrynin showed some of the cordiality on the last day of the visit. Kissinger's scheduled session with Brezhnev was delayed by a meeting of the Politburo. Afterward, Dobrynin told Kissinger, "Sorry about the delay, but I think you'll be pleased with the results." The Secretary was indeed pleased, but it took another eight hours of bargaining, including a long tête-à-tête with the Soviet Party Chief, to make sure.

Kissinger said later that during the head-to-head discussion, Brezhnev had laid out the most sophisticated Soviet position on strategic arms control that he had ever heard. And Kissinger, a connoisseur of Soviet strategic thinking, had not found much sophistication in their previous positions. Following the July Summit, he had told us, "The Russians are in a far cruder state of strategic thinking than we are," adding, "Every Russian proposal in history has been a lousy proposal." The Russians preferred to reject U.S. proposals and then wait for the Americans to come up with a new one.

If there was an unaccustomed sophistication in the Soviet negotiating position, however, there was a customary unsophisticated playfulness in the negotiating tactics of the Soviet leader. During one of the delegation-to-delegation meetings, Brezhnev fiddled with a toy cannon. The negotiations had been going on for about three hours; they were serious, intense, and sometimes tense. Both sides were throwing around doomsday numbers. At one point Brezhnev took the cannon apart, remarked on its intricacy, and then put it back together, explaining how well it was made to scale. He then put a toy shell into the cannon, pointed it at Hal Sonnenfeldt, and started playing with the lanyard. The negotiations went on. Suddenly Brezhnev yanked the lanyard. There was a tremendous bang and a big puff of smoke. Kisssinger, Sonnenfeldt, and the other Americans jumped in their seats. Brezhnev looked as pleased as a Soviet dissident with an exit visa.

This time the negotiations themselves did not blow up, and Kissinger left Moscow with an outline of the agreement on nuclear weapons ceilings that Ford and Brezhnev would announce in Vladivostok the following month.

The relationship between an American President and a Soviet Party Chief that had been established by Nixon and Brezhnev had to be started from scratch when Ford and Brezhnev met. However, in some unnoticed ways, not all that much had changed. Kissinger aide Bill Hyland recalled that during the 1972 Summit in Moscow, he and Sonnenfeldt had shared a Kremlin room with faulty plumbing. The toilet finally broke down and started making a lot of noise. At two o'clock in the morning, they got up and tinkered with it until they got it quiet if not fixed. Three years later, Hyland was staying at a room in a health spa at Vladivostok, and once again the plumbing failed. This time it was a sink. Some of Hyland's most vivid memories of the Soviet Union had to do with fixing the plumbing at odd hours. (Both he and Sonnenfeldt deny all association with the other White House plumbers, however.)

When Kissinger got to Vladivostok, he wanted to know from his Russian hosts where all the Chinese architecture was, since the Soviets referred to this area as the Far East and the Chinese laid claim to it. The Russians explained that it was they who had built up the area, not the Chinese. The surrounding drabness served as silent endorsement of their explanation. When Kissinger went to Peking right afterward, he teased the Chinese about the lack of

Oriental character in the Soviet port city. The Chinese did not share his amusement.

The Vladivostok meeting represented the last American-Soviet Summit as such during Ford's tenure in office, but the President did get together with Brezhnev one more time at a "mini-Summit" during the meeting of thirty-five heads of government at the conclusion of the European Security Conference in Helsinki in August 1975. The American entourage included the Secretary's son, David, who celebrated his fourteenth birthday in the Finnish capital. At that early age, he was already following in his father's quipsteps. Following a Kissinger briefing, David was asked what he thought. "About what I'd expect," he said. After a pause, he added, "Quite ordinary." The results of the Ford-Brezhnev talks themselves were quite ordinary as well.

The following January, Kissinger got off a plane at the VIP area at Vnukovo Airport in a lightly falling snow. The temperature had dropped below zero, and the Secretary was wearing a Russian hat he had picked up in Vladivostok. Gromyko, who greeted him, wore a fedora. This was to be Kissinger's last visit to Moscow as Secretary of State. For the first time on a Moscow visit, however, the official party included a representative from the Pentagon — a walking acknowledgment of the split within the Ford Administration over the proper negotiating position.

The beginning of a presidential election year did not seem a propitious time for concluding a new arms agreement with the Russians. In addition, the entire relationship between Washington and Moscow was clouded by the heavy Soviet and Cuban involvement in Angola. The Russian role in Angola clearly could not be explained away in terms of détente. Kissinger had originally argued, rather weakly, that the Soviets became involved in Angola to counter the presence of the Chinese there, not to exploit American weakness or confront the United States.*

Whatever the motivation of the Russians for being there, Kis-

---

*One of the most interesting explanations for the Soviet adventure came from an exiled official who claimed that the Politburo decided to send Cubans to Angola in retaliation for the failure of the Soviet Union to get trade benefits from the United States.

singer felt strongly that their presence had to be resisted. However, his efforts to continue funneling money secretly to pro-Western factions in Angola was thwarted by a leaderless Congress, which hallucinated over the prospects of another Vietnam. Kissinger, reduced to rhetoric, stated frequently that the United States would not tolerate the Soviet Union's adventurism in Angola, but there wasn't much he could do about it. Nor did he have any diplomatic cards to play, since the Russians were not getting much from the United States anywhere else. The Secretary of State worried aloud that "the impact on the Soviet Union, if they face us down there, would be very heady." Then, lashing out at critics of détente, he complained, "People want to be tough on the Soviets. Angola is the place to do it . . . not on the goddamned cubic content of the SS-19 missiles."

Angola represented precisely the kind of situation Kissinger had worried about during the Watergate period and then after Vietnam fell. "It's going to come, believe me," he said during an on-plane briefing in the summer of '75. How? "I don't know," he said, but he added, "You can't look that weak for that long in that many areas without paying for it, believe me. I don't know when or how that's going to happen." Later he was asked, if the Americans supported one side and the Russians backed another, "How are you going to avoid an endless proxy war in Angola?" His answer was flip: "By running the Soviets into the sea," adding, "and you can quote that." Nobody did. (Kissinger also warned presciently in one of those briefings that if Moscow's adventurism weren't challenged in Angola, there would be "Cubans all over Africa.")

Angola was thrust to the forefront of Kissinger's first meeting with Brezhnev in the Kremlin in January 1976. Right after the Soviet leader had patted Kissinger on the stomach and told him, "You're getting fat, Henry," a UPI reporter, Nick Daniloff, began asking questions. Daniloff had once been stationed in Moscow and spoke understandable Russian. Kissinger, a little uneasy, said to Brezhnev, "I hope he's more polite to you than he is to me."

"Comrade Leonid Ilyich," Daniloff said, "are you going to talk about Angola?"

"I don't have any questions about Angola," replied Brezhnev jovially. "It's not my country."

Kissinger interjected sternly, "It will certainly be discussed."

Gromyko noted dryly, "The agenda is always adopted by mutual agreement."

Kissinger persevered indignantly. "Then *I* will discuss it."

Brezhnev retorted jauntily, "Let Kissinger talk to Sonnenfeldt about that. Then there will certainly be no disagreement since they always agree with each other." And he laughed.

Back in Washington, Nancy Kissinger saw and heard the scene on television, and when Henry called her, she chewed him out for letting Brezhnev get the better of him in the exchange on Angola.

Kissinger later acknowledged that he didn't get much satisfaction in their private sessions either. He was bargaining from a position of weakness since the Soviet-backed forces were in a much better position on the ground. Kissinger's only real argument was to try to convince the Russians that their continued involvement in Angola might undermine public support in the United States for the whole policy of détente and that it would inevitably chill the atmosphere of American-Soviet relations. The arguments carried little weight. Kissinger also feinted at linking Angola to progress on the arms control negotiations, but he wasn't serious and the Russians knew it. SALT was too important for both of them.

However, the first Brezhnev-Kissinger encounter did not result in defeat all around. The press finally won a victory. We went though our customary hassle over how many of the reporters traveling with the Secretary of State would be allowed in. The Russians started with a figure of five, then upped it to eight during a bargaining session that lasted until one o'clock in the morning; finally, at the last minute, they agreed to let everybody in. If they demanded something in return at the negotiating table, we never found out about it.

Just before the January trip, one of the hardy perennials of the news business in recent years — the subject of Brezhnev's health — was blooming. The speculative grapevine was once again bearing reports of the Soviet leader's imminent retirement, forced or otherwise. Kissinger always treated the issue of Brezhnev's health gingerly, for obvious reasons. It was not the sort of issue on which he wanted to be quoted in any way, so he usually slipped away from a serious answer with a joke. Following the visit of the British Prime Minister to Moscow, Kissinger was asked if he'd had a report from London on Brezhnev's health. "Yes," he said, "we've had a report . . . Brezhnev was in fairly good shape." But he couldn't repress an addition. "He does have a few problems . . . like foaming at the mouth." And then Kissinger laughed uproariously.

After the Helsinki meeting in August 1975, Kissinger did note seriously — but not for attribution — that Brezhnev obviously was not as vigorous as usual. In January 1976, however, if Brezhnev was not well, he certainly did not show it. The stocky Soviet leader, at sixty-nine, appeared as robust and energetic as ever when he bounced into the Kremlin meeting room wearing an electric blue suit with two Hero of the Soviet Union red-ribboned medals on his chest.

Brezhnev's affability in public was matched by his playfulness in private. Once the talks got under way, he told the Americans he was following doctor's orders and had quit smoking. To demonstrate his will power, he opened a pack of cigarettes, sniffed them, and put them aside, saying he had conquered his desire to smoke.

But he had not conquered his inclination to joke with Hal Sonnenfeldt. According to the New York *Times,* as told to Bernie Gwertzman by Hal Sonnenfeldt,

> During Thursday night's four-hour Kremlin session, Mr. Brezhnev looked across the green felt table and noted Mr. Sonnenfeldt's gold watch valued at several hundred dollars.
>
> According to participants in the talks, Mr. Brezhnev demanded that Mr. Sonnenfeldt give him the watch. The Soviet leader examined it, expressed satisfaction with it, and put it on his wrist. In return, he gave Mr. Sonnenfeldt his inexpensive pocket watch.
>
> Mr. Sonnenfeldt protested at this "swap" and Mr. Brezhnev then wrote out with red pencil that he and Mr. Sonnenfeldt would again swap watches at another meeting. Perhaps, to ease the pain, he left the room and returned with a stainless steel watch valued somewhat more than the pocket watch.

The *Wall Street Journal* picked up the story and wrote an editorial about it, making it the great metaphor of détente, to show how the Russians were taking advantage of the United States at every turn. The story was also picked up in France and Germany, and the ultra–right wing Manchester *Union-Leader* carried a story about it the day President Ford arrived in New Hampshire to campaign for the Republican primary.

Unfair, claims Sonnenfeldt today, and he gives this version of what really happened. When Sonnenfeldt realized that Brezhnev wanted to keep his watch, he told the Soviet leader, "Mr. General Secretary, I'd be honored to have you wear my watch, but it has great sentimental value, and besides, I'm afraid I'd get in trouble if you kept it because it was a present from my mother-in-law, and if she knew I had given the watch to you, she might cut me out of her will." Brezhnev said *his* watch had great sentimental value as well. (Sonnenfeldt felt the sentimentality had something to do with the Russians' exchanging watches with Americans when they reached the Elbe at the end of World War II.) He then got up, left the room, and returned with a big turquoise box. He pulled out a calendar wristwatch and handed it over to Sonnenfeldt. "That is the deal," Brezhnev said. The deal, Sonnenfeldt now insists, turned out to be in his favor. He says the watch Brezhnev took was actually a slow-running Omega with a cracked crystal that had cost $110 at a PX. He concedes the pocket watch he got in return was not worth much, but it had a gold chain valued at between $150 and $200 by a jeweler's appraisal. And the stainless steel watch that Brezhnev also gave him was a Swiss Eternamatic worth twice as much as the Omega.

Since a U.S. official is not supposed to keep any gifts from a foreign government worth more than $50, Sonnenfeldt checked with the State Department Protocol Office for a ruling. The Protocol Office ruled that the Brezhnev note made the watches a "contingent" gift, and so Sonnenfeldt got to keep them. The pocket watch and chain, now encapsulated in glass, sit on a piano in the Sonnenfeldts' living room in a Maryland suburb of Washington.

Throughout the Kissinger period, Brezhnev used Sonnenfeldt as a foil in the negotiations just as Kissinger used Georgy Kornienko, a Soviet specialist on American affairs, as a foil on the Soviet side. Kissinger made Kornienko out to be a hard-line bureaucrat who pulled the wool over the Americans' eyes, and he used to claim that the Americans got Kornienko promoted to deputy foreign minister because they made so many concessions to him on communiqués. One advantage of using a foil was that Kissinger could make a serious point in a joking way, without forcing the Russians to react on the spot. Brezhnev did the same with Sonnenfeldt.

Kissinger often used his humor in Moscow to ridicule Soviet proposals that were in fact ridiculous. He was able to make his point without getting upset or angry — and without being harsh.

Brezhnev's playfulness, which had been unleashed by Kissinger's unconventional use of humor in diplomacy, became an unavoidable part of the Kremlin meetings. During one session, again while the interpreter was translating one of his statements, Brezhnev got up, left the room, and returned with a large briefcase. He put it on the table and opened it. It was full of whiskey bottles, and he poured a round for everybody at the table.

He was equally ebullient as a guest. At a dinner given by Nixon at Spaso House, the U.S. Ambassador's residence, baked Alaska was served for dessert. When the waiters came marching into the room with the flaming dishes, Brezhnev shouted to one of his cronies, "You've just been served hot ice cream, Comrade. These Americans can do anything."

For Brezhnev, food also became a part of the negotiating mix. He would frequently order something to eat to provide a breather during a Kremlin bargaining session. One of the most popular items on the Kremlin menu was a Russian sausage. The two sides used to toast each other with the sausages, dipping them first in mustard. The sausages looked like missiles, and so they lent themselves to numerous forgettable and forgotten jokes. When Brezhnev discovered the Americans liked the sausages, he used to threaten to starve them unless they made concessions in the bargaining. It was not the sort of thing Kissinger would make concessions for.

Brezhnev's love of gadgets also became apparent during the Kremlin meetings. In addition to the cigarette case with a timer and a box full of watches, he once showed up with a cigarette lighter that looked like the nose cone of a rocket. Inside, it had six lighters. Kissinger joked that it was a MIRVed lighter (that is, a lighter with multiple warheads) and would have to be made part of any agreement.

Brezhnev had not always been so playful and jovial in his dealings with his American adversaries, nor had the other Soviet officials. Pre-Kissinger, the relationship had been more rigid and the negotiating atmosphere more somber. But Kissinger's style had loosened up the Russians. Kissinger also spent a fair amount of time explaining the American system to the Russians. This was, after all, the first time there had been such intensive contact between Americans and Russians since the immediate postwar days, when Averell Harriman was the U.S. Ambassador in Moscow. The Kissinger style led to more frankness as well as more informality in the discussions. The Russians were less inclined to make set speeches straight out of *Pravda*. Less time was wasted on rhetoric and posturing. But the rhetoric and the posturing were not eliminated altogether, since they, too, figured as important elements in Brezhnev's negotiating style.

One member of the Kissinger party came away from his first exposure to the Soviet Party Chief shaking his head. "It's impossible," he recalls saying to the Secretary. "How can we ever get anything accomplished?" "Don't worry," replied Kissinger. "This is the way it always is. The next time, it will be half and half. In the third session, we can get down to business."

Brezhnev had demonstrated his theatrical flair during the 1972 Summit when he lambasted Nixon and Kissinger over Vietnam. The Americans figured he was showboating so that when a report of the meeting was sent to Hanoi, it would show that Moscow was not indifferent to North Vietnam's struggle. As soon as the Vietnam session was over, the clouds of contentiousness cleared, and a pleasant dinner followed.

During a difficult period in the talks in March 1974, Brezhnev acted like a "wild Banshee," in Kissinger's words. The Soviet leader exploded at one point, "I don't have to deal with you. You're a foreign minister!" At another point he stomped out of the room to dramatize his displeasure with the American position. Kissinger blithely wondered to Gromyko if Brezhnev's departure meant they should move on to the next item on the agenda. Gromyko diplomatically suggested it was time for a tea break. After the break, the negotiations resumed with Brezhnev sitting at his accustomed place, his theatrical exit forgotten.

Brezhnev's ability as an actor was less convincing than his talent as a storyteller, and he frequently used stories to make a point. Many of them fell into the shaggy dog category. One of them was, in fact, about a racing dog — a Soviet version of "The Tortoise and the Hare." It involved a dog that was nosed out at the finish line although it had been heavily favored to win. All the people who had bet on it complained to the owner. But the owner argued that his dog had made a major effort most of the way. As one of Kissinger's aides pointed out, that was Brezhnev's way of saying "Bullshit" when the American side promised to make "a major effort" on something the Russians were interested in.

Brezhnev also knew how to apply the needle more directly. On some occasions when Kissinger said something that was tough and did not move the negotiations forward, Brezhnev would boast that he had direct contact with Nixon and therefore knew that what Kissinger was saying was not correct.

Kissinger knew just as well how to needle the Russians. One way was to tell them how intelligent and astute Mao Tse-tung and Chou En-lai were. And he delighted in telling them often.

After leaving office, Sonnenfeldt told an interviewer, "Someday, when someone goes through the records of these meetings, he will be amazed by how much time was taken up in byplay. When you are engaged in serious business," he said, "that sort of levity is a big help." Neither side changed its basic policy because of the levity, as Ambassador Dobrynin once pointed out to me, but the humor relaxed the atmosphere and created a more propitious climate for making accommodations.

In addition to their joint appreciation of the use of humor in negotiations, Kissinger and the Russians were on the same geopolitical wavelength. The Soviet leaders tended to share Kissinger's perception of the world — "a bipolar constellation of forces arranged around the great powers," as one writer put it. The Soviet leadership also understood that Kissinger carried a lot of clout and they believed he delivered what he promised. Especially after the 1972 Summit. So the Russians felt comfortable with Kissinger.

The Russians were so comfortable with Kissinger that they even invited him in his presecretarial days to Zavidovo, the Soviet equivalent of Camp David, which foreign visitors seldom got to see. He described some of his experiences there at a White House briefing: "The hospitality was extraordinary . . . They took me on a new speedboat they have developed, which, with all respect to the General Secretary, is a rather harrowing experience — Mr. Ziegler said particularly with my weight load, which comes with ill grace — and he also gave me my first opportunity to go hunting, unsolicited."

Q: Did you get anything?
K: I acted as his special adviser.
Q: Did you fire?
K: No. I advised him about how to conduct the hunt.
Q: Where to aim the rifle, you mean?
K: In which direction. Ignorance of a subject has never kept a Harvard professor from offering theories . . .

The Soviet version of hunting is roughly equivalent to the Soviet version of sovereignty for Eastern Europe. The hunting blinds are set up near feeding areas. When the boars show up for food, the hunters blast away. The feedings are staggered so the "hunt" can take place at different times.

Kissinger was accompanied by Sonnenfeldt. The Russians provided them both with hunting outfits, which included jackboots. Ironically, Kissinger and Sonnenfeldt, two German-born Jews, looked like a couple of Nazi SS officers as they wandered around the hunting lodge. Sonnenfeldt did fire. Twice. And he killed a boar each time. Gromyko always referred to him as the "master huntsman" after that, but Kissinger was tauntingly skeptical. He claimed the Russians had put blanks in Sonnenfeldt's rifle, and a hidden Red Army marksman near the blind had actually fired the shots that killed the boars.

The hunting party didn't exactly rough it in the wild. The roads at Zavidovo had double strips of pavement so the cars and jeeps wouldn't get bogged down. Sonnenfeldt said the preserve reminded him of a wooded area in Germany where the dirt roads had metal strips, put there in the days of the Kaiser so the royal carriage wouldn't get stuck.

Kissinger came back from Zavidovo telling and retelling a favorite joke: When Brezhnev became the First Among Equals, his mother didn't believe it. In order to demonstrate his preeminence, he showed her his office in the Kremlin. Then he showed her his country dacha. Then he took her to the hunting lodge. He showed her his cars and speedboats. After seeing all this, his mother did indeed believe. "This is wonderful, Leonid Ilyvich," she said, "but what are you going to do when the Communists take over?"

Kissinger understood that much of the revolutionary zeal in the Soviet Union had given way to a Communist conservatism, and he based much of his policy on that transformation.

Many of his dealings with the other superpower did not take him to Moscow. Frequently he met in some "neutral" capital with the Soviet foreign minister, Andrei Gromyko, to discuss SALT, the Middle East, and whatever other issues happened to affect American-Soviet relations at the time.

One of the more rememberable, if not memorable, Kissinger meetings with Gromyko took place in Nicosia, in the days when Kissinger could still go there, before the Greek coup and the subsequent Turkish invasion. The Secretary of State was engaged at the time in the longest diplomatic mission of his or any other Secretary's career, the thirty-three-day shuttle between Israel and Syria. Although Kissinger would never admit to it, the United States was obviously squeezing the Russians out of the whole negotiating process in the

Middle East — even with one of their principal clients, the Syrians. The Russians, cochairmen of the Geneva Peace Conference on the Middle East, obviously didn't like it. But there wasn't much they could do about it without appearing to be totally irresponsible.

Kissinger joked at the time that the Soviets would obviously like to see him "institutionalize" American diplomacy; that is, stay at home and pay more attention to running the State Department, which he indicated he would do when he was first named Secretary of State. But he felt compelled every once in a while to throw the Russians a Middle East bone to chew on, and Cyprus was one of those times.

The host for the meeting in Nicosia was the President of Cyprus, Archbishop Makarios. And it was worth the price of admission alone just to hear Kissinger, with his heavy German accent and deep rumbling voice, refer to the archbishop as "Your Beatitude." In the middle of the Kissinger-Gromyko meeting, His Beatitude barged in — like a good Jewish mother, in the words of one Kissinger aide — and offered lunch. Gromyko wanted to keep on talking, but to no one's surprise Kissinger opted for eating, especially when he learned that the main course was one of his favorite dishes, Wiener schnitzel. The Wiener schnitzel proved to be excellent, and ever after Kissinger used to joke with Makarios, whom he neither liked nor trusted, that he was going to steal the archbishop's chef.

Most of the time Kissinger met with Gromyko outside of Washington and Moscow, however, the site was Geneva. While Switzerland may have been neutral, the Kissinger-Gromyko meetings seldom were. Just before Kissinger's arrival in February 1975, Brezhnev had blasted the Secretary of State's one-man brand of diplomacy in the Middle East, charging that "certain persons" were seeking to undermine Arab unity with "piecemeal solutions." When Gromyko and Kissinger appeared before the cameras at the conclusion of one of their sessions, an American reporter asked the Soviet foreign minister, "Who are those persons?" Gromyko sidestepped the question by pointing out that Brezhnev "did not mention any particular persons." But Kissinger wouldn't let him off the hook that easily. "I asked him the same question," the Secretary gibed. "I wanted to share in the condemnation."

Among the press observers on that trip was humorist Art Buchwald. During another of those picture-taking sessions, Kissinger pointed to the columnist and said to Gromyko, "I put him on the enemies' list. But then, he's kinder to you than to me — you should play chess with him sometime." "Ah," said Gromyko, "the famous Art. I have a book of your articles." He didn't say whether he had read it. Afterward, Buchwald confirmed that he did indeed play chess with Kissinger. "I beat him all the time," he said, "which I guess explains why we're losing the world." (I think he was joking.)

When Kissinger first started dealing with Gromyko, he felt that the Soviet foreign minister didn't know enough about weapons to be a "good partner" in the SALT negotiations, and so the Russians always had a special weapons expert sitting in. But eventually Gromyko learned about weapons, Kissinger said, and was able to talk about them with some authority. At one meeting, however, both men needed help on the basics. Gromyko was going on at great length about permitting a 15 percent increase in the size of certain missiles, and one of Kissinger's brightest weapons analysts, Jan Lodal, kept fussing about Gromyko's presentation. Kissinger thought Lodal didn't know what Gromyko was talking about and finally apologized to the Soviet diplomat for taking up so much time with intra-American discussions. Lodal patiently explained to the Secretary that he did indeed know what Gromyko was talking about: A 15 percent increase in dimensions led to a 52 percent increase in volume when cubed. Kissinger quietly asked Lodal, "Is that okay with us?" "No," replied Lodal emphatically, "that is not okay with us." Once Kissinger realized that Gromyko was trying to screw him, he set out to explain the fundamentals of solid geometry to Gromyko, who did not react warmly. Neither did Dobrynin, but when the Ambassador finally understood, he then explained it to Gromyko. About two hours of negotiating time went down the drain because the principals didn't have a solid grasp of solid geometry.

For Kissinger, Gromyko was the only Soviet leader who was not a "sleazy trader." One case of sleaziness involved a communiqué that the two sides had agreed on. Brezhnev said it couldn't be signed, however, until the Politburo had given its approval. When the communiqué came back from the Politburo, it had changes in it. One of Kissinger's staffers noted the changes, and the Secretary then pointed out to Brezhnev that he could not accept the document as amended. The Soviet leader demanded that the communiqué be signed as was, since it now bore the Politburo's stamp of approval. Kissinger adamantly refused and said he would have to report back to the President why there was no agreed-on communiqué. Brezhnev finally yielded. Gromyko smiled weakly at Kissinger and said, "I told them they wouldn't be able to get away with it."

In his dealings with the Soviet foreign minister, Kissinger once told us, "Ninety-nine percent of the conversation was business." The other one percent dealt with Gromyko's interest in nineteenth-century Russian foreign policy, with emphasis on Count Witte, the first Russian foreign minister, a contemporary of Bismarck. According to Kissinger, Count Witte was not as good as Bismarck, but good enough. He would probably say the same thing about Gromyko vis-à-vis his American counterpart.

Despite the "businesslike" atmosphere of their dealings, Kissinger made sure we knew he was wary of the veteran Soviet diplomat. A reporter once asked the Secretary if he had learned anything about reports of turmoil within the Kremlin during a session with Gromyko. "No," answered Kissinger, "he claims nothing is going on." Then, pausing for effect, he added, "And, as you know, he wouldn't lie to me." The sarcasm was as thick as the German accent.

In addition to their diplomatic jousting, Kissinger and Gromyko also took up gastronomic arms against each other when they met in Europe. Each tried to outdo the other when he was the host for a meeting. Gromyko had the built-in advantage of caviar, although Dobrynin once offered to provide the Americans with some caviar "on a lend-lease basis." The traveling press left it to the magazine reporters to find out what the menus were. The food provided some of the "color" they inserted into their voluminous files. At one of the

Geneva meetings, the Russians served salmon and Siberian meatballs. We later asked Kissinger what Siberian meatballs were. He had
no idea, but he didn't forget. When a reporter subsequently asked
him for the details of a reported disagreement with Gromyko over
the Middle East, Kissinger replied, "Siberian meatballs."

The disagreements over the Middle East, however, ran deeper
than Siberian meatballs, since the United States was supporting Israel and the Soviet Union was backing the more radical Arabs and
the militant Palestinians. At the conclusion of one long meeting,
Gromyko told waiting reporters, "Some of our positions were close
or coincided. It is no secret that on some questions our positions
didn't coincide." Kissinger chimed in, "I can't compete with the
foreign minister's oratorical skill, but I agree with his remarks."
After another meeting, when it was quite clear he and Gromyko had
disagreed, Kissinger ducked a direct answer by dredging up an old
line. "I'm not saying," he explained, "that we achieved a conceptual
breakthrough on the Middle East."

After Kissinger's surprise session with Gromyko on Cyprus in the
spring of '74, we used to ask him as a matter of course on subsequent
excursions through the area if he would confer with the Soviet foreign minister. It became a running gag. Before one of their scheduled
meetings in 1975, a reporter asked, "Why now?" Kissinger replied
maliciously, "Because I like to keep him informed." "Where are you
going to see him?" "Probably Geneva," he answered, then he
thought of a better answer. "How about Jerusalem? . . . the Old
City?" He broke himself up.

Despite Kissinger's efforts to keep the Russians at arm's length in
Middle East diplomacy, his frequent contact with them aroused
suspicions in Israel that the two superpowers were colluding to
impose a settlement. Kissinger replied to the charge with an outburst
of mock indignation. "The next Israeli who speaks of Soviet-Ameri-
can collusion will be dragged to my next meeting with Brezhnev,"
Kissinger declaimed. "He should have to sit through five hours of
that with Gromyko."

While trying to keep the Russians out, Kissinger was constantly trying to con them into believing they were in. One aide recalls that Kissinger always gave them a spiel about working together in the Middle East, conjuring up a rosy vision of a cooperative future, and as the Secretary of State was going into this routine with Gromyko for the fiftieth time or so, the Soviet diplomat actually allowed himself the luxury of an uncharacteristic smile. One of Kissinger's more ironic ploys with Gromyko was to needle him about his manner of expressing himself in Russian. Gromyko would never say, "It's acceptable." Instead, he would say, "It's not unacceptable." The irony was that Kissinger himself was a devotee of the double negative, and it was not one of his most unpredictable rhetorical devices.

Kissinger's dealings with Gromyko and Brezhnev paralleled his relationship with the top leadership in China; they transcended the function of the U.S. Ambassador in Moscow, just as his relations with Chou and Mao overrode the function of the U.S. envoy in Peking. There was another similarity. As in China, Kissinger relied entirely on a local interpreter — in this case, the slick and highly competent Victor Sukhodrev, who could translate with either an American or a British accent. As in China, using a local interpreter meant cutting in one less American on the action.

The "Washington connection" for Kissinger's supervision of American-Soviet relations was Anatoly Dobrynin, a sly, wily veteran who endured on Embassy Row longer than any other ambassador except the Ambassador from Nicaragua. Kissinger and Dobrynin had a unique working relationship — plus a direct telephone link. The Secretary once explained privately that he and the Soviet Ambassador "reach agreements in principle. We exchange ideas free from bureaucratic rigidity." If Dobrynin were to have left, Kissinger said, it would have been very difficult to reconstruct such a relationship.

Dobrynin also had a good sense of humor and, inspired by Kissinger, he allowed it to come into play. At an exhibition of Soviet photographs, Kissinger admired a picture of a veterinarian about to inoculate a bulldog. Dobrynin had it sent to him with the inscription: "Henry, Don't be too serious. Take it easy. Relax." Henry never did, especially with the Russians. Dobrynin also turned out to be the source of one of Kissinger's most quoted lines. The Soviet diplomat told him about a Russian peasant who became an ambassador. The peasant's friends wanted to know how to address him. "Since you are my friends," he said, "you don't have to call me Your Excellency. Just call me Excellency." Kissinger used a version of that at a news conference following his nomination as Secretary of State.

Soon after becoming Secretary, Kissinger received the Project HOPE Award for International Understanding at a formal dinner in New York. Dobrynin was there, and he gave the award-winner a gentle dig. "Congratulations, Henry," he said. "Imagine, in office only twenty-four hours and already winning prizes." Without missing a beat, Kissinger replied, "That, Mr. Ambassador, is the American way of life."

Dobrynin was, naturally enough, present at the ceremony on the eighth floor of the State Department when the new U.S. Ambassador to Moscow, Walter Stoessel, was sworn in. Just before the proceedings got under way, Kissinger turned to the Soviet Ambassador and asked, with mischief aforethought, "You want to hold the Bible?"

Throughout his last year in office, Kissinger dealt more with Dobrynin than with any other Soviet official. In that presidential election year, relations with the Soviet Union, like so many other controversial foreign policy matters, simply marked time. President Ford even went so far as to repudiate the word "détente," which had been oversold to the American public during the Nixon years — especially during the 1972 campaign — and which had come to connote "appeasement" to right-wing critics of the policy. Throughout 1976, Kissinger kept trying to come up with a joke about a suitable semantic replacement for "détente."

It was one of the major ironies of presidential politics that Gerald Ford and Henry Kissinger, two strongly conservative men, should come to be accused of somehow being soft on the Russians. Especially when one of Kissinger's diplomatic precepts was, Stick it to the Russians whenever you can. He might have phrased the concept somewhat more elegantly.

During one of Kissinger's early trips to Moscow, Brezhnev joked about sending him off to Siberia for taking a hard line in one of the negotiations. Kissinger retorted, "I should be a member of the Politburo since I meet with you guys so much." In those days, détente was still considered a political plus. But in 1976, Kissinger was regarded as a candidate for Siberia by some members of his own party, who felt that he should, indeed, be a member of the Politburo.

While Kissinger spent a lot of time joking and negotiating with Brezhnev and Gromyko, he didn't really like or admire the Russians, although he had to acknowledge their power, and he did recognize their determination to be treated as equals. He did not find them intellectually stimulating, and they were not the kind of people he would have spent time with off duty. He once told the Israelis he found the Russians to be "cowardly and inept" in their diplomacy. He also found them uncouth.

When he became interested in world food problems, Kissinger

" CHANGE IT TO 'AN EASING AND RELAXING OF TENSIONS BETWEEN COUNTRIES WHILE CONTINUING A POLICY OF PEACE THROUGH STRENGTH...,"

Mike Peters, with permission from *Dayton Daily News*

used to point out repeatedly that no Communist country in the world was capable of feeding itself. And he rankled about the general American perception of Russian strength, which he felt was exaggerated. At the same time, he recognized the Russians as tough. He used to observe regularly — and superfluously — that Brezhnev did not get to the top and stay there by being a "choirboy" in a system that had no procedures for orderly succession. And, while he didn't necessarily respect Gromyko's mind, he did respect his ability to survive. Well he might have. Long after Henry Kissinger was out of office, Brezhnev, Gromyko, and Dobrynin were all doing business at the same old stand.

The Middle East

A scorpion approaches a frog on the banks of the Nile River and asks, "Frog, how about carrying me across the river?"

The frog replies, "No way, scorpion. If I let you get on my back, you'll sting me and I'll die."

"Of course I won't," counters the scorpion. "If I sting you while I'm on your back, you'll drown, and I'll drown with you."

"That makes sense," says the frog. "Okay, get on."

The scorpion gets on the back of the frog, and the frog jumps into the river and starts swimming. Halfway across, the scorpion stings the frog.

Just before the frog sinks below the water, he looks up at the scorpion and asks plaintively, "Scorpion, why in the world did you sting me?"

The scorpion replies with a shrug, "This is the Middle East."

That parable came to mind the morning of October 6, 1973. I was asleep in my hotel room in New York, where I was covering the U.S. Secretary of State's fall pilgrimage to the United Nations General Assembly meeting. The annual meeting of UNGA rarely produces headline news unless a few presidents show up or there's a crisis somewhere. This particular UNGA featured the maiden address by the world's "most junior foreign minister," as Henry Kissinger then described himself to his colleagues.

While luncheons were traditionally given for the foreign ministers of other regional groupings (Israel was folded into the European luncheon), this was the first one ever for the Arabs. Since the 1967 Arab-Israeli war, the United States had not maintained formal relations with such key nations as Egypt, Syria, and Algeria.

The Kissinger luncheon seemed to signal his entry into Middle East diplomacy, an area he had shunned as national security affairs adviser at the White House. He felt his Jewishness might intrude on the Arab-Israeli conflict, and, unless superpower relations were involved (as during the Jordanian crisis in 1970), Kissinger remained on the Middle East sidelines. During Israeli Prime Minister Golda Meir's first visit to Washington, Kissinger did not sit in on her meeting in the Oval Office with President Nixon, as he did in those of other foreign leaders. He let his deputy, General Alexander Haig, handle that assignment. In general, the Middle East was one area that he generally left to Secretary of State William Rogers.

But once Kissinger became Secretary himself, he could no longer avoid the Middle East. Quite the contrary; while relations with Moscow and Peking prospered, Kissinger decided it was time for fresh American initiatives in the Middle East. The luncheon for the Arabs even set off wild speculation that he had already worked out a settlement in the Middle East, which was easily denied. But he *was* talking to the Egyptian and Israeli foreign ministers about holding talks in New York, with an American go-between.

Kissinger had already tried to dampen any unwarranted expectations about his diplomatic discovery of the Middle East. In one of his first news conferences as Secretary of State, Kissinger noted, with respect to the Middle East, "It would be a great mistake to assume that any one man can pull a rabbit out of the hat. The difficulties in the Middle East occurred not because the parties don't understand each other," he said, "but in some respects, because they understand each other only too well . . ."

On the Friday following the luncheon, the reporters covering Kissinger had been given their customary meager feeding by State Department spokesman Robert McCloskey on the thirty-fifth floor of the Waldorf Towers, near the Secretary's suite. The assistant secretary of state for Near Eastern and South Asian affairs, Joseph Sisco, walked into the virtually deserted briefing area. I invited him to lunch. He said he had already been invited, by Marilyn Berger of the Washington *Post,* but he added he was sure that Marilyn wouldn't mind if I came along. Wrong. Marilyn's annoyance at my inadvertent horning in on "her" luncheon with a source was assuaged, however, by a thick steak and a good bottle of wine at The Palm.

The source didn't have much to tell us anyway, except that there was no chance of another war in the Middle East anytime soon. Israel was even stronger now than she had been in 1967, and the Arabs would get clobbered again — and they knew it! But while we were lunching at The Palm, the scorpion was crawling onto the back of the frog on the banks of the Nile.

The next morning, Saturday, the telephone jolted me awake. A radio editor whom I didn't know told me war had broken out in the Middle East. I thanked the caller, hung up, and went back to sleep. Almost immediately the telephone rang again, and this time I came fully awake. Even before I picked up the phone I knew the message. It was the television assignment desk at NBC telling me that war had broken out in the Middle East. The rest of the day was spent chronicling the confusion of the American policy-makers.

Kissinger himself was awakened at 6:00 A.M. by a cable from the American Ambassador in Israel, Kenneth Keating, relaying an urgent request from Golda Meir to try to head off another war, which she said was imminent. He was not *totally* surprised. Earlier in the week he had asked for a special analysis of the situation. For the next several hours, he spent so much time on the telephone that he didn't finish dressing until noon. "Henry was still in his shorts and socks until eleven o'clock," recalls Eagleburger.

The history of what followed is well known. Heeding Kissinger's oft-repeated warning not to strike first, the Israelis nervously waited for the Arabs to come at them.

The October War of 1973 turned out to be no delayed replay of the June War of 1967. The Egyptians surged across the Suez Canal and cracked the renowned Bar-Lev line, the Israeli line of defense. The Syrians thrust into the occupied Golan Heights. The fighting was fierce and prolonged. The Russians began a giant airlift of supplies into Egypt and Syria. The United States eventually countered with a massive airlift of supplies into Israel, with only Portugal, of all America's NATO allies, allowing its bases to be used for transshipment.

King Faisal, angered by the American aid to Israel, angrily joined his fellow Arabs in an oil boycott against the United States and the Western world.

Israel painfully repelled the Syrians and Egyptians and encircled the Egyptian Third Army.

Kissinger was summoned urgently to Moscow to arrange a cease-fire that would save the Egyptian Army. On the way back to Washington, he stopped in Tel Aviv to nail down the standstill cease-fire. But the fighting continued, and the Russians threatened to send their own forces to save the Egyptians.

The United States ordered a worldwide military alert. Kissinger held a news conference and talked about ambiguous Soviet moves. President Nixon talked about a "firm note" from Soviet leader Leonid Brezhnev, but gave no details. Senator Henry Jackson spoke of a "brutal" letter from Brezhnev.

In the wake of the Saturday Night Massacre, skepticism about the motive for the U.S. alert became widespread. It appeared as though the Watergate-besieged President was trying to divert attention from his domestic problems. It was never precisely clear what role the President — who allegedly had gone to bed — actually took in ordering the alert: whether he took part in the decision-making or ratified a decision already made or whether he was simply informed of an action agreed on by Kissinger and Defense Secretary Schlesinger.

The Flying State Department.

The Boys on the Plane.

R. Valeriani – Owner
Tia Vieja – Second
Jabu Dancer – Third
6 Furlongs – L:12:4
Mutuals – 10.60 7.00 6.00

Henry the K.

Ronald Poulin, Up
Katherine Voss, Tr.
Oct. 15, 1976
Penn National
B. Pearl

Henry the K's four-legged namesake finally wins a race.

They did it all for him. The Air Force stewards on his plane once served McDonald's hamburgers and even got Kissinger to pose in a McDonald's hat.

Kissinger aide Winston Lord (far right) took notes during President Nixon's historic meeting with Chairman Mao Tse-tung in May, 1972, but Lord was cropped out of the pictures distributed by the Chinese to spare further embarrassment to Secretary of State Rogers, who was not invited to the meeting.

Henry Kissinger with two world leaders he respected a great deal — Communist party chairman Mao Tse-tung and Premier Chou En-lai, in Peking, 1973.

Soviet Foreign Minister Andrei Gromyko pointing at the author's tie in May 1975.

With "the plucky little king," Hussein of Jordan.

Syrian President Hafez Assad joked that he was the only Arab leader in the
Middle East who spoke English with a German accent (because of all the time
he spent with Kissinger during the 33-day Syrian-Israeli shuttle).

Kissinger, the first Jewish Secretary of State, reviewing an Arab Legion honor
guard in Amman.

Kissinger kissing Egyptian President Anwar Sadat and Israeli Prime Minister Golda Meir. The traveling press joked that while Kissinger was kissing the Arabs, he was really screwing the Israelis.

An emotional farewell at the State Department on Kissinger's last day in office.

Kissinger promised at a news conference that he would explain about the alert within a week. But he never did, publicly. A month later, a reporter asked Kissinger at another news conference to "tell us what led you to pledge [to make public] the documents on the U.S.-Soviet situation? Particularly, was it the American domestic turbulence at that time that encouraged you, with that short deadline which you gave?" Kissinger found refuge in humor: "It is a mistake to assume that everything that is said in a press conference is fully considered."

Later, during an in-flight session with reporters, Kissinger acknowledged he regretted having made his news conference pledge, and he explained he had backed away from it because he wanted to avoid a situation where it appeared he was flaunting the fact that "we confronted the Soviets and faced them down." So he decided at that stage of U.S.-Soviet relations that it was better not to disclose all the facts. "I confess I didn't think this through," he said at the news conference, and that's why he had promised to share all.

He also explained he didn't think the news of the alert would leak so fast. "In the Jordan crisis of 1970, we also ordered an alert, but it took two days before the press got it," he said. "Basing it on past experience, we figured it would be at least two days before the press got it this time. We were once on an SAC alert which didn't get into the press at all. We wanted the Soviets to notice it without a great deal of public attention."

As for the skepticism about the administration's motives, Kissinger said, "I think there has to be a minimum of confidence on the part of the people that their government would not play with their lives frivolously."

A couple of years later, Kissinger was able to joke about another facet of the alert. Responding to a question about the reopening of the Suez Canal at a Southern Governors Conference, Kissinger said, "I have seen statements that in 1973, the United States was affected in the conduct of the Middle East crisis by its fear of the Soviet Navy. This may have been true of our Navy; it wasn't true of our government . . . We all suffered," Kissinger said, "from the illusion that our

Navy was far superior to the Soviet Navy, and we conducted ourselves accordingly." And he milked them for yet another laugh: "We
may have been wrong, but we acted as if we were superior." And
then he explained that the reopening of the Suez Canal contributed
to the stabilization of the Middle East.

For the next two years, contributing to the stabilization of the
Middle East absorbed an enormous amount of Kissinger's time and
energy. As he pointed out at a luncheon he gave for Prince Fahd of
Saudi Arabia in mid-1974, "I think it is a very fortuitous and happy
coincidence that His Royal Highness and I should be visiting Washington at the same time . . . I had an opportunity to discuss his
itinerary with His Royal Highness, and I noticed that His Royal
Highness returns to the Middle East *after* I do."

Kissinger, who compared the Middle East to the Balkans before World War I, set out to do what was achievable, and he knew well the distance between the desirable and the achievable. "Usually when you talk about settlements," he once told newsmen privately, "you can say a good settlement is one with which both parties are equally happy. That is beyond reach in the Middle East. The best you can do in the Middle East is to make a settlement with which both parties are relatively equally unhappy.

"What we are trying to do is to strike a balance between the concerns [on both sides] . . . We are trying to give the Israelis enough of a sense of military security so that, in hysteria, they will not strike out and try to settle things before the balance shifts against them. We are trying to give the Arabs enough of a sense of dignity so that they do not feel that they are at the mercy of the Israelis, and we are trying to create DMZs [demilitarized zones] around Israel in order to remove some of these dangers which I mentioned, so that the Israelis don't feel that by withdrawing from conquered territories, they are merely moving their enemies close to their main centers of population." Kissinger also lamented that "the history of the Middle East is a history of missed opportunities."

For Henry Kissinger, the October War provided another opportunity in the Middle East, one he did not want to miss, and that surprise conflict set in motion one of the most extraordinary exercises of personal diplomacy this country or that region has ever known. After his stop in Tel Aviv on the way back from Moscow, Kissinger returned to the Middle East eleven times in two years.

His first trip produced an agreement to stabilize the cease-fire lines and to get Egyptian-Israeli negotiations under way.

The second trip led to the opening of a Middle East Peace Conference in Geneva.

His third trip engaged him in a unique brand of shuttle diplomacy and resulted in an agreement between Egypt and Israel on separating their tangled forces on the Sinai Front.

His fourth trip led to disengagement negotiations between Israel and Syria.

His fifth — and longest — trip produced a Syrian-Israeli disengagement. It took thirty-three days.

His sixth trip enabled a politically moribund President to take one more twirl across the world's diplomatic stage before exiting into exile.

His seventh trip attempted to lay out the strategy for the moderates to prevail at the Arab Summit in Rabat, Morocco.

His eighth trip attempted to repair some of the damage caused when the moderates did not prevail at Rabat, and when the Arab Summiteers designated the Palestine Liberation Organization the sole negotiating agent for the Palestinians.

His ninth trip set up negotiations between Israel and Egypt for a second disengagement agreement in the Sinai.

His tenth trip failed to achieve the agreement.

His eleventh trip did.

Of the traveling press, I was the only one who went eleven for eleven in the Middle East. Bernie Gwertzman of the New York *Times,* Bruce van Voorst of *Newsweek,* and Barry Schweid of the AP went ten for eleven, missing only the presidential trip. They could claim they dealt only with substance.

Kissinger also conducted a round of Middle East diplomacy in the summer of '74 in a highly unusual fashion — he stayed at home and the foreign ministers went to *him* — one at a time, of course.

He was intrigued — and challenged — by the complexities of the Arab-Israeli conflict. During one of his first missions, he commented, "At the beginning of the year, I was dealing with three Vietnamese parties. At the end of the year, I was dealing with one Jewish and four Arab parties. That's what Dante wrote about in *The Inferno.*" At the time, Kissinger described the Israeli-Egyptian negotiations as the "most difficult I've ever experienced." That characterization lasted only as long as the beginning of Israel's negotiations with Syria. The difficulty of the Syrian shuttle was then superseded by the second Egyptian-Israeli negotiations, which he said made all previous experiences look like "pattycake."

Shortly after the completion of the Syrian shuttle, Israeli Defense

Minister Moshe Dayan came to Washington, and I interviewed him on the *Today* program. Before we went on the air, Israeli Ambassador Simcha Dinitz and I were chatting. I noted that Kissinger had started out in the Middle East believing that Jerusalem would be the most difficult of all the Arab-Israeli problems to resolve, but after the Syrian-Israeli talks, he now felt that the Golan Heights would be the most difficult.

"That's typical of Henry," Dinitz said. "He always thinks the problem he was just working on is the most difficult."

"I guess that's so," I said. "Besides," I added, "he says he's got a solution for Jerusalem anyway."

Dayan and Dinitz did a double-take and sat upright in their chairs, as though I had just spilled coffee in their laps.

"What solution?" asked Dinitz. "What's the solution?"

"Well," I said, "on the plane, Kissinger told us that the main cause of the Jerusalem problem is the fact that King Faisal [of Saudi Arabia] wants to be buried there, so Kissinger says all you have to do is get Faisal to convert, and the problem is solved."

Both men smiled, then Dinitz said, "You tell Henry, Faisal doesn't even have to convert, we'll bury him in Jerusalem."

Dayan quickly added, "Look, tell him Faisal doesn't even have to die, we'll bury him in Jerusalem."

The most innovative feature of Kissinger's Middle East travel was shuttle diplomacy. It came about quite accidentally. On his third trip to the area, in January 1974, Kissinger was trying to get Egypt and Israel to agree to disengagement proposals, which he thought they would then convey to their official teams at the Geneva conference for negotiation. He told reporters it was not "likely" that he would function as a courier between the two countries. When he met with Anwar Sadat, however, the Egyptian President suggested that Kissinger "stay in the area" and make a personal effort to work out a disengagement agreement rather than leaving it to the technicians on both sides. Kissinger, astounded, asked, "Instead of negotiations in Geneva?" "For sure," replied Sadat. And that's how Henry Kissinger began flying back and forth between Aswan and Tel Aviv.

When Kissinger was later being pressed by a reporter about one of the more subtle points involved in the negotiations, he glibly tossed off a rationale for shuttling that stands up as well as any other. "If it could all be expressed on paper," he said, "they would be sending notes to each other."

Who coined the actual phrase "shuttle diplomacy"? The answer is lost somewhere among the shifting sands of the Middle East. The first known reference appeared in the New York *Times* under the by-line of Bernard Gwertzman, who wrote on January 11, 1974, about an "unorthodox bit of shuttle diplomacy." Barry Schweid of the AP wrote after the first round trip that Kissinger was "shuttling" back and forth. That same day, Assistant Secretary of State Joseph Sisco came to the back section of the plane a few minutes before taking off from Aswan and said in a loud voice, "Welcome aboard the Egyptian-Israeli shuttle!" Sisco, who had formerly been involved in UN affairs, was thinking about the Eastern Airlines shuttle between New York and Washington. Schweid, a New Yorker transplanted to Washington, was more parochial. He was thinking about the shuttle train between Grand Central Station and Penn Station in Manhattan. *Newsweek* correspondent Bruce van Voorst filed a line about "shuttlecock diplomacy." He's from Michigan.

Whatever the origin of the term, Gwertzman was certainly prescient about its future. After quoting Sisco's outcry, he wrote: "Mr. Sisco . . . was reflecting the feeling of most members of the party traveling with Secretary of State Kissinger that the shuttle had somehow become a permanent fixture in Middle Eastern diplomacy."

Shuttle diplomacy went hand in hand, of course, with step-by-step diplomacy in the Middle East. But whereas the shuttles were improvised, the steps were not. In order to proceed one step at a time, however, Kissinger needed a larger framework for the negotiations, so he conceived the Geneva Peace Conference as a negotiating umbrella for Middle East peace talks. And it took a considerable amount of mediating merely to get the umbrella up.

During all the preconference haggling over the wording of the invitations, Kissinger cracked, "This could well be the only diplo-

matic conference in history which begins before invitations are sent."
When Syria decided not to go to Geneva, Kissinger said sardonically,
"I don't think the Israeli Cabinet will have to meet in special session
to reaffirm *their* readiness to attend." En route to the opening session, Kissinger acknowledged the long odds at Geneva, but he took
an upbeat view: "With agony, good will, luck, and patience —
and I don't want to underestimate luck — you could just shape
something out of this."

In Geneva, Kissinger showed his determination to hold the middle
ground by quoting both Arab and Jew in his speech. He even showed
some linguistic daring by lapsing into Arabic to say, *"Eli fat mat,"*
which means, "The past is dead." His accent provoked laughter from
Egyptians watching on television. On the other side, he quoted the
Jewish sage Hillel, but without naming him: "If I am not for myself,
who is for me? But if I am for myself alone, who am I?" Afterward,
an Egyptian diplomat noted, "Kissinger was masterful. He used a
Jewish proverb to get at the Jews, and an Arab proverb to get at the
Arabs."

But Kissinger knew the past was not really dead — not yet. He felt
the Israelis could never really negotiate in Geneva with the rest of
the Arabs arrayed against them, since they were not secure enough
in the wake of the 1973 war to confront all of their problems at once
— withdrawal from the occupied territory, the Palestinian problem,
peace. Step-by-step diplomacy was designed to protect Israel from
facing all of its problems and all of its adversaries at the same time.
"It's in Israel's interest," he said then, privately, "that not all these
issues be handled simultaneously. It's better for them that we are
doing it rather than some international forum. You could argue that
what's being done now is the best means of keeping the pressures
tolerable on Israel." Ironically, however, a lot of Israelis wanted to
argue differently. They complained that Kissinger was putting too
much pressure on them to make concessions, and some eventually
even called for a return to the Geneva Conference.

It was clear that although Egypt and Israel were supposed to be
negotiating "directly" at Geneva, Kissinger's personal involvement

was needed because the two countries did not yet have any real experience in dealing with each other. And they still distrusted each other so much that they found it easier — and probably necessary — to negotiate through an intermediary. Kissinger, however, never considered himself a mere mediator. He originally thought of himself as a catalyst, an agent who made diplomatic interaction possible. But his role obviously turned out to be even more intense than that.

Shuttle diplomacy was made to order for Kissinger's style and talents. Flying among Middle Eastern capitals, he enjoyed one advantage that he could never quite achieve entirely in Washington. He alone knew what each side was saying and thinking at all times. And he was able to convey each side's thinking to the other in a part of the world accustomed to dealing with middlemen and back channels and emissaries rather than in direct, straightforward communication. A close aide gave the Secretary's role a wry cultural-geographical overlay: "He was about as conspiratorial as the people he was dealing with. They found a kindred spirit."

However, Kissinger was continuously suspected of talking out of both sides of the tent. And he resented such suspicions. When reports appeared that he told the Israelis one thing and the Egyptians another, he carped, "Contrary to what you see in the newspapers, you can assume I tell the same story to everybody. It's the only way I can survive for any length of time." In fact, Kissinger claimed on his way to Geneva, in reference to the oil embargo problem, "You may not believe it, but what I say in private is not very different from what I have said in public." And he was right. Some of us did not believe it.

Just before beginning the second Sinai shuttle, Kissinger explained to newsmen on his plane, "You know that my whole style of negotiations depends upon gaining the confidence of both sides and not ramming it down throats. Anything you ram down their throats makes you enormously vulnerable." And for the most part he did have the confidence of both sides. Israeli Foreign Minister Yigal Allon once welcomed Kissinger at the airport by remarking, "I couldn't think of any other person in the world today but Dr. Kissinger who could go to any Arab capital he wishes and from there go to Israel" with the eager concurrence of both sides, in the hope and belief that each would benefit by his mission. After he was out of office, however, Kissinger himself acknowledged (in an article written for *Time* magazine) that "no nation or leader will ever be totally certain whether an intermediary's account of the views of the opposing side reflects reality, gullibility, or his own preference. The mere fact that an intermediary was necessary — that direct talks were rejected — reflected and fueled the prevailing distrust."

Kissinger had one other extremely useful personal asset that made him a valuable shuttler. He was willing to take the heat from both sides. Each side said things to him that would probably have caused a breakdown in the negotiations if said directly to the other side. He served as a buffer for their anger and frustration, which, in turn, they moderated because they were dealing with the American Secretary of State rather than a hated enemy.

Not only were the perceptions different on each side. So was the very process of negotiating. Kissinger never expected it to be easy. As he explained, "When people have been shooting at one another for twenty-five years, the problem is not contracting. They don't rush into compromise."

In a way, however, it was easier for him in the Arab world — in Cairo and Damascus — than in Israel. Sisco once pointed out that "the Jerusalem stops were vastly more fatiguing than Aswan. You had to explain everything a half dozen times." But then, so are the people different: The Israelis apply Talmudic interpretations to every written word. They give much more weight to the components of the negotiation than to the personalities of the negotiators. The Arabs, on the other hand, place great faith in personal relationships, and once mutual trust has been established, the details of the negotiation are less important.

One important feature of Kissinger's catalytic mediation came to be known as "constructive ambiguity." When a reporter tried to pin him down on the difference of interpretation between Israel and Egypt over the nature of the Geneva Conference, he burst out, "For

Christ's sake, leave everyone their face-saving formula! If it pleases the Israelis to consider it direct if they are in the same room with Egyptians and Sadat prefers to call this indirect if somebody else is there, what the hell difference does it make?" That kind of pragmatism and flexibility also helped his shuttling efforts. He entered the negotiations with a flexible scenario. There was no ideological involvement, no interfering preconvictions. He believed that what worked was what worked. As an aide once explained, "The secret of Kissinger's success is that he combines American pragmatism with German thoroughness." Plus a lot more.

How did Kissinger himself see his role? He once told us, "My contribution can be in shaping their perceptions and in influencing their positions before they get to each other, or even later, so that they come closer to each other's position." He was always careful to allow each side to project what it wanted. He constantly made the point that he couldn't allow himself to be in the position of acting as a "lawyer" for either side. He was also careful not to insert his personal recommendations into a negotiation until he felt the parties themselves had exhausted their own possibilities for bridging gaps.

Don Wright, *The Miami News*, The New York Times Syndicate

"In negotiations," he explained, "if you put down specific proposals before you know where you're going, it is almost suicidal." In a self-deprecating aside, Kissinger himself later remarked on his technique, "In any negotiation, there's a deadlock. In my case, I talked so much, nobody noticed."

Whenever he had a spare moment — and even when he didn't — he would break away from the negotiating shuttle to fly to other Arab capitals to explain what he was doing and why. This was done so that "they realized the difficulties that arose were due to the objective nature of the problem . . . rather than to this or that failure on the part of the United States."

On a day when his schedule included meetings with King Hussein in Amman, President Assad in Damascus, and Prime Minister Rabin in Jerusalem, Kissinger observed, "Nobody will say I'm on a government-paid vacation."

All that travel reflected his serious concern that if his Middle East peace mediation failed, either the Arabs or the Israelis — or both — would hold the United States responsible in general and Kissinger in particular. "If I've learned one thing in this job," he said, "it is that you cannot bank good will. You can be a hero today and a villain tomorrow."

Apart from the immediate results, Kissinger's diplomacy had a psychological impact that was significant and probably enduring. Henry Kissinger made the Arabs respectable in America. Until the 1973 war, the Arabs were perceived as backward, inept, bumbling, loud-mouthed, laughable, and pro-Russian. The image was accurately projected in an offbeat way by a Washington delicatessen that celebrated the Israeli victory in the 1967 war by offering a new item on its menu, the Nasser sandwich. It was half chicken, half tongue — with Russian dressing. Kissinger himself acknowledged that he thought of Anwar Sadat as a "clown" following Nasser's death. Stories about the latest coup d'état in Syria were thrown away in American newsrooms, and Hafez Assad was hardly a household word. Or, as ABC's Herb Kaplow punned on the first trip to Damascus, Hafez Assad is better than no Assad at all. Saudi Arabia was a flashback to the fifteenth century, and only Jordan had some respectability because of King Hussein's frequent visits to Washington.

But Kissinger's constant travel to Arab capitals, the pictures of him with Arab leaders, and his positive descriptions of them in his briefings helped change the American concept. And so did simple exposure. While the time spent by the traveling press corps in Arab capitals did not turn them into instant Arabists, it did help them to see — as Kissinger did — that there were indeed two sides to the story, and the heavily pro-Israel bias in the American press began to be moderated.

One top Middle East hand said that Kissinger achieved success in the Arab world because "he had an instinctive ability to deal with the Arabs. He knew how to reach them — in their sense of national pride, their strong sense of the individual. Kissinger used to say, 'The Arab world is the last place where there are heroic individuals. This isn't an organizational society . . . It's a society where individual personality makes a difference and is important.' "

Kissinger seemed ambivalent about the personalizing of Middle East diplomacy. He kept complaining that some other way should be found to negotiate, but he never found it. After the second round of talks between Israel and Egypt had broken down, one of his staffers sought to console him, saying, "I just want you to know how much I share your personal disappointment. We feel terribly let down. We know how hard you've worked and how much you've tried." Kissinger quickly replied, "This is not anything personal. Don't get me into this."

Yet, on the flight out of Israel, Kissinger commented stoically, "There is no question that it will be argued that it was my fault. That's fair enough because if it succeeds, I get the credit." The Secretary's irritation flared, however, when a reporter said, "A lot of Israelis ask, 'What about Kissinger? What is this going to mean to him?' Can you throw it around a little bit?" Kissinger replied angrily, "No, I cannot throw it around. It is totally indecent to discuss the question as though I am running around the Middle East for my own position. I think that's a disgrace."

Although Kissinger may not have been "personally" involved, his person certainly was. Israeli Prime Minister Yitzhak Rabin told me, "I don't believe any of the agreements would have been reached without shuttle diplomacy. I don't think anybody else could have done it. Only by using shuttle diplomacy could he get both sides to create the atmosphere that in itself made agreement possible, even [transcending] real issues. None would have been possible without Kissinger's stamina."

The Secretary's stamina was legendary. The Middle East shuttles were brutally fatiguing for almost everybody except the central figure. The shuttles were almost like military campaigns. John Maclean of the Chicago *Tribune* recalled lyrically in print:

> For journalists, traveling on those early, successful shuttles was an unmatchable experience. It was like being part of a Shakespearean history play, speeded up by modern technology.
>
> The untidy, everyday world of wives and children, debts and uncut lawns, disappeared. Instead, you became part of a vital force, exhausting and exhilarating at the same time.
>
> Living history unfolded in a wave which swept all before it. Petty matters of hotel reservations, food and beverage were handled by others. You were free to become part of the "flow," the word psychologists use to describe this sense of absorption.

Kissinger himself and the members of his party were caught up in the "flow" more than anyone else. As one close aide recalled, the Secretary "was much more pleasant to work with on these trips than back in Washington. It was fun to deal with him on an uninterrupted problem, which got all his concentration." Another top official said that although the members of the Kissinger team occasionally got brusque with one another because their nerves were frazzled or time was short, seldom was heard a disagreeable word. "Among professionals," he said, "it was an incredible human experience. The people became so close to each other that you could divide labor with just a word. There was no arguing, no false pride, for example, about who would draft a message or other menial jobs." The temperament of the people around Kissinger was important. Instead of picking up his turmoil, they calmed it down, spread it out, cushioned it.

Two of Kissinger's brightest and hardest-working aides were the assistant secretary for Near Eastern affairs, Alfred "Roy" Atherton, Jr., and Harold Saunders, a former NSC staffer who became deputy assistant secretary of state and eventually director of the State Department's Bureau of Intelligence and Research. They were both calm, extremely soft-spoken men, who came to tolerate Kissinger's outbursts.

"Calm" and "soft-spoken" would not be used, however, to describe Joe Sisco, the hard-driving assistant secretary of state for Near Eastern affairs whom Kissinger later named as undersecretary for political affairs, the number one job in the Foreign Service for a career officer short of the Secretary's chair (although Sisco had never served overseas). Sisco described himself as a Mediterranean, by which he meant volatile and volcanic. And on occasion he would let go, screaming at Kissinger, "What the fuck do you think you're doing?" Kissinger would reply indignantly, "You can't talk to the Secretary of State like that." And Sisco would shout back, "When you act like the Secretary of State, I'll talk to you like the Secretary of State." Or at least that's one overheard version. During an especially bumpy descent on one of the early shuttles, Sisco was thrown against the Xerox machine, which he grabbed to keep from falling. "Quick," shouted a staffer, "turn it off! We can't take more than one Sisco at a time."

One official recalled that the shuttles were characterized by a great esprit de corps among the American team. Everyone felt tremendous pride in what he — and his country — were doing. "There's no other government in the world," the official said, "that would even have tried to do that sort of thing. People were buoyed by the exhilaration of a mission, even at the purely mechanical level."

Kissinger often disguised his own feelings about the shuttles with humor. Wandering to the back of the plane after one trying stop, Kissinger exclaimed, "When I leave this job, I can become the director of an insane asylum. I've been well trained for it." At times, we felt like the inmates.

Israel

It took only a cookie and a cigarette to dramatize the enormous gulf that separated Israel from its geographic neighbors. The time was early December, and Kissinger was visiting Israel for the first time with accompanying press. He had just completed a swing through the Arab world, including the first trip to Damascus by an American Secretary of State since the 1950s.

I was walking down the hall where most of the members of the press had rooms in the King David Hotel in Jerusalem. Marilyn Berger of the Washington *Post* was just leaving her room. A maid was inside cleaning. Marilyn had bought some sesame cookies during the stopover in Damascus, and she offered one to the maid. But the maid refused to take one. "Not if it comes from Syria," she said.

Two days earlier, I had been riding in the back seat of a car provided by the Syrian government. Hank Trewhitt of the Baltimore *Sun* was riding in the front seat as we sped from the airport to downtown Damascus at speeds up to ninety miles an hour. Trewhitt was smoking, and he offered a cigarette to the driver in primitive sign language. The driver refused. Trewhitt tried to persuade him, but he was adamant. Finally the driver said, "Israel," with the Arabic inflection that makes it comes out Iz-ray-*el,* with the accent on the last syllable.

The maid in Jerusalem and the driver on the road to Damascus personalized the Arab-Israeli conflict for me much more vividly than any briefing paper or history book.

In fact, for newsmen, part of the exhilaration of the shuttling was precisely that ability to go directly across forbidden frontiers, to spend the day in the Arab world and the night in Israel and compare notes in a way that no other journalists could do.

During the shuttle, Kissinger spent much more time in Israel than in the Arab countries. One reason was simple convenience. The communications were better, and the accommodations were, too. Another was political. He had to spend more time haggling with the Israelis, who, unlike the Arabs, struggled with a democratic form of government. He once joked, "I see more of your Cabinet than my own."

Whereas Kissinger could deal directly, and alone, with presidents and kings in the Arab world, he had to deal collectively with a team of individualistic negotiators in Israel, or at times with the entire Cabinet, many of whose members disliked each other intensely. The animosity between Prime Minister Yitzhak Rabin and his challenger for primacy within the Labor party, Defense Minister Shimon Peres, was no secret, and it was frequently on display in the negotiating sessions.

During the first Egyptian-Israeli shuttle, Kissinger once returned to Jerusalem well past midnight rather than stay in Aswan so he could begin the time-consuming negotiations with the Israelis early the next morning.

The large delegation-to-delegation meetings were not only time-consuming, they were often histrionic as well, and at times the Israelis seemed to be performing for each other, positioning themselves politically. Kissinger used to lament in private that "Israel has no foreign policy. It only has domestic politics."

To illustrate that point, an American diplomat revived an old story, probably apocryphal, about Golda Meir's visit to Washington when she was foreign minister during the Kennedy years. She was talking to Attorney General Bobby Kennedy, who explained how the United States had become so tolerant that "we now have a Catholic President. Maybe," he said, "in twenty years, we'll even have a Jewish President." "We already have one," replied Golda. "It doesn't help."

One top Middle East hand recalled that while Kissinger used to "joke with the Israelis, more often he was emotional or irritated — and so tired. At times," he said, "Kissinger got just plain mad at the Israelis for being unreasonable, shortsighted, and obtuse about their own interests. He'd get mad at them as a government and he'd get mad at them as individuals across the table for not pulling together." Yet, remembers another aide, "there was a family atmosphere — we didn't have to question each other's basic motives, and therefore we could fight. There *were* fights, but it was always like fighting in the family."

Kissinger himself once described the Israelis as "exhausting negotiating partners." He said, "Periods verge on being obnoxious because of the pettiness and pressure and psychological warfare. They put out stories that they know you are going to betray them." But Kissinger showed understanding: "In a historic sense, you have to say, 'They may be right . . .' Their margin of survival is so narrow that unless they make themselves impossibly difficult, they may be driven right over the precipice altogether . . . They have a deep sense of historic tragedy . . . and they are in mortal danger right now. They do face an actively hostile world in which we are the only ones who are pursuing policies generally parallel to their interests."

Prior to the Geneva Conference in December 1973, Kissinger felt the most important part of his preconference diplomacy was his visit to Jerusalem. The Israelis seemed to be working themselves into a state of hysterical paranoia. Kissinger had a long talk with the Cabinet at Foreign Minister Abba Eban's home and then with the General Staff the next morning. He came away struck by the Israelis' sense of isolation. "They're a people who fled from the ghettoes of Europe to set up their own country in the Middle East," he said, "and now that country has itself become a ghetto internationally." As an example of Israeli anxiety, he cited Ambassador Simcha

Dinitz's perceived need to talk to him "ten times a day" when they were in Washington.*

Leaving Geneva after the opening session of the conference, Kissinger spoke again with great feeling about Israel's problems. "The country has gone through a great psychological trauma," he said. "On October fifth, its position was unassailable — militarily invulnerable, diplomatically untouchable. Three weeks later, all that had changed. It was heartbreaking," he went on, "to go there and see how totally dependent Israel is on the United States."

He talked about the "horrible dilemma" facing Israel in choosing between its options, that is, security versus the risks of a peace settlement. But he had no doubt about Israel's survival, at least not publicly. He told a magazine interviewer at the end of December 1974, "The United States — and finally, in the last analysis, Europe — will not negotiate over the survival of Israel. This would be an act of such extraordinary cynicism that the world would be morally mortgaged if it ever happened. But it won't happen."

Apart from his own analysis of the Israeli national psyche, Kissinger was probably influenced by a conversation that Golda Meir recounts in her autobiography, *My Life*. Mrs. Meir was in Washington in October 1973, talking about the problems of the cease-fire lines in the Sinai. "They were not easy or pleasant talks," she wrote, "but then we were not discussing easy matters . . . At one stage I said to him, 'You know, all we have, really, is our spirit. What you are asking me to do is to go home and help defeat that spirit, and then no [American] aid will be necessary at all.' " Kissinger constantly returned to the question of "spirit" whenever the issue of American pressure on Israel was raised. He reflected Mrs. Meir's concern about the "breaking" of Israel's spirit, which he felt would crack its will to resist and lead to the disintegration of the Jewish state.

---

*That was something of an exaggeration. But Dinitz did have a direct "hot line" telephone to Kissinger's office, and he used it often. Before becoming Ambassador, Dinitz was known as "Golda's Kissinger," a bright, articulate, charming, witty, wisecracking adviser to the Prime Minister. In Washington, he worked as hard as Kissinger did and with a single-mindedness that made him effective with a large constituency that included Congress and the American Jewish community as well as the Executive Branch of the U.S. Government.

Ambassador Dinitz recalls a time when the United States and Israel were having a "difficult argument, and when some people were blaming us for intransigence, and Kissinger said, 'The Jews have not survived five thousand years because they were soft.' "

Still, Kissinger frequently felt the Israelis sacrificed their long-term interests for short-term benefits that provided only fleeting advantage. As one top aide put it, "Henry really honestly felt that he knew what was the best thing for the Israelis, and he was right, in that sense."

Whatever his private frustrations, he did not shy away from joking in public about the difficulty of negotiating with the Israelis. At the end of his first visit to Jerusalem with a full entourage, he brought Abba Eban aboard the plane for a quick tour before leaving. In the press section, Kissinger explained with amusement that Eban had once defined objectivity as ".one hundred percent agreement with Israel's point of view." Kissinger later amused an American Jewish audience by recounting that story and adding, "I thought Eban was joking when he made that remark. I realized later that he was threatening me."

"ANYTHING! I'LL SIGN ANYTHING IF ONLY YOU PROMISE TO GO HOME!"

Kissinger's difficult dealings with the Israelis were typified in an incident during the second Israeli-Egyptian negotiation on disengagement in the Sinai. One of the most disputed issues involved an uninterrupted access road for Egypt through Israeli-held territory to the Abu Rodeis oil fields. After Kissinger had presented the Israeli proposal on the issue, he found that the line the Israelis had drawn for the road was under water at all times, even at low tide! His reaction was quite predictable. When the Israelis put forward their map documenting their supposed withdrawal from the Mitla and Gidda passes in the Sinai, American officials checked it carefully and found that the Israeli line went right through the middle of the passes. Once the explosive anger had passed, however, Kissinger used to laugh about it in the retelling.

Of all the Israelis, Golda Meir was clearly Kissinger's favorite. During one of their disputes, Mrs. Meir finally said in exasperation, "Look, what do you want from me? I was born in the last century." Kissinger replied with a puckish smile, "The nineteenth century is my specialty."

Golda's specialties were strength and leadership, and Kissinger respected and admired those qualities. A close associate recalls that during the late stages of the Syrian shuttle, Kissinger went to Jerusalem with a new Syrian proposal on the number of troops to be permitted in the limited forces zone. The figures were way too high, and the Israelis blew up. Kissinger lectured them on how important it was to keep the Syrians engaged in the peace process — engaged in disengagement, as it were — and to put the question of numbers in perspective by taking a look at the next step. Golda went off for twenty minutes with her negotiating team, then came back and said, "Go get the best numbers you can."

However, his frequent bouts of exasperation in Israel extended to her as well, especially when she would go back over the history of the Jews in Europe before getting to the matter at hand. That was one of her ploys to counter the "dire consequences" ploy of Kissinger. Her presentation troubled and irritated him, and since he too had been a Jew in Europe, he found it somewhat superfluous, not to say annoying. One of Mrs. Meir's closest associates said she frequently let the Secretary of State know that while "there's no greater expert on American policy than Kissinger, on Israeli policy, she had her Ph.D." And she once twitted him, "The United States will never be alone. Israel will always be with you."

In *My Life,* Mrs. Meir described her relationship with Henry Kissinger as "very complicated," but it was clear the respect and admiration were mutual:

> At this point [October 1973] the outstanding personality in the Middle East became not President Sadat, or President Assad, or King Faisal or even Mrs. Meir. It was the U.S. Secretary of State, Dr. Henry Kissinger, whose efforts on behalf of peace in the area can only be termed superhuman. My own relationship with Henry Kissinger had its ups and downs. At times it became very complicated, and at times I know I annoyed and perhaps even angered him — and vice versa. But I admired his intellectual gifts, his patience and his perseverance were always limitless, and in the end we became good friends . . . I think that possibly one of the most impressive of Kissinger's many impressive qualities is his fantastic capacity for dealing with the minutest details of whatever problems he undertakes to solve.

Kissinger genuinely regretted Mrs. Meir's departure from the Prime Minister's office, although he joked that his favorite regime in Israel was a caretaker government. "There's nothing more stable than a caretaker government," he said, "since the ministers can't resign."

We once asked Kissinger whether it was easier dealing with the Sabras (native-born Israelis) than with the old generation. "Easier," said Kissinger; then after thinking a bit, he added, "and harder. For them the existence of Israel is not a miracle but a fact. This group," he continued, "is humanly less warm than the generation of Golda. But they are 'Mideast.' You can't be sure that the world map in Golda's head is not centered in Europe. For Rabin it is more matter of fact that the center is Israel."

The Secret Service agents were also sorry to see Golda go. She used to leave the negotiating sessions, and like a good Jewish mother, she checked to make sure they had coffee and cake and that every-thing was comfortable for them during their long waits.

Mrs. Meir's successor was Yitzhak Rabin, a military hero and former Chief of Staff who had known and worked with Kissinger during a long stint as an Ambassador in Washington. But Kissinger found Rabin somewhat indecisive and not too straightforward, and he felt Rabin overanalyzed everything. He rather liked the new defense minister, Shimon Peres, whom he found more direct and open.

Given Kissinger's compulsion for flicking his poison tongue, his critiques of various Israeli personalities quickly found their way back to the principals. He felt Eban didn't count for a great deal in Israeli political councils, and he also thought the foreign minister's elo-quence was unfortunately matched by his prolixity. When this got back to Eban, he was personally hurt by it, but the effects were not long-lasting. Rabin was once offended when he heard that Kissinger had described him as a "peasant general" at a time when the Jewish people needed a Rothschild.

Kissinger's criticisms of individual Israeli leaders were generally made to other Israelis or to the Arabs, but never to the press. We did hear him make the point more than once that while the "farmer-soldier" had played a vital role in the founding of the State of Israel, he was no longer sufficient for the country's current needs. But he never personalized "farmer-soldier" to us.

By the same token, Kissinger was the target of criticism within Israeli circles, although government officials were cautious about going after him head-on. Usually they did it by selective leaks, which either distorted the facts or gave a partial version of an unflattering story.

On a nonofficial level, Israelis who didn't like what Kissinger was doing repeated a joke that portrayed him as a zookeeper. When he was asked about his qualifications for the job, he said he could make the lion and the lamb lie down together and he went on to prove it. He got the job, and the zoo became so renowned that people came from all over the world to see the lion and lamb lie together. Even

Kissinger's mother eventually showed up. She watched in amazement and then asked her son how he did it. "It's easy," said Kissinger. "Early every morning, before anyone comes, I put a new lamb in the cage." For the Israelis, the moral of the story was unmistakable; they were the new lambs.

As Kissinger's popularity in Israel waned, some of the criticism became more public, and even Moshe Dayan, who lost his defense portfolio when Rabin took office, criticized the Secretary's tactics in an article for an American magazine. Kissinger seemed genuinely puzzled. "If you read the record of my conversations with Dayan when he was in office," Kissinger said on the plane, "you'll find that he was more supportive of my efforts than any other Israeli leader, and in a more sweeping way than anybody is now talking about." Kissinger also thought Dayan the most innovative of all the Israeli negotiators, although he described him as "an acquired taste."

Dayan was a part of the Israeli negotiating team for the first two agreements — with Egypt and Syria — along with Prime Minister Meir and Foreign Minister Eban. Eban served as a kind of a diplomatic point man. He met Kissinger at the Tel Aviv airport, and during the hour-long drive to Jerusalem, the Secretary of State would fill him in on what had happened on his previous stops. In turn, Eban would brief the other Israeli negotiators and their aides, so that by the time the formal meetings began, the Israeli side was up to date on the general situation.

The limousine ride to Jerusalem was not only a diplomatic convenience, it was a preference. The first time Kissinger arrived in Tel Aviv with his full entourage, helicopters were waiting to take the entire group to Jerusalem. The Old City, seen from the air by night, with artistic lighting illuminating thousands of years of history, was a breathtaking sight. But Kissinger hated helicopters, especially helicopters that were buffeted by the wind on their way to a small hilltop landing pad in Jerusalem. The limousine replaced the chopper after that, although when large-scale demonstrations were staged against him during the second Israeli-Egyptian disengagement negotiations, the choppers made a comeback because of security.

The road to Jerusalem was marked with periodic reminders of recent history — the agonizing birth of the State of Israel. Significant dates were painted on rocks, and the wreckage of burnt-out trucks and armored cars had been deliberately left by the roadside — and repainted — to serve as dramatic memorials to the courage of the young nation that was almost overrun in its first days.

But Kissinger seldom showed any interest in the landscape. He wanted to talk business with his Israeli counterpart. However, on an early trip, when the car passed a building that stood in semi-isolation in the hills at Latrun, Kissinger asked Abba Eban what it was. Eban told him it was a Trappist monastery, and he explained that only one man was allowed to talk for all the monks inside. "Just like the State Department," quipped Kissinger.

Following a brief ceremony at the airport and the ride to Jerusalem, the Secretary's arrival ritual usually ended with the Grand Entrance Scene at the King David Hotel.

The lobby was roped off to allow clear passage from the front door to the elevators. As soon as the limo arrived out front, the television lights would go on as though it were an opening night. Kissinger would burst through the front door, flanked by half a dozen bodyguards, and, smiling and waving, he would stride briskly past another dozen Israeli agents while the cameramen filmed, the photographers clicked, the guests applauded and jockeyed for a better position behind the velvet ropes for a look, and while radio and television reporters tried to slow him down to get a few words on tape or film. Then he would disappear into one of the two main elevators near the reception desk. The other members of the party would dash to get into the other one, since the elevators were often held on the sixth floor while Kissinger was there, and missing the second elevator meant a long wait.

There was a lot of grumbling about the accommodations at the King David, but Kissinger himself had a huge suite on the sixth floor, with a large living room and purple furniture. It offered a splendid view of the Old City and the Valley of Kidron, which used to be a no-man's-land before Israel captured East Jerusalem from Jordan during the 1967 war.

When Kissinger looked out of his window, he could literally see the physical embodiment of the intractable conflict he was trying to resolve.

The suite did not have a balcony for enjoying the view, and that suited the security men just fine, since the hotel was within sniping distance of the Old City. (Two rockets were once found on a nearby hill aimed at this corner of the building.)

However, Kissinger was occasionally concerned about another kind of security. Although there was never any evidence that the Israelis bugged the Secretary's suite, he and Sisco sometimes took precautions anyway when they discussed highly sensitive matters. They would lean far out of the window overlooking the Old City and whisper. Of course, that did them no good at all if the windowsill were bugged.

The hotel itself deserved a footnote in history. It had served as the headquarters for the British Army when Palestine was still under British mandate, and one wing of the hotel had been blown up by the group of terrorists led by Menachem Begin, the long-time leader of the political opposition who eventually became Prime Minister.

Judging by the food at the King David, it's easy to be convinced that the explosion did permanent damage to the kitchen, which never recovered. But then, Israel was not known as a gastronomic paradise anyway. Kissinger used to wonder aloud "how a nation of a million Jewish mothers can turn out such lousy food!" Yet he didn't do badly at the table there. One hotel official recalled "he normally had two soft-boiled eggs and rolls and croissants and a little cheese and coffee for breakfast, plus vegetables and herring. He liked everything." The hotel used to stock his suite with fruits and cookies and petits fours, which, the official said, "were always gone."

Kissinger once told a Jewish audience in New York, "In recent years, I have had, as you can see [referring to his girth], the opportunity that every Jewish mother dreams of for her son — to do something for the peace of the world and never miss a meal."

The King David was strictly kosher, a circumstance that undoubtedly had something to do with the caliber of the food. Marilyn Berger once good-naturedly put the finger on me in print when I violated the rules by buying a hamburger and a grilled cheese sandwich at the poolside snack bar and then combining them into a cheeseburger. When Kissinger wanted a better meal, he and Dinitz would slip away to a downtown Italian restaurant, La Gondola, to eat before a negotiating session, even though a meal might be served at the session itself.

During Kissinger's frequent sojourns in Israel, a new Hilton hotel was completed, and the management went after the lucrative Kissinger party business, arguing that the U.S. Secretary of State should stay in an American-owned hotel, that security would be easier (true), and that it was more comfortable and more conveniently located, since it was closer to the Prime Minister's office and the Knesset, the Israeli parliament (also true). A public relations battle ensued as well as a private relations battle. The manager of the King David wrote a personal letter to Kissinger, imploring him not to move, and one story said Kissinger's aged parents were even contacted in New York in an effort to enlist them on the side of the King David.

Eventually, the struggle seemed to acquire political overtones, as though Kissinger's transfer to the Hilton would somehow symbolize a lessening of American support for Israel itself. Once the King David was wired to accommodate all of the traveling party's needs, however, it was unlikely he would move out. The closest he came to moving was during the second disengagement negotiations between Israel and Egypt, when demonstrators camped outside the King David and bellowed through microphones all night long. Kissinger called Dinitz at 4:00 A.M. and told him that unless the shouting stopped, he was moving to the Hilton in the morning. Dinitz replied he couldn't do anything about it. As it turned out, there weren't enough available rooms at the Hilton, anyway.

The security precautions at the King David extended to the cleaning women, who were always accompanied by security agents when they entered Kissinger's suite or other sensitive areas. If the maid who cleaned Kissinger's room had inadvertently seen something sensitive, it would not have mattered. She was illiterate, a Jewish immigrant from Iraq. Nevertheless, somebody once pointed out for the sake of historical perspective that at the Congress of Vienna, the maids were spies of Metternich.

A woman named Judith was in charge of the cleaning women. As part of the hotel staff, she had a security button. Even so, whenever she went into Kissinger's suite to make sure the maids had done a good job, the security men went with her. Judith came to personify the Israelis who disliked and distrusted Kissinger. She opposed the idea of giving back the Mitla and Gidda passes in the Sinai and returning the Abu Rodeis oil fields to Egypt as part of the second disengagement agreement. So she stopped smiling at Kissinger, who told Atherton, in front of Judith, "She doesn't like me anymore." "You said it!" said Judith. Only in Israel.

Judith did like Nancy Kissinger, and she once asked her, "How can a nice girl like you have a husband like that?" According to Judith, Nancy smiled graciously and replied, "He's not that bad."

When Kissinger was in town, the King David became, naturally enough, a political hot spot. It was not unusual to find a Cabinet minister or other high-ranking official in the ground-floor coffee shop. A reporter once spotted Abba Eban in the lobby at 1:00 A.M. and noted that he had lost weight. "Yes," he said, "that's Kissinger's doing." Moshe Dayan wrote in his autobiography that after leaving the Secretary's room at one-thirty in the morning following a private meeting, "I was almost dropping from fatigue, but Kissinger appeared as sprightly as ever."

While Kissinger often conferred privately with Israeli officials at the hotel, all of the negotiating sessions took place in the Prime Minister's office in an unpretentious building about fifteen minutes away or in the private home of one of the Cabinet ministers. The most impressive setting was Dayan's home in the suburbs of Tel Aviv; in the back he had a mini-museum of archaeological treasures, most of them dug up by Dayan himself.

Kissinger always tried to manage to have at least one session with the Prime Minister alone so he could get a feel for what Israel's bedrock position might be and so he could explore certain issues in a way that would not provoke prolonged debate in the larger councils.

In the group sessions, Kissinger "played the role of an extremely talented teacher put in charge of a class of disturbed children," as one Israeli leader later described it. One of the Secretary's aides recalled that he operated "at several levels. One minute he was the U.S. Secretary of State. The next moment, he was Professor Henry Kissinger, consultant to the government of Israel."

One Foreign Ministry official said, "Kissinger taught us some facts of life we didn't like to hear. But he did it in the kindest way, in the way we would have preferred." Rabin remembers him as "a compulsive talker — so full of ideas and knowledge he liked to share it with somebody. And he had to be the star in every talk."

The Israelis were initially amused by the way Kissinger would make his exposition, then turn to his aides and say, "Wasn't it that way?" as though they would disagree. But the amusement turned to exasperation, and finally one of the Israeli negotiators told him, "Please, stop asking for their approval. We believe you."

However, the Israelis did not always believe — or at least they did not always believe everything. "It's not that he lied," said one prominent Israeli diplomat. "He had a unique ability of explaining every situation in the manner most pleasing to the one who heard it. We trusted him," the diplomat added, "but with the necessary discount."

Deputy Prime Minister and Foreign Minister Yigal Allon, a former Kissinger student at Harvard, told me, "I would like to say that I trusted him to the extent that I could trust the foreign minister of any other country. I trusted his friendship, but not always his judgment. I never doubted I was talking to a friend of Israel. He was loyal to Israel in his way."

Rabin recalled that "Kissinger had a Metternichian system of telling only half the truth. He didn't lie. He would have lost credibility. He didn't tell the whole truth. He stressed certain points he wanted out of proportion to the proportions of the parties.

"He was a good manipulator of people and situations. He created a kind of personal relationship with those with whom he negotiated, so that regardless of the fact that everyone knew he didn't tell the whole truth, he created a kind of intensive relationship that forced people to be in a way committed to him."

Shimon Peres remembered that "if you didn't listen exactly word by word, you could be carried away by what he said. But if you listened word by word, he wasn't lying."

Kissinger frequently arrived late for his meetings with the Israeli negotiators, but he would never apologize. They assumed he had been delayed by phone calls to Washington and that he was more likely to make sensitive calls to the United States from Israel than from the Arab countries.

However, said Eban, "there was no one breathing down his neck from Washington . . . Kissinger was plenipotentiary. He occasionally would say he had to discuss something with the President, but clearly he was in charge."

Joe Sisco endorsed that view. "Kissinger," he said, "was a de facto President. It was terrifying in a way [the presidential situation in Washington], but Kissinger was a terribly responsible person."

Kissinger often began a meeting by telling amusing or derogatory stories about the Arabs (just as he told the Arabs amusing stories about the Israelis). He once cracked that if someone told him the Arabs were with him a hundred percent, "that's when he would start looking for the knife."

However, the Israelis never quite believed the stories Kissinger told about Egyptian Foreign Minister Fahmy or Minister of War Gamasy storming out of a meeting in anger or his accounts of private meetings with President Sadat, who had to have "tremendous concessions to keep Fahmy on board." (Kissinger also claimed that Fahmy, for his part, had talked Gamasy out of resigning at one critical point.) They felt that was part of the Kissinger act.

Kissinger flattered the negotiators by contrasting the efficiency he found in Israel to the renowned inefficiency of the Arab world. In one session, he told an aide to go get an important document, then added for the benefit of his hosts, "The Israelis probably have it on microfilm already anyway."

As usual, he used humor to relieve tension, but his stamina was a more important negotiating tool. "He relied on his stamina," said Eban, "as a tactic in the negotiations, continuing through day and night, especially when there was a readiness to conclude something and the question was how to finalize it."

Once a negotiation was under way, "Kissinger's main strength was logical analysis," in the words of one of the participants. His technique, said another, "was to give us a picture of the predicament of the other side, what was the limit of their domestic consensus. He never rejected outright what the Israelis suggested. He would just say that it couldn't be accepted by the other side." "He would never argue directly," recalled still another. "Instead, he would say he was in complete agreement with what you said, and only then would he explain why he opposed what you were saying."

"There was no pressure," said Allon. "You had the feeling that time was unlimited . . . he tried to persuade you." One of the Secretary's top Middle East aides concurred. "I didn't see any pressure in the way he operated. Dipping into the mode as professor-consultant, he shared the traditions, customs, and heritage of many of the people around the table. 'Let me analyze this for you,' he would say. 'If you do this, you will have that . . . If you do not have an agreement, then you will eventually face isolation,' pointing out the alternatives down the road which they themselves were not willing to confront. He'd point out that all of the forces that converged against Israel in 1973 would join together again. He did it not in the sense of using pressure or a threat, but in pointing out reality."

Kissinger was quite accomplished in presenting his version of the Apocalypse. However, one Foreign Ministry official remembered that "Kissinger tended to overplay his hand, to exaggerate in describing the apocalyptic future which Israel faced unless it did exactly what Dr. Kissinger prescribed for it. It was very impressive the first time, less so the second time. He kept repeating it, yet every time the performance was as fascinating as if you heard it for the first time."

The Israeli negotiators even concocted a "Kissinger lexicon," which defined some of his favorite words: "suicidal" meant "difficult"; "impossible" meant "unlikely"; "difficult to get" meant "achievable"; "I will see what I can do" meant "I already got that concession long ago."

Apart from his formidable negotiating talents, Kissinger enjoyed one other overriding asset. He represented the United States of America. As Eban pointed out, "There was a unity between the power of the United States and Kissinger's virtuosity. Another American would not have been as successful as he was, and Kissinger would not have been successful if he had represented Luxembourg."

As an American, Kissinger was able to offer the parties compromises that they would not offer each other. In fact, the deadlock in the first Israeli-Egyptian negotiations was broken when both sides said they were more willing to sign an American proposal than one offered by the other side. The sticking points turned out to be somewhat less negotiable than Kissinger anticipated, but he was not concerned how it looked for an American Secretary of State to be shuttling back and forth between two Middle Eastern countries that were haggling over numbers like rug merchants. His view was, if it brought peace, it wouldn't matter how it looked.

At one point, it looked as though Kissinger was shuttling between sickbeds. In Aswan, Sadat was suffering from bronchitis, and in Jerusalem, Golda Meir was suffering from shingles, a painful nerve disease. Kissinger commented, "I guess I make her nervous."

When Ambassador Kenneth Keating greeted Kissinger at the airport, he joked, "You shouldn't try to go to bed with Golda; she has shingles." Ambassador Dinitz quickly added, "You shouldn't try to go to bed with Golda even if she didn't have shingles." For Mrs. Meir, it was no laughing matter.

The first time Kissinger saw Keating in Jerusalem, he told the former New York senator jokingly that he would never again be appointed an ambassador. The reason was simple: "Everywhere you go, a war breaks out." Keating had previously served in New Delhi, and while he was there, an Indo-Pakistani war broke out. His transfer to Israel was followed by the October 1973 war. Keating, the politician turned diplomat, advised Kissinger to give the matter some second — and Machiavellian — thoughts. "Perhaps," he said, "there's someplace in the world where you wouldn't mind having a war." Kissinger laughed and said after instant reconsideration, Keating might be reassigned within a week.

When the Egyptian-Israeli disengagement was just about completed, a surprise snowstorm draped a couple of inches of snow over the bright sandstone city of Jerusalem. I imagined that Golda Meir had once said to Kissinger, "It will snow in Jerusalem before I sign an agreement with the Egyptians!" It snowed, and she signed.

The snow infused the city with an unusual beauty. It also paralyzed its operations. The city's hilly streets were virtually impassable. Meetings had to be delayed and their sites changed, all of which slowed down the process of consultations that Kissinger was trying to finish by the end of the day.

The power went out at the King David, and the electric typewriters stopped producing four originals of all documents. Kissinger was screaming and ranting. An emergency generator was wheeled in by Arab workers who didn't speak much English. Communications between them and the staff quickly broke down. Sisco and Tom Pickering, of the Secretariat, plugged the generator into the wrong socket; the only light they produced was a shower of sparks and the generator shorted out. Finally, the secretaries managed to borrow manual typewriters and type as best they could, spurred on by the Germanic voice that kept bellowing, "Where the hell are the documents?"

The manager of the King David, Avraham Weiner, was one of the first people who knew an agreement was imminent besides the negotiators themselves. But not because of the typing. He got a call from the Prime Minister's office "to bring champagne," and as he astutely noted, "Champagne you don't drink for nothing."

The snowstorm caused a special problem for the television reporters. It prevented us from driving to Herzliya, about an hour and fifteen minutes from Jerusalem, so we had to broadcast from the studio in Jerusalem itself, where there were no color TV facilities. Our reports were broadcast in black and white. We were driven to the studio on the snow-covered roads in open jeeps, and we had to thaw out before going on the air.

The snow had slowed down Kissinger's departure from Jerusalem. Since the roads were unmanageable, the Israelis laid on a train from Jerusalem to the airport. The Israeli Army provided a two-and-a-half-ton truck to carry the Kissinger party's baggage from the King David to the train. But the truck was trapped in an alley behind the hotel by a bakery truck, whose driver had hot bread to deliver and who refused to let the baggage truck out. The Americans drove the bakery truck out of the alley themselves and left it in the street so they could get the baggage to the train on time.

John Maclean of the Chicago *Tribune* wrote poetically of the journey: "As the train passed miles of orange groves, its passengers saw a picture of the waste brought on by war.

"With farmers away at the battlefronts, overripe and rotting oranges made brilliant colored dots on the white carpet of snow. Partridges strutted among the oranges, in their own way as arrogant as victorious soldiers viewing the enemy dead."

On arrival, the train stopped several hundred yards from the airport. The people who were handling the baggage — Chuck Reilly, the State Department officer in charge of travel logistics, his aides, U.S. Embassy employees, and U.S. Marines — had to work in mud up to their knees. The Marines may have trained for the mud, but the Foreign Service officers certainly had not. But neither snow nor mud, et cetera, would keep Henry Kissinger from the punctual completion of his appointed rounds.

The members of the Kissinger party left not only with a feeling of great accomplishment, they also carried away an offbeat gift, the origins of which lay in a telephone call from Joe Sisco to his wife in Washington. Jean Sisco told her shuttling husband that they had been invited to a bar mitzvah by Sheldon Cohen, the former director of the IRS, and she suggested that it would be appropriate to give Cohen's son a gift from Jerusalem. Sisco solicited ideas from Embassy people. One official recommended that he buy a version of the Old Testament reproduced as a series of newspapers. Sisco liked the idea, bought the volume, and took it to the next negotiating session to get Golda Meir and the others to sign it. They all did, and Mrs. Meir began leafing through it, with Dayan kidding her, saying she didn't know anything about the Old Testament. The Israeli Prime Minister held up the start of the session for about fifteen minutes while she looked through the volume. She was so taken with it that she gave a copy to all of the negotiators at the final session. They spent an hour getting everybody's signature in all the copies, with the Prime Minister reading headlines out loud and Kissinger and Eban wisecracking about them. Thus, the Old Testament written in newspaper fashion became a cherished memento of the first Egyptian shuttle.

At the time of the simultaneous formal signing ceremonies in Egypt and Israel, Kissinger was literally up in the air. He had carefully arranged to be in neither country. After he left, Abba Eban toasted the agreement by saying, "These were the easiest negotiations ever conducted by Israel with the United States."

When copies of the agreement had been passed out, Kissinger sighed to newsmen on his plane, "When you look at it, it's hard to see where the hours went." An aide familiar with the Great White Way calculated that there were a hundred miles traveled for every problem solved.

On the way back to Washington, "the senior American official" said, "At the moment, Kissinger has no plans to involve himself in any further 'shuttle diplomacy.'" Oh yeah? One month later, Kissinger was back in the area, trying to arrange disengagement negotiations between Israel and Syria.

Just before we left, I reported that the Arabs had passed the word that if Kissinger would follow up the Sinai disengagement with a similar effort involving Syria, the oil embargo would be lifted. When Kissinger boarded the flight leaving Washington, someone asked him about the story. "Talk to Valeriani," he replied sarcastically. "He thinks he's got the best sources in town." One of my colleagues whispered to me, "He just confirmed your story."

His petulance was not based entirely on the fact that the story had not come from him. He did not want to appear to be running errands for the Arabs as the only way to get the oil embargo lifted, especially since he kept arguing that oil diplomacy and Middle East diplomacy were separable and indeed separate.

Embargo or no embargo, the Israelis absolutely refused even to consider negotiations with Syria until they received the list of Israeli POWs held by the Syrians. After stopping in Damascus, Kissinger went on to Jerusalem to see Golda Meir. In a moment of deep emotion, he delivered the list to her. Golda cried. The list contained sixty-three names, and the Israeli Cabinet described itself as "very pleased" to find so many were still alive.

As the Secretary of State left Israel, he was handed a bunch of flowers — dahlias and bird-of-paradise — with a note: "Thank you very much, from the Families of Israeli Prisoners in Syria." Said Kissinger, "The flowers remind us that foreign policy affects human beings."

A week after Kissinger returned to Washington, the oil embargo was lifted.

When the Secretary of State headed back to the Middle East at the end of April 1974, he envisioned a new shuttle of from two to three weeks. And whatever he thought about the Aswan-Jerusalem shuttle, he knew in advance that this one would be difficult. "This is more delicate, more complicated, more uncertain than any other trip I have taken," he said en route on the plane. "This has the potential of being an anguishing week." Week?

In addition to the complicated military issues, the Israeli-Syrian negotiations were burdened with a tremendous psychological handicap: the enormous mistrust between the two countries. And the geographical maneuvering room was limited, since the Golan Heights did not parallel the expanses of the Sinai for making complex territorial arrangements. Besides, the Syrians were extremely reluctant even to discuss making compromises with Israel over territory that they insisted was theirs. As Kissinger pointed out, "For the Syrians to talk to the Israelis at all, it's a tremendous wrench." From the Syrian point of view, the very fact of negotiations was a major concession.

There was another complication. The Israelis had never previously given up any land they had captured and cultivated, which was what they were being asked to do.

Kissinger saw other complicating factors. "The Israelis look at it as a military problem," he said. "We have to put it into the strategic and political context." This was another variation of the Kissinger theme that almost any agreement between Israel and Syria would be a significant achievement in itself. He thought it was more important politically to have an agreement and maintain the movement away from war than to worry too much about the specific dimension of the agreement or its terms.

On the Syrian side, he said, "Nobody wants to be the first Syrian to negotiate with the Israelis, especially when they don't know the outcome." Beyond that, Kissinger pointed out, "the Syrians have no negotiating experience. They have a different concept of what a negotiation is. They want me to do everything by myself. I cannot seriously say what they are asking me to do." By the time Kissinger left the area, the Syrians had had plenty of negotiating experience. And so had he.

The Israelis had become increasingly anxious about the Secretary's developing friendship with the Arab world, and when he arrived in Tel Aviv to start the shuttle, he tried to put them at ease about the negotiations with Syria: "I have come here not to discuss concessions, but to discuss peace," he said in his airport statement. "The issue is not pressure, but a lasting peace."

The Secretary's arrival statement was all business, serious and somber. The light touch was added this time by Foreign Minister Abba Eban: "We have come to Lod to welcome Mrs. Kissinger, who is on her first visit to Israel," he said. "To our pleasant surprise, we found out that accompanying her is the Secretary of State, and we welcome him, too." Kissinger reciprocated the humor at a reception. He felt somewhat embarrassed by the Arab men's custom of kissing each other and holding hands, but out of politeness and diplomatic requirement, he had done what was expected of him on his trips to the Middle East. When the subject came up at the reception, Kissinger looked at Israel's foreign minister, then said, "The reason the Israelis don't get better treatment is that Eban doesn't kiss me."

Kissinger's first order of business in Jerusalem was to introduce Nancy to Golda Meir. Then began the longest overseas mission ever for an American Secretary of State — thirty-three days. He flew to Damascus twelve times and to Jerusalem sixteen times, with side trips to Egypt, Jordan, Saudi Arabia, Algeria, and Cyprus.

Sooner or later, almost everybody in the party came down with diarrhea, and the doctor on board ran out of Lomotil, an effective antidiarrhetic. The most popular drink on the shuttle became a "Lomotil cocktail" — a pill and a glass of water. Even Kissinger was afflicted. As his plane was taking off on one of the many flights from Tel Aviv, he saw a giant American C-5-A cargo plane landing, and he quipped, "They're bringing in another shipment of Lomotil for us."

His personal aide, David Gompert, lost 20 pounds on the shuttle, and he was a lean 165-pounder to begin with. Kissinger himself had no such luck.

The State Department doctor on board was Martin Wolfe, an easygoing specialist in exotic internal disorders. Kissinger liked to joke with him. On his first trip to the Middle East, he turned to Wolfe and said, "Are you really a doctor or are you just following me around?" He soon found out Wolfe was really a doctor.

The Israeli press, always on the lookout for sidebar stories during the Kissinger trips, eventually discovered Dr. Wolfe. A *Ma'ariv* reporter wrote an article, "The Shadow of Dr. Kissinger — Dr. Martin Wolfe." The article included a line saying, "The doctor never travels without large amounts of Lomotil and Demerol in his bag in case Secretary Kissinger has intestinal problems." Dr. Wolfe wrote to the author of the article, pointing out that the drug he carried was Donnatal, not Demerol. Demerol, he explained, was a narcotic and addicting, and, wrote Wolfe, "if I gave Dr. Kissinger as much Demerol as the author claimed, he'd be considered a dope addict and I'd be considered a pusher." After a while, it seemed as though the negotiations were a narcotic and everybody had become an addict.

The gulf between the two countries was immediately apparent. Kissinger took the Israelis a Syrian proposal calling for an Israeli withdrawal from all of the Golan Heights — back to the 1967 lines. The Israelis exploded. "That shows Syria doesn't really want an agreement," they said. "No," explained Kissinger, trying to soothe them, "that's just a negotiating position." "Fine," snapped Foreign Minister Eban. "Then we'll draw our disengagement line through downtown Damascus."

The apprehension about the opening gambits was not eased on the Israeli side by Kissinger's belief that the Israelis would probably have to make the first move since they were the ones who occupied Syrian territory and who would therefore have to do the withdrawing.

Kissinger had predicted beforehand that the negotiations would be "murderously tough." They were made even tougher when Palestinian terrorists seized an Israeli school at Ma'alot and held the children as hostages, to be exchanged for other Palestinian terrorists in Israeli jails. Israeli forces stormed the school and freed most of the hostages, but not before the Palestinians killed several of the children. Israel retaliated by bombing Palestinian camps in Lebanon.

During the siege of the school and the subsequent air strikes, the negotiations were suspended, and Kissinger stopped shuttling for a while. With unaccustomed time on his hands in Jerusalem, he had a massage at the hotel. In the small world department, the masseur was Steve Strauss, whose mother went to the same synagogue — Adath Yesharin in Washington Heights, New York — as Kissinger's parents. While Strauss massaged Kissinger, the two men talked about the incident at Ma'alot. Strauss remembers saying, "It's a pity we have the terrorists in jail so they could be exchanged. We should have killed them all instead." Kissinger agreed, then quickly amended his view. "That's what Mrs. Kissinger thinks."

The subject turned to Arab leaders. Kissinger described Sadat as "very sincere . . . he wants peace." King Hussein, he said, was "a very reasonable fellow." At that point, Mrs. Kissinger walked in and added, "He means well," referring to Hussein. Strauss was not impressed, and he noted acidly, "George Bernard Shaw wrote that the worst thing you can say about somebody is that he means well."

They also talked about the Secretary's shuttling. Kissinger asked, "What do you think about peace with Syria?" Strauss replied, "I think every Israeli would be willing to give ten years of his life for peace." Kissinger followed up with, "How about ten kilometers?" Strauss answered, "If it was real peace, I think they'd go along with it." "And what about the West Bank?" Kissinger asked. "Not one inch!" thundered Strauss. Kissinger delighted in telling and retelling a shortened version of that conversation for the next few years.

Strauss also said he told Kissinger that if the Secretary kept coming back to Jerusalem, Israel would invoke the Law of Return and draft him into the army. Kissinger borrowed that line as well.

Strauss recalled that Kissinger's first massage was less substantive. "What do I do?" the Secretary asked the masseur. "Undress," said Strauss. Kissinger shot a glance at the Secret Service agent with him. "Do you have to be here through the whole performance?" he asked. "I'll wait outside," the agent said. Kissinger indulged in a bit of gallows humor. "OK," he said. "If he kills me, I'll yell."

After the tragic Ma'alot interlude, the shuttling resumed, and despite a negotiating "breakthrough" — agreement on the location of the disengagement line — the pace did not accelerate. Kissinger noted, "Both sides are negotiating each minor aspect of this accord with the tenacity with which they negotiated the disengagement line."

Bruce van Voorst of *Newsweek* started signing the cables to his editors "the Flying Dutchman," as though doomed to spend eternity roaming the Middle East.

As the mission got longer, patience and tempers got shorter. Kissinger and the Israelis shouted at one another. After one outburst by Mrs. Meir, the Secretary noted that it was he who had to face Syrian President Hafez Assad the next day, not Golda. "And I can tell you," he said, "it's not a pleasant mission."

Much of the haggling focused on the Golan Heights town of Kuneitra. Kissinger argued that no agreement was possible unless the Israelis vacated it. The Israelis were reluctant to do so. The Syrians insisted Israel also give up three surrounding hills as well. Israel adamantly refused. During one of his outbursts, Israeli transcripts show that Kissinger complained that Israel was doling out little pieces of territory as though it were a personal favor to him, "as if I were a citizen of Kuneitra, as if I planned to build my house there."

Information Minister Shimon Peres wrote Kissinger a note explaining why "we love the hills," tracing Israel's fondness for strategic heights to Biblical origins: "The Lord is God of the hills, but he is not God of the valleys" (1 Kings: 20, 28).

When the negotiations got down to the minutest details, Kissinger complained, "I don't want to become the desk officer for Syria, disputing the number of guns in every square kilometer." But in effect, he did. As Golda Meir pointed out in her memoirs, "There wasn't a road, a house or even a tree there about which he didn't know everything there was to know. As I said to him then, 'With the exception of the former generals who are now members of the Israeli Cabinet, I don't think we have a single minister who knows as much about Kuneitra as you do.' " That had never been one of Kissinger's principal ambitions.

Part of Kissinger's problem in Jerusalem was persuading the Israelis they could make a deal with Assad. The Secretary of State came to like and respect the Syrian President, and he was constantly trying to interpret to the Israelis the logic of Assad's position in a Syrian context.

Four weeks after he had left Washington, Kissinger advised us that four weeks were enough for the Secretary of State to be on the road, and if there were no agreement within the next forty-eight hours, he would suspend the talks for ten days or two weeks while both sides reviewed their positions. But then the White House dropped a bombshell. A spokesman said President Nixon had asked Kissinger to stay as long as necessary to get an agreement. In the words of one of his closest aides, Kissinger was really "pissed off."

The White House announcement undercut his long-standing thesis that the United States must not look as though it wanted an agreement even more than the parties did. It fueled speculation that Kissinger was pushing both sides into an agreement in order to give Mr. Nixon a diplomatic victory he could use in his battle to fend off impeachment, since a Syrian-Israeli agreement would pave the way for a Nixon visit to the Middle East. Kissinger also worried that he had lost a valuable negotiating tool — the threat of breaking off the talks. He felt the major impact of the White House statement was to make the Syrians more obstinate and therefore to delay the conclusion of the talks by at least forty-eight hours.

When it appeared the mission might end without an agreement despite the White House announcement, Mrs. Meir had a "farewell" luncheon for the Secretary of State and thanked him for his efforts and, most of all, she said, for his "understanding" of Israel's position. Despite the apparent failure of the mission, Kissinger had not lost his sense of humor, as he responded, "The foreign minister many months ago told me that Israel would conduct its negotiations with its characteristic tenacity. I didn't know what he was talking about, or I would not be here . . .

"We have had occasions when, after talking about Kuneitra for several weeks, I sent two members of my team out there to take a look at it, and one of them came back and said, 'Imagine what they're doing now — they're pushing Kuneitra toward the Syrian frontier.' They had seen some bulldozers at work.

"We have gotten to know every hill on the Golan Heights and many other problems, and we have also learned what was to us first an intellectual decision has now been transformed into an emotional necessity; that the progress that has been made must not be lost and that whether or not this last trip to Damascus will bring the agreement that is so close, we will continue the effort until this first step toward a lasting peace will have been concluded . . ."

Despite the weeks of haggling, Kissinger's sense of humor managed to survive in the private sessions as well, but barely. At the Israeli end of the shuttle, bowls of dried fruits and nuts were always plentiful, so much so that there was never enough room on the tables to lay the maps out flat; they were always draped over the fruit and nut bowls. Kissinger, a compulsive *nosher,* always acquitted himself admirably at the table, and the nuts and fruit became a part of the negotiating folklore among the participants.

At what appeared to be the final session in Jerusalem, Kissinger announced that the American delegation had decided to award prizes to the members of the Israeli team. Rabin won a "prize" for eating more nuts than anyone else. Peres was commended for his courtesy in passing plates. Dayan won an award for his artistic peeling of apples and oranges. Eban won the award for eating the most nonsalted almonds. But Allon won the prize for eating the largest number of salted and nonsalted almonds. For other members of the team, there were awards for the person who always started eating before the Americans sat down and for those who ate dried fruits and not nuts. The shuttle had indeed gone on a long time.

When another round trip to Damascus apparently failed to break the deadlock, Kissinger decided to send Sisco to Syria to be there when a joint statement was issued to announce the suspension of the mission. But when Kissinger went to see Prime Minister Meir for the supposed final time, he wondered aloud if he shouldn't go to Damascus instead of Sisco. Mrs. Meir said she didn't dare ask him to go back another time, but she pointed out that if Sisco went, there was surely no hope of keeping the negotiations alive; if the Secretary went, there would still be some chance of success.

Sisco agreed, and Kissinger decided to take off shortly after word had gone out to the pilots of his plane that he would spend the night in Jerusalem. The new word came on extremely short notice.

At the airport, the television reporters raced to put something on film to satellite to the United States, since there was not enough time to make arrangements for shipping film out of Damascus. Barrie Dunsmore of ABC was still in front of the camera when the rear stairs were wheeled away. If he thought Kissinger would not take off without him, even at the cost of a minute or two, he was wrong. The Secretary bounced up the stairs and gave the crew its orders: "We're going." The front door had already closed and the stairs were just starting to move away when Dunsmore raced up them and pounded on the plane. The door opened, swallowed him up, and closed again. The ABC camera never stopped rolling. It made for an amusing closing piece on the *ABC Evening News.*

As the plane taxied toward takeoff, one of the crew members

looked out a window and saw Chuck Rude, the chief steward, riding in a catering truck along the flight line. It was not a serious loss — the food, not Rude.

Even though it was well after midnight when Kissinger returned to Israel, he had sent a message from his plane that he wanted to meet with the Israeli negotiators. The meeting took place at two-thirty in the morning, and Kissinger told them they had a deal.

The agreement was celebrated later at a victory party, carried live on Israeli television, near Prime Minister Meir's office. After the documents were signed, Kissinger kissed her on the cheeks. "Oh," Mrs. Meir said on national television, "I didn't know you kissed women, too." After thirty-three days, it sounded hilarious.

At the airport, Foreign Minister Eban uttered the words the Kissinger party was desperately eager to hear. "Ladies and gentlemen," he said, "I have an announcement to make. The Secretary of State will not be coming back tonight." But Kissinger wouldn't go along: "Mr. Foreign Minister, knowing how carefully you choose your words, I have to pay particular attention to the insistence with which you point out that I shall not return this evening, and given our past experience of having made so many final departure statements, I just wouldn't count on it completely."

A week later, the cover of *Newsweek* depicted Kissinger in the costume of Superman. Kissinger was wearing a supersmile when the editors gave him the original sketch.

After time out for the Nixon visit to the Middle East and the Arab Summit at Rabat, the Secretary of State turned to a new round of negotiations between Israel and Egypt. He tried to set it up through regular diplomatic channels, but the problems were too complex to deal with at long range, and both sides told him he would have to go back to the area personally to get the talks started.

A new government had taken office in Israel, but it had not taken hold, and a growing sense of uneasiness there clouded the negotiating atmosphere.

Egypt was insisting that Israel vacate the strategically located Mitla and Gidda passes in the Sinai and return the Abu Rodeis oil fields, which the Israelis had been pumping since 1967. In return, Israel demanded from Egypt a formal declaration of nonbelligerency, which Kissinger advised them was not attainable as such.

En route in February 1975, the Secretary took wry note of a certain lack of enthusiasm in Israel for his latest diplomatic exercise. "I think if I told them I wouldn't be back for three months," he said, "they wouldn't send an El Al plane to get me." When questioned about the possible terms of compromise, he replied pragmatically. It depends, he said, "on what the quid pro quo is. I'm not trying to build a summer house on the Egyptian side of the line, so I'll consider anything. But I just don't know."

"Why," a reporter wanted to know, "do the Israelis consider a piece of the Sinai so important, why are they so emotional about it, when it's still far from the 1967 border?" "Talk to Marilyn's boyfriend about any hill," advised Kissinger. "You try to get a hill away from Gur and you know you've had a struggle." The reference was to General Mordechai Gur, the Israeli Chief of Staff, who Kissinger thought was a source for Marilyn Berger.

At a dinner marking the end of his visit to Jerusalem, Kissinger discussed the problem facing Israel. He emphasized how difficult it would be to relate the tangible issue of territory to such intangible qualities as the legitimacy and the acceptance of Israel and the desire for peace. He stressed the need for good faith in this round of negotiations, but good faith was not in good supply in Jerusalem then. The Secretary also acknowledged the growing skepticism about him in Israel, and he tried to take the curse off with humor. He noted that members of the political opposition had come to the dinner "to study the depths which human depravity can reach."

But not only the political opposition was skeptical. The new defense minister, Shimon Peres, had talked publicly about delaying the talks. A reporter asked Kissinger, "What possible motivation could Peres have for trying to delay this when it's so obvious time is not on their side?" Kissinger's reply gave some insight into his own domestic position. "If you're a politician," he said, "the time you're interested in is the time in which you're surviving. Leo Durocher said, 'Use your best pitcher today; tomorrow it may rain.' And so you have a complicated situation in Israel of all these people maneuvering."

Some Israeli politicians were even suggesting that it would be better to revive the Geneva Conference than to negotiate a second agreement with Egypt. Kissinger interpreted those suggestions as an attempt to "get through the U.S. elections. They sure as hell don't want to go to Geneva to settle rapidly." A reporter asked, "Are you talking of the U.S. elections for a new President — or a new Secretary of State?" "I don't think necessarily either," he said. "I don't think they are against *me,* but ambivalent. They will be against *anyone* who has to produce movement." Kissinger had gone to the heart of the Israeli opposition against him.

A couple of weeks later, he climbed aboard his plane at Andrews Air Force Base to try again "to produce movement" in the Middle East. He was in high spirits. A reporter asked, "Did you hear that Elliot Richardson hired a New York *Times* man to be his press spokesman?" Kissinger shot back, "Not Tony Lewis, I hope."

Another asked, "Was there anything to the Jack Anderson piece in the *Post* this morning?" It quoted from allegedly classified material. Another Kissinger joke: "I wish he'd let me see my secret cables, because they sure didn't get to me."

What about American contacts with the PLO? (The Israeli reporters in Washington and a couple of the Jewish reporters on the plane never failed to ask about contacts with the PLO or a change in policy toward the PLO.) "It's all true," Kissinger said with a wicked smile. "We're going to announce it on Passover so it gets a bigger play."

When the traveling party reached Israel, Foreign Minister Allon was waiting at the airport with an unusual appeal. He urged newsmen not to "speculate, but to report only what was officially announced." He might just as well have asked the Israeli Cabinet to stop arguing.

Protestors were demonstrating in the streets as Kissinger arrived in Jerusalem. Some of them carried signs reading: MR. KISSINGER, WE DON'T WANT YOU HERE. "I'm glad to see the demonstrators," he said sarcastically to an aide. "I was afraid they were starting to like me in Israel." Then he added, "At least they call me Mister."

Prime Minister Rabin had arranged a dinner at his home for Kissinger and the members of the new Israeli negotiating team. They were all prepared for a lengthy siege. As they were going into the dining room, Peres joked, "Mr. Secretary, this is not the Last Supper." "You're telling me?" replied Kissinger.

From a journalist's point of view, it was a curious shuttle. If you listened to the Egyptians, there was no way it could fail. If you listened to the Israelis, there was no way it could succeed. And if you listened to Kissinger, you couldn't be sure, although his use of the word "glacial" to describe the pace of progress was a significant tip-off.

Halfway through the shuttle, the Kissinger plane made history of sorts. It flew directly from Amman to Tel Aviv, over the Jordan River, rather than circling out over the Mediterranean — the first time a plane had been permitted to fly that route. When the plane landed in Tel Aviv, the crowd of waiting Israeli dignitaries was much larger than usual. But they weren't waiting for Henry. As Allon told him, "I hope you know your way to Jerusalem. I'm waiting to welcome President Ephraim Katzir back from his first trip to the United States."

During any negotiating trip to the Middle East, Kissinger tried to avoid staying in Israel on a Saturday, the Jewish Sabbath, since he couldn't get any work done with Israeli officials during the day. He usually tried to get out of town by Friday night. On the first Friday night of the March 1975 shuttle, however, he didn't make it out of town, so he left the next morning, driving through Jerusalem when all the stores and restaurants were closed and all the streets virtually deserted. On the way to the airport, an Israeli official told him the story of a British officer, a veteran of the British mandate over Palestine, who returned to Jerusalem twenty-five years later. It was a Saturday, and the officer looked around in surprise and said, "By Jove, they still haven't lifted the curfew!"

About a week into the shuttle, correspondents were working in their rooms at the King David when they heard a knock at the door. When they answered, there stood Nancy Kissinger with her security guards and a couple of Israeli women, inviting them to a fashion show of bikinis in another room of the hotel. Despite the allure of models in bikinis, the reaction of most of the correspondents — including the men — was, who needs it? But since Nancy was obviously making a personal effort, most of us showed up, although it certainly seemed incongruous, sitting in that room watching two shapely Israeli women swirling around in bikinis and matching capes while covering a mission to bring peace to the Middle East.

Meanwhile, back at the negotiations, things were not going well. The main sticking point was Israel's insistence that Egypt make a written and public pledge of nonbelligerency to Israel. The Israelis felt the Egyptians were negotiating with the United States, not with them. As Peres pointed out sardonically, "We are not going to marry the father-in-law. We are going to marry the girl."

As if there weren't enough problems, a reporter asked if the Israelis were ready to agree to some statement about the Palestinians. Kissinger, who constantly griped that the press paid more attention to the Palestinians than anybody else, replied, "I don't believe the Israeli Cabinet on Sunday will accept writing something about the PLO into the agreement." And he underscored his sarcasm with a derisive chuckle.

As the pace slowed down and the chances for an agreement receded, Sisco chimed in at a Kissinger briefing that he thought both sides were reaching the limits of what could be done in the present "framework." "There's no possibility of a deal as the Israelis just defined it," Sisco said. The Secretary teased him about his outspokenness. "Let Sisco talk," he said, "and I'll move my lips." Just before the end, a reporter asked Kissinger if he were "upbeat." "Upbeat is wrong," he replied. "Downbeat is also wrong. I'm just beat." So were we all.

On the second Friday night of the shuttle, Kissinger once again found himself in Israel, this time with the final proposals from Egypt. The Israeli Cabinet took a Sabbath break, and Kissinger decided to take a sightseeing break, although the decision was not made until very late. It was 2:30 A.M. when the Israeli Foreign Ministry got the word to have helicopters ready for an 8:00 A.M. departure for Masada, the ancient hilltop fortress overlooking the Dead Sea, where more than two hundred Jewish fighters and their five hundred sixty dependents committed suicide on the eve of Passover, A.D. 73, rather than surrender to the fifteen thousand men of the Roman Tenth Legion who surrounded them.

The helicopter landing at Masada had a little more suspense than usual. Only a short time before, former West German Chancellor Willy Brandt had been flown there, but upon landing, the brakes hadn't held, and a gust of wind had carried the chopper right to the edge of a steep precipice, where a restraining wall stopped it. When we arrived, however, there was no wind; a hot sun blistered the hilltop, and the temperature flirted with the hundred-degree mark. Kissinger put on sunglasses, and somebody gave him a two-tone clownish hat to protect his head. The hat, called a kova tembel hat, had the words "Shalom, Israel" printed on it.

The Secretary was given the grand tour of Masada by the most knowledgeable man possible, archaeologist-soldier Yigael Yadin, who made the original find and supervised the digging. The two men kept up a steady stream of archaeological chitchat and jokes and puns. Yadin pointed out that his archaeological team had included a number of young Israeli women who preferred to work in bikinis in the intense heat. "I don't know whether they were more interested in exposing the present or revealing the past," Yadin joked.

He explained that he was not a religious man, but he said he had to think twice after digging below the floor of a ruin and finding the pages of a manuscript with only one passage of Ezekiel still legible: the prediction of the resurrection of the dry bones of Israel. "I understand," Yadin said to Kissinger, "that's a phrase you often use yourself." "But I do it sarcastically," replied Kissinger good-humoredly.

Referring to articles and allegations that Israel had a Masada complex — that is, that Israel was willing once again to commit national suicide rather than make concessions for peace — Yadin argued, "I don't think Israel has a Masada complex. The only Masada complex" — he pointed to a large ruin — "is that complex of buildings."

He also explained that recruits for Israel's armored brigades are brought to Masada to take their oath of allegiance. And they pledge, three times, that "Masada shall not fall again." (Israeli paratroopers take their oath at the Wailing Wall.) Speaking professor to professor, Yadin added, "Masada is a reminder and a challenge to remember what should not be." He went on to point out that King Herod had built the fortress on the rock of Masada not only as a protection against the Jewish people; he was also worried that Cleopatra would persuade Anthony to give her the entire area. "I'm sure — to quote you — that they had 'constructive talks,' " Yadin said to Kissinger. Kissinger shot back, "They never got a framework." ("Framework" was a favorite Kissinger word during the negotiations. Nobody was ever exactly sure what it meant.)

Yadin was concerned about tiring Kissinger, but the Secretary wanted to see everything. The only way to get to one of the finds, the hanging palace with three terraces, was down a stairway with one hundred fifty steps. Yadin told Kissinger puckishly, "We don't have to do it in one leap. We can do it step by step."

During the excavations, Yadin said, his team found fifteen broken wine jars with inscriptions in Latin, giving the names of the consuls of that year, 20 B.C., and the name of the owner of the Italian vineyard from which the wine had come, in the Brindisi area. I asked Yadin if 20 B.C. was a good vintage. Ted Koppel recalled a line from *A Funny Thing Happened on the Way to the Forum*: "Was the year zero a good year?" But Yadin had an answer. He said he had gone to Rome to talk to scholars to find out if 20 B.C. was a special vintage. There were no records. He concluded that the wine jars provided evidence that Herod had finished building his fortress in that year and had the wine brought there either to celebrate completion of the work or simply to stock the wine cellar.

Yadin had also guided Nancy Kissinger around Masada, and she told him Henry had once said that if she did not see Masada, she would not understand the sum of the problem of the Jewish people.

Yadin later wondered why Kissinger, a Jewish Secretary of State, had gone to Masada on the day he was waiting for a crucial decision from the Israeli government. Was it a pilgrimage? he asked himself, or was it an expression of interest by a scholar or tourist? "Was he so cunning as to emphasize to the Israelis to beware," Yadin said to me, "or was he trying to fortify his Jewish conscience? I didn't ask," Yadin added, "but the Jewish argument of Masada was very much in his mind that day. He asked very few questions of an archaeological nature."

That night the negotiations collapsed, and unfortunately for Kissinger, the pictures that accompanied the page I stories around the world showed him at Masada, wearing that silly, pointed hat with the now-ironic words, "Peace Israel."

During the fateful, final session of the Israeli Cabinet, a courier brought an urgent cable from Washington. It was a message from President Ford, warning of the consequences of failure to reach an agreement. Dinitz read it and passed it on to Rabin. The Prime Minister read it aloud, then angrily told his colleagues, "This is an ultimatum. We cannot bow to an ultimatum. If we give in now, our credibility will be damaged — our credibility with the Arabs, with the United States, and with world Jewry."

During the discussions, Dinitz was called out of the room for an urgent phone call. The familiar voice with the German accent asked if the message from Ford had arrived yet. It had. Kissinger urged that it not be read to the Cabinet. "Too late," said Dinitz. "I didn't think the meeting would last so long," lamented Kissinger. "It's Friday night." Dinitz told him the Cabinet was still in session and was likely to continue for a few more hours. "The mood," Dinitz said, "is not good." Kissinger said he was going out to eat and asked Dinitz to call him when it was over. He went back to La Gondola. The call came before he had finished his dessert. It was all over.

The Secretary went immediately to the Prime Minister's office to meet with the Israeli negotiating team. According to the Israelis,

Kissinger said he had nothing to do with the presidential message, but Rabin said he didn't believe him. Kissinger said grimly, "Let's not kid ourselves, we've failed." And he laid out the dire consequences of the failure — for Israel, for the United States, and for the Middle East. The four Kissingers of the Apocalypse were riding again.

As Kissinger lamented the breakdown in the negotiations and discussed the future course of U.S.-Israeli relations as well as Israel's relations with the American Jewish community, two people were deeply moved. One was the Israeli stenotypist, an attractive woman in her forties, who had been born in America and who had gone to live in Israel after marrying an Israeli. She seemed to understand what had happened from both an American and an Israeli perspective. She was almost in tears. And the other person as deeply moved was Kissinger himself.

Before leaving Jerusalem, the Secretary called on Mrs. Meir. He privately longed for the days when she had headed the Israeli negotiating team. In her modest apartment in Ramat Aviv, a suburb of Tel Aviv, Mrs. Meir served tea and consolation as well as homemade cookies. She told him she supported Rabin in his decision, but she pointed out, "Henry, it's still two to one in your favor."

Prime Minister Rabin went personally to the airport to see Kissinger off and to thank him for his efforts. Kissinger, on the verge of tears for the first time in public, said, "This is a sad day for America, which has invested much hope and faith, and we know it is a sad day also for Israel, which needs and wants peace so badly . . . As we leave, we wish the people of Israel all the best."

Kissinger was indeed sad and disappointed, but he and his team were also deeply annoyed and irritated with Israel's stand since the entire negotiating scenario had been closely coordinated with Israel. On the flight home, Kissinger talked about the shuttle that failed:

"The major thing I want to make clear before you all go off is that I am not assessing blame on either side. It was a situation in which the negotiations broke down because neither side had enough maneuvering room to make the concessions that were necessary or to make the decisions that were necessary to break the back of this. Or you could say," Kissinger summed up with ad-libbed eloquence, "tragedies sometimes occur when both sides, following the laws of their own nature, produce precisely the consequences they fear most."

Kissinger suggested that step-by-step diplomacy was finished, and the United States announced a "reassessment" of its policy in the Middle East. President Ford had alluded to such a reassessment in his message to Rabin. The Secretary of State insisted throughout this period that "in no way are we considering the punishment of any country." But in Jerusalem, Rabin said, "Reassessment, hell, it's simply pressure." The reassessment had been recommended in a National Security Study Memorandum (NSSM), known as "nissim" for short. (Ironically, *nissim* is the Hebrew word for miracle.)

For the Israelis, the danger of the "reassessment" did not involve the fundamental question of military aid, which they knew they would eventually get. The real danger was that the United States would go public with its own plan for the overall settlement in the Middle East and then return to the Geneva Peace Conference with all the Arabs present and leave the Israelis diplomatically isolated. Much later, Kissinger told newsmen on his plane, "Without the reassessment, we would have lost the Arabs."

During this period, Matti Golan, the diplomatic correspondent of *Ha'aretz,* finished his book, *The Secret Conversations of Henry Kissinger,* subtitled *Step-by-Step Diplomacy in the Middle East.* It was clearly a hatchet job, and although Golan had apparently benefited from the leak of transcripts of negotiating sessions, the book was full of inaccuracies. On Kissinger's first visit to Jerusalem following its publication, he frequently noted after saying something to Israeli officials, "I hope this will not be published in the next book."

Ironically, Kissinger himself was soon accused of some selective leaking of his own. An article by Edward R. E. Sheehan on Kissinger's step-by-step diplomacy appeared in *Foreign Policy.* It was a generally favorable account, and it included what appeared to be verbatim quotes from MemCons — Memoranda of Conversations.

At the time, the Secretary of State was embroiled in a dispute with a congressional subcommittee over his refusal to provide classified documents about Cyprus, and the timing of Sheehan's article was enormously embarrassing to Kissinger, although substantively flattering.

Two of Sheehan's principal sources were Kissinger aides Roy Atherton and Hal Saunders. They had not actually shown the author classified material, but they had apparently read to him from the MemCons. It was widely assumed that Kissinger had authorized them to do so, even though he claimed he was "thunderstruck" when the material appeared. Atherton, ever loyal, said later that the Secretary of State had never really "focused" on the Sheehan project.

There was nothing magnanimous in Kissinger's subsequent reaction. The Secretary of State officially reprimanded Atherton and Saunders for leaking classified material. Neither man suffered from the reprimand, however, and one State Department veteran even commented afterward, "The Secretary who succeeds Kissinger might think a reprimand from him is really a recommendation."

Don Wright, *The Miami News*, The New York Times Syndicate

Much later, on another Middle East mission, Atherton walked through the press section of the plane on his way to the bathroom. He was wearing a white shirt. Immediately afterward, Saunders walked through, also wearing a white shirt. One of the reporters made some comment about "two peas in a pod." Whereupon Barry Schweid of the AP cracked, "Well, they always did leak together."

Not long after the failure of the Sinai II talks, Senator Henry Jackson called for an end to what he termed "this Mickey Mouse shuttle diplomacy" and said the parties should go to the conference table. Kissinger was asked to comment on that remark before a meeting of the American Society of Newspaper Editors. He said he understood Jackson's problem of having to campaign for eighteen months (for the presidential nomination). Then he added, "With respect to the last point, of getting the parties around the conference table, during World War Two, somebody suggested that the way to deal with the submarine problem was to heat the ocean and to boil the Axis subs to the surface . . . So the man was asked how to do this, and he said, 'I have given you the idea. The technical implementation is up to you.' "

The parties did not go to the conference table. Instead, cables began arriving from both Cairo and Jerusalem, urging Kissinger, in effect, to pick up where he had left off.

On a flight to Europe, a reporter asked the Secretary if it was "now up to the Israelis to make a decision." "You know the Israelis," he replied knowingly. "All I would need to say now is that I think they have to make a decision, and I guarantee a three-week stalemate."

For a while, Middle East diplomacy went through a new phase of negotiations — between Israel and the United States. Rabin went to Washington. Dinitz flew secretly to the Virgin Islands to confer with the vacationing Secretary of State. And Kissinger and Rabin arranged to cross paths in Germany in the summer of 1975. Their three-hour session in Bonn provided the final impetus for another round of shuttle diplomacy, but there were still difficulties to be overcome, and an American reporter asked the Israeli Prime Minister about them after the meeting. Rabin responded, "I am not going to elaborate about details. I believe for the time being, the statements that have been made are enough. You are going on the plane; you'll get an opportunity to . . ." Laughter drowned out the rest of his answer. Kissinger broke in: "It may produce a senior official familiar with the Middle East." It did.

The combination of the U.S. "reassessment," Egypt's economic difficulties, the promise of considerable American largesse to Israel, and the general lack of enthusiasm for reviving the Geneva Peace Conference soon had Kissinger on the Middle East road once again.

In late August 1975, the last of the Kissinger shuttles got under way with a fixed deadline: The Secretary had to be at the United Nations to deliver a speech on September 1. Arriving in Tel Aviv, the Secretary departed from practice. He read his arrival statement from a prepared text, leaving nothing to misinterpretation. "I know these are not easy times for Israel," he said. "I know also that relations between Israel and the United States have gone through a difficult period. This has ended, and we have emerged from our dialogue strengthened in our friendship and determined to pursue common policies. Peace in the Middle East depends on many factors, and both sides must make a contribution."

"The difficult period" he referred to had not ended, however. While Kissinger was speaking at the airport, thousands of protesters were demonstrating against him in Jerusalem, blocking streets and snarling rush-hour traffic. Armed soldiers were posted all along the road from the airport to Jerusalem, but they were just a decoy.

For the sake of security, the Secretary of State was flown by helicopter from the airport to the soccer field of the YMCA, then driven the couple of hundred yards to the King David Hotel. The area around the hotel was blocked off to all but official traffic, and the usually tight Israeli security for a Kissinger visit was even tighter.

On the night of his arrival, Kissinger and the rest of his party were invited to a light supper at the Knesset (Parliament), up on a hill overlooking Jerusalem. The blintzes had been made personally by Leah Rabin, the wife of the Prime Minister. We left the hotel in a heavily escorted motorcade that followed a twisting maze of back streets and dirt roads to escape the demonstrators, many of whom carried umbrellas as a silent Chamberlain-like symbol of "Kissinger's sellout." Once the motorcade reached the Knesset, however, the demonstrators quickly sealed off the dirt roads as well, and the party was virtually trapped there. Nobody could leave. The police wouldn't even let the newsmen try to get back to file their reports. When it was obvious that the demonstrators were not going to go away, the Israelis regrouped the motorcade and made a run for it. Some of the protesters did approach the Secretary's limousine, but Secret Service agents with their .45s out of their holsters made sure nobody got too close.

The demonstrators were not allowed close to the King David Hotel either, but they found a way to overcome their strategic disadvantage. They shouted anti-Kissinger slogans through bullhorns all night long, despite the best efforts of the police to shut them up.

The next morning, Kissinger paid a return visit to Yad Vashem, the memorial to the victims of the Nazi holocaust. No press was allowed. The visit seemed to be designed to reassure all those demonstrators that Kissinger was not really selling them out.

In his first meeting with the Israeli negotiating team, Kissinger made light of the demonstrations. "I'm from Harvard," he reminded them, "and I'm used to that." Later, in a private session with newsmen, Kissinger spoke more seriously. He claimed again that he was not bothered by the demonstrators, and he said he felt they would eventually come to see that a new Sinai agreement was in the best long-term interest of Israel, that Israel's strategic security would not be reduced significantly, and that its political position would be improved.

One demonstrator who did not agree was Menachem Begin, the leader of the right-wing opposition. When Begin met Kissinger at a reception in Israel, he pointed out, "I knew you about as long as Allon did . . . since 1962." And he added with needling courtliness, "We had a few slight differences of opinion." The differences were no longer so slight, and Begin organized a mass rally to demonstrate opposition to a new Sinai agreement.

For this round of talks, there was a new player on the American side, Ambassador Malcolm Toon, who was assigned to Israel after the death of Ken Keating. Toon had a reputation as a hard-nosed diplomat. He was known for his tough anti-Soviet views and he was not regarded as an Israeli sympathizer. His appointment was seen in Israel as another sign of pressure from Washington.

About an hour after the talks began, Kissinger called a recess. The Israelis were being negative, and the Secretary met with his advisers in a separate room. Stomping up and down, he ranted that "those sons of bitches are out to get me, they're trying to bring me down." He told Toon and Sisco to send a cable to the White House saying he was going home. Toon was baffled. Nobody said anything. Finally, the Ambassador spoke up. "Do you want me to go along with you, or do you want me to tell you you're wrong?" he asked. He conceded that he was the "new boy on the block," but he said he had been there long enough to believe that there would be an agreement and "it will be the agreement you want." Sisco agreed. "Mac's absolutely right . . . you'll get a good agreement." For Toon, it was a quick lesson in Kissinger's modus operandi.

Later in the mission, the Secretary returned earlier than scheduled from Egypt. Toon raced to the airport, arriving just in time to see Kissinger's helicopter taking off. The Ambassador then drove to Jerusalem, following an Israeli official's car, and reached the Prime Minister's office at about the same time as Kissinger. When they all hooked up, Israeli Ambassador Dinitz joked to Kissinger in front of Toon, "Since your Ambassador was not at the airport to greet you, I was on hand to represent him." Kissinger cracked, "You mean, my *former* Ambassador!"

Apart from the complexities of the negotiation itself, the mission was further complicated throughout by the security considerations. Whenever possible, Kissinger was transported in a helicopter, and the meeting sites were constantly shifted.

At one point, Kissinger ran into General Arik Sharon, the extremely hawkish general who had led the Israeli crossing of the Suez Canal. As they shook hands, Kissinger said, "So this is the most dangerous person in the Middle East?" Sharon smiled. Those were the same words he had used about Kissinger just a few days before.

From the time he began his shuttle, Kissinger's diplomacy and the demonstrations against him dominated the headlines in Israel, but relief was on the way. He was soon outglamorized on the domestic scene when Elizabeth Taylor and Richard Burton flew in for their first visit to Israel. They also stayed at the King David, but, for a change, they didn't get the best suite in the house. Kissinger already had it. Kissinger naturally invited them up for a chat. He knew Liz, but didn't know Dick. Nancy didn't know either one, but she was obviously not star-struck. She was in bare feet, a "ratty sweater," and jeans when Liz and Dick came to call. Liz was dressed to the teeth.

Defense Minister Peres arranged a small dinner party at his apartment in suburban Tel Aviv for the Burtons, who were later going to drop in on the Kissingers. The Secretary of State reportedly told the minister of defense, "I understand we are both paying host to the Burtons this evening. Let's make a deal. You take Dick and I'll take Liz." Ever the negotiator.

One of the tricks of the negotiations was to allow Israel to claim one length for the passes and Egypt another, so the Egyptians could claim that as far as they were concerned, Israel had withdrawn from the entire length of the passes, while the Israelis could claim they still retained the eastern ends.

Despite Kissinger's deadline, the amount of time required to get the two sides to finish all their nitpicking took longer than anticipated, and Kissinger was not able to get back to New York to deliver his speech to the Special Session of the UN General Assembly.

As the negotiations went down to the wire, Rabin asked for a break in the talks so that he, Peres, and Allon could see Kissinger alone in the Prime Minister's office to discuss some further details. Although it was 3:00 A.M., Kissinger agreed. As they walked toward the office, Peres said to the Secretary, "You know, of course, it will be three against one." "If Sisco were with me," Kissinger rejoined, "it would be four against one."

The final session lasted until six in the morning. Allon said later that Kissinger exerted a "spiritual influence more than a political one" at the end. "Everybody else was exhausted and nearly broken," he said. When Kissinger and Allon finally emerged, a handful of reporters was still waiting. "Well, as you can gather," said Kissinger, "there were a few minor technical problems that required attention." That line provoked a lot more laughter from the fatigued newsmen than it should have.

When Allon declined to say whether the Cabinet would approve the draft agreement, a reporter asked, "All of you seem to be exuding nothing but good will this morning. You are certainly not going to recommend that it be turned down, are you?" Allon replied, "Well, let us keep you waiting a little bit longer and you'll find out later — late afternoon." Kissinger interjected, "The keepers are going to come for us any moment anyway."

Another reporter wanted to know if Kissinger was going to bed now, since he looked so energetic. The Secretary got a big laugh with a straight line: "I am thinking of going to bed now." Allon quickly pointed out that Kissinger still looked so vigorous because "he was well treated tonight, you see." When Kissinger returned to the King David, an American in the lobby thanked him. "Any genius could have done it," he replied.

Later that day, more than five months after walking out of the Prime Minister's office, despondent over the breakdown in the Israeli-Egyptian negotiations, Kissinger was back in the same office, toasting the signing of a new agreement with Israeli champagne.

During the long, final session, Lars-Erik Nelson of Reuters was the only traveling correspondent still waiting outside the Prime Minister's office when the meeting finally broke up. Everybody else was back at the King David, sleeping or waiting for Kissinger to return. Other reporters still waiting at the Prime Minister's office included three American Jews living in Israel who represented ABC and the two wire services, AP and UPI. At about half an hour past midnight, a Foreign Ministry spokesman, Gad Ranon, came out and said, "We're going to accept it. There are a lot of details they're still talking about, but the decision is to accept." And he gave the details about the withdrawal, the warning stations, and so on. The three American expatriates immediately began attacking the agreement as a bad deal, a betrayal of Israel's security. Nelson said, "Thank you." Ranon looked at him and nodded, so Nelson walked away and filed. When he finished, he returned to the waiting area, where the three other newsmen were still arguing. Nelson ended up with a beat of more than an hour — a huge margin for a wire service.

The official who passed word of the Cabinet's readiness to accept had formerly been the press spokesman at the Israeli Embassy in Washington. In addition to his Embassy extension, he had a direct-line telephone as well, which most newsmen used to call him. We were all on a first-name basis with him, and we all pronounced it God. Once, Jim Anderson of Westinghouse Broadcasting dialed Ranon's direct number and asked, "Is God there?" A woman's voice at the other end answered, "Mister, I think you want Dial-A-Prayer."

After the agreement was signed, President Ford issued a statement complimenting Kissinger on "one of the greatest diplomatic achievements of this century." En route to Washington, a reporter teased the Secretary of State about the comment, asking Kissinger the historian if he really thought it was "one of the greatest diplomatic achievements of this century"? The answer came from Kissinger the humorist: "Why only this century?"

In a highly unusual gesture, Ford and Vice President Rockefeller were waiting at Andrews Air Force Base to welcome Henry home.

Even before we had left Washington, Kissinger was referring to the new U.S. aid commitment to Israel as a "new order of magnitude." The figures turned out to be staggering — about $2 billion a year, compared to a range of between $300 and $600 million before that, not counting the special $2.2 billion emergency appropriation during the 1973 war. This was clearly a case of Dollar Diplomacy, although Kissinger insisted he had "never seen political concessions for economic aid in any major negotiation."

After Kissinger's return, John Chancellor and I had a two-way conversation on the air, and I used the words, "It was the best agreement money could buy." Israeli Ambassador Simcha Dinitz called me the next day to complain — the only direct complaint I ever had on a diplomatic report. Dinitz felt my line reinforced the impression of people who thought that Jews would do anything for money.

After the successful Sinai II shuttle, Kissinger did not return to the Middle East. A bitter reaction throughout the Arab world left Egypt temporarily isolated, and election-year politics left Kissinger — and his Middle East diplomacy — rather isolated as well. So the Middle East marked time while the United States elected a President. American Jews generally supported the challenger, Jimmy Carter, against an incumbent administration that they would soon come to regard as benign for all their differences with it at the time.

In a 1976 speech to the American Jewish Congress, Kissinger jokingly took note of his differences with the American Jewish community — and with some Israelis: "Rabbi Hertzberg has delicately referred to some occasional disagreements — usually directed, if I understand them, not at things that I have done — but of things that I am suspected of planning." The audience was charmed.

"And I realize also," Kissinger said, "that there is a peculiar difficulty of conducting foreign policy vis-à-vis a country of three million people and six million opinions. It came to expression again as Prime Minister Rabin was here, and the Israeli press — which, as all of you know, is a wild group of individualists, united only by a common paranoia — kept asking me what we had achieved. And it presented a very profound dilemma for me, because if I said this was true that we had achieved substantial agreement, I ran the risk of undermining his position ... But if I indicated that there was some slight possibility of disagreement, which would not have been true, it would only have confirmed all the suspicions with which the journalists came here to begin with."

He got the laughs he was aiming for, but the patter raised once again the intriguing question of Henry Kissinger's Jewishness and how it affected — or did not affect — his Middle East diplomacy. On

his first overnight visit to Jerusalem, in December 1973, Kissinger
went to Yad Vashem, the memorial to the Jews killed by the Nazis.
The Israelis take all of their important foreign visitors to the shrine
to help them understand what Israel is about.

For Kissinger, the visit had particular relevance. Gideon Hausner,
who administers the shrine, had dug out a lot of material from
Kissinger's birthplace, Fuerth, where, he said, "the Kissinger name
figured prominently." Hausner showed the Secretary books from
Fuerth and Frankfurt that listed the names of members of the Kissinger family. Kissinger asked that no press be allowed in while he
was visiting Yad Vashem. Outside, a cold hard rain pummeled the
hillside memorial. A person who was inside said that Kissinger
bowed his head as a cantor sang a mournful chant in front of the
eternal flame. He refused to talk about his feelings afterward, not
even during the off-the-record session on the plane. But an American
official who was present described Kissinger as absolutely silent and
almost "paralyzed." "Something traumatic had been disturbed," he
said.

Many Jews felt that Kissinger was certainly ambivalent, if not
downright defensive, about his own Jewishness. They pointed out
that he was sworn in on a Saturday, the Sabbath, that he took his
oath of office on a King James version of the Bible, that he worked
on Yom Kippur, the holiest day of the Jewish calendar, and that his
second wife was a non-Jew. Kissinger's parents made a concession
to their own Jewish orthodoxy by attending his swearing-in ceremony on a Saturday, but they did observe the injunction against
riding in automobiles on the Sabbath by walking to the White House
from their hotel.

Suspicions about Kissinger's Jewishness were reflected in a dou-
ble-edged joke the Israelis told about him — and themselves —
after his first visit to Jerusalem. Golda Meir, the story goes, took
Kissinger to the Wailing Wall, one of the holiest of all Jewish religious places. "What do you do here?" asked Kissinger. "You pray,"
said Golda, "and your prayer goes directly to God." So Kissinger
went to the Wailing Wall and prayed, "Let there be peace in the

Middle East." Then he went back to where Golda was watching and said, "That's wonderful." "I told you so," said Golda. "In fact," said Kissinger, "I'd like to do it again." "Fine," said Golda. "Go right ahead." Kissinger returned to the Wailing Wall and prayed again: "Let there be peace in the Middle East, let Arabs and Jews stop fighting one another and live forever in peace." Then Kissinger went back once more to where Golda was watching. "Marvelous," said Kissinger, "I feel like I'm really getting through." "Do you want to do it again?" asked Golda. "I do," said Kissinger, and he returned to the Wailing Wall to pray: "Let there be peace in the Middle East, let Arabs and Jews stop fighting one another and live peacefully side by side, and to get peace, let the Israelis withdraw from the Sinai and the Golan Heights and the West Bank." At that point, Golda turned to one of her aides and said, "Look at that schmuck — talking to himself beside a pile of stones!"

At the very outset of Kissinger's venture into Middle East diplomacy, there was apprehension in the American Jewish Community that the only place pressure could be applied was in Jerusalem. In response, the Secretary met constantly with prominent American Jews to try to convince them he was acting in Israel's best interests.

He argued that Israel had to exploit the current negotiating opportunities because time was not on its side. Down the road, he said, the Israelis would be at a military disadvantage because they would lose hundreds, even thousands, of men if they had to fight a series of wars. In addition, he constantly pointed out that Israel had become confined to a "diplomatic ghetto" once most countries decided to side with the Arabs because of the influence of oil, and he emphasized that the Israelis had to get out of their international ghetto just as they had escaped from the ghettoes of Europe. At the same time, he made the point that as the Secretary of State of the United States, whatever he thought of his religious background, he kept it to himself.

His aides acknowledged that many Jews found it hard to accept a situation in which a Jewish Secretary of State was welcomed by such bigoted enemies of Israel as King Faisal of Saudi Arabia. But

Israeli Foreign Minister Yigal Allon pointed out that if Kissinger was to function effectively as a mediator, he had to have the trust of the Arabs as well.

The main concern in Israel was that because of his background, Kissinger would bend over backward to be fair to the Arabs — at Israel's expense — and there was constant debate about whether he could be "trusted." This concern was expressed facetiously in a cartoon in the Israeli newspaper *Ma'ariv,* which was reprinted in the English-language Jerusalem *Post.* It showed an Israeli soldier racing toward an air-raid shelter, with the caption: "Kissinger's coming." Kissinger told an Israeli newspaper editor he had been amused by the cartoon, but he also expressed concern over some of the attacks in the Israeli press doubting his impartiality.

Prime Minister Meir once called a group of Israeli editors together and told them in private that she thought they were being unfair to the Secretary of State, and she asked them to moderate their criticism. In her memoirs, Mrs. Meir discounted Kissinger's Jewishness. "I don't think it either aided or hindered him in all those months of negotiations," she later wrote. "But if he was emotionally involved with us, such an involvement never reflected itself, for one moment, in anything he said to us or did in our behalf."

Abba Eban felt Kissinger's Jewishness was "part of the intimacy that he and the Israelis had with each other . . . There was a kind of inner understanding, a tragic experience. We weren't going to compromise our security and he wasn't going to be responsible for compromising our security." Dinitz thought "his Jewishness was a part of his own personality. It had to influence his performance positively because he did have a special feeling for the history of the Jews. . . . On the other hand, he often had to be careful and lean over backward so his judgment did not appear to be colored by his faith." Allon also found him detached from his Jewishness in an analytical way. "I think he did want to be responsive as a man who cared for Israel," Allon told me, "not only as an American, but as an American Jew. But he wanted to be free to determine what was good or what was bad for Israel, like any other Jew." Peres was as pragmatic about Kissinger's religion as Kissinger was about everything else. "If you have a horse," Peres said in his epigrammatic way, "you don't worry about his color. He is a white horse. If he gallops, he gallops."

One of the State Department's top Middle East experts had no doubt that "Kissinger was fundamentally committed to Israel's security. He used to cover it up and joke about it, but I think he felt very deeply his Jewish roots . . . In this relationship, he sometimes would get very angry at them [the Israelis] just because they were being shortsighted and were adopting policies which would be destructive of their long-term prospects." Rabin sensed that "his tendency was first to put the blame on Israel when Israel didn't do more."

Ironically, Israel, the Jewish state, was the only place in the world where Kissinger heard ethnic slurs. Demonstrators opposed to any Israeli pullback jeered at him when he arrived at the Prime Minister's office during the Syrian shuttle, calling him "Jew-boy." (President Nixon had allegedly used this term in referring to Kissinger, according to a Washington report on the White House tapes.) Kissinger later took note of the irony, but he was deeply hurt. The jeering reminded him of his boyhood days in Fuerth, and he asked the Israelis to have it stopped. The demonstrators were moved farther back the next time the Secretary arrived at the Prime Minister's office.

Kissinger once asked Steve Strauss, the American-born masseur at the King David, "What do the Israelis think of me?" Strauss answered, "A lot of them think you have forgotten who you are and where you came from." Kissinger replied, "I could never forget that."

This sensitivity was rarely on public display, but Ken Freed of the AP has a vivid recollection of one occasion. President Ford's visit to Poland in 1975 included a wrenching tour of the German death camp at Auschwitz. In the building where Jewish women were housed the night before they were taken to the gas chambers, Freed was overcome. He started to cry and almost collapsed. One person grabbed his elbow and helped him stand. It was Kissinger.

The Secretary did not escape Jewish demonstrators even in his adopted homeland. Two weeks before the presidential election, as Kissinger began addressing the Fiftieth Jubilee dinner of the Synagogue Council of America in New York, he was interrupted by shouting members of the militant Jewish Defense League.

But ten days before Kissinger left office, the American Jewish community paid tribute to the first Jewish Secretary of State at a luncheon that turned into a nostalgia trip. It was given by the conference of presidents of major American Jewish organizations at the Hotel Pierre, where Kissinger had first agreed to serve Richard Nixon. Max Fischer, a wealthy, politically active businessman who happened to be out of the country, sent a telegram reading: "I must mention that as Secretary of State, you created an openness to the Jewish community which they have never had since Israel was established."

Rabbi Alexander Schindler noted,

He may have been objective, but he was never detached. "How can I, as a Jew, do anything to betray my people?" Many of us have heard him say these words, and these words were not lightly spoken . . .

May our appreciation, as we express it, ease that moment of parting which must be difficult for him — even though assuredly there must also be a part of him which senses a release, a gladness to be "rid of us" as well.

Let's admit it, we were at times exasperating. Even as we will continue to be exasperating, we can do no otherwise.

Perhaps, Dr. Kissinger, you will remember us with exasperation tinged with affection.

As usual, Kissinger eased into his serious remarks with humor. He first expressed his "appreciation for the thoughtfulness of the Presidents' Organization in insuring that every speaker here would have an accent . . . I have dealt with the Presidents' Organization throughout my term as Secretary of State," he said,

and I need not tell you that they are composed of a rugged group of individualists, united only by a wary suspiciousness of all forms of government.

I have had also the privilege of dealing with the Israeli Ambassador, who is the Ambassador of the only country in the world where the representative in Washington can be criticized for having too close a relationship with the Secretary of State.

Now, as I understand it, the Ambassador has been accused, at the risk of his political career — I would think correctly — as being a friend of mine. All I can tell you is, I don't know how he treats his opponents.

"You and I have gone through a great deal together in recent years," he went on,

and I thought that if this meeting made any sense, it would be if I spoke to you from the heart about some of the considerations on my mind . . .

I thought it was important for the future of Israel and for the future of the Jewish people, that the actions that the U.S. Government take were not seen to be the result of a special, personal relationship, and that the support we gave Israel reflected not my personal preferences alone, but the basic national interests of the United States, transcending the accident of who might be in office at any particular period.

I have never forgotten that thirteen members of my family died in concentration camps, nor could I ever fail to remember what it was like to live in Nazi Germany as a member of a persecuted minority . . .

I believe, however, that the relationship of Israel to the United States transcends these personal considerations.

The support for a free and democratic Israel in the Middle East is a moral necessity of our period, to be pursued by every administration, and with a claim to the support of all freedom-loving people all over the world.

And Kissinger mended some fences as well. "Rabbi Schindler pointed out that maybe I am glad to be rid of this group, but I do not believe I will ever be rid of this group." They laughed and applauded. "And frankly, I do not want ever to be rid of this group — though I may retract this in a few months."

Once Kissinger left the scene, he was missed in Israel. Yitzak Rabin gave me this retrospective summing up: "He was a person of great talent. He really penetrated the problem. He knew the limitations, he knew the personalities, he knew the situation, he had a creative mind. It was a real pleasure to work with him."

SEVEN

Egypt

By the time Henry Kissinger became Secretary of State, he had already visited China, the Soviet Union, Southeast Asia, Israel, and dozens of world capitals. But the first Jewish Secretary of State had never set foot in an Arab country. By the time Henry Kissinger became ex–Secretary of State, he had spent more time in Arab countries than any of his predecessors. The Arab-Israeli war in October 1973 had seen to that.

Shortly before the war broke out, Kissinger told Arab foreign ministers at a New York luncheon, "We recognize the present situation is intolerable to the Arab world in the long run." And he promised to try to make it less intolerable. His guests were impressed. Within days, however, the situation in the Middle East had become virtually intolerable for the United States. The wreckage of America's relations with the Arabs left over from the 1967 war was compounded when Saudi Arabia and other long-standing friends of the United States imposed an oil embargo in retaliation for massive American aid to Israel during the 1973 war.

The Secretary had been invited by President Anwar Sadat to stop off in Cairo after his visits to Moscow and Israel to arrange the cease-fire at the end of the 1973 war, but he had declined. He felt the time wasn't quite ripe for that move.

Sadat sent his minister of tourism, Ismael Fahmy, to Washington to talk to Kissinger about postwar efforts at negotiation. Kissinger grumped about having to deal with a minister of tourism. He was used to playing in a bigger league. When word of Kissinger's grumbling got back to Cairo, Fahmy was upgraded to acting minister of foreign affairs, and he was eventually promoted to the minister's job on a permanent basis.

Kissinger delighted in reminding Fahmy that he had "made" him foreign minister, and he also delighted in retelling the sequence of events to other people in Fahmy's presence. Fahmy, a feisty, dapper little man with an ego to match Kissinger's, finally had had enough. At a State Department luncheon in 1974, when the Secretary started to tell the story again, Fahmy interrupted to complain, "Henry, every time I'm invited, you tell the same story." Henry relented, but he soon came up with a new story. After he got into political hot water in the United States, he said he would leave the State Department and become foreign minister of Egypt, and he added that Sadat had already approved the idea. Fahmy didn't appreciate that story, either.

When Kissinger scheduled his first trip to the Arab countries in November 1973, he decided to wade in rather than plunge. Cairo was not the first stop; the trip began on the friendlier Arab soil of Morocco and Tunisia. Kissinger's aura and his reputation as a skillful negotiator and a Nobel Peace Prize winner helped clear the way for his entrance into the Arab world. That first trip was extraordinary in many respects, as Henry Kissinger, a Jew, was received by Arab leaders who had spent much of their life trying to destroy the Jewish state of Israel. He not only introduced himself to them, he immediately began to build trust among them as he sought to revive American influence in the area.

The airport for Kissinger's first landing in the Arab world was appropriately named: Bab Salam (Peace Gateway) Airport in Rabat.

Rabat turned out to be a crashing success for Joe Sisco, the hard-

driving assistant secretary of Near Eastern affairs. When Kissinger
and his party first arrived at the presidential palace, they were taken
to the King's sitting room, where they sat in ornate, red velvet-
covered chairs. When Sisco sat, he really sat. The chair gave way,
so Kissinger's first meeting with an Arab leader began with one of
his top aides sprawled on the floor. Neither Sisco nor Kissinger's
diplomacy was hurt, however, and when the Secretary of State visited Rabat a year later, King Hassan greeted him by asking where
Sisco was. His Majesty immediately pointed out that he had ordered
new chairs for his sitting room so that Sisco could take a seat with
confidence. Sisco eventually showed up and did.

Traveling as the Secretary of State for the first time, Kissinger got
his first exposure to the benefits — or curses — of protocol, which
had been denied him as a mere White House aide. The Royal Palace
Guard — Berbers wearing baggy scarlet and green uniforms and
wielding sabers and halberds — turned out to welcome him. Kissinger was always more adept at negotiation than protocol, and when

Dwane Powell, *The News and Observer*, Raleigh

the ceremony was over, he didn't quite know what to do. So he extended his hand toward the leader of the honor guard, who was holding a scimitar. Kissinger almost shook hands with the sword.

He was not overly impressed with the honors due him. At the next stop, as he straightened his tie before descending the ramp, he cracked that he had to "review another camel brigade."

The next stop was Tunis, which had been added to the itinerary after Kissinger received word that President Bourguiba felt offended that he was being bypassed. The stops in Morocco and Tunisia were intended to have a political impact far beyond their borders. Kissinger later told newsmen privately that he wanted to demonstrate to Israel that even the ultra-moderates now identified with the hardliners on such issues as the Palestinians. As usual, his travel was neither accidental nor incidental.

The terra incognita of Cairo was next, and the flight from Tunis was not without tension. Kissinger tried to relieve it by coming to the press section of the plane and demanding, "Hey, where's the MiG escort you guys promised me?"

In all the Kissinger travels, the first arrival in Cairo stands out for the sheer drama of the occasion. The plane landed an hour late. The airport was pitch black as the big 707 rolled to a stop. Egypt was still on a war footing, and Cairo was blacked out. The cease-fire in the Sinai wavered daily. American-Egyptian relations had been broken since 1967. Sadat himself was an unknown quantity. Before Kissinger's arrival, officials at the American mission and the Secret Service advance team had advised the Egyptians not to permit newsmen out on the ramp, but to keep them behind barricades. The Egyptians ignored the advice. Dozens of soldiers and plainclothes police set up a security ring around the plane instead.

As the Secretary emerged, the bright television lights flashed on, a horde of photographers, cameramen, and reporters closed in, and the security ring collapsed like the Sinai defenses in 1967; while screams and curses in Arabic filled the air, Kissinger's Secret Service agents struggled desperately to keep him from being mobbed. In the resulting chaos, Spanish Ambassador Manolo Alabart, who represented U.S. interests in Egypt at the time, was knocked down and trampled. Only his dignity was hurt. It was one of the most anxious moments the security agents ever had.

As we made the long drive into Cairo, we could see signs of wartime everywhere. Sandbags guarded doorways. Car headlights were shaded by blue or black paint. At the Nile Hilton Hotel, windows were crisscrossed with tape, to prevent shattering, and painted blue. For newsmen there was another sign of war. All of our copy had to be given a stamp of approval by Egyptian censors before it could be filed or broadcast.

Kissinger's first historic meeting with Sadat took place in Tahirah Palace in suburban Helopolis, and it began with nonhistoric chitchat. Kissinger said, "I had a very interesting time with Mr. Fahmy in Washington." "Yes," responded Sadat, "he told me about it." The two men then met alone in a Louis XV drawing room while members of their delegations conferred outside on the lawn. It established a pattern that was repeated frequently.

Afterward, Kissinger, Sadat, and Fahmy posed for pictures. A reporter asked, "Is it war or peace?" "We must await the answer of our friend, Dr. Kissinger," replied Sadat, establishing another practice of deferring to the Secretary during question-and-answer sessions. Kissinger took his cue and ad-libbed to the galleries beyond Cairo, "I think we're moving toward peace."

An Egyptian reporter asked, "Do you expect an interruption of arms supplies to Israel?" Sadat once again deferred: "Ask Dr. Kissinger." Kissinger tried humor. "Luckily, I didn't hear the question." The reporter persisted: "I'd be happy to rephrase it." Kissinger persisted as well: "And I'd rephrase the same answer."

Later, an anxious American diplomat stationed in the U.S. Interests Section in Cairo wanted to know what had happened at the meeting. Roy Atherton answered simply and profoundly, "They liked each other."

When Sadat succeeded Gamal Abdel Nasser as President of Egypt, Kissinger tended to dismiss him as a "clown," another loudmouthed lightweight who postured ridiculously. But after the Egyptian President threw out the Russians, Kissinger became somewhat intrigued and decided to take a closer look. Three years earlier, Kissinger told a group of reporters in California that one of the principal goals of American policy in the Middle East was to expel the Russians from Egypt. The use of the word "expel" caused a lot of controversy at the time, but when push came to shove, "expel" came to pass, although it seemed to be more Sadat's doing than Kissinger's.

In their first face-to-face meeting, Kissinger decided that Sadat was "going for peace," as he himself once told me. Prior to the Secretary's arrival, the Egyptians were screaming that the Israelis had violated the cease-fire agreement and moved beyond the October 22 lines. But Kissinger found that Sadat did not want to talk only about forcing the Israelis back to the October 22 lines, the issue of the moment; he wanted to talk about the big picture and what lay ahead.

Months later, Kissinger told us on the plane, "Look, there are few national leaders with whom you can discuss ten years of [the future]. In fact, with Sadat, you can come closer to it than with anybody else."

One of Kissinger's top aides explained later, "Kissinger made a judgment at that first meeting with Sadat that this was a man on whom we could build our peace strategy. This was the only person who seemed to understand our conceptual approach . . . That was as much insight as I ever had about Henry . . . He instinctively saw the qualities in the man and the opportunities in the situation, and in his mind, he made a decision on the spot. He was not hampered by preconceptions. He could make a very quick adjustment and exploit the moment, exploit the opportunity. He could see a situation through in his own mind — he saw at once what the next step would be. He has the instinctive intelligence to see things that other people have to think through step by step. People who say he basically has the mind of a genius — they're right."

Kissinger's initial impression of Sadat was reciprocated by the Egyptian President. Sadat wrote in his autobiography:

Our first session of talks took three hours. The first hour made me feel I was dealing with an entirely new mentality, a new political method. For the first time, I felt as if I was looking at the real face of the United States, the one I had always wanted to see — not the face put on by Dulles, Dean Rusk and Rogers. Anyone seeing us after that first hour in al-Tahirah Palace would have thought we have been friends for years. There was no difficulty in understanding each other.

From the beginning, Kissinger usually dealt directly with Sadat — alone. One reason was that he felt that Foreign Minister Fahmy and the Chief of Staff, General Gamsay, got bogged down in details and tended to string out the negotiations. Sadat made the major decisions, and the Secretary then worked out the details with Sadat's subordinates. It was not an arrangement that pleased Fahmy, and it was not especially satisfying to Kissinger's aides, either, since he never briefed them fully on his conversations with Sadat. That was part of the Kissinger style. Only he knew the whole picture.

Kissinger amused the Egyptians during the first visit by telling "war stories" about urgent Israeli appeals for tanks and ammunition in transatlantic calls during the war. The stories flattered Sadat; "his" October War had scared the Israelis. The stories were also designed to ingratiate Kissinger with his Egyptian hosts.

Although the Egyptian President had been denouncing the United States for its support of Israel only two weeks earlier, he and Kissinger agreed on a restoration of American-Egyptian relations "in principle." Sadat obviously wanted to have in Cairo a senior American diplomat who could get through to Kissinger in a hurry. But he did not want to appear to be moving too fast toward the United States in the eyes of his brother Arabs. And so the highly unorthodox device of a resumption "in principle" was devised. It appealed to Kissinger's sense of diplomatic innovation.

Egypt's decision reflected a growing Arab conviction that only Washington would be able to persuade, or even force, Israel to change its policies, that only Washington would one day be able to get Arab land back for the Arabs.

The principal short-term result of Kissinger's visit to Cairo was a six-point plan for stabilizing the cease-fire lines. Since Israel was not on the itinerary, Joe Sisco was sent to Jerusalem to get Israel's concurrence. Kissinger jokingly referred to the uncertain nature of Sisco's mission by telling newsmen that disclosure of details of the plan would have to await Sisco's return — "if Joe ever does."

Reporters kept pressing the Secretary to describe the six points as a Kissinger plan, but he declined. Should it be called the Sisco plan? "Only if it fails," observed Kissinger. Later, he refined his position. "If it becomes known as the Sisco plan," he said, "then I'm certain Joe will enjoy becoming head of a passport office — somewhere."

One of Kissinger's hallmarks was to lay the groundwork very carefully before going on a trip, and the first visit to Cairo was hardly an exception. He had prepared himself very thoroughly in his Washington meetings with Fahmy. But he had not been briefed on the famed "Cairo Tower," which rises meaninglessly from Gezira Island, across the Nile from the Hilton Hotel. The tower was built with three million dollars slipped to Nasser by the CIA in the early 1960s. According to Miles Copeland in *The Game of Nations,* one of Nasser's aides suggested building

> a structure, roughly modeled on the Sphinx, that would consist of two large statues on the Gezira side of the Nile, facing the site where the Hilton Hotel would one day be built; the one behind would be a large head featuring a particularly large nose; the one in the front would be a hand of proportionate size with the thumb adjusted to the nose and the four fingers extending skywards. Nasser thought the idea very good but lacking in subtlety. Instead, he ordered "something unidentifiable, but very large, very conspicuous, very enduring and very expensive — costing, oh, say, something in the neighborhood of three million dollars." The result is the "Tower of Cairo" which we American friends of Egypt see across the Nile every morning as we breakfast on our balconies at the Nile Hilton.

We all see it, all right, but we never had breakfast on our balconies, since if you ordered room service at the Nile Hilton, breakfast was likely to turn up around lunchtime.

Copeland also pointed out that the Egyptians themselves came to refer to the tower as "Roosevelt's erection," after Kermit Roosevelt, a CIA official who was instrumental in promoting the three-million-dollar slush fund for Nasser.

Kissinger did not get such a colorful description of "Nasser's Needle" when he asked Fahmy about it. The Egyptian foreign minister mumbled something about a television tower.

On that first visit to Egypt, Kissinger established another custom that he followed on almost all of his subsequent visits: He went sightseeing. And Cairo has some of the best sights in the world — the pyramids and the Sphinx. They were ready-made for Kissinger quips.

After posing for "just one more" in front of the Sphinx, he sighed to photographers, "Now can I turn around and look at it?" Conscious of complaints from reporters about a lack of information, he added, "I hope you are clear in your minds which one is the Sphinx." While Kissinger was viewing the pyramid at Giza, one of his aides cracked, "Henry's looking it over . . . he wants one for himself." Not

Mike Peters, with permission from *Dayton Daily News*

precisely. He told a reporter, "Now this is the kind of press center I need."

For unknown reasons, the Egyptians refused to allow the entire traveling press corps to accompany Kissinger to the pyramids, and so a press pool went along, which included Herb Kaplow of ABC News. Near the pyramids, Kaplow had to fend off a camel-pusher, who took pictures of people on his camel for a couple of bucks or as much as he could get. "Why not?" said the man, who wore an Arab headdress and a flowing robe. "David Brinkley was on my camel."

Kissinger the historian was genuinely interested in Egypt's historical treasures. Kissinger the diplomat benefited thereby. The Egyptians were pleased, not only that he showed such interest, but that he was so knowledgeable about the places he visited. They were doubly pleased when Nancy proved to be knowledgeable as well. The Egyptian daily *Al Akhbar* summed up Kissinger's triumphant first visit: "Like Metternich, Kissinger has been able to restore links which had become as fragile as glass, and to induce flexibility in relations which had become as stiff as steel. Nobel-man Kissinger has proved his capability for this unique type of activity . . . Massive bridges between America and Russia, America and China . . . Tomorrow, it may be the restoration of bridges between America and West Europe, the day after tomorrow between Israel and the whole Arab world."

Israel approved the six-point agreement, and within a month Kissinger was back in the Middle East, hoping to get something from Egypt and Israel to "grease the wheels" at the Geneva Conference — perhaps an agreement of principles to guide the disengagement negotiations. He foresaw the possibility of going back and forth between Egypt and Israel a couple of times, but he did not envision a prolonged "shuttle" until Sadat suggested he remain in the area to wrap up the disengagement agreement himself.

Sadat was recovering from bronchitis and had gone to Aswan on the Upper Nile, six hundred miles south of Cairo, to rest in the gentle winter sun. Aswan was certainly an ironic site for one end of the shuttle. It was best known as the site of the Aswan High Dam, the massive project that the Soviet Union financed after Secretary of State John Foster Dulles canceled American participation in its construction. Their aid gave the Russians a big foot in the Middle East door; now Aswan became the site of a negotiation designed in large part to close that door, with the Russians left outside.

The signs of Soviet influence were pervasive. American diplomats were transported in Russian-made Volgas and Czech-made Skodas during the Kissinger visit. And shortly before the Secretary of State arrived, a 250-foot-high concrete lotus flower commemorating Soviet-Egyptian friendship had been dedicated. The friendship did not endure as long as it took to complete the monument to it.

The dam itself had been dedicated in 1971, and the Egyptians wanted to show it off to Kissinger. He was not ungracious. "I think it is spectacular," he said when he saw it from a bridge where he could feel the spray from the huge gushes of water below. And he listened patiently while an Egyptian official recited the dull statistics of the dam. The official noted that the bed of Lake Nasser, which stretched behind the dam, was so deep that five hundred years would pass before sediment could fill it and render the dam useless. Kissinger, thinking ahead as always, commented, "Then you'll be in trouble in five hundred years." The Egyptian official was prepared. "But we expect that modern technology will find a solution to the problem within a hundred years," he said.

The Kissinger party was housed at the New Cataract Hotel, which stood, appropriately enough, next to the Old Cataract Hotel. The new hotel had been built by the Russians, which meant it was cramped and drab. It contrasted greatly with the Old Cataract, which stood decaying in Victorian splendor, a massive structure of dirty crimson brick and ornate sandstone. It had high ceilings and an elegant, faded, domed dining room (where we were served bad-tasting Nile fish). It also had a broad veranda for taking a spot of tea or a nip of gin or a Stella beer while looking across the river at the granite cataract that gave the hotel its name. Sailboats and feluccas slipped silently across the brownish water of the Nile, and in the distance, the sun bounced off the large white villa of the Begum

Khan, who placed a rose on the nearby tomb of the late Aga Khan every day. Nightfall infused the stretch of desert beyond with a sense of mystery and romance. And for those who got up early enough in the morning, the sights in Aswan included Ambassador Hermann Eilts's Egyptian bodyguard, who did his yoga exercises in the garden near the pool of the New Cataract every morning at dawn.

Kissinger was himself an early riser, but not that early. However, one morning he wanted to go for a walk around seven o'clock, but he wanted to do it quietly, without an entourage. He asked his bodyguard, Walter Bothe, if they could sneak out of the hotel without alerting the phalanx of Egyptian security guards. Bothe thought they could. But as soon as they hit the street, the Egyptians mobilized — armored cars, motorcycles, troops brandishing machine guns, the whole array. Kissinger decided to take his walk anyway, but he kept it short — and brisk.

When they got back to the hotel and into the elevator, Kissinger exploded at Bothe. But Bothe shot back, "Look, Mr. Secretary, I'll make you a deal. I won't interfere with diplomacy, and you don't interfere with security." Kissinger looked at Joe Sisco, who was swallowing a laugh. "Okay," Kissinger said to Bothe, "I guess you got a deal."

The Old Cataract provided the setting for Agatha Christie's *Death on the Nile*. The maitre d'hôtel was seventy-five-year-old Charles Bayer, a man who had learned firsthand about death and disaster. When he worked at the King David Hotel in Jerusalem, one wing was blown up, and he barely escaped death. He then moved to Shepheard's in Cairo; the hotel was destroyed by fire. The Old Cataract was his next employer, and the people who knew Herr Bayer wondered when catastrophe would strike there. Instead, the worst thing that happened was its inundation by a huge press corps. The old hotel housed the "press room" and the "communication" facilities, all of which were minimal.

Bayer did avoid one potential disaster. He personally supervised the preparation of Kissinger's breakfast. He didn't trust the Egyptian chefs to do it right each time.

In stark contrast to the teeming and the tumult and the frenzy of

Cairo, Aswan was a sleepy city, full of green palm trees, white houses, scarlet flame trees along the riverbanks, and cool breezes that bore the scent of jasmine. Sadat's lodging in Aswan was a sandstone house set amidst bougainvillea on a bluff high above the original Aswan Dam, built by the British in 1902. Sadat liked it there not only for the setting; he was less accessible than when he was in Cairo, and he wanted to concentrate fully on the negotiations.

The first Kissinger-Sadat encounter took place in a latticework gazebo just outside the villa overlooking the Nile. (The film editors later complained about the "spotted" quality of the faces, which had been crisscrossed by the shadows of the latticework.) Sadat and Kissinger subsequently spent so much time alone that Sisco and Ambassador Ellsworth Bunker occasionally tossed blankets on the lawn and napped al fresco.

From the very start of the negotiations, it was apparent that Sadat had considerable respect for Golda Meir. The members of the American delegation did a double-take when they found out — not because of the sentiment, but because of Sadat's expressiveness. "That woman has balls," he said admiringly.

Kissinger felt at the outset that Sadat's ambitions for an agreement were overreaching, but the Egyptian President's optimism was eventually justified. Kissinger later told us that Sadat often showed more flexibility than his aides, whom he had to overrule at certain crucial times to keep the talks going.

One of the overruled aides was Foreign Minister Fahmy, who had a graying mustache and a hard-line attitude toward Israel. But he, too, was optimistic from the outset. Just after Kissinger's arrival in Aswan, Fahmy told the American reporters, "Your Secretary of State, when he sticks his fingers into something, generally brings it to a successful conclusion, and I think he will this time."

Apart from the diplomatic benefits, the first Middle East shuttle provided a boon for Aswan's tourist industry. Foreign visitors stayed away in droves following the October War, but the hordes of American and Egyptian officials, plus the dozens of newsmen, took up the slack.

The American diplomats in Cairo and the members of the advance team had all gone to Aswan expecting a short stay. But the "short stay" dragged on for three weeks for the American ground support personnel, who did not fly back and forth. Three weeks in Aswan became a very long time.

The nontraveling Secret Service agents, whose nocturnal habits were severely curtailed in a place like Aswan, devised their own system for getting out. They awarded points for certain activities, with 10 points needed in order to leave. A successful suicide was worth 10 points. An unsuccessful suicide meant forfeiting all previously accumulated points. Other activities were:

Dropping an empty Stella bottle on Fahmy's head from the balcony on the seventh floor — 1 point.

Sexual relations with a camel — 2 points.

Sexual relations with a Nubian maiden — 3 points.

Sexual relations with an Egyptian soldier — 5 points (they were better looking than Nubian maidens).

Overpowering a felucca crew and commandeering the boat — 7 points.

Eating within smelling range of one of the visiting Russian tourist groups — 1/2 point.

Three weeks in Aswan became a very long time indeed.

Two young members of the American staff from Cairo, April Glaspie and Beth Jones, achieved a kind of sexist fame for themselves during the Aswan shuttle. After his first two visits to the Middle East, Kissinger had griped about too much starch in his shirts, especially in Cairo. It took three more washings, he joked, before he could button them. In Aswan, the all-important job of handling Kissinger's laundry was entrusted to Foreign Service Officers Glaspie and Jones. They proved worthy of the task, and Kissinger began praising them ad nauseam for managing to get his shirts done right. Aswan, he used to say, was the only place where a U.S. Embassy officer was able to get his shirts done properly, without starch. Little did he know that everybody in Aswan had his shirts done without starch. There wasn't any starch in Aswan. April Glaspie referred to herself jokingly as the Embassy's laundry officer. But praise for lowly junior officers in any fashion from the Secretary of State would not hurt their promotion records.

Later in the year, at a ceremony in Cairo, he publicly thanked the much-put-upon employees of the American Embassy for having spent so much of their life accommodating his demands on the numerous trips. He paid special tribute to Beth and April. "I've been coming here more often than I can remember in the last year, and you've all been taking very good care of me. These young ladies here," he said, "have been bossing me around in such a way that I'm a strong supporter now of women's liberation, which, as I understand it, gives men equality."

To prepare for Kissinger's visit to Aswan, the small staff at the American mission in Cairo had been given just forty-eight hours' notice. And since they were advised that Kissinger would not be staying long, they didn't go out of their way to worry about communications. As one official said later, "We never did that again!"

When the Secretary's plane was not on the ground in Aswan, the Americans had no classified communications, so any messages from Washington or from the Kissinger party in Israel went first to Cairo and then by a tenuous open telephone line to Aswan. Even the Top Secret and NODIS (No Distribution) traffic traveled this open, uncoded route. The secretaries wrote the message down, typed it up in their fifth-floor rooms at the New Cataract, and had it delivered to the Egyptians on the third floor. The short-handedness of the staff led to a lesson in shorthand for political officers. The secretaries were so overwhelmed with the flood of messages, they taught the political officers some elementary shorthand to help them transcribe the messages more quickly.

On one memorable occasion, Arthur Houghton, a political officer who was manning the fort in Cairo, called Aswan to say that the Kissinger party had some procedural questions that required an urgent answer. The Aswan staff duly took them down and was in the process of typing them when Omar Sirry, of the Egyptian Foreign Office, showed up on the fifth floor, saying, "The answer to those questions is . . . ." The Egyptians had been listening to everything over the open telephone line.

When the agreement was finally reached, the signings in Israel and Egypt had to be precisely coordinated. To make sure of the communications, the Americans in Aswan turned the crank on the old-fashioned, hand-cranked telephone in their office and opened a line to Cairo seven hours before the designated signing time. The line went from Aswan to Cairo to the Operations Center at the State Department in Washington to Jerusalem. If at any time the Egyptian operators detected silence on the line between Aswan and Cairo or between Cairo and Washington, they immediately cut it and took the next call on their list, since calls were stacked up for as long as twenty-four hours at times. And since most of the Egyptian operators did not speak English, appeals for return of the broken line were usually fruitless. (The broadcasters struggled with the problem throughout the shuttle. Any pause in the conversation with London or New York meant we lost the line we had waited several hours to get.) Much of the burden of keeping open the Aswan-Cairo-Washington-Jerusalem line fell to the laundry specialists, Beth Jones and April Glaspie. They talked with young officers in Washington about the weather and baseball (although Beth didn't know anything about baseball). They read poetry, they read from the Bible — since it was the New Cataract, they read from the New Testament — they read administrative regulations — all of which succeeded in keeping the line open until everything was signed and the first Sinai disengagement agreement was a reality.

When Kissinger paid his farewell call on Sadat, a new ritual was born. The Egyptian President told the American Secretary of State, "You are not only my friend, you are my brother." And he kissed Kissinger on both cheeks. The quips were never-ending after that.

Kissinger was not surprised, however. Before his visit, he had asked Arabists in Washington about the practice of fraternal kissing. He understood that the symbolism was useful in Egypt and elsewhere in the Arab world; it indicated he was a person accepted by the leadership. But he never seemed entirely at ease. On a later mission, when he was accompanied by his wife, he returned to Aswan and hugged Fahmy before kissing Nancy. Another time, he shook hands with Nancy after hugging Fahmy.

His self-consciousness displayed itself in joking. During one of his departures from Egypt, he gave Fahmy a bear hug on the ramp and told Ambassador Eilts, over the foreign minister's shoulder, "When I trust you as much as Ismael, I'll hug you like this, too." Later in the year, he went to Cairo to see Sadat, who was again in bed with bronchitis. En route, a reporter asked, "Are you going to risk kissing Sadat with his cold?" "If I don't," replied the amused Secretary, "there will be an international incident."

One of Kissinger's rewards for working out the disengagement agreement was a visit to Luxor the day after the signing. Once again, the Embassy whiz kids took off to prepare the way. They first had to get permits from the Egyptian government, since foreigners were still not allowed on the road between Cairo and Aswan. Once they had taken care of the accommodations at the Winter Palace on the Nile, their main problem was the transportation. The governor of Quna was determined that Kissinger should ride in the best car in the area, and the governor's version of the best car in the area was a 1957 pink Cadillac with huge tailfins. The two staffers managed to locate a white Mercedes, and they diplomatically persuaded the governor that it would be more appropriate than the pink Cadillac.

Their next problem was the American flag flying outside the hotel for the Kissinger visit. As they pointed out to the manager, Egypt and the United States did not yet have formal diplomatic relations, so it was not appropriate to fly the flag. The manager of the hotel reluctantly had it taken down.

There was one problem they failed to cope with. At 7:00 A.M. the morning after the Kissinger party arrived, an Egyptian pilot flew his MiG low along the Nile past the Winter Palace and then soared skyward, breaking the sound barrier with a boom that sounded as though the war had resumed. Not even the fatigued shuttlers could sleep through that kind of noise. How loud was it? It was so loud that Secret Service agent Walter Bothe reacted by rolling out of bed and pulling the mattress on top of him; he thought the hotel was under attack.

Since the trip to Luxor had been arranged on short notice, some of the details normally handled by an advance team had to be put off to the last minute. There wasn't time beforehand, for example, to make sure that the cars in the motorcade taking Kissinger to the Valley of the Kings across the river were all numbered for quick access and easy organization once the traveling party arrived.

In order to get to the motorcade, the party first had to cross the Nile in a small ferry. As Kissinger walked aboard, he saw Dick Smith, from the American mission in Cairo, standing on the dock. He nodded a greeting. Smith smiled and nodded back. Just before the ferry pulled out, Smith jumped on the back and rode across. As it pulled up to the other side, Smith jumped off and raced up the hill to check out the motorcade. He was relieved, and surprised, to find everything properly arranged. Kissinger was also in for a surprise. When he got to his limousine, there was Dick Smith holding the door open. The Secretary did a double-take, then asked, "How did you get here?" Smith gave him a Kissingerian response: "Like any good Foreign Service officer, I walked on the water, sir."

During the tour, an extraordinary number of men in peasant dress lounged on the high crags overlooking the valley. They were Egyptian security men in disguise.

For the Secretary of State, the Luxor visit turned into something of an ego trip. Having negotiated an agreement between Egypt and Israel, having been kissed on both cheeks by Sadat and anointed his "brother," Kissinger was now a folk hero on the streets, and Egyptian men in galabias and women in black robes clapped their hands and shouted his name as his motorcade drove by. One little-known result of the successful shuttle took place in Beersheba, Israel. A Bedouin tribesman went to the local registrar following the birth of a seven-pound son and announced, "I want to express my gratitude, and so please call the boy Dr. Henry Kissinger Hassan Abargad, of the Abargad Bedouin tribe."

When Kissinger returned to Egypt a month later, one change was immediately apparent. Sadat, an Army general, was wearing civilian clothes for the first time since the October War. The Egyptian President told inquiring newsmen that the civvies were meant to symbolize a new era in view of all that Kissinger was doing to bring about peace in the Middle East, although he added that he did not yet regard the war as "over." However, he never again wore his uniform during a Kissinger visit, and he became a figure of elegance in his well-tailored, pinched-waist dark suits and expensive accessories. He also smoked his pipe more in public. Irreverent newsmen dubbed it his "lucky pipe" for no good reason.

In addition to Sadat's clothes, the February 1974 visit marked another turning point. During an early morning ceremony, the American flag was raised over the U.S. Embassy on Latin America Street for the first time in seven years. The Americans and the Egyptians also began talking about an exchange of visits between President Sadat and President Nixon. At the flag-raising ceremony, Kissinger spoke of Egypt's "great leader." The public language was a reflection of a private ritual. After the first disengagement agreement, Sadat took to calling Kissinger "The Miracle Worker," with the accent on the second syllable in "miracle." (People at the American Embassy also began referring to Kissinger the same way, but with a sarcasm missing from Sadat's inflections.)

Whenever Sadat had a small lunch or dinner for Kissinger, the ritual was always invoked. At one of these dinners, there were just four couples: the Sadats, the Kissingers, the Fahmys, and the Eiltses. The Egyptian President once again toasted "The Miracle Worker," saying, "You did it, Henry, you worked the miracle . . ." And Kissinger replied, as he always did, "No, Mr. President, it was you who did it, it was because of your statemanship and wisdom and vision . . ." As they went into their act, Mrs. Sadat leaned over to Ambassador Eilts and whispered, with a combination of amusement and exasperation, "There they go again!"

Those dinners with the Sadats were intimate and familylike. After leaving office, Kissinger recalled that during meals in the President's home, all the members of his family emphasized how much they wanted peace. Kissinger was convinced that the sentiments were genuine, that an entire family could not be programmed to say what they did.

Sadat, who was extremely careful about his diet, always ate the same thing at lunch — a gelatinous, starchless macaroni. His wife used to lament to the guests, "He's on a strict diet. All this wonderful food we prepare, and he doesn't eat any of it."

With Kissinger now virtually a member of the official Egyptian family, for the first time his hosts took him to see a contemporary institution as renowned in Egypt as the pyramids at Giza. They took him to the Sheraton to see Najwa Fuad, the queen of the belly dancers. That's not the description she uses for herself, however. She prefers "Oriental dancer." It's not the classic belly dance, but it'll do. She has taken the traditional dance and modernized it, making it more Western in the process. She is the biggest thing in Egyptian show biz, and while Egyptian show biz may not be a hot ticket in the United States, it's the biggest thing on the Arab circuit, especially since Beirut went under.

When I heard that Kissinger was going to dinner at the Sheraton, I decided to tag along as a spectator. Few of my colleagues did likewise, and I felt afterward that they had missed something. So when I returned to the hotel at about two in the morning, feeling fine, I wrote the following report:

> The Kissinger party arrived at the Sheraton Hotel at 10:05 and proceeded directly to the bar on the top floor, which commands an imposing view of the Nile Hilton across the river.
>
> After Foreign Minister Ismael Fahmy bought a round or two, everybody made his way to an elongated table placed strategically near and perpendicular to the dance floor.
>
> Secretary Kissinger sat in the last chair nearest the dance floor. He was facing the Nile Hilton panorama.
>
> The rest of the party was arranged haphazardly toward the salt at the other end of the table.
>
> The dinner, as far as could be ascertained, was uneventful. It consisted of cream of chicken soup, grilled shrimp, veal chops masquerading as

grilled veal cutlets, an assortment of vegetables, plus hummus, yogurt and cucumber salad, followed by a dessert of ice cream and cigars (Havanas for those who could cadge one from Fahmy, as Kissinger aide Larry Eagleburger is wont to do).

All this was accompanied by Pharaoh wine. (It was a good Pharaoh, but not a great Pharaoh.)

At approximately 10:45, a Middle Eastern facsimile of "My Way" gave way to a rhythmic, erotic explosion of sensuous sounds . . . a spotlight drilled the smoky cabaret air, and Najwa Fuad undulated out of the darkness in a Scheherazaidic costume.

If you squinted, you saw Rita Hayworth. Nobody squinted.

The motions which followed defy verbal description.

Full breasts rallied tantalizingly against a black halter which restrained but did not restrict. Hips gyrated. Long auburn hair flashed. There may have been some hand movements, too.

The music climaxed. Go to black. Najwa Fuad undulated back into the darkness.

She reappeared in a yummy muu-muu with jangles jangling in all the jangley places.

Your Secretary of State watched intently, almost stolidly, his face masking any lascivious impulses which may have made him wonder why Le Duc Tho never brought him to a place like this. His lap remained inviolate.

Meanwhile, elsewhere down the line: Ambassador Hermann Eilts was enveloped in the darkness, the camera eye of his mind perhaps focusing on the fleshy undulations on stage and then dissolving into a red, white and blue flag undulating in the breeze not long after dawn the next morning — the first time the American flag will have flown over Cairo in seven years.

Ambassador Ellsworth Bunker's interest was unflagging.

Eagleburger moved his chair back for an unobstructed view. So did Winston Lord, another Kissinger aide. Propriety impedes further characterization of their behavior.

Still another Kissinger aide, Peter Rodman, sat erect with a cigar jutting from squared jaw. Cigar well chewed.

Undersecretary of State Joseph Sisco managed to respond to woman whispering beside him without losing concentration.

Deputy Assistant Secretary of State Roy Atherton did not divide his attention.

Ambassador Robert McCloskey successfully fought disinterest.

National Security Council aide Hal Saunders appeared diplomatically noncommittal.

State Department spokesman George Vest got up from his seat below the pepper and gaped with open mouth.

Only Secret Service agents Walter Bothe and Charlie Potts seemed uninterested. Resisting all temptation — or else succumbing to advancing age — they focused on the audience in a posture of almost unparalleled devotion to duty. Bothe occasionally sneaked a glance stageward in the name of security.

Postnavel comments:

Kissinger: "Now that diplomatic relations have been restored, we should have an immediate cultural exchange program, and she gets the first visa."

Richard Hottelet, CBS News: "Najwa Fuad is to belly-dancing what Pablo Casals was to the cello."

Eagleburger: Unaccustomed silence.

Vest: "I wish they had given me a better seat."

Marilyn Berger of the Washington *Post* was present in a red caftan.

When Kissinger read the pool report, he said, "Valeriani has talent when he finds a subject he's interested in. God knows it isn't foreign affairs."

One of the staffers told me later that following the performance, Kissinger turned to his aides and said, "You are all going to be locked in your rooms tonight."

Despite the restoration of diplomatic relations, Najwa Fuad never did make it to the United States.

But Richard Nixon made it to Cairo to certify the vast improvement in American-Egyptian relations. During the presidential visit, Kissinger was assigned a bedroom and sitting room all done up in pink ruffles, with matching frills, in the Ras el Tin Palace in Alexandria. Nervous Embassy staffers tried to get it changed, but they couldn't. Kissinger never complained. His room was close to the

President's. It was also on an upper floor, away from the cockroaches that overran the lower-floor rooms, where female staffers slept on desks to avoid them. Nixon's quarters had a Chinese motif, with huge dragon faucets and a sunken bathtub. If any symbolism was intended, it was inadvertent.

Nixon was by then almost totally preoccupied with saving his presidency, and during the return dinner he gave for Sadat, the two men hardly talked. Several American officials were brought in from other countries for the Nixon trip, including Dick Smith, who had been reassigned from Egypt to Pakistan. The Secretary recognized him in a Kissingerian way: "I've already said good-bye to you."

After Nixon resigned, Kissinger's first foreign trip was to the Middle East. He felt he had to go back promptly to make it clear that the new President was committed to keeping the negotiating process alive.

Ford personally went to the airport to see him off. "He's a very unusual Secretary," the President said, "on a very important mission." Kissinger noted that it was "the first time in a long time that one can go on a mission with an America that is at peace with itself."

Since his trip occurred during the Moslem holy period of Ramadan, he got in a lot of sightseeing, for the Arab leaders did not work during daylight hours in observance of Ramadan. In Cairo, he went to the Citadel, a walled city–fortress sitting on the only hill in the Egyptian capital. It was built in the Middle Ages by Saladin, the leader of the Arabs' successful campaign to expel the Crusaders from Palestine. One of its main attractions was the Muhammed Ali Mosque (named after the father of modern Egypt, not the heavyweight fighter). Kissinger donned light green felt slippers to go inside. Everyone else was given tan felt slippers. Once inside, a blast of prayers from the muezzin made him jump. The muezzin later came out and embraced and kissed the abashed Secretary of State, who mumbled, "Thank you."

Kissinger also toured a Coptic museum, and since he was running late, the curator started speeding up his presentation, trying to cram everything into a short period to make sure he gave the Secretary his whole fund of knowledge before he left. But Kissinger advised his host to slow down. "I'm relaxed," he said, "because I know nothing can happen until I get there." It sounded like a motto for his travels in the Middle East.

Although he used to say, in his double-negative way, "My life would not be unfulfilled not to travel," he felt that his constant personal involvement was necessary to nurture the delicate process of negotiations between Arab and Jew.

Early in 1975, after several months of laying the groundwork, the Secretary of State revved up his Middle East shuttle once again and took off for Aswan to begin negotiations on a second disengagement agreement between Egypt and Israel in the Sinai. Sadat now had still another reason for repairing to Aswan. The first disengagement agreement had been concluded there. Why not Sinai II?

The Kissinger mission began with a bang, literally. The pilot of the 707 couldn't see the runway and hit the power just before the plane touched down an hour and a half late at 1:30 A.M. Under the glare of the television lights, the Secretary told the already-tired press, "I will do my very best. I plan to stay in the area until we have achieved definite progress." During an on-plane briefing a couple of days later, he said he was ruling out another thirty-three-day shuttle. But conscious of the difficulties involved, he joked, "I'm still going to be ruling it out on the thirty-second day."

The Egyptian hyperoptimism about the mission was reflected in a cartoon printed in *Al Ahram,* Cairo's leading newspaper. It depicted officials waving Kissinger through the customs line with the caption: "Never mind opening your bags, we know what you have in them." But they didn't. When a reporter told Kissinger that the Egyptians were predicting 80 percent probability of success, he undercut the forecast with humor. "By their standards," he said, "this is profound pessimism." One of the prime purveyors of optimism was Foreign Minister Fahmy, partly as a means of setting up Israel for the blame if an agreement was not reached. But American reporters had come to the conclusion that Fahmy, as a news source, was something less than reliable.

Kissinger's new shuttle happened to coincide with a visit to Aswan by a tour group that included some prominent Americans; among them was George Ball, a former undersecretary of state and a reputed contender for Kissinger's job in a Democratic administration. A reporter wondered, "Why is George Ball here?" The incumbent Secretary of State amused himself with his answer: "He's looking over my room to see if the accommodations are any good." Then he added, "President Ford sent me a note saying, 'Don't get worried, George Ball is on a private visit.' "

As always, Kissinger did some touring of his own. Fourteen months earlier, during the previous Aswan shuttle, he had sailed to the ancient temple of Philae, which had been submerged by the waters that rose behind the completed High Dam and which was being reclaimed by a United Nations project. A reporter noted then, "Seeing this whets my appetite to come back as a tourist." Kissinger, well aware of the negotiating difficulties that lay ahead in the Middle East, advised wryly, "Don't worry. We'll see them all before we're through." He turned out to be almost right, though we never got to see Abu Simbel, another great temple saved from the waters of Lake Nasser.

The delicacy of the negotiating situation restrained Kissinger from disclosing many of the details of the talks, but under pressure from the correspondents he did provide some of the flavor.

"Ninety percent of the talking is done by Sadat and me," he said. Sisco interrupted, "Every now and then I say a word, but at my peril." Ignoring the peril, Kissinger resumed, "Fahmy is very acute in pointing out what the practical meaning of certain things might be and the diplomatic ramifications. And very professional. Gamasy talks only of military subjects. He's much more assertive than he was in any previous meeting. The previous defense minister was not very assertive. Gamasy is very military, very professional. We talk for an hour and a half, then Sadat and I meet alone and sort of review the intangibles of the situation. I say, 'Let's forget what the phraseology is, have I understood this properly?' And he tells me — on a human level. That's to help me understand what he's really after, so that we don't communicate or convey the wrong framework. I must be sure what he can take, must have. On the American side, we know what we're after — Joe is sort of the counterpart of Fahmy. Sometimes, so much depends upon an interpretation of what is possible that I may ask Joe afterward, 'You sat in. My view is, this is what the Israelis can do, this is what they can't. Give me your impression.' "

A reporter interrupted to ask, "Does Joe ever disagree?" Sisco: "I'll tell you one thing — not in front of Sadat. It would be disastrous!"

While the details of the talks were not forthcoming, Kissinger signaled the mood by using words like "painful" and "glacial" to describe the negotiations. But he managed to keep his good humor to the end. Just a couple of days before the breakdown, a reporter reminded him, "Yesterday, you said you had some sense of the duration of your negotiation. Any better now?" Kissinger laughed as he replied, "It will either be very long or very short."

Another reporter asked, "Does it depend upon the Israeli response?" Kissinger, conscious of suspicions among the pro-Israeli reporters that he was unfair to Israel, turned to Sisco and joked again, "I know what they're reaching for now — now I'm blackmailing the Israelis again." Then he replied seriously, "At some point, at some place, it will become apparent that it can either be done, or that it cannot. That is mathematically certain . . . At some point, we have to decide whether at this pace, it's really worth it, and whether that will be in Israel or whether I go back to Aswan again depends upon what I hear in Israel."

During one session in Aswan, Kissinger, who later talked about the "paralysis" in Israel, told the Egyptians that when he talked to the Israeli negotiators, they just sat there like "mummies." It's not known if the Egyptians took offense at the denigrating reference.

After a break in the talks, when Kissinger was informed that negotiations were resuming, he remarked to an aide, "Just as I'm regaining my sanity, you're sending me back into that madhouse."

Signals also came from Sadat. He told a news conference halfway through the shuttle, "I shall not agree to nonbelligerency as long as there is any foreign soldier on our land, and I said that doing so

means that I am inviting them to stay, so I think this is quite clear."
The questioning got sharper, and Sadat got testier, until he finally
said it was "really absurd" to discuss such matters as commerce
between Egypt and Israel at this stage.

An Egyptian reporter wanted to know, from Kissinger, "Do you
believe at this stage the Palestinians would participate in these talks
concerning their future?" He ducked the question with an answer
reflecting his pained desire to see the conference end. "I think," he
said, "the two press corps are competing in asking provocative questions." The news conference did end one question later. Not long
afterward, the shuttle itself ended on a sour note.

The U.S. "reassessment" diplomacy that followed the collapse of
the negotiations included a meeting between Presidents Ford and
Sadat. Up to then, Ford had not been personally identified with
Middle East diplomacy, but presidential intervention seemed to be
the only good way to revive American policy initiatives in the area.
It provided a convenient cover for what everybody really wanted to
do — to try again to negotiate another partial agreement in the Sinai.

Before the meeting, Kissinger was asked at a news conference:
"President Sadat has said publicly now several times that he intends
to press President Ford for an answer to what the American position
is on supporting Israel, either in the present situation or back to the
1967 borders. What will the President say to President Sadat, or what
do you think about that question?" Kissinger replied, "If I tell you
that, maybe President Sadat won't come to the meeting."

The two presidents decided on Salzburg, Austria, as the meeting
place, since they both planned to be in Europe on other business in
the summer of 1975.

Ford's introduction to personal diplomacy in the Middle East was,
fortunately, not a reflection of future policy. As he deplaned from Air
Force One, his knee buckled, and he fell down the steps. Nothing
that happened afterward topped the entrance scene.

The Austrians provided a castle, the Salzburg Residenz, and the
two presidents conferred in the throne room. The Austrians had
offered two other castles as well, but they had been subjected to

peremptory rejections by each side. One of them was known as Watercastle, which the Americans disdained for obvious reasons. The other had too many stairs for Sadat to climb.

The meeting turned out to be all sweetness and light, and the report that Ford and Sadat had hit it off well was also calculated to put pressure on Israel. But there was precious little information about the meeting itself. When it was over, the two presidents held a news conference in the courtyard of the Residenz during a downpour and exchanged pleasantries with the press.

I wrote the following report for my own amusement:

> Standing beneath nonnuclear umbrellas in the rain-soaked courtyard of Salzburg's historic Residenz [sic], President Ford and President Sadat confirmed today that they had indeed met.
>
> Diplomatic observers observed that the two presidents apparently did not have enough sense to come in out of the rain.
>
> Egyptian sources insisted the United States had insisted on staging the presidential statements in the open-air setting of the Residenz [sic].
>
> White House sources insisted Egypt had insisted on the open-air setting.
>
> Deputy Press Secretary William Greener emphasized the United States had nothing to do with the rain. But he would neither confirm nor deny that it was Austria's fault.
>
> Press Secretary Ron Nessen denied that it was raining.
>
> Later, at a news conference where he did not threaten to resign, Secretary of State Kissinger explained the setting for the Ford-Sadat statements had been negotiated step by step, and he left the implication that if anybody was tó blame for the rain, it was probably Israel.
>
> Kissinger maintained the rain was a pain but in the main had not had a concrete impact on the nonnegotiations, which were not too concrete, either.
>
> Kissinger also confirmed that the name of the Residenz [sic] was the Residenz [sic].

Following the meeting, Kissinger held a news conference at the Kongress Haus Press Center, not far from where he had threatened to resign more than a year earlier. Most of the same reporters had been in Salzburg then, and Kissinger confronted the memories with head-on humor: "I need hardly say how much I have been looking forward to having another press conference in Salzburg." He milked it for yet another laugh. "I have been rehearsing for it for a year."

The questioners included veteran Washington *Post* correspondent Murrey Marder, who was known as an incisive Kissinger-baiter with whom the Secretary liked to banter. Marder was not known as a concise questioner, as he demonstrated once again in Salzburg: "Mr. Secretary, that certainly was not a happy, exhilarated-looking group in the courtyard today, the two presidents and those of you who were standing with them. It did not, by any means, look like it had lived up in any way to President Sadat's talk of this meeting marking a historic moment." Marder continued, "Can you say whether, from your perception, the Egyptian leaders had much higher expectations which could not be fulfilled because of the American timetable? And secondly, can you tell us whether the deadline of the expiration of the mandate in the Sinai is pressing with any urgency on your considerations?"

A smartass reporter shouted, "Question?" meaning he wanted the Secretary of State to repeat Marder's long statement.

Kissinger took the cue: "As I understood Mr. Marder's conclusions, He formed the impression that this was not a happy, exhilarated group that he saw standing in the courtyard at the Residenz — and that is the name of the place — and he wondered whether the expiration of the mandate in the Sinai might have been pressing on the consciousness of the unexhilarated group that was standing there.

"If I can be frank and not be offensive to you ladies and gentlemen," Kissinger said, "you didn't look like a pretty exhilarated group to me, either . . . And it could be that the atmospheric conditions had something to do with it because I don't know how you show exhilaration when somebody holds an umbrella over you and rain is pouring down your back. But I am just beginning my lecture . . .

"Basically, we thought it was a very constructive meeting. It was not intended to reach any specific conclusions. It achieved that purpose . . . It was not intended to reach any precise conclusions that would lead to any immediate negotiation. It was, however, very positive, very constructive, and I think it provides the basis for useful talks with the Israelis."

Kissinger concluded, "I really think, Murrey, that your impression was just not right." Marder: "You often do." Kissinger: "That is true, but it never seems to affect what you write." Murrey agreed.

Two months later, the grounded Kissinger shuttle was reactivated, and the Secretary of State took off for the Middle East for what turned out to be the last time. Kissinger challenged reports that an agreement was virtually in the bag before he left, but his position was undercut by a telltale addition to his entourage: David Kennerly, the official White House photographer. It was obvious that Kennerly was not going along to make a photographic record of another failure for the Ford administration.

The symbolism of Aswan had not worked during the previous shuttle, so Sadat was content to conduct the negotiations from his

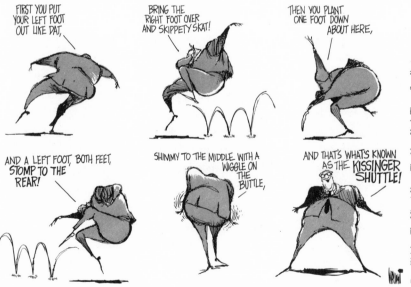

villa on the Mediterranean at Alexandria, the sprawling Egyptian port founded by Alexander the Great in 33 B.C. It was not a new site for Kissinger. He had conferred there with Sadat at the beginning of the Syrian shuttle. But it wasn't easy to get to. The Air Force 707 couldn't land at Alexandria, so it put down instead at Jianyklis, a military air base in the middle of the western desert, about fifty miles from the coast.

On that first visit, at the end of April 1974, the Egyptians provided a helicopter for Kissinger and the other American officials for the journey to Alexandria. But the traveling press was herded into a ramshackle bus, and we spent two hours on a hot, dusty road. We were not in the best of moods when we finally arrived at what seemed, briefly, like an oasis — the Palestine Hotel. It didn't take us long to organize our own Palestine Liberation Organization. We longed to be liberated from the Palestine Hotel. We failed.

The Palestine Hotel Information Sheet prepared by the U.S. Embassy gave us the first tip-off. It read in part: "There is a room service station near 407, 507, and 607. They can provide simple services (bottled water, coffee, etc.) immediately, but more complicated chores (meals, for example) take considerable time. If you are pressed for time, do not count on room service to bring meals at the exact time you desire. Room service does, however, provide Continental breakfasts *relatively* on time." What the information sheet failed to point out was that the Palestine Hotel staff had obviously been trained by the Russians at the Intourist School for efficiency.

The Palestine Hotel notwithstanding, Alexandria immediately became one of the favorite spots on the Kissinger itinerary for almost everybody except the Secretary and the other officials who took part in the negotiations. That's because it was close to Abou Kir and the Zephyros restaurant, which sat on the beach hard by the Mediterranean, which supplied its fare. The fish were so fresh they were still flopping on a table when we went back to select the one we wanted grilled for dinner — after the prawns and lobster, also fresh, also grilled. Local color was provided by wandering vendors selling black market items, such as soap, toothpaste, and toilet paper, and by beach urchins selling seashells by the seashore or playing recorders.

One night, after lots of seafood and an equivalent amount of wine, we taught one of the boys with a recorder to play "Hava Nagila," a popular Israeli dance. It was not the usual musical fare in Egypt.

As we left the restaurant, other children surrounded us, begging for change. Barry Schweid, who thought Israel was being pressured into a bad deal in the negotiations, looked at one of the urchins and said, "Don't worry, kid, we'll be back tomorrow and give you Haifa and twenty-five piasters."

Curiously, the security at Alexandria itself was tighter than anywhere in Egypt. Sadat's villa, the Maamoura Palace, fronted on the sea and was surrounded by a large expanse of lawn and flowers studded with palm and eucalyptus trees. The credentials issued by the American Secret Service for the traveling reporters and by the Egyptian Foreign Ministry for everybody else were not sufficient to get in. We had to have a credential with a picture on it as well. All vehicles were stopped at the gate of the grounds, and anyone entering had to walk the several hundred yards to the villa itself.

The lawn at Maamoura was the scene of much of the public activity. Sadat, wearing a pin-striped lounge suit, greeted Kissinger there with the customary embrace and kiss on both cheeks. Most of the impromptu news conferences took place there. Marilyn Berger began one of them by asking, "Mr. President, there was a report before we started coming here today that Egypt has requested a larger number of troops in the limited forces zone, numbering twelve thousand. Is that correct?" Kissinger wanted to keep it light. "I don't know why you give her a visa," he said. Sadat replied, "I do not know where you get this information." Kissinger added, "She tried it already on me, Mr. President."

Another reporter asked, "Mr. President, do you feel that Israel has raised some unexpected demands in the course of this week?"

Sadat: "They are always raising hell, as you say in America."

Reporter: "Mr. President, can you imagine, having come this far, that failure is still possible?"

Sadat: "Believe me, as I have seen and as has happened during the

March mission, it may come to this. But not from the Egyptian side. We are quite ready and we are quite understanding. But I do not know what goes there on the Israeli side."

Reporter: "Well, the only conclusion we can draw then, sir, since you say you are ready for an agreement and no difficulties are being raised from your side, the only conclusion we can draw is your suggestion that there are difficulties being raised by the Israeli side?" Kissinger couldn't resist stepping in. "Unless," he said, "they are raised by *my* side."

At another impromptu news conference, Kissinger again tried to take the sting out of tough questions from American reporters by explaining, "You see, Mr. President, what I have to go through four times a day."

Afterward, he introduced one of the tough American questioners to Sadat. "This is Bernie Kalb, Mr. President," he said. "He's Marvin Kalb's brother. Marvin doesn't travel anymore because he has a bad back." Then, in a joshing attempt to sound menacing, he added, "And if Bernie keeps asking questions like that, he's going to have a bad back, too."

At the outset of the shuttle, Kissinger acknowledged that the "odds are that it will succeed." But he kept warning us that it could also fail. Nobody in the press took him seriously.

He did not make his usual claim that this was the toughest negotiation he had ever been engaged in. Instead, during one of the on-plane briefings, he labeled it the "weirdest negotiation I've ever seen." Why? "Stuff keeps popping out all the time," meaning that both sides were raising issues that had not previously come up in the discussions.

Much of what the agreement would contain had been thoroughly aired in the press before the shuttle even began, but there was a lot of talk about secret agreements, which Kissinger declined to discuss. Likewise Sadat. When a reporter on the plane reminded Kissinger that "Sadat said there would not be any secret agreements," Kissinger did a dumbstruck number on the reporter. "For God's sake," he said, "do you think he should say, 'I'm making a secret agreement with Israel?' When you guys ask him questions that involve political suicide for him, what do you want him to say, 'I'm making a secret agreement'?"

Sadat himself had replied to the question by saying, "Ho, ho, ho . . . no secret agreements." Sadat's frequent "ho, ho, ho" was later replaced linguistically by "for sure," and playful reporters eventually had a pool on how many times Sadat would say "for sure" during a news conference.

Lars-Erik Nelson of Reuters had a vivid recollection of the shuttle's end game: "On the next to last day of that same shuttle, we were in Alexandria, preparing to fly back to Israel. It was the make-or-break day after spending two weeks going back and forth between Jerusalem and the New Palestine Hotel. Either a deal was going to be done or it was not. The bulk of the press was taken out to the airport, but a four-man press pool plus Dana Schmidt [of the *Christian Science Monitor*], who had once again missed the bus, was taken out to Sadat's summer house on the beach to be helicoptered back to the plane with Kissinger. We were seated outdoors, on a patio on the west side of the house, as Kissinger and Sisco argued with Sadat and Fahmy inside. The impression was that Sadat wanted to make a deal, but Fahmy, concerned with Arab unity and solidarity, was skeptical. As we sipped our glasses of orange juice, the sun turned bright orange and sank toward the western horizon. Suddenly, from around the corner of the house, Kissinger and Sisco appeared, flanking Fahmy and leading him on a long walk through the garden. Sisco towered over Fahmy on his right, and even Kissinger, on his left, was slightly taller. They were clearly giving him the hard word, laying down the law. It looked for all the world like Mutt and Jeff in a police station, the two Americans working over the suspect who refuses to break down and talk.

"There was a desert vulture high overhead, flapping its wings desperately in the off-sea breeze and getting nowhere. He hung as though pinned to the sunset sky, flapping furiously and unable to go forward. Kissinger and Sisco and Fahmy came back from the garden. Kissinger then spotted us for the first time and said, in what he hoped was a whisper, 'My God, has the press been there all the time? Make it look good . . .' His voice carried to us. He smiled and waved, as did the others. Later, on the plane, he told us that the Egyptians had bought the deal that afternoon. Now it was up to the Israelis."

The deal was bought on the basis of the stationing of American technicians at early warning posts in the Sinai. That was the key element that made a new agreement possible.

When Kissinger returned to the lawn of Maamoura for the initialing of the agreement, studio television cameras were in place to carry the ceremony live on nationwide Egyptian television. A table covered with green baize was set up on the lawn for the ceremony. Even the participants represented a compromise: a military man because Egypt insisted it was a military disengagement agreement and a diplomat because Israel wanted to emphasize the political nature of the agreement.

Before Kissinger returned to Alexandria, President Ford had called President Sadat, but as all of us who had tried to communicate from Alexandria knew, the connection was not the best, and their conversation sounded like a Bob Newhart routine:

FORD: President Sadat?
SADAT: Hello, this is President Sadat.
FORD: How are you this morning, President Sadat? I'm calling you to congratulate you on the important role you played in the negotiations that brought about this agreement.
SADAT: Hello, hello . . .
FORD: I hope you hear me better now. Allow me to express, with emphasis, in the name of my administration, our appreciation for your political skills, in spite of the opposition and the critics, and the spirit you have brought to the negotiations. I am most grateful for your leadership and I hope to continue to work with . . .
SADAT: Hello, hello . . .
FORD: Hello, do you hear me, Mr. President?
SADAT: No, I don't hear you very clearly.
FORD: I know that we both know that a stalemate or a deadlock in the Middle East could bring about a catastrophe and we appreciate your

leadership in the negotiations with Secretary Kissinger and the Israelis. We are all thankful and as we are going to continue to work together personally and both our administrations . . .

SADAT: Hello, hello . . .

FORD: I hear you well, Mr. President. I hope that you can hear me, Mr. President.

SADAT: Hello, President Ford?

FORD: I can't hear you, Mr. President.

SADAT: Is this President Ford speaking?

FORD: Yes, this is President Ford.

SADAT: Go on please.

FORD: The line unfortunately is very poor and I don't hear you well. Allow me to say, if I may in spite of the difficulties, that Mrs. Ford and myself are hoping Mrs. Sadat, your children and yourself will visit Washington in the coming autumn. I am sorry I cannot hear you, the line is very bad, but I hope you can hear me and my remarks from the U.S.

SADAT: Hello, hello . . .

The line suddenly improved, and Sadat thanked President Ford for his message.

FORD: I couldn't hear each word distinctly, but I understood the spirit of your kind and encouraging words.

SADAT: I want to add one point, Mr. President.

FORD: Yes.

SADAT: I want to stress the importance of . . .

FORD: Unfortunately, I can't hear you. The line is very bad, I hope it's better over there.

SADAT: I hear you very well.

FORD: Have a nice day. I understand Henry will be with you shortly.

SADAT: I am expecting him.

Sadat praised "the sincerity and tireless efforts of Dr. Kissinger" and concluded, "I consider this a turning point in the Arab-Israeli conflict and a step toward peace based on justice." Sadat left the initialing to subordinates, but it was he who did the talking at the news conference that followed. He summed up the shuttle by saying, "Dr. Kissinger has had a helluva time there and here."

After the news conference, Bruce van Voorst of *Newsweek* approached Sadat with maps signed in Israel by Kissinger, Prime Minister Rabin, Defense Minister Peres, Ambassador Dinitz, and Chief of Staff Mordechai Gur. He asked Sadat to sign as well. Sadat looked up at the reporter with a wide smile and said, "I don't think that would be a good idea."

Sadat had told the news conference the next step in the Middle East should be another interim agreement between Syria and Israel, and Kissinger confirmed that the United States was ready to explore the possibility of more Syrian-Israeli negotiations. But the vehemence of the Syrian reaction to another separate agreement between Egypt and Israel shot down the next potential shuttle before it could ever get off the ground.

When Kissinger left Alexandria, he did not return again to the Middle East as Secretary of State.

With a second Sinai agreement safely on the books and the presence of American technicians manning early warning stations approved by Congress, Sadat finally visited Washington in October 1975. In addition to the extravagant White House tributes — and an invitation to Sadat to address a joint meeting of Congress — Kissinger laid on one of the most lavish lunches ever seen on the State Department's eighth floor. The guest list read like a *Who's Who* of American achievement, and the caterers served an elegant luncheon, including cold poached salmon and several wines. At the end of the lunch, however, waiters moved among the crowd with humidors, passing out cigars. They were King Edwards. This country may need a good five-cent cigar, but King Edward is not it. American cigar-smokers were even more appalled than the Havana-puffing Fahmy. It was a detail that the nonsmoking Kissinger had overlooked.

The end-of-luncheon toasts came from the by-laws of the Kissinger-Sadat mutual admiration society, although they did not precisely repeat their "Miracle Worker" ritual.

Kissinger forwent his customary humorous warm-up as he said,

"I have always believed that once we have analyzed all the clauses of all the agreements, that the most important contribution that our honored guest made was to understand that the process of peace was in the first instance a psychological problem, and that what was needed was a climate of confidence between the United States and the principal parties and between the parties themselves."

Sadat responded, "When I met Dr. Kissinger for the first time and we started dealing with each other, it was a turning point in the history of the conflict in our area. We needed one in whom we can put our confidence in the United States so that he can bear the responsibility and break the snow and go forward toward a peaceful solution built on justice. After one hour of discussion with Dr. Kissinger, for the first time we felt as if we were old friends. And since that time up to this moment, I am proud to say that working together, we have achieved something that couldn't be achieved in a whole generation."

Looking back on the Kissinger shuttles, one American Ambassador in the Middle East recalled, "Even with all of its problems, it was a great time. It was exhilarating for those who were in on it . . . He shouted on occasion . . . he did not suffer fools gladly . . . But he had style, he had flair . . . Kissinger was something to experience."

Syria

President Hafez Assad of Syria still tells visitors he spent so much time with Henry Kissinger that he's the only Arab leader in the Middle East who speaks English with a German accent. It's a line he borrowed from Kissinger himself.

The Secretary of State knew that his strategy in the Middle East could not succeed without Syria being part of the negotiating process. He also recognized early in the game that Assad — and Syria — had become the new repositories of Arab nationalism — and romanticism — following the death of Nasser, and so Kissinger courted Assad assiduously in an effort to neutralize him, if not to proselytize him.

It was not an easy assignment. Syria was easily the most radical of the so-called confrontation states — the Arab countries that bordered on Israel and that actually fought against the Jewish state. Libya and Iraq and Algeria were certainly more radical, but they generally just made a lot of noise in prodding their Arab brothers into combat while they safely remained hundreds of miles away.

Kissinger was not sure exactly what to expect in December 1973, when he became the first American Secretary of State to visit Damascus since John Foster Dulles twenty years before. Syria had been diplomatically estranged from the United States since the 1967 war, and it was unknown diplomatic territory, although it was known to be a principal base of operations for Palestinian terrorists. A tremendous sense of excitement — and some anxiety — fermented aboard the Secretary's 707 as it approached the Damascus airport. The anxiety involved physical as well as political concerns. The plane had to fly fairly low over a large Palestinian camp during its landing approach, and the tragedians aboard pointed out that one well-placed rocket by a PLO "crazy" could make world headlines that none of us would be around to read. It was not especially comforting to watch the Secret Service men don bulletproof vests just before landing.

The newsmen got off first. One agent cracked to John Barton of the UPI, "We're testing the water." Then, more grimly, he patted his "attaché case" and said, "If I hit the side of this thing, you hit the dirt. No questions — because I may not be alive to reply." It all seems melodramatic in retrospect, but the security people never made a trip to Damascus without worrying and without feeling relieved when they left.

Kissinger's arrival was in keeping with the state of relations: austere. And local newsmen were not allowed to film it. The Secretary of State was greeted at the foot of the ramp by Abdel Halim Khaddam, one of the few foreign ministers in the world whom Kissinger literally looked down to when he talked. But Khaddam was as fiery as he was short. As they shook hands, the Secretary said, "Finally, we have an opportunity to meet." The greeting had a slight bite to it. Khaddam had boycotted Kissinger's luncheon for Arab foreign ministers at the United Nations two months before, and he had stayed away from the Secretary's speech to the General Assembly as well.

Even before they drove away, the plane was cordoned off by Syrian soldiers wearing red berets and carrying submachine guns over their shoulders. On a later visit, one of the soldiers was startled out of his beret when Kissinger walked up and shook his hand. "I have to shake hands with my guardian," he said. Familiarity eventually bred less security, and the cordon was dropped after Kissinger's visits became commonplace.

As is often the case in countries with volatile politics and frequent coups, the airport was located far from the capital, about twenty-three miles away. While a military helicopter hovered overhead, Kissinger and Khaddam left the airport in a motorcade that raced toward Damascus at speeds of up to 90 miles an hour. The entire route was patrolled by plainclothes security agents stationed at fifty-yard intervals.

In making the advance arrangements, American Secret Service agents had said they were concerned that they had no way of identifying the plainclothesmen, all of whom were armed. (Some of the agents felt the biggest threat to Kissinger existed within the ranks of the secret police itself.) The Syrians told the Secret Service agents that none of the roadside sentinels would pick up a gun unless necessary. Each would keep a rifle at his feet. "What happens if we see a sentinel holding a rifle?" the Americans wanted to know. The Syrians, confident of their discipline, replied matter-of-factly, "If you see anyone holding a rifle, shoot him!" The agents never saw anyone holding a rifle.

The most tension-filled part of the drive came just before reaching Damascus, where the road ran right between two large Palestinian camps, one housing refugees who evacuated the Golan Heights during the October War, the other containing about fifty thousand Palestinians who had been refugees much longer.

The Syrians provided cars instead of the usual bus for the traveling newsmen, but for once, a bus might have been preferable. The Syrian drivers, like a playful school of porpoises out on a lark, all seemed eager to outrace each other, and they all kept passing one another at high speed for no good reason — unless they were simply showing off or engaging in a subtle form of intimidation of their passengers.

The combination of the competitive drivers and the Palestinian camps guaranteed that the ride to and from the airport was never a relaxing experience, although it certainly became routine during the thirty-three-day shuttle.

i am henry
fly me to damascus

On that first visit, only the black humorists among us were amused when we later found out that Kissinger had been taken into the city by an alternate route — we were part of a decoy motorcade — and if there had been an attack of any kind, it would probably have been made against us.

For security reasons, Kissinger's car took a different route every time. One night, on the way back to the airport, the motorcade was passing through an exceptionally dark section of the city — there wasn't even a street light — when the road got bumpy; suddenly there was a screech of wheels and the flashing of taillights, and the motorcade jolted to a halt, with some of the cars turning sideways. The driver of the follow-up security car, which tailed the Secretary's limousine as close as a foot away, stopped in a straight line without even nudging the car in front.

Agents Walter Bothe and Charlie Potts leaped out of the follow-up car before it came to a complete stop and raced to take up positions by the doors of Kissinger's car. Bothe carried an Israeli-made Uzi submachine gun; Potts, a Georgia boy, had a shotgun. Bothe could see Kissinger, his eyes wide open, his nose pressed against the glass, trying to look out. The agent figured in his mind that "they" had successfully blockaded the motorcade, and now "they" would come after Kissinger. Sure enough, shapes began to materialize in the darkness.

Inside the limousine there was deathly silence, broken only when Kissinger cracked to Khaddam, "Don't worry, Mr. Foreign Minister, they'll protect you, too."

Bothe could hear voices, and then, from the other side of the car, he heard Potts's slow Georgian drawl, "Y'all better get your asses away from this here car." Bothe, on the other hand, began screaming a string of four-letter and twelve-letter (hyphenated) curses at the shapes in the darkness, warning them to "get the hell out of here."

The shapes turned out to be curious people in the neighborhood who wondered why all the cars were stopped there. They didn't understand Bothe's four-letter words or Potts's drawl, but the tone of voice was unmistakable, so they didn't get too close. Another agent quickly came back and explained that a Syrian policeman had hit a bump and his white Honda 450 had gone out from under him, causing everybody to brake.

Kissinger reveled in describing this incident at his next meeting with the Israelis in Jerusalem. The Uzi that Bothe had waved around was prominently featured in the Kissinger version, although the agent's language was diplomatically bowdlerized. The Secretary later kidded Bothe, "You certainly made an enormous contribution to international understanding and good will out there."

Kissinger's purpose in going to Damascus the first time, in addition to reestablishing some kind of American-Syrian rapport, was to persuade the Syrians to endorse a Geneva Peace Conference on the Middle East. Unlike Cairo, which was sunny and balmy in December, Damascus was gray and cold, with a political climate to match. The Syrians showed little enthusiasm for the whole negotiating approach, mostly because of internal domestic pressures.

The ruling Ba'ath party did not accept the existence of Israel, and negotiations would amount to de facto recognition. In fact, the only time Israel was mentioned in the press or in broadcast news reports, it was referred to as "southern Syria" or "Occupied Palestine." (When newsmen talked to their home offices from Syria and some other Arab countries, they used a code name for Israel, such as "Dixie," to avoid the risk of having their line cut off by some irate censor.)

Soon after we arrived, the Syrians took the newsmen to see the former Soviet cultural mission, which they said had been destroyed by an Israeli bomb during a raid in what was obviously a residential neighborhood. They had turned the wreckage into an exhibit for visitors. But the ruins of the bombed-out Russians elicited little sympathy from the visiting Americans.

The influence of the French colonization of Syria was immediately apparent as the Secretary of State went to the unimposing "presidential palace," an undistinguished white stucco building near the foot of Mount Kessioun (not far from the spot where Cain is supposed to have slain Abel). It had formerly been an apartment building, but its entrance was now flanked with gendarme shacks painted red, white, and blue — the colors of the *tricoleur.*

Kissinger quickly found out that Assad had a good sense of humor. The Secretary introduced Joe Sisco to the Syrian President by describing him as "the most powerful man at the State Department." The only reason he brought Sisco along, Kissinger explained, was his concern that if he left him in Washington, he might stage a coup d'état. "One day," Kissinger said, "I arrived at my office in the State Department and found Sisco in there measuring the rugs and the curtains. I figured he was planning to take over."

Assad, who had come to power himself through a coup d'état and then survived longer than any other Syrian President in a country where coups had been epidemic, laughed out loud. He took Kissinger aside and wanted to know, "Is he really a problem for you? Maybe," he suggested, "we can do something about him." Kissinger had to assume that was a joke, and he did. The Kissinger-Assad meetings thereafter usually contained some reference to "Sisco's coup."

At one of the first sessions with the Syrian leaders, Kissinger, still a bachelor, played on his reputation as a "secret swinger." "You lift the oil embargo," he said, "and I'll give you three phone numbers. On second thought, that's no good. You can put the embargo back anytime you want, but if I give you the phone numbers, I can't get them back."

Beyond geopolitics, Kissinger seemed genuinely intrigued and fascinated and amused — and at times exasperated — by Assad, a former Air Force general in his mid-forties. After their first couple of meetings, Kissinger described him as "very intelligent, extremely engaging, with a good sense of humor." We attributed the glowing description to Kissinger's usual practice of characterizing local leaders in the most favorable terms in the hopes that the flattery would find its way into print and then back to the descriptee. And it usually did. But Kissinger's perception came to be shared by most of the traveling party. And more than a year later when Kissinger said on the plane, "I take Assad seriously. He's extraordinarily clever," nobody disagreed with him.

Kissinger also found that Assad "makes these turns in conversations that are weird." His conclusion was based on an early experience, when he was discussing with the Syrian President the draft of a letter of invitation to the participants in the Geneva Peace Conference. Giving a tactical nod to the Syrians' reputation for toughness, Kissinger said to Assad, with gentle sarcasm, "I don't want you to concede too quickly, since the Syrians have a reputation for being easy negotiators and agreeing right away."

He then explained the Israelis wanted any reference to Palestinians taken out. "Okay," said Assad. The Israelis also wanted to postpone a ceremonial role for the UN. "Okay," said Assad. And so it went, paragraph by paragraph. An American official who was there said afterward of Kissinger, "I could tell by his eyes, he was saying, 'Jesus Christ, what is this?'"

After they had breezed through the entire letter and Kissinger was ready to go, Assad spoke up. "I only have trouble with one sentence," he said. "What's that?" asked Kissinger. "The one that says we've agreed to attend the conference," said Assad. "We haven't." Kissinger, according to one participant, "about fell out of his chair."

The Secretary eventually came to learn that the Syrians could be full of other surprising twists and turns. As he once put it flying into Damascus, "I don't know what's going to happen here, but I'm sure whatever it is, it will be a little bit nuts!"

Just before one of the early visits, he got a message from the American mission saying that the only thing certain about the schedule was that there would be no dinner. But as his plane was approaching the Syrian capital, he got another message from the American mission saying the only certainty about the planning was a dinner with the foreign minister.

While Syria was a country where prophecy was usually unrewarding, it was generally safe to predict that a Kissinger-Assad meeting would not be brief. The first one was startling in its length. American officials, expecting a two-hour meeting, arranged to have the American reporters and other members of the traveling party taken to the plane with that time frame in mind.

We newsmen were accustomed to long waits, but none of us was prepared for that December night at the Damascus airport. After the first hour, the routine griping intensified into serious griping. After the second hour, the griping turned to amusement. Then it dissolved into booziness. After four hours, it became the subject for jokes and wild speculation. And then we began to wonder if we weren't missing a story, like the kidnaping of Henry Kissinger in Damascus. Even some of his aides began showing anxiety as the delay stretched out. He finally showed up five hours later than originally expected. Messages had been sent hourly to Amman, where King Hussein was waiting to have dinner with him. (They finally ate after midnight.)

More than a dozen of the Syrian plainclothesmen who guarded the route to the airport were taken to the hospital for treatment of exposure and chill. And the long delay produced a long string of now-forgotten lines about kidnaping. The subject came up again during a conversation on the flight back to Washington. Glancing at his agents nearby, Kissinger made light of the security problem. "I'll probably get knocked off on the way in from Andrews," he said.

A later experience in Damascus was no joking matter. Kissinger was planning to visit one of the world's largest mosques, the historic Omayad Mosque in the teeming, covered *souk* (marketplace) in the morning, following a round of talks with President Assad. But when the talks again ran longer than expected, Kissinger postponed his visit to the mosque so as not to delay too much his departure for Israel. The postponement may have kept him alive. Palestinian extremists had planned to assassinate him on his way to the mosque; American officials learned of the plot after Kissinger left. For security reasons, they never did say how they found out about it or who was involved.

Later, commenting on the extension of his talks with the Syrian President, Kissinger said, "Assad may have saved my life." However, if the Syrians knew about the plot, they never told the Americans directly.

One reason the Kissinger-Assad talks ran so long was the Secretary of State's professorial instinct. While he found Assad highly intelligent, he also found him limited in his knowledge of the world in general and the United States in particular. And so he frequently reverted to his role as the Harvard professor who directed a seminar on national security affairs for foreign leaders. He sometimes spent the first hour of a meeting discussing American constitutional processes or current diplomatic events, in effect, tutoring Assad about the world beyond Syria's rather parochial society. He even briefed him on the strategic arms limitation talks with the Russians, Syria's chief arms supplier. During one of the SALT briefings, Assad playfully proposed that the two superpowers spread their weapons around the Middle East in an even-handed way. "We'll store them for both of you," he joked.

Assad occasionally lectured on his own, tutoring Kissinger in Arab history from a perspective he had not shared before. Assad spoke from the point of view of a soldier, which he was. And Kissinger spoke from the point of view of a historian, which he was.

During the long Syrian-Israeli shuttle, the seminars occasionally provided relief at times of deadlock. An American official who sat in on these sessions said the two men "enjoyed each other," and he was sure that Assad deliberately prolonged the meetings because Kissinger was such an enjoyable, eye-opening experience for him in a section of the world where mind expansion is associated principally with hashish. Assad was also fascinated by Kissinger's accounts — often humorous — of his meetings with the Israelis. One American participant feels certain Assad "discounted them to some extent. But he just enjoyed them." Assad later told author Edward Sheehan that Kissinger used to refer to Golda Meir as "Miss Israel" and "the beauty of Jerusalem."

Kissinger also came to appreciate Assad's straightforwardness. He once told us, with amusement, "Where Sadat understood you have to fuzz things up because nobody could live with the answer, Assad says frankly, 'You're fuzzing things up!' "

State Department Arabists believe that one reason Kissinger got along so well in Damascus was that "the Syrians were flattered that Kissinger, someone of extraordinary importance and intellectual capacity, came to see them." For his part, Kissinger found Assad to be "a challenging interlocutor." His assessment may have derived in part from his determination — some felt it was compulsion — to win over adversaries.

Whatever Kissinger's sentiments about Assad, he was not charmed by Assad's capital city, and his first night in Damascus was almost his last. The Secretary of State and his top aides were put up in a government guest house near the presidential palace. Their quarters were cramped and inconvenient for communications; Kissinger had already acquired a taste for more grandeur as well as instantaneous communications. Sleeping was difficult because light flooded into the bedroom through a transom. A secretary was summoned from the small American mission in Damascus and told to block out the light. She improvised with some black velvet she had bought to make a skirt. But Kissinger wasn't going to get much sleep anyway.

At the crack of dawn, a tremendous blast of noise rattled through the guest house. Aide Larry Eagleburger bolted out of bed. He had gone to sleep only about three hours earlier, when the Kissinger-Assad talks of that night had finally ended. When the shock wore off and his head had cleared, Eagleburger realized that the "noise" was coming from a nearby mosque where the muezzin was calling faithful Moslems to prayer at the first light of day. As he sat on the side of his bed in a room reverberating with the sound of prayer, Eagleburger heard a knock on his door. He opened it. "There," he remembers, "stood this short, fat German, pleading, 'Can't you get them to stop that?' "

When Kissinger saw Assad later that morning, he informed the Syrian President, "I'm looking for a less demanding religion."

The Secret Service agents were even more pleased that Kissinger did not spend more nights in Syria, and not only for security reasons. The Syrians thought nothing of assigning two or even three agents to the same room — with only one bed. The other one or two agents had to sleep in a chair.

Before he first went to Damascus, Kissinger had promised the Israelis that he would try to get a list of the Israeli prisoners held since the October War. Based on previous experience, the Israelis were extremely concerned about the fate of the POWs in Syrian hands. When Kissinger was told beforehand that a top Syrian official had said it would be a "big mistake" to raise the question of Israeli POWs on his first visit to Damascus, he dismissed the advice. "I've made mistakes before," he said.

Kissinger knew the Israelis wouldn't even consider negotiating with the Syrians until they got the list, and he knew the Syrians were opposed to providing the list unless they got something in return. But he was still not prepared for Assad's comeback when he said, "If you give me the list, I'm sure you can start negotiations with the Israelis." Assad looked him in the eye and remarked, "Then I'll have *two* problems!" The humorous reply gave Kissinger new insight into the difficulty of arranging Syrian-Israeli negotiations, and he later told us that the Syrian leader who negotiated with the Israelis "is not going to be a hero in Syria."

Kissinger came away from his first visit to Damascus with the impression that the Syrians were "pretty tough guys," but he felt his talks had been "extremely amiable" and that he had made a good beginning. The follow-up was good as well, and Kissinger felt encouraged by the Syrian reaction to the first disengagement agreement between Egypt and Israel.

During that first trip to Syria, reports popped up frequently in periodicals back home that he was about to marry Nancy. He brushed them aside by joking that if he married anybody, it would be Joe Sisco, since he was spending most of his nights with him.

The reports finally came true in March 1974, just after the Secretary returned from Moscow. On the flight to Washington, a reporter asked him point-blank if he was getting married, and he replied, "Absolutely!" Everybody laughed and left it at that. But he meant it, and it was true. Exceptional candor from Henry Kissinger had proven too much to cope with.

The Secretary of State honeymooned in Acapulco, and a month later he hit the road with his new wife. That next trip was no honeymoon. It was the shuttle between Israel and Syria that lasted thirty-three days. As Kissinger said later, "Just writing arrival statements is a full-time job." He also quickly found out that on his arrival, he was no longer the only attraction. He lamented, not seriously, "Since I started taking Nancy along, nobody photographs me anymore."

The Secretary of State found the experience of negotiating with the Syrians a unique one. When his traveling doctor asked him if he needed anything during this period, he had two favorite replies: (1) "What do I do about foaming at the mouth?" (2) "Yes, you can get me a straitjacket."

One account of a negotiating session claimed that a shirtsleeved Kissinger stormed out of the meeting in Damascus and shouted, to no one in particular, "How can anybody do business with these people?" before he returned to the negotiations. In more diplomatic language, Kissinger once told an in-flight briefing, after Khaddam constantly reopened issues he thought had already been agreed on, "Meetings with the Syrians are always dramatic."

During another on-plane briefing, he described Assad's unusual negotiating technique. "In my experience with Assad," he said, "he jumps over the precipice and hopes to find a tree to hold on to." He told Assad the same thing, elaborating with a joke about a man who falls off a cliff and grabs a tree on the way down. He prays for help. A voice comes from above, saying, "If you have faith, just let go and you will be saved." The man, wild-eyed, raises his head and pleads, "Is there anybody else up there?" The Syrians cracked up.

When Kissinger resorted to humor in negotiations, he liked to have a foil for his jokes. In Damascus, his favorite foil was Khaddam, who thought of Israelis the same way Saladin thought of the Crusaders. To break the tension of a difficult session, Kissinger once proposed, "I'll take Khaddam back to Israel, and Golda will cook dinner for him." When the Syrians insisted that the Israelis had to accept one of the negotiating points, Kissinger jibed, "I'll take Khaddam back with me. He can convince Golda." And he teased the foreign minister with lines like, "Golda would like his pretty blue eyes."

Like everything else on that shuttle, the Kissinger lines were a little overworked by the end of the thirty-three days.

The Secretary also teased his Arabic interpreter, Isa Sabbagh, a serious, stern-faced Arab with a graying Vandyke beard, although he never did pronounce his first name right (it's pronounced Eesa, but Kissinger always called him Eye-sa). "Are you translating the same jokes I'm telling you?" he used to say. Then he'd add, "I don't care if you are or not — you get the desired reaction." He once told the Syrians, "He's the one person I cannot fire. He knows too much about me already." Sabbagh said he was "thinking about joining the ranks of your biographers." "That's what worries me," Kissinger shot back.

Kissinger's use of humor apparently encouraged Assad to respond in kind. When the Secretary took to Damascus an Israeli proposal for dividing the Golan Heights town of Kuneitra into three parts, one for them, one for the Syrians, and one for the UN, Assad reacted with heavy sarcasm. "Quick," he said, "bring me a pen so I can sign it immediately."

Kissinger had explained to the Israelis that there would be no agreement unless they withdrew from Kuneitra, and they eventually agreed to do so, although they insisted on maintaining control of three surrounding hills. "If they like hills so much," Assad remarked sardonically, "we'll build them some farther back." It was the kind of line Kissinger would appreciate.

The proposals that flew back and forth with Kissinger often infuriated the other side. In a burst of evenhandedness on board his plane, he once pointed out that "you can't have successful negotiations unless both sides are equally unhappy." He then looked down at his watch and joked, "It's six o'clock. I only have six hours left to make the Syrians furious."

Neither side wanted to make the kind of compromises necessary to reach an agreement. As the negotiations dragged on, Kissinger noted wearily, "I'm dealing with two countries that do not specialize in making concessions." Syria, like Israel, had not had much experience as an independent state. Syria became independent only in 1941 and then had to fight off French efforts to reestablish control following World War II.

A couple of weeks into the shuttle, the Soviet Union announced that Foreign Minister Gromyko would be visiting Syria. Kissinger teased Assad about the visit, saying he expected Gromyko to be wined and dined, after which the two governments would issue a statement criticizing the United States and "interim" settlements in the Middle East, and then Syria would get a new supply of Soviet warplanes.

Kissinger agreed to meet with Gromyko, but not in Damascus; they compromised on nearby Cyprus. The Soviets, who were co-chairmen of the Geneva Conference, disliked Kissinger's solo diplomacy in the Middle East, and they wanted a piece of the negotiating action. The Secretary felt the Russians had not gone out of their way to help the negotiating process up till then, but he knew they were able to cause problems if they really wanted to, and in order to avoid unnecessary complications, he was willing to give them a more visible — if not more active — role. At their meeting in Nicosia, Gromyko complained noisily about Israel's negotiating stance and demanded that the Israelis retreat from at least half of the Golan Heights. Kissinger casually advised the Soviet foreign minister that *he* should go to Jerusalem the next day and tell the Israelis what to do. Gromyko returned to Moscow instead.

As early as the third trip of the shuttle, American officials began talking about the possibility of suspending the mission to give each side more time to reconsider its position. Kissinger complained that "everything is a guerrilla war on each side. At some point, it's counterproductive for me to stay. I don't want any winners and losers. I don't think the Syrians have done a great deal of staff work. Many just freeze when figures are raised."

Assad began expanding his delegation, a move Kissinger viewed as positive since it widened the area of responsibility for decisions and also exposed more high-ranking Syrian officials to Kissinger's persuasiveness. On the other hand, it slowed down the pace of the talks by reinforcing Assad's tendency to haggle over every point. Unlike Sadat, he did not make the major decisions and leave the details to subordinates. As Kissinger later pointed out, "Every issue was contested with a tenacity that I find unequaled in my experience." And he also griped, "It's no longer a question of concept, but of haggling."

After seven round trips, Kissinger again considered suspending the mission, but, he said, "both sides are pleading with me to go on. There's no question that without our being here, this wouldn't get done. There's no way of getting this done by diplomatic channels." And he added, "If I had to do it again, I'd do it again the same way."

Meanwhile, back at the State Department, officials were kept busy juggling Kissinger's calendar, and meetings with the Spanish foreign minister, the Japanese foreign minister, a Saudi Arabian economic delegation, and the foreign ministers of the Central Treaty Organization all had to be rescheduled, some of them for the third and fourth times.

Three times Kissinger was ready to read an announcement suspending the negotiations without an agreement. But each time one side or the other found "a tree to hang on to" after jumping over the cliff. One weary staffer climbed aboard the plane one day and said out loud, "I've been thinking about hijacking this plane. To Washington," he added wistfully.

When it appeared there would not be an agreement, potential farewell lunches were scheduled in Israel and in Syria. In Damascus, the site was the comfortable U.S. residence in the Abu Rumaneh diplomatic section of the city. The idea of such a luncheon was unprecedented, since government ministers would not ordinarily attend a social function in the residence of a country with which Syria did not have diplomatic relations. It was a sign of improving American-Syrian relations if not negotiating progress.

One of the guests was Defense Minister Mustafa Tlas, a forty-four-year-old major general who looked thirty-five. He was a handsome, debonair officer with a chest full of medals and considerable personal appeal. Kissinger, producing some of his own charm, said, "I don't know what the seating arrangement is, but don't let him sit next to my wife."

In his toast, Kissinger carried his humorous gibes at Khaddam from the private meetings into the public forum. "When I first met the foreign minister," he said, "his natural affection for anything American nevertheless had to give way to some suspicion engendered by six years of isolation." He turned to the shuttle: "It has been a difficult negotiation, eased somewhat by the natural conciliativeness of both sides." On a more serious note, he promised to keep working for a Syrian-Israeli agreement, which he predicted would eventually be reached, and he praised Syria's "constructive" role.

After twelve round trips between Israel and Syria, Kissinger still did not have a disengagement agreement. His diplomatic road show had turned into a melodrama with no final act, and he found himself in precisely the trap he had hoped to avoid — shuttling back and forth between the two countries so often that it appeared he was being exploited by both sides. He stayed out there so long and changed his deadline for ending the talks so often that it did indeed seem, as some critics charged, that the United States wanted a disengagement agreement even more than the two countries directly involved.

Kissinger's fifty-first birthday began during a session with Assad that lasted five hours, until three in the morning. But he didn't get the present he wanted most, although a still optimistic staffer said later in the day, "We've ordered the cake — a map of the Syrian-Israeli border and one word: Peace!"

After the meeting with Assad, the Secretary conferred with his negotiating team. They concluded the talks were hopelessly deadlocked. A cable to that effect was sent to Israeli Prime Minister Golda Meir. Another cable went to American officials in Israel, instructing them to have the Secretary's bags packed for the return trip to Washington. And a statement announcing suspension of the negotiations was drafted.

After a few hours' sleep, Kissinger went back to see Assad alone to tell him he was going home. They spent about an hour working on the draft of the communiqué announcing the breakdown in the talks. Finally, as they were walking toward the door of Assad's office, the Syrian President said, "What a tragedy that this should fail after all this effort." Kissinger quickly picked up on that. "Does it really have to?" he asked. "Well," said Assad, "what is necessary, what could we do?" "Forget some minor points and concentrate on basic issues," advised Kissinger. "I have the rest of the day free . . ."

Another cable went to Mrs. Meir, canceling the birthday luncheon she had planned for Kissinger, and several hours of intensive talk with Assad followed. But the pieces of an agreement still did not fall into place. As Kissinger left Syria on his birthday, he said, "This is my last visit to Damascus on this trip," and he announced that Sisco would return the next day to discuss what might happen next.

Despite the announcement, there was a small birthday celebration on the flight to Israel anyway, and the traveling newsmen gave him a card hand-drawn by UPI's Dick Growald. It read: "By a vote of 8–6, we wish you a happy birthday." We also gave him a poster, which showed a smiling, waving Kissinger above the caption: "I am Henry. Fly me to Damascus." It was supposed to read, "I'm Henry," as a takeoff on the National Airline ads then, but the Israeli printer was more literal than we anticipated. (Also more expensive, since we had to pay double-overtime for the rush job. Each of us also kept a copy of the poster, which Kissinger eventually signed individually.

"Fly me to Damascus" turned out to be an apt phrase for Kissinger's thinking when he returned to Israel. While talking to Mrs. Meir, he decided to give the mission one more try. He returned to Damascus himself instead of sending Sisco, and shuttle number thirteen proved to be the lucky one. The draft announcement of suspension became a historic curiosity piece. The cameraman who filmed the Kissinger-Assad meetings came out of the final session with a clue to the successful conclusion. For the first time, he said, Assad looked directly at the camera and smiled.

One of the measures that finally sealed the agreement was the stationing of a United Nations force in a buffer zone on the Golan Heights. The Israelis insisted that the name of the force include the word "disengagement," while the Syrians demanded it include the word "observer." And thus was born the United Nations Disengagement Observer Force, which became UNDOF, the world's newest

acronym. Kissinger was enormously amused by the haggling between the two sides over the name. "It has taken five thousand
years," he mused, "for civilization and the mind of man to devise
something called UNDOF." And he chuckled deeply.

Whenever the time for Syrian renewal of the mandate for UNDOF
came up, Kissinger used to think back to the Syrians' negotiating
technique and point out that one way to guarantee that they would
not approve a renewal until the last minute was to try to press them
on the issue.

As he boarded his plane to leave Damascus for the last time, he
shook hands with the chief of the American mission in Syria, Tom
Scotes, and whispered, "It takes a Jew and a Greek to get the Middle
East straightened out." He ended the thirty-third day of his mission
at the same time he had ended most of the previous thirty-two
— at 2:00 A.M. — but now at Andrews Air Force Base.

Following Kissinger's return, Sisco and I appeared on the *Today*
program, and Sisco was asked how a typical shuttling day had gone.
He replied, "In this particular instance, as Dick will verify, an early
morning arising, meeting with the Israelis in the morning, an hour's
ride to the airport, an hour's flight to Damascus, a half-hour's ride
again to the guest house where we met, long meetings — six to eight
hours — with President Assad, the same flight back to Damascus,
usually a midnight meeting with the Israeli officials, winding up
about two in the morning, and then our work began in terms of
preparation for the next day." He added, "Don't ask me what we did
with our spare time."

A member of the plane's crew recalled that he had watched farmers in the rolling hills outside of Tel Aviv "cut, rake, and bale the
wheat, plow the ground, and plant new seed. The wheat was beginning to come up when he finished."

The disengagement agreement paved the way for President Nixon
to include Syria in his tour of the Arab circuit in the summer of '74,
and although diplomatic relations had been resumed in a practical
sense, the formal announcement was timed to the presidential trip.

The President's flight into Damascus was eventful. As the presidential jet was approaching the capital, Kissinger aide Larry Eagleburger was writing a note to the Secretary about the scenario at the airport. He had just scribbled, "You will get off the plane right after Mrs. Nixon," when the plane suddenly went into turns and dives. Up front, the pilot, Ralph Albertazzi, had seen blips on his radar, and he took major evasive action.

Since this was the President's plane, Eagleburger was not concerned about the sudden motion. But then he looked at Kissinger's NSC aide, Brent Scowcroft, an Air Force general. He was "white as a sheet." Kissinger, who was not especially fond of flying in the first place, was gripping a table so hard his knuckles were white. Eagleburger suddenly figured it might be serious. But although he was in a state of near-panic at that point, he resumed writing the note to Kissinger as soon as the plane leveled off. "You will get off the plane right after Mrs. Nixon . . . I hope." The blips turned out to be Syrian escorts that the Americans had not known about beforehand.

The visit was brief. The all-military welcoming ceremony at the airport was correct and restrained, in keeping with the lack of formal diplomatic relations. Following the airport ceremonies, Assad and Nixon drove off at high speed in the U.S. President's limousine. The motorcade raced through downtown Damascus, with the two presidents standing up and waving to a crowd that was friendly, demonstrative, and fairly large, considering the long period of estrangement between the two countries and the fact that, for security reasons, the route had not been publicized beforehand.

Once relations were officially restored, career officer Richard Murphy became the first American Ambassador in Damascus since 1967. Murphy was a hard worker who didn't allow for a lot of time waiting at an airport, even for the Secretary of State. But he cut it too close on one visit when Kissinger's plane got in twenty minutes early. As Kissinger got off and spotted only Khaddam, he said to the Syrian foreign minister, "I'm very happy to see you. My own Ambassador has broken relations with me." But there were no recriminations.

Kissinger's visit to Damascus following the change in American presidents was highlighted by one of the most bizarre incidents of all of his travels. The Secretary had just said his good-byes in Egypt, and as the plane was taxiing onto the runway at the Cairo airport, he was standing in the aisle in the rear section, chatting with newsmen. Suddenly, there was a loud noise in the rear galley. It sounded like a loud slap, and I was sure it was a shot. The stewards yelled for a doctor. Agents jumped from their seats and rushed Kissinger to his compartment, where they made him lie flat as they quickly drew the shades on all the windows. Dr. Martin Wolfe dashed to the rear and found one of Kissinger's bodyguards, Walter Bothe, lying in the galley, bleeding from his head and arm. "Don't worry about me," the agent said. "Check the Secretary!"

The rest of us sat in our seats, stunned and bewildered, wondering what had happened. Other agents quickly found out. As Bothe was getting a cup of coffee in the galley, an Uzi submachine gun had fallen from an overhead rack and gone off. The bullet grazed Bothe's nearly bald head and clipped his arm. Another inch, and it would have been bye-bye, Bothe. The agents also found a bullethole in the ceiling of the plane, but the pilot said it would not cause a problem for the plane's pressurization system or endanger the aircraft in any other way. So we took off half an hour late, with Bothe lying in a bunk over the rear seats, his head and arm bandaged.

"You were damned lucky," Kissinger told him, adding, "We were all lucky. He's the only one of my original agents left. He's a sweetheart." (Bothe became one of Kissinger's private bodyguards after the Secretary left office.) Once Kissinger was assured that Bothe was all right, his humor took over. After take off, he needled Bothe, "Walter, I know you want to get off my detail, but you didn't have to shoot yourself to do it."

Later, Bill Sprague of the Voice of America commented that the incident had been designed to demonstrate how fast fourteen newsmen could jump from a sitting position into the overhead racks.

In addition to grazing Bothe's arm and head, which required six stitches, the bullet also put a hole through one of Joe Sisco's suits, which had been hanging in a plastic bag in the rear. When a staffer who didn't like Sisco heard about it, he remarked sardonically, "Too bad he wasn't in it."

A couple of days later, Bothe, his head still swathed in bandages, was something of a minor celebrity as he stood guard in the lobby of the King David Hotel in Jerusalem. He was even asked for his autograph. And he commented, "The trouble was, it took all of my hair with it."

Later at a dinner party in Washington, a guest nodded in the direction of Bothe and asked, "Is that the one?" Kissinger replied, with mock pride, "I'm the only person in the world who would have as a bodyguard a man who, when he decides to shoot himself at a distance of six inches, misses."

In Damascus, in the wake of Nixon's resignation, Kissinger found the conspiratorially minded President of Syria questioning the Secretary's own survival. Assad reasoned that Nixon had been removed from office not only because of his own corruption, but also because of pressure by the "Jewish-Zionist conspiracy," which wanted Ford to become President because of his long, unwavering record of staunch support for Israel. And since Kissinger had been a major factor in shaping the Nixon administration's policy in the Middle East, how long could the Secretary of State himself manage to hold on? Kissinger assured him that the new President had the utmost confidence in the old Secretary of State.

A few months later, when American policy in Southeast Asia was beginning to disintegrate, Kissinger again found Assad in a rather conspiratorial mood. The Syrian President cited the example of Cambodia as evidence that the Arabs could play a waiting game in the Middle East — anticipating that American support for Israel would eventually erode as well.

During this March 1975 visit, Assad held one of his rare news conferences for the traveling press. Despite their frequent presence in his capital during the shuttle, the American reporters had never met with the Syrian President. We eventually asked Kissinger to intervene on our behalf. He did, and Assad finally sat down with us, playing with his worry beads as he skillfully answered questions through an interpreter. The visit was taking place during a break in the negotiations between Israel and Egypt on the second disengagement agreement in the Sinai, and Assad stressed Syria's opposition to another separate deal. He preferred a return to the Geneva Conference.

He also got in a subtle dig at the Egyptians when a reporter asked if Syria would sign a peace treaty with the Israelis if they agreed to withdraw from the Golan Heights. Assad noted that the pertinent UN resolutions on Middle East negotiations did not refer to peace treaties, and he added, "We are not enamored of peace treaties — nor of those of friendship. What is important is to move toward a condition of peace and not just to sign treaties."

Assad, the leader of a country constantly portrayed as a client of the Soviet Union, was craftily pointing out that it was Egypt, not Syria, that had signed a Treaty of Friendship with the Russians. When he met privately with Kissinger later, he wanted to know if we had understood his needling point. Kissinger assured him that he had educated us well in the perception of such nuances.

It did not require an appreciation for nuances, however, to understand Assad's reaction when Israel and Egypt finally reached a second agreement. He charged that step-by-step diplomacy was really "foot-by-foot diplomacy," and he wanted no more of it. He even turned down overtures for a meeting with President Ford.

Just prior to one of Kissinger's last visits to Damascus, a reporter wanted to know what would happen. "It will be a warm, constructive, and useful talk," he joked, "and I'll be glad to be out of it."

After the August 1975 trip, he was "out of it," although I doubt that "glad" described his true feelings.

Saudi Arabia

As the Secretary of State's plane was approaching Riyadh for the first time, Kissinger walked to the rear compartment and scanned the fourteen reporters sitting there, seven of whom were Jewish. "Do we have any WASPs on board?" he asked. Saudi Arabia's reputation for anti-Semitism underlay the joking tone in his voice.

Only a couple of reporters raised their hands. "WASPs," Kissinger cracked, "are an endangered species." And he suggested it would be a good idea to "let Keatley get off the plane first." The *Wall Street Journal*'s Bob Keatley, a studious blond reporter in his late thirties, looked more WASP-ish than any other member of the press corps. After leaving Saudi Arabia, Kissinger took to teasing the Jewish reporters on board by "threatening" to make them get off first on the next trip to Riyadh. One of them finally complained he was overworking the joke, and he stopped.

Even though Saudi Arabia was not a direct participant in the Middle East negotiations, Kissinger included it on his itinerary on every swing through the area. The Saudis had a lot of influence because of their oil and their money, and Kissinger carefully nurtured U.S. relations with the Desert Kingdom.

Kissinger also regarded King Faisal, like President Sadat, as the kind of moderate Arab leader he hoped would benefit by negotiated agreements in the Middle East at the expense of the more radical elements.

Kissinger knew what to expect in Riyadh, more or less. Before setting out on his first Middle East expedition, he had conferred with a former American Ambassador to Saudi Arabia, who told him, "You have an obstacle to overcome. King Faisal is anti-Jewish. He always says, 'How can I be anti-Semitic? We are a Semitic people.' But he is anti-Jewish." The Secretary of State came to find that out for himself. One of the Jewish reporters once asked Kissinger privately, "Does Faisal hate only Zionists, or does he hate Jews?" Kissinger didn't hesitate: "He hates Jews!"

The former Ambassador had also told Kissinger not to be "put off by Faisal's dour visage and manner," and he advised him that "whenever Faisal was thinking of a rejoinder, he picked lint off his robe." Above all, he cautioned Kissinger that whatever he said to Faisal, he should be prepared to stand by it and to fulfill any promise, since Faisal attached great importance to a man's word.

So Kissinger was prepared, but not fully, for their first meeting. The King's visage and manner were indeed dour as the two men posed for pictures, sitting side by side on white and gold upholstered armchairs beneath dazzling chandeliers in the state room of the Saudi monarch's Al-Mazaar Palace on the outskirts of the desert capital. The King wore flowing black robes and a white Bedouin headdress. Kissinger was in his blue business suit with a blue polka-dot tie. Outside, aged Bedouin retainers in ankle-length greatcoats, armed with golden scimitars and curved daggers and with bandoliers slung across their chests, stood watch.

The Secretary of State leaned across the small marble-topped table between him and the King and through an interpreter conveyed greetings from President Nixon.

The King noted, gratuitously, "These days he has a lot of problems." That was the small talk, but it had a large meaning. The Saudis didn't know much or care about Watergate, but they were concerned that the President was in so much trouble that he might not be able to follow through on whatever Kissinger was trying to do.

The fact that Kissinger was Jewish did not spare him from Faisal's routine diatribe against Jews, Zionism, and Israel. Faisal's line was quite simple: The Jews were out to take over the world. It was they who had created the Communist Party, and in the parts of the world they did not already control, they infiltrated governments and held high positions. He also pointed out that Golda Meir had been born in Russia (Kiev) as a way of underlining the link between communism, Zionism, and Israel.

One of his aides recalls that "Kissinger was sardonically amused by the comments Faisal and the Saudis would make about Zionism, Israel, and the Jews, not offended."

Kissinger's sardonic amusement was reflected in the anecdotes he told afterward. During one of Faisal's lectures about the Zionists, Kissinger diplomatically tried to change the subject. "I saw a painting at the far end of a long, smoke-filled hall, and I asked, 'Is that a landscape of Saudi Arabia? I really do like the desert.' The King replied, 'That's the Holy Oasis.' It was," Kissinger said, "like going into a Catholic home and seeing the Virgin Mary on the wall and saying, 'Is that your aunt?' That remark probably caused a three-month extension in the oil embargo."

An Israeli Cabinet minister recalls Kissinger telling him about his first meeting with Faisal. The Saudi monarch greeted him by saying he was receiving him not as a Jewish person but as a human being. Kissinger said he responded by saying, "Some of my best friends are human beings."

But it's more likely that the reported repartee reflects what he thought about saying rather than what he actually said, since none of Kissinger's aides remembers his ever cracking a joke with Faisal. In fact, "dour" went with Faisal as automatically as King did, and the Saudi monarch was one leader whom Kissinger never characterized as having "a good sense of humor."

Kissinger also liked to recount his first dinner with Faisal. Ambas-

sador Jim Akins, who looked as Saudi as the locals with his clipped
beard and mustache and stern visage, told the Secretary beforehand
not to expect a "serious discussion." During the meal, Faisal again
launched into his anti-Zionist tirade, delivering the whole litany, full
of the familiar vitriol. Afterward, Kissinger asked Akins, in amused
amazement, "Is that your idea of light dinner conversation? I'd hate
to see what you consider an argument." Akins cautioned, "It will get
worse." And it did.

However, as Kissinger's visits to Riyadh became regular, the
King's tirades subsided, and the Secretary was able to report to the
Israelis with great glee, "I'm getting along with Faisal so well now
that he's picking lint off *my* clothes!"

Kissinger had found out at first hand what was already in his
briefing books, that Faisal never made the distinction between Zionism as a political movement and the Jews as a people. For Faisal and
the Saudis, it took some adjustment in their mind set to deal with
an American Secretary of State who happened to be a Jew, since to
them Jews were Zionists and enemies.

The delicacy of dealing with the Saudis was made clear from the
outset. Joe Sisco had peeled off from the Kissinger party in Egypt
and gone to Israel, planning to rejoin the group in Saudi Arabia. It
was not easy to get from Tel Aviv to Riyadh; complicated connec-
tions were necessary for commercial travelers. Since Sisco flew in a
U.S. government plane, the Saudis allowed it to land without asking
where it had come from.

The anti-Zionist diatribes notwithstanding, Kissinger was well
received in Saudi Arabia. His acceptance was signaled symbolically
at the end of his first visit in November 1973. The Saudi foreign
minister, Omar Saqqaf, a sad-faced man with a short gray beard and
soulful eyes, clasped the Secretary's hand as they walked from the
airport lounge to the plane. This common gesture in the Arab world
was a new experience for Kissinger — and for Kissinger-watchers.

Saqqaf told reporters, "We found that the man was sincere." The
reticent, soft-spoken foreign minister had clearly come under the
Kissinger spell, and his farewell statement during a later Kissinger

visit was inordinately long-winded. Saqqaf concluded, "I have always been . . . a man of few words; I don't know what has happened to me; maybe the presence of our friend is inspiring. Let me end by wishing him every success, bon voyage, and we welcome him anytime."

In advance of any visit to Riyadh, Kissinger always used to point out that Saudi Arabia, apart from its vast oil riches, was the guardian of orthodox Islamic faith and exercised a great deal of moral influence with the Arab countries involved in the Middle East negotiations. In his more flippant moods, he would also point out, "You'd be surprised at how much moral influence sixty-five billion dollars a year can give you."

Kissinger knew that Faisal was an important figure from an economic as well as a diplomatic point of view, and in typical fashion, he wanted to get out the word that he had a favorable impression of the Saudi King. After the first couple of meetings, he told newsmen on the plane, "King Faisal always has the face of the desert. He's a very serious man. He takes words seriously and he chooses words seriously. He's intelligent . . . he understands the world in which he lives, the world in which he must succeed."

Kissinger also described Faisal as "quite a savvy guy." But the savviness was extremely limited, and Kissinger later observed, "He's a feudal lord, a skillful manipulator within the Arab context." He added at another point, "If it weren't for his money, Faisal would be a feudal ruler of a rickety kingdom, like the King of Libya."

The traveling newsmen were quickly exposed to some of the more "rickety" parts of the kingdom. A little old red bus that would have been a museum piece anywhere else was waiting at the airport to haul us around. The first place it hauled us was the Sahari Palace, a hostelry that resembled the first part of its name considerably more than the second. When Kissinger heard about our accommodations, he cracked, "The Sahari Palace? Is it part of the Las Vegas chain?" It was a long way from Las Vegas — in every conceivable way.

When we first walked into the Sahari Palace, we passed through an elongated lobby to an area where the press room had been set up, and we got our first indication of what the international telephone service was going to be like when we heard Juan de Onis of the New York *Times* roaring into a telephone. A reporter nearing his deadline raced to a typewriter and started writing, then quickly turned to de Onis and asked in an annoyed voice, "Do you have to shout so loud?" De Onis turned from the phone and shouted even louder, "No, goddamnit, I'm just doing this because I enjoy it." And then he resumed shouting into the telephone.

The two telephones available for international service were connected by land to the small Emirate of Bahrain on the Persian Gulf, where the calls were then relayed to the United States. The wait was unpredictably long, and the print journalists who didn't trust the Telex operators had to spend an extraordinary amount of time dictating stories to their home offices because the quality of the line was so poor. The broadcasters simply went through the motions. They were lucky to be heard, let alone understood, at the other end.

Bernie Gwertzman of the New York *Times,* who has a rather large chest, not to say stomach, cavity, bellowed his story until the walls reverberated; one reporter heard him on the third floor of the hotel. But back came the voice of a New York dictationist, "Can you speak up, please?"

As bad as the telephone service was, it did at least exist. When the members of the Kissinger advance team arrived in Riyadh to make the arrangements for his first visit, they toured the royal guest house and found it quite satisfactory; it had a total of four telephones, including one in the bathroom. However, they were not hooked up to anything. The advance team installed its own telephone communications to the Embassy and to the plane.

On that first visit, the telephones and the automobiles almost seemed out of place in Riyadh. Visiting Saudi Arabia was somewhat like stepping into a time capsule and being transported back to the sixteenth century. Bedouins traded in live hawks on street corners. The few women who appeared on the streets at all were always completely veiled. The outdoor toilets in "downtown" Riyadh were primitive.

At the Royal Palace, one of the most striking figures was the royal executioner, a leathery old man with creases in his dark chocolate face. He wore an Arab headdress and a bandolier slung over his robe. When he smiled broadly for the photography buffs, he revealed a mouth rich in gold. And he carried a huge scimitar. When we were told that thieves still had their hands cut off for stealing, we wondered what the punishment was for adultery.

But a few months and billions of petrodollars later, the cityscape began to change. The impact of oil wealth on the communications system in particular was quite audible. The Saudis bought equipment to hook into the global satellite network, and they hired outside experts to train Telex and telephone operators. The communications in Saudi Arabia went from the worst on the Arab circuit to the best before Kissinger was through shuttling.

Not only the telephone system became more sophisticated. So did the personnel. On all of our visits, our calls were placed by young Saudi men wearing kaffiyas and galabias. Some of them wore Pierre Cardin jackets over the robes. But on one visit after the new system was installed, the chief of the telephone bookers came out looking Western-style cool. He wore trousers with a jeans cut, a sport shirt, a baggy sweater, and shades above the requisite mustache and goatee.

While we were chatting with him, he wondered if somebody would be willing to make a few dollars by bringing a video cassette player on his next visit, since the customs service didn't check the Kissinger party. Why, we wondered back, did he want a video cassette player in Saudi Arabia? Well, he explained, on his last trip to the States, he had bought video cassettes of *Deep Throat* and *The Girl Behind the Green Door* and had smuggled them into the country, only to find out there were no video cassette players in Saudi Arabia, and he had no way of viewing them. We did not see him on subsequent trips.

There were, of course, no X-rated movies in Saudi Arabia. There were no movies of any kind. And certainly no gambling or drinking in public. This puritanism was an obvious target for Kissinger's worldly humor. Just before landing in Riyadh on one trip, he came to the rear of the plane, and with a malevolent grin on his face, he asked, "So, what are you going to do tonight?" And he chuckled because he knew the answer.

During all eleven visits to Saudi Arabia, Kissinger always made the point that he was trying to keep Middle East diplomacy separate from oil diplomacy. And during all eleven visits, the members of the traveling press were skeptical. (He probably thought we were my-OPEC about the subject.) At one point, the skepticism had a physical manifestation. On the flight into Saudi Arabia in March 1974, Kissinger advised the traveling press not to expect any "breakthrough" on the oil embargo, although an OPEC meeting at which the embargo was scheduled to be lifted was less than a week away. Kissinger didn't want to take any chances on rocking the OPEC boat by having more oil stories appear in American newspapers.

Two reporters decided to commemorate the lack of a "breakthrough" with a sardonic reminder. They went to a nearby gas station and bought two quarts of oil for about one third the price in the United States. (As for gasoline, it was only 12 cents a gallon.) On the plane, they gave a quart to Kissinger as a symbol of his non-oil policy.

However, oil diplomacy and Middle East politics were kept separate in one significant regard. After the October War, the Saudis — and other Arabs — tried to link a phased relaxation of the oil embargo to a phased Israeli withdrawal from occupied Arab territory. Kissinger regarded that formula as a form of blackmail, since the implication was that the United States would be rewarded with more oil as it pressured Israel to give up more territory. He felt that such an arrangement would subvert the American role as middleman, and he warned the Arabs that they needed a peace conference to get their land back more than the United States needed Arab oil.

He also kept explaining over and over that the primary thrust of American oil diplomacy was toward organizing the consuming countries, and therefore there was no real reason to discuss oil prices in depth with the Saudis. In short, he had a very weak energy hand to play, and the Saudis knew it.

In reality, so did Kissinger, but virtually every time he left Riyadh,

he claimed he had assurances from the Saudis that they opposed any increase in the price of oil. But the price invariably went up at the next meeting of OPEC. Our skepticism eventually produced a standard joke on the flights out of Saudi Arabia. Kissinger would say the Saudis told him they were against a price rise, and a reporter would ask, "So, how much is the price going up?"

It wasn't long before Kissinger himself was joking about it. While sightseeing in Egypt in the fall of 1974, he visited the Papyrus Institute, a museum on a barge anchored in the Nile. Its founder-director was giving him the guided tour, showing him how papyrus was made and explaining that a large supply of the raw material had recently been discovered in the Sudan. Papyrus, he explained, is a perennial plant and would be available long after the world's oil supply had been depleted. "Just don't raise the prices," Kissinger joked. "My nerves are not good."

After a visit to Taif, where the Saudi royal family was spending the summer, Kissinger was asked about his discussions on oil.

"They're going to lower prices," he said, anticipating the reporters' jibes. "Listen," he went on, "I made a joke to an Arab minister a few weeks ago, saying, 'Every time you talk about lowering oil prices, they go up.' And he took it as a statement of our policy." He was vastly amused.

Oil diplomacy was complicated early in 1975 by intimations of American military intervention in Middle East oil fields. The intimations came in oblique comments by Kissinger and Ford, and the resulting controversy was intensified by an article in *Harper's* suggesting that the only way to break the oil producers' cartel was through the use of military force. The Saudis thought the magazine article had been officially inspired, and they were visibly exercised when Kissinger went to see them in March, during a break in the unsuccessful negotiations between Egypt and Israel. The Israelis were then demanding the Egyptians make a public pledge of nonbelligerency, which they refused to do.

Before leaving, Kissinger offered public reassurance to the Saudis. "I would like to state categorically here," he said at the airport, "that our relationship with Saudi Arabia is based on friendship and cooperation in which threats, military or otherwise, play no part, and we base our relationship on cooperation and not on confrontation." The acting foreign minister, Sheik Ahmad Zaki Yamani, replied, "We heard the official views about the fantasies of the newspapers, and articles written by certain groups of writers, and we are pleased they are now in public. We thank you for your efforts and wish you best of luck."

On board the plane, a reporter congratulated Kissinger on achieving a nonbelligerency statement with Saudi Arabia. "You guys are a cynical bunch," Kissinger said not unkindly, "and a bit paranoid." He went on to say that in his private talks with the Saudis, he did not retract his statement that military force would have to be considered in the event the industrialized Western world faced "actual strangulation" because of an oil shortage. "But don't repeat this, for God's sake," Kissinger implored. "This is just for your understanding."

Acting Foreign Minister Yamani was actually the minister of

petroleum. He was bright, articulate, Harvard-educated, and charismatic, which meant he got a lot of press attention. For some reason, Kissinger seemed to resent Yamani's popularity. He claimed to like Yamani personally, but he always put him down, emphasizing that when he met the members of the royal family at receptions — and there were a lot of royal members — Yamani was always "somewhere in the back of the room" or "far down the list."

Kissinger himself was originally suspect in the eyes of the Saudis, and one of Ambassador Jim Akins's primary jobs was to dispel the Saudis' suspicions, to persuade them that Kissinger was an honorable man who was not blindly pro-Israel because he was Jewish and who would put American interests above Israeli interests. But Akins and Kissinger were themselves bound to clash. Both were extremely intelligent, headstrong men, with oversized egos, but Kissinger had the higher rank, and Akins did not survive the Kissinger era at the State Department. Eventually he lost his post in Saudi Arabia and resigned from the Foreign Service.

During Kissinger's first meeting with Faisal, Joe Sisco told Akins that the Ambassador didn't have to attend the session. "Fine," said Akins. "My resignation will be typed by the time the meeting is over . . . How can you expect me, having just presented my credentials, to function if you keep me out?" Akins then raised the matter with Kissinger, who said, "Of course, come along."

Another of Akins's prime assignments was to work toward getting the oil embargo ended. The Saudis were essential to the effectiveness of the boycott, and they were influential in determining when it would be removed. One American diplomat recalls that some of the State Department's instructions on this were "hysterical." Akins was told to tell the Saudis that the State Department would release some documents "proving duplicity" if they didn't lift the embargo. Akins passed along this threat in an informal way to Foreign Minister Saqqaf, saying he just wanted to give an indication of the mood in Washington, but adding that he was going to try to get his instructions changed. Saqqaf counterwarned that if the department released embarrassing documents, so would the Saudis. The matter ended there since Akins's instructions were indeed changed. But Saqqaf later told the American Ambassador that the issue had been raised with King Faisal, and the Saudi King said that if the United States had carried out its threat, he would have broken relations.

In February 1974, Akins had a meeting with Faisal at which the Saudi leader seemed responsive to American requests for an end to the embargo. Akins sent a top-secret cable to Washington about Faisal's attitude. When, a few days later, the cable appeared in a newspaper column, the Saudis taunted the American Ambassador, asking, "What will we see in the papers next?" American officials who were in the Saudi capital at the time felt the leak caused the embargo to be prolonged.

The end of the embargo had been forecast publicly by the Nixon administration so many times — unsuccessfully — that an exasperated Kissinger finally said during one of his on-plane briefings, "The best way to get the goddamned embargo lifted is for me to say on the record, 'I don't give a good goddamn if they lift the embargo or play cards on March tenth.'" He said that off the record. And they did lift the embargo on March 10, although they kept on playing the price card for several months to come.

As other Arabists had done, Akins also tried to impress upon Kissinger the importance of personal relations in Saudi Arabia. He told the Secretary about Foreign Minister Saqqaf's disappointment with Joseph Luns, the former foreign minister of the Netherlands who became Secretary-General of NATO. At the time of the October War, Saqqaf thought he had a close relationship to Luns. But when the Dutch diplomat made a speech that Saqqaf considered anti-Arab, the Saudi foreign minister was stunned. Saqqaf later told Akins that Holland was singled out among the nations of Europe as a target of the oil embargo specifically because of that speech.

Akins was eventually replaced in Riyadh by veteran diplomat William Porter, who, ironically, shared some of his predecessor's feelings about the Secretary. After Porter retired, he gave a pointed speech in Washington, in which he said, "It is worth repeating that the U.S. government should cease sending high-level envoys to the Middle East before the home front is properly prepared. Every government in that region keeps close tabs on the congressional state of mind concerning Middle East developments. As one of the more outspoken foreign ministers put it to an American visitor who repeated several times that he had the President's complete confidence and backing, 'Yes, yes, Mr. Secretary, I'm sure of it. But you haven't said anything about Congress.'

"The arrivals of our special envoys in small countries are rather splendid occasions," Porter went on, "but alas, they do not always improve our image. The planners of such expeditions seem to have little regard for the natural modesty which is the hallmark of our people outside of Washington. Their idea seems to be to overwhelm our hosts with officials, mountains of baggage, and the noise of scores of walkie-talkies.

"We've seen planes disgorge as many as ninety-five people, including the head man, his administrative team, his substantive team, his blood plasma team, his security guards, the gentlepersons of the media, and of course, the caterers."

Although Porter certainly had Kissinger in mind, he was thinking more of Treasury Secretary William Simon, who reportedly had once insisted that his entourage for an overseas trip include at least one more person than Kissinger's.

While Kissinger's entourage remained large, his clout with the Saudi government eventually diminished, especially after the death of Saqqaf and the assassination of Faisal. In fact, some otherwise intelligent and sophisticated Saudis even came to suspect American implication in the deaths of the two men. They pointed out that the foreign minister had died in New York and that the King had been assassinated by a member of the family who had recently left the States.

By the end of his Middle East hegiras, Kissinger's diplomacy had been somewhat discounted by the Saudis. They realized that he was not going to deliver the Israelis, that the Arabs were not going to get their territory back, that the Jewish settlements would not be removed from occupied lands. Nevertheless, the Saudis remained fascinated with him to the end.

Jordan

A Kissinger visit to Jordan cannot be reconstructed on paper. It had to be seen and heard to be appreciated. Of all the countries he visited — almost sixty as Secretary of State — none of them gave him a bigger welcome or a more colorful sendoff. Whenever Kissinger's plane landed or took off from the Amman airport, a band and honor guard of the Arab Legion gave a performance straight out of *Lawrence of Arabia.* After the U.S. and Jordanian national anthems had been played, Kissinger reviewed the honor guard. While the band played a slow waltz — in three-quarter time, naturally, for the British hand-me-down ceremony — the Secretary of State tried to master the little hesitation slide required to stay in step with the music.

In his first effort, Kissinger looked like a hippopotamus on a tightrope. The newsmen and staffers managed to smother their laughter, but they guffawed in recounting "The Kissinger Waltz" afterward. They shared their hilarity with the Secretary himself, who allowed as how he didn't quite have the hang of it.

Once the funny part was over, the musicians uncorked their bagpipes, and the legionnaires passed in review with a snappy heel-and-toe-stepping and arm-swinging panache. The ceremony made for great television pictures, and Kissinger's visits to Jordan probably got a little more air time than they deserved because the pictures were so good.

A member of the Kissinger party commented to Bernie Gwertzman, "It's crazy, isn't it? An Arab King honoring a Jewish-American official, with his British-style band playing its Scottish bagpipes to a desert background."

One reason for the big show may have been that Zaid Rifai, the Prime Minister, was a former student of Professor Kissinger at his Harvard seminar for foreigners. A more important reason was that King Hussein, an annual visitor to Washington, admired and respected Kissinger.

The United States and Jordan had been friends for a long time. The Jordanians had not broken relations with Washington like the rest of the Arabs, and Jordan even got some American military assistance, although not as much as it would have liked.

Hussein, a courageous survivor on the Hashemite throne, was known in the lexicon of American journalistic clichés as the "plucky little king," PLK for short. (That was like JLP, which was shorthand for "just and lasting peace," a standard phrase in all arrival and departure statements as well as aftermeal toasts in the Middle East.) During flights into Jordan or waiting periods on the ground, some newsmen occasionally amused themselves by trying to coin substitutes for the PLK cliché. Lars-Erik Nelson of Reuters was a prolific competitor. He came up with "Lilliputian Levantine leader" and "mighty minuscule monarch" and even "hearty half-pint Hashemite." None of them ever caught on. (It was Nelson who once described the journalist's craft as "the creative application of clichés.")

The King was not only plucky. He had a lot of flair and showmanship. On our first visit, he took the controls of a helicopter to fly Kissinger to the airport. The Secretary, who appreciated helicopters only slightly more than camels, plagiarized Abraham Lincoln with his reaction: "If it hadn't been for the honor, I'd just as soon have walked." On another visit, Hussein buzzed the airport in his chopper during the farewell ceremony on the ground. Kissinger looked up and waved, obviously pleased he was not in the helicopter.

Hussein, wearing casual sports clothes, also flew Henry and Nancy on a trip to historic Jerash, the ancient Roman stronghold in the Jordanian interior. Kissinger learned about the perils of small talk during that trip. He told newsmen afterward, "The King flew Nancy and me at treetop level. When I said I didn't think he could fly so low, he dropped down even farther." The Secretary laughed in a way that indicated he wouldn't do that again.

As another courtesy to the Secretary of State, Jordanian jet fighters usually escorted his plane out of Jordanian air space.

When Kissinger began his regular tour of the Arab circuit, Amman was still an important stop. Jordan attended the December 1973 Geneva Peace Conference, and Kissinger explored the possibility of arranging negotiations between Jordan and Israel to follow the pattern of Israel's negotiations with Egypt and Syria. But he never managed to get them together, although he kept warning the Israelis that if they didn't deal with Hussein, they were going to end up confronting the Palestine Liberation Organization. And sure enough, at the Arab Summit in Rabat in the fall of 1974, the PLO was named the sole negotiator for the Palestinians. That decision virtually removed Jordan from the active negotiating picture.

Following the Rabat Summit, some reporters became virtually obsessed with the PLO question, and their suspicions that Kissinger would move to make contact with the organization's leaders never abated. At one point, Kissinger complained during an in-flight briefing, "I keep getting badgered about the Palestinians by everybody except the Arabs." Following a visit to Damascus, a reporter wanted to know if Kissinger had met with representatives of the PLO. "Absolutely!" he replied with a straight face. "But not with Yasir Arafat, only with a deputy." The reporter remembered that Kissinger had also answered "Absolutely!" when he was asked if he was getting married, and nobody had paid heed. He pressed the question. The Secretary once again restated the unchanged policy that no American officials would meet with PLO representatives until the PLO recognized Israel's existence.

Although Jordan became an "odd man out" in the Middle East negotiating line-up, Kissinger never stopped visiting Amman when he went to the Middle East. And it was not because of the airport ceremonies. He hoped that Hussein could eventually be brought back into the negotiating process. He kept telling the Arabs that they had "a choice between making declarations and making progress" on the Palestinian issue. They chose declarations. At another point, he said waspishly, "They [the PLO] have the mandate. Now let's see what they can do with it." He knew the answer. The Israelis would not deal with the PLO.

Kissinger always thought that Hussein was the most moderate of the Arab leaders and that "Jordan would be the easiest part of the problem to settle if it weren't for the National Religious party" in Israel, which insisted that Israel had a Biblical claim to sovereignty over the West Bank — Judea and Samaria.

And so Kissinger always made a point of seeing Hussein so it wouldn't appear that Jordan had been excluded from the negotiating process, even though Jordan had indeed been excluded. He also wanted to reassure Hussein, and everybody else in the area, of continuing American support.

In addition to staging colorful airport ceremonies, the Jordanians also ferried Kissinger around in a splendid cream-colored Bentley limousine. On the first visit, Kissinger posed grandly beside the limo and said with as much truth as wit, "It's nice to know that some countries know how to treat me in the manner to which I'm accustomed."

When he spent the night in Amman, he usually spent it at a royal guest house. As in so many places where the Kissinger party stayed, the plumbing stopped working one night. Kissinger complained to the Embassy, and administrative officer Perry Linder showed up at about two in the morning. "Who are you?" Kissinger wanted to know after Linder had fixed the plumbing. "A plumber?" "No," said Linder. "I'm a Foreign Service officer attached to the Embassy."

Despite the lack of a wider audience, Kissinger couldn't resist. "It's nice to meet an FSO who knows what he's doing," he said.

As befitted a king, Hussein also maintained royal quarters in Aqaba, a resort area on the Gulf of Aqaba, and he occasionally invited Kissinger to visit him there. (Kissinger went to Aqaba more than once but never learned how to pronounce it. He called it Ak-waba instead of Ah-kaba.) The gulf scenery was enchanting, but the communications were frustrating, if not impossible. Most of the print copy was sent by special Embassy courier to Amman, several hours away, for transmission from there, with an information officer riding shotgun to make sure it was actually sent in reasonably intelligent form. Telephone communications were virtually out of the question, although everybody kept trying and some occasionally got through.

The King had a bowling alley and a pinball machine at the palace in Aqaba, and the Kissinger staff set up the radio-teletype in the pinball machine room. The radio-teletype depended on lines from Amman, and it quickly went "Tilt." It turned out yards of gibberish all night long until the staff gave up and went to the bar. Thereafter, on visits to Aqaba, the staff relied on the plane's communications system and forgot about the palace.

The only line from Aqaba to Amman was a bare wire strung on telephone poles across the desert. But every night, at sundown, birds roosted on the line, disrupting the communications. So royal orders went out, and the next time Kissinger showed up in Aqaba, the Jordanian Army organized a special unit that spent the night chasing the birds off the line. I always wondered if the members of the unit got a special campaign medal, such as a distinguished shooing cross with tailfeather clusters.

It was in another Jordanian town that Kissinger earned the sobriquet "Henry of Arabia." Specifically, it was Petra, the "rose-red city half as old as time." It's one of Jordan's major tourist attractions, and Hussein had urged Kissinger to see it from the time of his first visit. The Secretary's escort for the occasion was Prime Minister Rifai, who showed up for the outing looking indeed like a tourist, wearing a Trumanesque blue and yellow sport shirt. Kissinger was conspicuously overdressed. He wore a blue business suit, white shirt, and tie.

They flew from Amman to a spot near Petra in a French-designed Alouette helicopter. The only ground approach to the ancient town is through a narrow mile-and-a-half-long gorge set between soaring cliffs. It was strewn with rocks and boulders, and Rifai playfully offered Kissinger his choice of conveyance for the bumpy journey — camel, donkey, or mule. The Secretary rejected all three, so Rifai provided a Land Rover, which wasn't all that much more comfortable, especially since Kissinger was suffering from the "Damascus bug," as he described his malady to newsmen.

Petra is carved out of red sandstone, and it's an archaeological gem, loaded with monuments and tombs from the Nabatean and Roman periods. Kissinger, ever the antiquities buff, peered into the tomb known as Khazneh, or Treasury, so named because of the local belief that a treasure is buried somewhere inside, and despite his leather-soled shoes, he walked up a two-hundred-foot stretch of rocks to the Tomb of the Urn, a huge crumbling structure with two floors of vaults. "It's a great place to visit," he said, "but I wouldn't want to live here."

At a rest house, Rifai made photographic history. He placed a kaffiya, the red-and-white-checked Bedouin headdress worn by Arabs, on Kissinger's head, and the photographers snapped away. Thinking ahead to his next stop, Israel, Kissinger cracked, "It will make a great picture for my arrival tonight." Then he added, "My father [an Orthodox Jew] will really be proud of me."

To spare the Damascus-bugged Kissinger the long, bumpy ride out of Petra, the Jordanians flew a helicopter right into the city. Looking at the surrounding cliffs, Kissinger reworked the line he had used at the airport on an earlier visit. "If it weren't for the honor," he said, "I'd just as soon take a camel."

When he got to Israel that night, a member of the Israeli negotiating team let him know that the headdress had not gone unnoticed. "I watched you on Jordanian television," he said, "and I see that you have become an honorary Arab leader."

Kissinger's unorthodox diplomatic style — and his multilayered personality — once came into play in Jordan through the presence of another American diplomat, Dean Brown. Brown was a short, colorful, feisty former Ambassador to Jordan whom Kissinger later designated as a special U.S. representative in war-torn Lebanon. At the State Department, Brown was known as one of Kissinger's few "abominable No men," the few who talked back.

After retiring from the Foreign Service — against Kissinger's wishes — Brown visited Jordan, where he stayed in a private home. Just before leaving Washington, he had been interviewed by a New York *Times* reporter. Brown claimed the reporter distorted what he really said, and the resulting article came out critical of Kissinger, especially on his handling of the Syrians.

While in Jordan, Brown got a call from the Embassy, saying two telegrams had arrived for him from the State Department. The first was from Roy Atherton, the assistant secretary of state for Near Eastern affairs. It said, in effect: The Secretary has asked me to tell you how terribly annoyed he is at you over the interview in the New

York *Times,* how destructive it is of American policy, and he would like an explanation. The second cable, which was numbered consecutively, meaning it had been sent immediately after the other one, was marked "Personal for Dean Brown from HAK." It said, in effect: While you're in Jordan, I'd appreciate it if you would go to see King Hussein and say certain things — from you, not from me — but you can hint that we talked about it. And the cable listed the things Kissinger wanted Brown to say about the Middle East negotiations.

In the Middle East, Kissinger was indeed a "kindred spirit."

ELEVEN

Press I: Kissinger Versus the Media

Henry Kissinger, a slender, owlish-looking Harvard professor, had just been appointed the new Assistant to the President for National Security Affairs. President-elect Nixon announced the appointment at the Hotel Pierre, his transition headquarters, in New York City. During the news conference that followed, Herb Kaplow, who soon became the *NBC News* White House correspondent, asked Kissinger about his reputation as a "hard-liner." Kissinger denied being a hard-liner. As soon as the question-and-answer session was over, Kissinger went looking for Kaplow to follow up his denial on a more personal basis. For the next eight years, Kissinger applied that kind of personal touch to his relations with the press.

Henry Kissinger was fascinated, intrigued, and challenged by the press. He read virtually everything that was written and broadcast about him. While he was traveling, the State Department sent him several pages of cables daily containing the coverage of the trip by both the print and broadcast media. His omnivorous interests extended even to the comic pages. "Any word from 'Doonesbury'?" asked one message from Africa.

The standard trip cable read:

All posts are reminded to: 1. Send telegraphic summaries local press reaction of Secretary's visit both before and after visit, and

2. Send a collection of press clippings of local coverage of visits to Funseth S/PRS by air pouch as well as any summaries of radio and TV coverage.

He missed nothing. After spotting a story noting that he was seldom satisfied with his breakfast on the road, he said aloud in his office, "I see people have been unveiling my breakfast habits." The remark was not directed at anyone in particular; he just wanted his staff to know he hadn't missed the item. And he once marveled to a magazine reporter who had written about "a hole in his Sulka socks" that he himself didn't know what kind of socks he was wearing. They had been a gift from Nancy.

Kissinger missed nothing that was written about his associates, either. After an overblown column carried a misleading report about a so-called Sonnenfeldt doctrine, Kissinger grumped meaningfully, "If we ever have a new doctrine around here, it won't be called the *Sonnenfeldt* doctrine." And when his energy aide, Tom Enders, was the subject of a highly favorable sketch in *Newsweek,* Kissinger cracked to newsmen, "One more puff job like that, and Enders will be deputy chief of mission in Chad." (Enders did somewhat better; he became Ambassador to Canada.)

In modern times, only Lyndon Johnson rivaled Kissinger in his determination to know every word said or printed about him. Part of their motivation was egomania. But Kissinger also knew that the press helped shape his image, which he considered important in the conduct of diplomacy. "In my experience," said a former State Department press spokesman, "no public official was as persuasive, informative and effective in his personal dealings with the press as Kissinger was." And he added significantly, "Furthermore, Kissinger worked at it harder than anybody else."

When he traveled — which was always — he briefed reporters incessantly on the plane, although it should be pointed out that we complained when he didn't. We were there, of course, to cover a story in which Kissinger was always a central figure. The long sessions on the plane often resembled seminars as much as briefings, with the world's foremost diplomat expounding on current events, the recent past, history, negotiating styles, and his relations with various world leaders, including, on occasion, American presidents he had known — from Kennedy through Ford.

There's no question that he tried to shape the news and "manipulate" the press. All politicians do that, but few are as skillful as Kissinger. Barbara Walters neatly captured an essential element of his effectiveness: "You always have the feeling," she said, "that he's told you ten percent more than he has to."

Bernie Gwertzman, the best of the contemporary diplomatic reporters, pointed out: "In the role of supplier of information . . . Mr. Kissinger has often been maligned. He is often portrayed as a manipulator, dispensing to the 'puppets' of the press only that which furthers his own ends. This is only partially true. Like all officials, Mr. Kissinger does 'declassify' what he thinks helps him out. But he is not by nature able to control himself that well. He cannot just reveal this much and not any more. He is a very talkative man, who when the mood strikes him is apt to go far beyond what he intended. His anecdotes are often earthy, his language crude, and his portrayals of world leaders embarrassingly frank. Away from Washington, Mr. Kissinger is particularly voluble."

Anybody who traveled with Kissinger found him to be a compulsive talker. He frequently wandered back to the press section to chat after the more formal briefings were over. He exchanged one-liners with the newsmen and occasionally discussed the latest Pinter play he'd seen in London, but the subject always turned quickly to substance, with the reporters pressing for information and Kissinger enjoying the limelight as he verbalized thoughts that were percolating in his mind and that often appeared later in news conferences or speeches. The chitchat was one of Kissinger's forms of relaxation. As Jim Anderson noted, "Kissinger doesn't play golf. His hobby is talking to us." Although Kissinger deliberately cultivated the press as an obviously useful avenue of communication, the chitchat was not a one-way street.

He found the traveling press corps to be made up of mostly intelligent people who understood what he was talking about, who would challenge him in ways his subordinates would not, who could appreciate his jokes and joke back without worrying if they topped him, and, most important, who could give him a feel for what others were thinking — in Congress or in the countries he visited. He got valuable feedback through us. Gwertzman thought Kissinger "would feel lonely without the press. He likes the press as a sort of sounding board."

Kissinger's intensive interest in the press had still another aspect. He obviously had a stake in the process of disseminating information, but he was genuinely intrigued by how the process worked, even when it did not work to his advantage. Former spokesman George Vest explained, "Sure he wanted to exploit. But the press wanted to exploit him, so that's not original. The key to Henry is that the press really did interest him. He found the business of articulation fascinating — how to say something and how it would be written or reported."

That fascination was personalized following a Kissinger meeting with Le Duc Tho in Paris, when the United States and Vietnam issued a communiqué of only four terse sentences. Afterward, Kissinger almost couldn't wait to get at the press on his plane. Eyes twinkling, he threw down a challenge with an air of jovial defiance: "Let's see you make a lead out of that!" In the same "one of the boys" manner, he told us after leaving Dacca, "You guys can't spot history being made. You missed it completely in Bangladesh."

In his dealings with us, Kissinger usually counted on the articulated logic of his own analysis to influence how something would be written or reported, but at times he became impatient and tried to steer reporters in a certain direction, especially when he was involved in delicate discussions in the Middle East. Prior to an Arab Summit meeting, he virtually appealed to the reporters' patriotism. "Really," he said, "you people could do a national service by writing this one with some care. I'm serious . . . it's not to make the administration look good or bad. This is not an administration thing. But this is really a very ticklish thing . . . and frankly, more ticklish than I realized before I came out here." At another point on the same trip,

he said, "I told you I did not expect to have a diplomatic announcement at the end of this trip. And I still don't expect that. But it's up
to you how you analyze it. It does not mean that there's no progress
made." He added, with a humorous touch, "You can try to explore
some very elusive remarks from me and write them very profoundly."

During an Egyptian-Israeli shuttle, when public statements on
both sides seemed to conflict with Kissinger's briefings, the Secretary
explained, "On this trip, what you have to understand is that everybody has to position himself vis-à-vis many audiences. Now you can
report it all very literally or try to understand it . . . I cannot say a
hell of a lot more than I have been saying. Look at the trends, rather
than what people say." Kissinger sometimes forgot, however, that
daily journalists wrote daily stories, not articles for *Foreign Affairs
Quarterly.* For most newspapers, nuances were what closed on Saturday night.

When the complaints about the lack of information rose high
enough, Kissinger always retreated into a promise to provide a
tutorial on the whole negotiation after it was over. But after it was
over, there was a different story to write about, and the tutorials were
seldom given. They'll no doubt appear in his own book.

On the trip that followed the Arab Summit, he advised, "Write
what your convictions are, but if you all put out pessimism and
gloom, you may trigger something in Europe." Most reporters did
indeed write what their convictions were.

The briefings did not automatically produce a story. Sometimes
they provided material to fill out a story or information to be filed
away or to be followed up and developed into a story later. But they
always provided insights into Kissinger's mood, his thinking, or
his mode of operations, and therefore, they were almost always
helpful.

When Kissinger was on the road, he didn't forget about the home
front. He sometimes sent cables to the White House giving instructions on how the press secretary should brief on certain international
issues. And he often instructed his State Department aides to set up

luncheons with prominent columnists like James Reston of the New York *Times* or William F. Buckley, Jr., of the *National Review.*

Columnist Joseph Kraft, who had a stormy relationship with Kissinger, has a remarkable example of his cultivation of the press. After Kraft had written an article that Kissinger didn't like, he told his secretary he didn't want to talk with anybody about it. That night, Kraft's phone rang at home. His wife said, "It's Haig" (Kissinger aide Alexander Haig). Kraft didn't take the call. The phone rang again. It was Kissinger. Kraft still refused to take the call. A little while later, the doorbell rang. It was their Georgetown neighbor, Henry Kissinger, with flowers in his hand for Mrs. Kraft.

It was not always flowers and sunshine, however. Kissinger used to denounce Kraft in the semiprivacy of his office as "that poisonous prick." And the Secretary's aides claimed that if Kissinger refused to see Kraft, the columnist would then write a derogatory article out of pique.

For his part, Kraft said he left standing instructions with his secretary never to take a call from Kissinger before 10:00 A.M. because "before that he is too bitchy and crotchety."

Although Kissinger was not the first Secretary of State to take reporters on his travels, none of his predecessors had tried to use them so determinedly or involve them so intimately in his missions. One aide described the press as "an extension of his diplomatic operation." Israeli leader Shimon Peres summed it up best: "Kissinger arrived long before his plane did," meaning that the press reports of his background briefings provided early warning signals of what to expect when he arrived.

During the first Egyptian-Israeli disengagement negotiations, Kissinger relied on the press to report his words in a way that would impart a sense of momentum to the shuttle. He claimed the negotiation was 50 percent completed, then 80 percent completed, then only 10 percent remained to be worked out. He was subtly sending word to the negotiators on the other side that it was up to them to keep things moving.

On a flight to Teheran, Kissinger praised the Shah of Iran as a "political leader of world class." The phrase found its way into wire service stories and perhaps helped repair some of the damage caused when Treasury Secretary William Simon referred to the Shah as a "nut." (At his farewell news conference, with Simon sitting nearby, Kissinger noted that the Treasury Secretary "added immeasurably to, shall we say, the complexity of our foreign policy . . . by calling the Shah of Iran a nut. He then protested that he had been quoted out of context. My question to my friend Bill Simon is, 'In what context *can* you call a foreign head of state a nut?' ")

The generally favorable press reporting of Kissinger and his exploits eventually provoked charges in post-Vietnam, post-Watergate America that the press had rolled over and played dead for the dogged Secretary of State. Most of the critics were outsiders with little knowledge of daily journalism or people who bore personal grudges against the Secretary. And they generally failed to comprehend a basic element of the coverage, which columnist Kraft discussed on a public television program: "He's performed. He's performed very, very well. I know there's a myth around to the effect that by some kind of manipulation and advertising techniques and PR skills, you can develop a good press. I don't think you can. He does not do it by the charms of Zsa Zsa Gabor. He does it mainly by performance."

Nick Daniloff, a thoughtful reporter for UPI, said at the time Kissinger was traveling, "You can certainly say a clubbiness, a coziness, exists on Kissinger's plane, but it is a natural kind of clubbiness. We are all pretty well educated people interested in foreign affairs, and we are all rubbing shoulders, drinking together. There is a certain feeling of ease, but I wouldn't say it includes a suspension of critical faculties."

There's no doubt that when we were faced with conflicting views, we tended to give Kissinger the benefit of the doubt, for a variety of reasons. He had the advantage of arguing *his* case at close hand, using all the persuasive logic for which he was known. Beyond that, his record of candidness in the briefings lent weight to *his* arguments. And his track record was excellent. He proved more reliable over a period of time than any other single individual we dealt with.

The questioning on the plane was polite but direct, and while I acknowledge that some of us occasionally took something off our fast balls, the hard questions were always asked. They weren't always answered, but as Lars-Erik Nelson observed, "There is no way you will ever satisfy the press. There is always going to be that difference between what the government says and what is actually happening. We understand the necessities for diplomatic confidentiality. That doesn't mean we accept it in every case, but we do understand it."

Inevitably, considering the pressure-cooker atmosphere of some of the more delicate Middle East negotiations, tension built up between Kissinger and the reporters, who sometimes felt they weren't getting enough information or who resented being beaten on their own story by leaks in other capitals. At times, Kissinger sought to relieve the tension with humor. He once threatened to get a new airplane for his next trip, one with a "detachable press compartment." Later he decided, "I'm going to send you all on the next Skylab. I can do with ninety days of peace." At other times, Kissinger's impatience flared. On one Middle East mission, he complained, "You people are trying to push me constantly into saying things that are going much too far." During the second Israeli-Egyptian shuttle, he answered testily when asked about something Sadat had said: "You know, you people are in the unusual situation of being able to screw up everything by going too far."

There were flare-ups on both sides. On the same mission, one of the reporters finally complained out loud, "I must confess that at this point, I haven't got the foggiest idea of what's going on in the negotiations. We're all writing about 'concrete ideas.' It's a parody," the reporter said, "of both journalism and diplomacy. Isn't there some way that you can give us some idea of what you're talking about?" Kissinger responded by complimenting the quality of the reporting up to that point.

Kissinger's basic view about briefing on foreign policy was that "the objectives should be open, but the tactics have to remain confidential."

The openness of his discussions with the press astonished foreign diplomats who occasionally sat in on them. British Ambassador Peter Ramsbotham said he was amazed at the Secretary's forthrightness, as did Canada's minister of external affairs, Mitchell Sharp. One of Kissinger's former NSC aides, Dick Solomon, a China specialist, marveled, "If we told you guys as much as Henry did, we'd be hanged!" And it's Henry who would have done the hanging.

Kissinger was daring with humor as well as substance. Leaving Washington after complex talks with Soviet Foreign Minister Gromyko on limiting strategic nuclear weapons, a reporter asked why President Ford had met with the Soviet Ambassador, Anatoly Dobrynin. Kissinger paused, then said slowly, "We had to get some technical competence into the discussions." He let it sink in, waiting for the laughter, then pointed to a reporter who was taking notes and shouted with mock exasperation, "Go ahead. Write it down!" Then to the rest of us: "He'll kill me."

Throughout his travels — and throughout his government career, for that matter — Kissinger was dogged by suspicions of double-dealing, which he repeatedly tried to dispel. "If what I'm trying to do succeeds," he said during an early trip, "then the parties concerned will soon be sitting down together, comparing notes . . . To give them distorted versions of reality would be suicidal."

The same was true, Kissinger insisted, in his dealings with the press. He told an ABC interviewer in June 1974, "If you mislead the press consciously once, and you're caught at it, your credibility is destroyed forever. I don't consciously mislead. And I try not to manipulate it. Because it's a long-term relationship that I have to be interested in and because again, in this time, the confidence of the public in their leaders is more important than whether they agree with one particular policy."

At least once that we know about, Kissinger did mislead consciously, i.e., lie. And he got caught at it. In early 1974, he indicated he was going to Damascus to get the list of Israeli POWs from President Assad to deliver to Prime Minister Golda Meir, but he already had the list before leaving Washington. (When he was asked point-blank later if he did indeed have the list before leaving Washington, he answered squeamishly, "Substantially, yes.") He later sought to justify his action by explaining at a news conference, "We had a profound humanitarian problem, which is that we had been given the list on a confidential basis. We had told of the fact that we had this list to only the highest leaders on the Israeli side, and we were afraid that the prisoners would not be released if we did not follow the sequence that had been suggested to us . . . As soon as we had been given the go-ahead to release the list, we explained to the press exactly the circumstances in which it had been obtained." The reporters involved argued that under those circumstances he should have refused to discuss the matter at all rather than lie, even in a good cause.

One reason for reporters' suspicions on the trips was that Kissinger seemed to be overly cautious in his assessments of what could happen. Obviously, he didn't want to build up expectations he couldn't fulfill. And it was obviously tactically better to achieve a success with the appearance of a surprise than to have it discounted in advance.

After the first couple of trips, we began needling him, "If you say the chances are fifty to one, we make it eight to five." Kissinger himself started telling others, "If I say one in a thousand, I mean three to two." And he also needled back, telling the traveling contingent, "If I declared the millennium, you'd all write it was only for nine hundred ninety-nine years."

The "revisionist" piece about Kissinger's information practices was written by Bernie Gwertzman in the New York *Times* on March 14, 1976. "Ironically, for one who begrudgingly has shared his wealth of information with other officials," Gwertzman wrote, "Mr. Kissinger has been an extraordinarily liberal benefactor to reporters. No Secretary has been more forthcoming in discussing world issues both publicly and in the nonattributable guise of 'senior official.' His speeches have generally been meaty, his press conferences provocative, his background sessions to the point."

Kissinger was especially sensitive to press criticism, not only because it bruised his ego, but also because it tarnished his image and prestige. And since he believed strongly that the ability to conduct foreign policy depended in large part on the perception of others, he worried about how criticism affected that perception. As he once explained with an incisive ad lib, "At some point, you can't have foreign policy without authority. Foreign policy is the sum total of what other countries perceive your authority to be."

His reaction to criticism took many forms. Sometimes it was characteristically humorous. During a panel discussion at a Washington luncheon in mid-1975, he jokingly dismissed the criticism as "totally unjustified." He was asked if he felt the "recent criticism of you in the press is unfair," and he responded, "Well, of course, unless there was some hope for a terminal date to my efforts, the morale of my associates would disintegrate completely." He then picked up on the laughter and applause that followed. "Are those some of my associates applauding?" he said.

Sometimes his reaction was generic, and he would philosophize about it on the plane. When a reporter complained about a lack of information, he responded, "My problems aren't the same as yours. You need hard news, and I need eventual progress." Similarly, he once observed, "The press measures success or failure only against concrete results. Another measure is whether there's quiet or relative quiet."

Sometimes his reaction to the criticism was personal. He once told Nick Daniloff of UPI, whom he respected, "Mr. Daniloff, you are a receptacle into which garbage has been poured."

AP reporter Ken Freed wrote: "There is a legend that Secretary of State John Foster Dulles carried American foreign policy in his hat. There is a feeling in the State Department now that Henry A. Kissinger has it under his thumb." Kissinger later remarked caustically to Freed, "I thought you were a serious reporter, until now."

Kissinger called me to complain about a report I had done on television that criticized the information policy at the State Department. After telling me the report had been "brought to his attention," he said, "When you accuse us of deliberate deception — "

I interrupted to point out that I had not done that, but Kissinger interrupted back, saying, "Well, I would hope you feel that if we are deceiving you, we are intelligent enough to do it deliberately." And then he turned more serious, explaining the problems from his point of view, but conceding, in reference to one of the examples I had used, "We goofed."

If his telephone calls were meant to be intimidating, they seldom achieved their purpose. In the heady atmosphere of post-Vietnam, post-Watergate Washington, a complaint by a high government official was treated like a journalistic merit badge. Bernie Gwertzman observed, "I haven't found that you are punished if you displease Kissinger. In fact, there is the theory that the more you criticize, the more information you get because he wants to convince you. If a reporter wrote that Kissinger had cut him off, it would *make* him in this town — an automatic Pulitzer Prize."

Apart from that, as Marvin Kalb of CBS pointed out, a Kissinger telephone call was not so much a complaint as an explanation. "There's no shrill voice, no shouting," said Kalb, "rather more a Harvard professor's patient effort to demonstrate the error of your ways."

However, when Kissinger occasionally called a reporter to his compartment on the plane to chew him out for a story that annoyed him, there could be plenty of shrill voice and shouting and attempted intimidation. He once blew up at Bruce van Voorst of *Newsweek,* saying, "If you really believe your information, then our relationship is at an end." Van Voorst, who never figured he had a special relationship anyway, was a bit shaken. But the next time they were together, Kissinger acted as if the confrontation had never taken place.

Sometimes Kissinger's reaction was conveyed indirectly, through an aide. Bob McCloskey, whose jack-of-all-trading for Kissinger included advice on press relations, called me after I had interviewed Assistant Secretary of State Philip Habib for an *NBC News* television special. One of my questions was: "Is the Secretary's personal prestige one explanation for our continued efforts to support Cambodia?"

Habib answered, "No." The question and answer never appeared on the air. McCloskey knew that, but he was under orders from the top to call. And so he pointed out solemnly, "Dick, there are some people around here who feel this was an ugly question." I argued that it was a legitimate question, and I never heard any more about it.

Sometimes, Kissinger's reaction to criticism was personalized in a way that was obviously — and naïvely — calculated to trade on his relationship with the traveling reporters. He occasionally called Bernie Gwertzman to complain about stories written by others in the New York *Times.* "Don't call me," advised Gwertzman. "Call them."

While Kissinger was on his first African journey, he was criticized in an editorial in the Chicago *Tribune,* which accused him of selling out South Africa. Kissinger sent a cable back to the State Department, instructing Larry Eagleburger to discuss the editorial with the *Tribune*'s diplomatic reporter, John Maclean, who had nothing to do with the paper's editorial page. Later, on a domestic trip, Kissinger came to the rear of the plane and saw Maclean typing. "What the hell are you doing?" he asked in a gruffly joking way. "Writing another editorial for the Chicago *Tribune?*" It was, Maclean said, the first time Kissinger had ever paid any attention to him.

When Maclean signed up to go on Kissinger's second African journey, he did not make the list. He told the press aide who called him, "It's extremely unfair that Kissinger would attack me in front of my colleagues about an editorial in the Chicago *Tribune,* and to let me know through others that he felt the Chicago *Tribune* was ill informed about his policy, and then refuse to allow me to go on the next trip to Africa. I think that's insupportable." So, on second thought, did Kissinger. MacLean was added to the list.

To my knowledge, Kissinger never took his complaints over the heads of the reporter on the beat. Nor, one of his closest aides said, did he ever call a reporter and ask him to handle a story a certain way out of "friendship."

Kissinger was not only criticized by the press, he criticized in return. He twice delivered formal critiques to an audience of newsmen. The first time was an awards ceremony for the late Chicago Daily *News* reporter Peter Lisagor. Kissinger warmed up his audience by explaining that he had rejected a suggestion that he say what he really thought of the press "because I felt this was not an occasion where the use of profanity would be seemly." In a more serious vein, he said, "I think it is important to remember that endless scrutiny — without some minimal element of understanding — can lead to a massive undermining of public confidence in the very institutions of government. Skepticism is healthy, and condemnation often deserved, but no free nation can long exist if its people lack faith in its essential justice. And in an imperfect world, one cannot demand perfection as the price of confidence." He also expressed skepticism about the climate of scoop-happiness in contemporary Washington: "Effective journalism, in the area of foreign policy at least, is not measured so much by the wealth of information discovered as by the weight of superior analysis."

He returned to the subject of the press at a farewell appearance at the National Press Club, where he stirred the substance with dashes of humor:

You and I have been reasonably good protagonists. The jokes and the conflicts, the cooperation and the pain that we have had over the past eight years reflect the fact that under our system, the press and the government are natural partners that nevertheless need each other. Both are powerful institutions attempting to serve the public interest by their own lights, and according to their own legitimate purposes. The aim of the Executive Branch is to govern and lead and to implement public policy; yours is to illuminate, question, and analyze. The fact that we are generally right and you are generally wrong does not change the basic elements made up on both sides of respect, fear, deference, and the attempt by each side to get the better of the other.

Nor can it avoid the difference in perspective inherent in the two points of view. I know how exciting it is for reporters to be given access to arcane classified documents, even though they are usually appallingly written and generally incomprehensible. I, of course, hold the view that the real essence of our foreign policy was to be found in the series of speeches I have given around the country. These, of course, have often been slighted (I consider anything except running the full text as being slighted) — I suspect because they were unclassified. But I have one consolation. If you had had all the classified documents that were available to me, you would be as confused as I was.

We shall not settle this debate here — all the less so since after January twentieth I hope to profit from the leaks which you print. This may be the occasion to say that for all my needling, I have admired the objectivity, the honesty and the fundamental fairness of the press corps which covers the Department of State and the White House. They are the most amusing and perceptive collection of outrageous individualists that I have known. They have, at times, left me breathless with exasperation. But they have sharpened my wits as well. They have made me concede, in sentimental moments, there may be something in Thomas Jefferson's claim that were it left to him to decide between a government without newspapers or newspapers without a government, he would prefer the latter. Luckily for all of us, Jefferson never had to pronounce himself regarding television.

We have had — to put it mildly — an intense experience, and we are now at the end of our time together until late January 1981. As a result of the extraordinary record of discourse between us, we understand each other better. And if I may be so bold, I believe that our discourse has also served the American people, for they know more, as a result, about the role and responsibilities of this nation in the world — perhaps more at times than I wanted them to know.

There were other times when he betrayed a grudging admiration for the profession of those who wrote about him. One such time occurred when Ken Freed of the AP asked a visiting foreign minister a series of difficult questions outside the hotel room where he and the Secretary had met. Kissinger watched with growing discomfort, and after the minister left, he turned to Freed and said with feigned anger, "You have to act like a barracuda every time, eh?" And then he chuckled appreciatively.

One aspect of reporting that drove him up the wall, however, was the unauthorized "leak," the unofficial revelation of information, sometimes classified, in the media. He wanted the State Department to be a ship that "leaked" only at the top. Aides were amused to see him begin a department staff meeting by berating somebody for having leaked a story that had, in fact, come from him. "This was Henry's way," recalled one official, "of letting you know that he was in full charge of press management."

Non-Kissinger leaks brought retribution. After three classified cables appeared in print within a two-week period in late 1974, the Secretary ordered a cutback in cable distribution, and all traffic moved to a higher classification. Even cables from the department to his plane on such routine subjects as his projected daily schedule in Washington were marked NODIS, i.e., top secret. The leaks tended to have an anti-Kissinger quality, since they were generally designed to get publicity for views that challenged or dissented from existing policy.

However, Kissinger never understood that not all stories that he didn't want published were the results of deliberate leaks. Often they resulted from old-fashioned reporting. A good reporter simply picked up a fact or a small piece of a story or perhaps even started with a logical theory and then birddogged his sources incessantly until he pieced the whole story together, or most of it.

Like everything else, even Kissinger's obsession with leaks eventually provided a target for his own humor. Asked in London if a certain newspaper report was accurate, he joked, "I am reaching the point now where I read the newspapers before my cable traffic because they have a better selection."

A different, if not better, selection of cables was presented to Kissinger by the members of the traveling press during a birthday luncheon they gave him at Claridge's on May 27, 1976. At the time, Kissinger was having his troubles at home and abroad. Ronald Reagan was challenging President Ford in the primaries, and the Republican right wing was trying to make Kissinger a political hot potato for the Ford camp. *Newsweek* had just published excerpts from *The Final Days* containing the account of Kissinger kneeling and praying with the distraught Nixon. Arms control negotiations with the Russians were in a holding pattern, and so was Middle East diplomacy.

With all this in mind, we picked up on Kissinger's complaint that we saw his classified traffic before he did, and we read off the following sheaf of cables:

The Hon. Henry Kissinger Secretary of State of the United States of America
Dear Henry:

Many happy returns. I'm talking about Oregon, Kentucky, and Tennessee, of course. Take your time coming back. There's not much doing here anyway. Hope to see you sometime in late August. Until then, I'm behind you one thousand and one percent.

Jerry

Henry Kissinger Claridge's London Great Britain
Dear Dr. Kissinger:

As I said in Bakersfield last night I hope you spend your next birthday in the obscurity you so richly deserve.

Ronnie

The Hon. Henry A. Kissinger, London
My Dear Dr. Kissinger:

On this deeply spiritual day, I would like to affirm that while I am not willing to retain you in the Cabinet, I would be quite happy to look for something for you at the University of Georgia.

Jimmy

Henry Kissinger in London
Dear Henry:

I want you to know that on this day I'm praying for you.

Dick

The Hon. Henry Kissinger Secretary of State of the USA
Dear Henry:

Happy Birthday and Mazeltov. How come we don't hear from you anymore?

Yitzhak

The Hon. Henry Kissinger Secretary of State of the USA
My Dear Brother Henry:
   Happy Birthday. Praised be you and Allah. How come we don't hear from you anymore?

                                                                    Anwar

The Hon. Henry A. Kissinger Secretary of State of the USA
Dear Comrade Henry:
   Happy and peaceful birthday. We know why we don't hear from you anymore.

                                                                  Regards,
                                                                  Leonid

Henry Kissinger c/o Claridge's Hotel London
Dear Henry:
   Happy Birthday, but I still want to know what's the story with Liv Ullman?

                                                             Love and kisses,
                                                                    Nancy

We had debated among ourselves beforehand whether to include the "Nixon cable" because the subject was so sensitive. We needn't have bothered. Kissinger, who privately enjoys that kind of give-and-take needling, immediately zeroed in on precisely that cable. "I must point out," he said, "that some of those cables did not quite have the ring of verisimilitude. We all know, for example, that when the former President prayed, he did not pray alone."

When it came to talking to the press, Kissinger did most of it alone. Access to the Secretary of State — or perhaps it should be *his* access to the reporters — was more than ample. It was often said, accurately, that Kissinger was his own press spokesman, although a number of officials held the title during his term of office. Most of them belonged to the Harpo Marx School of Spokesmanship. Bernie Kalb of CBS once described a government spokesman as a man who, when you ask him what time he has, looks at his watch and replies, "What time do *you* have?"

The spokesman at the State Department is, technically speaking, the department's principal liaison with the press, and he conducts a daily briefing in Washington, giving the department's views on a variety of matters and fielding reporters' questions. His instructions on what to say come from the Secretary or the heads of regional bureaus, but in Kissinger's case, they came mostly from him, and he kept his spokesmen on a short leash. Kissinger took joking note of that practice at his farewell news conference. "It will be hard to replace my daily sessions with the department's press spokesman prior to his daily briefing," he said. "I will be sorry to be deprived of the opportunity to instruct him each day on the virtues of frankness, honesty, and openness." The newsmen laughed at the self-deprecating sarcasm, but they had never found the policy itself to be amusing.

The most respected press spokesman at the State Department in recent times was Bob McCloskey, who had survived even the Viet-

A birthday present from the Boys on the Plane in May 1974, during the Syrian-Israeli shuttle.

nam era under Dean Rusk and then William Rogers, and his reward was his appointment as Ambassador to Cyprus. But when Kissinger became Secretary of State, he wanted an old pro around to advise him on press relations — or perhaps to help him neutralize the press — and he recalled McCloskey to Washington. The old pro was not exactly overjoyed to leave his Embassy and take over the briefing burdens once again — at State and then on the road. But he did. As he later pointed out, "We had an exchange of views in Washington when Henry Kissinger became Secretary of State. I went in to see the Secretary with my views and I came out with his views."

But even McCloskey was not immune to the new skepticism of Washington journalism. When we were in Israel in the spring of 1974, a rumor circulated that the Secretary of State was flying back to Washington secretly to receive Nixon's resignation. McCloskey denied the story. "Where is Kissinger?" some of the traveling newsmen wanted to know. "In his suite at the King David," replied McCloskey. "We'd like to have one of us allowed to go upstairs and see him physically," the newsmen said. McCloskey was outraged. So was Kissinger. The request was rejected out of hand.

McCloskey made it clear he did not want to remain in the spokesman's job, and he was named assistant secretary for congressional relations early in 1974. Kissinger noted at the swearing-in ceremony, "There are several theories for the appointment of Bob McCloskey to his position. One is that you have to have an Irishman take an oath at least once a year if you want to be sure of his actions."

McCloskey's replacement was George Vest, a senior career officer who was recommended by Larry Eagleburger, another close adviser on press relations. Vest himself did not have direct experience in press relations, but he had done a commendable job handling the briefings for the American delegation at the European Security Conference. His appointment was announced shortly before his fifty-fourth birthday, which fell on Christmas Day, but the job turned out to be no gift assignment.

Vest was an honorable man, but he was not a Kissinger insider, and before long, he found he was not physically capable of standing the daily abuse of working for Kissinger at close range. On his first overseas trip with the Secretary, the compulsive shoppers among the press corps (who spent hours in Middle East bazaars) bought Vest a set of worry beads, which Middle Easterners twirl constantly between their fingers to relieve tension. Vest told Kissinger, "If you don't think I need these, you don't understand the situation." (The shoppers bought Kissinger a black Egyptian whip, which fit his personality as well as the worry beads fit Vest's.)

Following one especially severe chewing-out in the Secretary's seventh-floor office, Vest emerged and stretched out full length on the floor in the anteroom in front of the secretaries. Afterward, he went to Eagleburger and said, "I will not tolerate this humiliating abuse anymore." The job had begun to affect his health, and he left it after only a few months.

Kissinger showed bureaucratic sympathy. He named Vest director of the Political Military Bureau at the State Department, a top post. (Vest went on to become assistant secretary for European affairs.)

Vest's successor was Robert Anderson, Ambassador to Dahomey (now Benin). He discussed the impending appointment in the only official telephone call ever made between Washington and Dahomey. Kissinger presented him at a news conference in April 1974. "First of all," the Secretary said, "I'd like to introduce a new victim for your torments, Ambassador Anderson, who has taken over as spokesman for the department, and whom I know you will treat with the gentleness, generosity, and warmth that is characteristic of the State Department press corps." Kissinger's words were prophetic. Anderson soon became a "victim" for torments all right, most of them coming from the Secretary himself. He stuck it out for eighteen months without the respect of the Secretary of State, the press, and many of his departmental colleagues.

Anderson is best remembered by some of us for a night in Vienna. Since he was neither informative nor popular with the press, he was not invited out to dinner by reporters, as other officials usually were, when Kissinger was on the road. During the Secretary's meetings with Gromyko in Vienna, Ken Freed of AP, Lars-Erik Nelson of

Reuters, and I were having dinner at the Hotel Imperial with Arthur Hartman, the assistant secretary of state for European affairs, and Anderson tagged along. The food was first class, but Anderson didn't get to finish his meal. Before we had ordered dessert and coffee, he was paged, and he left and never came back. The rest of us ate our desserts, drank our coffee, smoked a cigar, and then paid the bill, which included Anderson's dinner. When we arrived back at the press center, Anderson had just finished briefing the press on the Kissinger-Gromyko talks. We were almost too shocked to be angry.

The telephone call that Anderson had received during dinner told him to return to the press center to brief, but he didn't bother to pass along that information to us. And so Freed, Nelson, and I, who had not only eaten dinner with Anderson but had also paid for it, were the last to be able to file on the only meager story of the day.

When Kissinger began looking for a successor to Anderson, he turned to the press corps. He offered the job, in succession, to Ted Koppel of ABC, to me, and to Jerry O'Leary and Smith Hempstone of the Washington *Star.* For a variety of reasons, none accepted. It was generally thought that Kissinger, who was then at the nadir of his popularity and becoming an open target for the media, wanted a newsman in the job to neutralize the press for a while, to co-opt the media, as it were. When he offered me the job, I was seriously tempted to take it in order to see diplomatic events at close range from the "other side." But the tenure was questionable. Election day was not that far off, and Gerald Ford did not look too electable. In addition, I felt deep down that Kissinger would still function as his own primary spokesman, and I didn't relish the prospect of constant battles with him over information policy, among other things.

He finally settled on another career officer without previous press experience, Robert Funseth, the political officer at the U.S. Embassy in Canada. Funseth tried hard in a losing battle. He seemed to have an antipress chip on his shoulder when he took the job, and he was generally disliked at first by the reporters who covered the department. But he did try to get out more information, and while he was never popular with the press, he stopped being unpopular.

And, of course, Kissinger did indeed go on being his own spokesman for the most part. When he became Secretary of State, it seemed that he would have to abandon his White House anonymity and speak most of the time "on the record." He did not. Instead, he gave those "U.S. officials" who used to speak at the White House a promotion paralleling his own. They became "a senior U.S. official" in Washington and "a senior U.S. official traveling aboard the Secretary's plane" on the road. Kissinger used that cover to enable him to speak more freely in a way that would not require a formal reaction by foreign officials or foreign ministries.

His on-plane briefings were always "on background," which meant the material could be used, with quotes, but the source could not be identified by name.*

In the early days of Kissinger travel, the rules of attribution were not clearly delineated, and the initial confusion caused occasional problems. Just prior to the Secretary's second visit to Saudi Arabia, spokesman George Vest, chatting in the aisle of the plane, said he thought there was a fifty-fifty chance that progress would be made toward the lifting of the oil embargo against the United States. A wire service reported his remarks, quoting "senior U.S. officials." The stock market went up seventeen points the next day. Talk about the power of the press!

When Vest returned to Washington, his wife told him that the next time he said something like that, the least he could do was to notify her ahead of time so that she could buy some stock. Kissinger was not nearly so amused. He blew up higher than the market. But Vest told him three people had to share the blame: the spokesman for being speculative, the reporter for jumping to conclusions, and the Secretary for creating a general atmosphere of optimism. That was

---

*In addition to "on the record" and "on background," other classifications for attribution in standard journalese are "deep background" and "off the record." "Deep background" means that the information may be used, but without direct quotes and without any attribution. A reporter handles deep background information by writing, "It is understood that . . ." or "Newsmen have been told . . ." or he can simply report the information on his own, e.g., "The official American position is . . ." "Off the record" means that the information is strictly for the reporter's information and is not to be used in print or on the air — in any way.

the last time, however, that anybody on the plane except Kissinger himself was quoted as a "senior U.S. official."

The "senior U.S. official" was created seriously, but he was not always treated seriously. He was a natural target for Art Buchwald's satiric typewriter. "The only thing that every journalist must agree on when traveling with Mr. Kissinger," Buchwald wrote, "is that you may not identify the person who gives background briefings on the plane by name. You can't even say high U.S. official with wavy hair, horn-rimmed glasses, and German accent who had his garbage stolen last weekend. The only attribution permitted is 'a senior American official on Dr. Kissinger's plane'; and since I took the pledge, I don't want anyone guessing who that could be."

Bob Schieffer, a White House correspondent for CBS, had a field day with the "senior official" gambit in a "First Line Report" on radio:

> Guess who is in Germany to take a few days off and watch the soccer matches? Why, Senior American Official, that's who. You remember him, of course? He's the anonymous fellow who often shows up in various parts of the world where Henry Kissinger happens to be visiting.
>
> No one knows his name, but we do know several things for sure. He apparently has wide contacts throughout the American press establishment because when he calls a news conference, all of the important reporters show up. And one thing is absolutely certain: Senior American Official knows a lot about U.S. foreign policy.
>
> It comes as no surprise, then, that Senior American Official is in Germany this week, since Kissinger is also there. Kissinger isn't talking while he's in Germany; he's taking a few days' rest. But Senior American Official is talking . . .

Kissinger himself poked fun at his nameless shadow. When a reporter quoted a "senior American official" in a question at a news conference, Kissinger interjected, "There are too many senior officials speaking on background."

When Kissinger was challenged to justify the practice, he replied with a mixture of seriousness and humor. "The problem that exists when fourteen or fifteen members of the press travel with the Secretary of State is quite different from the relationship of the Secretary with the press here in Washington," he said. "When there has to be a daily briefing, it can be done in two ways — either by a spokesman on the record or by some of the chief actors on background. And in the particular circumstances of a delicate negotiation, I think that this arrangement has worked reasonably well — as long as the senior official and the Secretary agree with each other." If there was any confusion about the latter point, he noted at another news conference, "My experience is that the high official almost always agrees with the Secretary of State."

Some of the traveling reporters came to feel that the guise provided an excessively convenient hatch through which to escape the public record. They also felt it was misleading and a little too tricky, since virtually everybody except their readers knew who the "senior official" was. And they became bolder and bolder in their efforts to unmask the "senior official" to their readers.

As early as Kissinger's second trip, Murrey Marder wrote in the Washington *Post*: "The fig leaf of attributing what Kissinger says to the accompanying press aboard the plane to a 'senior American official' or a similar euphemism, for diplomatic protection . . . should be transparent to every sophisticated reader." Not long afterward, Bernie Gwertzman wrote in a "Reporter's Notebook" that "on each leg of the journey, he [Kissinger] invites the group, fourteen on this trip, to his office in the front of the plane for a 'background briefing.' That means he himself cannot be quoted, and whatever he says must be attributed to 'a senior American official' or something like that." Gwertzman's colleague Craig Whitney took this revelation a step further by writing in the spring of 1976: "The inevitable 'senior official aboard Mr. Kissinger's plane' — Mr. Kissinger himself — conducts a briefing on nearly every leg of the journey."

Yet, when a network filmed Kissinger conducting one of his on-plane briefings for a documentary about him, the print journalists protested that television was perverting the "background" rule.

The traveling reporters tried to blow the cover by another route. They asked Kissinger some of the same questions at public news conferences that they had asked in the background briefings. He was sometimes amused by the gambit, and in Teheran and again in New Delhi he turned to the local official seated next to him and explained that what the reporters were trying to do was to get him to say on the record what they knew he had already said on background. And he did.

On Kissinger's final overseas trip — to NATO in December 1976 — the lame-duck Secretary of State ended the career of the "senior official" he had made so famous. He said he did not want to talk substance and appear to be giving advice to his successor, and so he did not want anything he said attributed to old you-know-who. He

Freeman Martin, *The Milwaukee Journal*

HENRY KISSINGER'S "SHADOW," SENIOR U.S. OFFICIAL, RETIRES.

suggested that what he said should be attributed to "a State Department source" instead. One unsentimental reporter suggested that Kissinger's remarks should be attributed to "a has-been official." (The old stand-by, "unimpeachable sources," had lost some of its appeal during the Nixon administration. Personally, I always thought it would be fun to cover the Vatican one day and quote "infallible sources.")

The demise of the "senior official" got as much attention as the activities of the man he shadowed. I broadcast a report saying, "The senior U.S. official who always travels aboard Kissinger's plane was retired today on a flight to Brussels." Jim Anderson of the UPI wrote: "The famed 'senior American official,' an institution in American journalism and diplomacy during the Secretaryship of Henry Kissinger, quietly passed away Tuesday at the age of three." Barry Schweid of the AP filed: "America's second most famous diplomat — the 'senior U.S. official' who always travels aboard Secretary of State Henry A. Kissinger's jet — disappeared Tuesday somewhere across the Atlantic."

On the return trip — Kissinger's final flight as Secretary of State — a reporter asked him, "What will you tell [incoming Secretary of State Cyrus] Vance about the press?" He thought for a while, then replied revealingly, "I'll tell him that you bleed easily."

Press II: The Boys on the Plane

Henry Kissinger's promotion to the seventh floor of the State Department made him one of the best journalistic beats in the world, if not *the* best. Reporters like to be where the action is, and for more than three years, most of the diplomatic action was where Kissinger was.

Vietnam was over. Watergate was good while it lasted, but Kissinger lasted longer. The White House under Richard Nixon turned into a police beat. Under Gerald Ford, it was a dead beat.

The Kissinger beat provided a steady stream of stories with substance, variety, color, glamour, personalities, travel, wit, adventure, and even conflict — without the daily risk of being shot at. If you covered Kissinger, you were on the nightly television news programs and the morning news programs or your by-line appeared on the front page of your newspaper with regularity.

But it wasn't easy. Darius Jhabvala, the gentle Parsi who worked for the Boston *Globe,* once cryptically compared the job of covering Kissinger to "trying to track sirocco. You don't know where the wind comes from, but it seems to blow away the locusts." Bruce Van Voorst was more epigrammatic. "Nobody covers Henry," he said; "you chase him."

Following a weekend of hyperkinetic Kissinger travel, I tried to recapture the frantic pace in a film report for the *Today* program:

All Voiceover K. — Faisal film (Arikan)	FRIDAY NIGHT — RIYADH — NINETY MIN-UTES WITH SAUDI ARABIA'S KING FAISAL . . . SOME MOVEMENT TOWARD GETTING OIL SHIPMENTS RESUMED, BUT ONLY IF THERE'S PROGRESS AT PEACE CONFERENCE . . . (:10)
K. dep. from Riyadh (Arikan)	ONE POSITIVE SIGN: FOREIGN MINISTER SAQQAF WALKS KISSINGER TO PLANE, TELLS NEWSMEN HE CALLS HIM "HENRY." (:07)
Ludlow Airport exteriors	SATURDAY NOON — DAMASCUS — NO FILMING PERMITTED AT AIRPORT FOR FIRST VISIT BY AMERICAN SECRETARY OF STATE IN TWENTY YEARS . . . (:08)
K. — Assad (Ludlow)	SIX AND A HALF HOURS OF TALKS WITH SYRIA'S "TOUGH GUY" PRESIDENT HAFEZ ASSAD . . . FOUR HOURS LONGER THAN SCHEDULED . . . BUT NO WORD ON ISRAELI PRISONERS OF WAR . . . (:10)
K. — Hussein (Falletta)	SATURDAY MIDNIGHT — AMMAN — KING HUSSEIN HOLDS UP DINNER FIVE HOURS WAITING FOR KISSINGER TO ARRIVE FROM DAMASCUS . . . (:08)
K. dep. from Jordan (Falletta)	SUNDAY MORNING — ROYAL SENDOFF FROM AMMAN . . . ARAB LEGION MARCHES WITH BRITISH ACCENT (:05) (Sound up :05)
Pool Film	SUNDAY AFTERNOON — LEBANON — A FIVE-HOUR STOPOVER . . . OBSCURE AIR BASE USED FOR TALKS WITH LEBANESE LEADERS BECAUSE OF SECURITY WORRIES IN BEIRUT . . . (:09)

| K. — Meir | SUNDAY EVENING — JERUSALEM — HARD-NOSED TALKS WITH PRIME MINISTER GOLDA MEIR TO NAIL DOWN FINAL DETAILS FOR PEACE CONFERENCE. (:08) |
| K. Entering and disappearing behind door | MONDAY MORNING — MORE TALKS WITH ISRAELI LEADERS . . . THEN ON TO LISBON, FOLLOWED BY MADRID ON TUESDAY, PARIS ON WEDNESDAY, GENEVA ON THURSDAY, WASHINGTON SOMETIME.

RICHARD VALERIANI, NBC NEWS, EN ROUTE WITH SECRETARY OF STATE KISSINGER (:15) |

As Kissinger jetted around the Middle East and the rest of the world in his Boeing 707, the surrogate Department of State, he often viewed his contingent of reporters as his mirror on the world. At times, he tended to feel downright possessive about "his" reporters, and as somebody once said, he displayed them as generals show off their elite units. The reporters continually disabused him of this notion.

During a picture-taking session in Golda Meir's office in Jerusalem, the Secretary turned to the group of newsmen and introduced us, almost grandiosely, to the Israeli Prime Minister. "These are the fourteen reporters who are with me," he said. Jim Anderson of UPI cracked, "Not all of us are *with* him, Madame Prime Minister. Some of us are *against.*" Kissinger joined in the laughter.

Ken Freed of the AP once dashed from his hotel room after midnight in Brussels to get some quotes from a foreign leader who had just conferred unexpectedly with Kissinger. Freed threw on jeans, a sweat shirt, and basketball shoes. "What's the matter?" Kissinger jibed, "have you no feeling for the dignity of my office?" "I'll do better the next time," Freed responded.

The next time occurred several hours later, following a breakfast meeting between the Secretary of State and another foreign minister. Freed couldn't resist the temptation to show up in the same outfit — with one addition. He put on a tie over the sweatshirt. It was a put-on indeed. After the foreign minister left, Kissinger growled at

Freed, "That's much better." And he playfully tightened the tie like a noose.

The traveling contingent occasionally served as a safety valve for small talk when other subjects for chitchat were exhausted. Once, in Vienna, while Kissinger and Gromyko were posing for pictures, he pointed me out to the Soviet foreign minister as the part-owner of a horse named after him. Gromyko, not to be outdone in the irrelevance department, pointed to the yellow tie I was wearing and quoted a Russian saying to the effect that a tie like mine was one that helps you find your way in the fog. The photographs flashed around the world by the wire services that day showed Gromyko pointing his finger and Kissinger looking in the same direction, but the captions made no reference to my yellow tie.

On his domestic excursions into the American "heartland," Kissinger liked to use the traveling newsmen as a foil for his humor. He told a news conference in the Midwest, "I hope the local press realizes that the Washington press here not only asks the questions, but gives the answers." He milked it for another laugh: "What they really do at our press conferences in Washington is not so much elicit information, but to give me a grade, about how well I do."

In Milwaukee, one of the traveling reporters wanted to know what the Secretary was learning in his talks with community leaders. "Do you find anything, any insights, that you don't get back in Washington?" the reporter asked. Kissinger replied, "For the benefit of the local press, the Washington contingent that is here is trying to get me to say something that will make great news in Washington; namely, an admission by me that I can learn something from anybody."

Although we were not part of the "official" Kissinger entourage, others came to regard us virtually that way. In many countries, particularly in Israel and Egypt, local reporters raced to interview us as soon as Kissinger had finished his arrival statement. An Israeli newspaper once described us as the "best-informed press corps in the world."

During a Kissinger-Gromyko encounter in Geneva, I was even interviewed by Bulgarian television. I never had occasion to find out what my ratings were in Sofia, however, since that was one of the few capitals the Secretary of State never visited. In Washington, high-ranking State Department officials sometimes called me on the phone following my return from a trip to ask if Kissinger had talked on the plane about their area of responsibility, and if he had, would I mind telling them what he said.

In addition to the hours of briefings on the plane, we asked for — and often got — a briefing from American diplomats residing in the various capitals. The quality varied, depending on the quality of the diplomat and his sense of security in his job. Naturally enough, the more intelligent the diplomat and the more secure he felt, the better the briefing.

Just as important, traveling with Kissinger gave us an uncommon access to officials of the host country on the ground — kings, presidents, prime ministers, and other high-ranking officers. We may not have always received a totally objective presentation, but we certainly got firsthand exposure to their thinking. The host governments frequently invited us to official functions such as dinners and receptions, which gave us another opportunity to ply our trade, since officials were sometimes more open after a glass of wine in a casual setting.

We were so constantly immersed in diplomatic environments that we learned things almost by a process of photosynthetic journalistic osmosis.

One of the more exotic official functions to which we were invited was a cruise on one of the world's great rivers, the Zaire River, formerly the Congo. The host was Mobutu Sese Seko, Zaire's President for Life. As part of his nation-building effort, Mobutu tried to peel away the overlay of Belgian colonial culture on his country and restore African "authenticity." That's why "Congo" became "Zaire"; that's why "Joseph Mobutu" became "Mobutu Sese Seko"; and that's why the menu for a luncheon aboard the presidential houseboat included wild boar, manioc leaves, baked bananas, and a number of other "authentic" delicacies from the African cuisine.

The wines, however, escaped the authenticity campaign. They

were vintage French, and they were outstanding. Scott Sullivan of *Newsweek,* a self-proclaimed oenophile after six years on assignment in Paris, spent much of the afternoon after lunch polishing off some of the best Saint-Julien he had ever drunk. Jerry Schechter of *Time,* another bon vivant (the magazine guys were more accustomed to gracious living than the daily journalists), was enjoying a superb Château Figeac, and he had drunk enough of it to stop a waiter, en route to the head table, carrying a bottle of wine wrapped in a napkin. Schechter unwrapped the napkin, and when he saw that the head folks were drinking Château Lafite Rothschild, he simply appropriated the bottle. (I wondered afterward if there was an authentic African word for chutzpah.)

In addition to wining and dining us on occasion, host governments more frequently tried to propagandize us. During the Israeli-Syrian shuttle, both sides ferried us to the Golan Heights to bolster their negotiating arguments. During the second round of Israeli-Egyptian negotiations, the Israelis flew us in helicopters close to the strategic Gidda and Mitla passes in the Sinai. The Chinese took us on a tour of their underground bomb shelters to show us that they were prepared for a Soviet attack. The Russians plied us with vodka in an effort to find out what Kissinger was "really" thinking. One American reporter, familiar with Russian ruses, drank from the same bottle as his Soviet hosts and discovered they were drinking water. He complained, and they switched to the Stolichnaya.

On the initial trip to the Middle East, the host governments in the Arab world insisted on picking up the tab for our hotel rooms. Their generosity probably had more to do with traditions of Bedouin hospitality than with an appeal to our venality. But some of the correspondents absolutely refused to accept the gesture, and the hotel lobby was a scene of mass confusion in the morning at check-out time, as American reporters, rushing to get to their press bus on time, argued with a cashier who was under orders not to take their money. The cashiers won the first round handily, but on subsequent trips, U.S. Embassy officers were instructed to emphasize that the newsmen insisted on paying their own way.

Following the rejection of Hashemite hospitality in Amman, the members of the press learned that there were no single rooms available on the next visit to Jordan, and whether by design or by coincidence, we all had to share rooms with a colleague. Three of us — including me — were even tripled up. What's worse, I lost the coin flip for the beds and ended up on something resembling a cot. But we didn't get that much sleeping time, anyway.

Hotel controversies were not limited to fighting with cashiers to make them take our money. Sometimes we complained that they tried to take too much. The uncertainty of Kissinger's itinerary occasionally forced the local Embassy to book hotel rooms for an extra night in order to ensure available space when we arrived, and we ended up paying two nights' rates for one night's stay. This caused more arguments at the cashier's counter. Barry Schweid once lamented that he paid for two hotel rooms a thousand miles apart on the same night and didn't get to sleep in either one.

One of the more amusing hotel episodes involved Dana Adams Schmidt of the *Christian Science Monitor,* who miscalculated during an overnight stop in Paris at the Hotel Crillon. Each room had a "mini-bar," a small refrigerator containing beer, wine, champagne, and whiskey miniatures as well as snacks and soft drinks, all for sale at exorbitant prices. But Schmidt thought the contents were a gift of the house, and he stashed some in his suitcase before leaving. The rest of us world travelers snickered derisively when we found out, but Schmidt had the last laugh. He never got a mini-bar bill. Ironically, if newspapers drank, the *Christian Science Monitor* would be a teetotaler.

The *Monitor*'s reporter was not a regular on the Kissinger plane. The cast of press characters varied from trip to trip, but from the outset, nine news organizations were hard-core regulars: three television networks, NBC, ABC, CBS; two wire services, AP and UPI; two news magazines, *Time* and *Newsweek*; and two newspapers, the New York *Times* and the Washington *Post.* The British news agency, Reuters, eventually gained a regular seat on the plane, and the hard-core nine became ten. And one seat was always allocated to the Voice of America or the United States Information Agency. The other three or four press seats rotated among various other newspapers, with special guest appearances by an occasional columnist or author. The press seats were always oversubscribed, so foreign reporters or small-town newspapers were almost never included.

The only newspapers from "west of the Appalachians" that were frequently represented were the Los Angeles *Times* and the Chicago *Tribune.* The geographical designation was a touchy point with the *Tribune.* Spokesman George Vest once referred to it as the only newspaper "west of the Mississippi." *Trib* correspondent John Maclean quickly corrected him. "You people who work for Kissinger know more about the geography of the Middle East than of the Middle West," Maclean snapped, pointing out that Chicago is 165 miles east of the Mississippi.

Kissinger personally approved the list of correspondents, although the process was virtually perfunctory, since he wasn't going to deny a seat to the major news organizations and he had no say on the correspondents those organizations chose. But he could, and occasionally did, make a seat available for journalistic friends, such as Henry Brandon of the *Sunday Times* or Pierre Salinger of *L'Express.*

The collection of all those newsmen — a captive audience in the rear of the plane — attracted Kissinger like a magnet. He was full of restless energy, and during any long flight, he wandered back frequently to chat, usually wearing a baggy sweater and soft slippers. Ken Freed of the AP pictured him this way: "There was always something incongruous about this five-foot, seven-inch fat man as he acted out a role often stereotyped as belonging to a slender, gray-haired fellow with aquiline nose and Ivy League wardrobe. Kissinger was routed in his battle against an appetite for candy and pretzels. His ever-expanding stomach drooped over his belt, his buttons often appeared ready to burst and his shirttail often was pulled out of his pants. In informal times, he usually was seen with his hands tucked inside his waistband."

The chatting invariably turned to matters of substance, and in the early days, a Kissinger briefing consisted of him talking in the aisle with fourteen reporters clustered around him, draped over seats, clogging the aisles, trying to hear something more than the drone of the engines. While Kissinger was chatting with us on one of the first trips, an Air Force pilot of the frustrated disc-jockey school began doing a tourist-guide number over the plane's intercom. The Secretary of State was interrupted in midsentence. He buzzed an aide, and the intercom went dead for the next few hundred thousand miles of flying. It wasn't until the plane was flying over the Himalayas in bright sunlight, offering a splendid panorama below, that a pilot dared to use the intercom again to recommend the sights to his passengers.

Even without the intercom, half of the reporters could hear only about half of what Kissinger was saying in the noisy airplane, and we suggested to the spokesman that improvement was needed in the logistics of the briefing. One aide suggested a bullhorn, which Kissinger tried once and quickly abandoned. It was hardly an instrument of intimate discourse. He sounded more like a drill sergeant or police chief than a Secretary of State.

We then suggested that Kissinger invite us forward to his office-in-the-sky for the formal briefings, and he acquiesced. The new arrangement proved more satisfactory not only for the press, but also for the stewards, who had not been able to serve meals while the Secretary was standing in the clogged aisle.

It soon became apparent, however, that the arrangement in Kissinger's office needed refinement. As soon as the press spokesman announced that the Secretary was ready, the reporters jumped out of their seats and made a mad dash up the aisle, literally knocking into each other at times in their rush to get the seats up front, closest to Kissinger, where the hearing was better and, more important, the opportunity to ask questions was much improved. Those who sat back near the galley were almost always shut out from the better seats, since they had the longest distance to travel. After making a spectacle of ourselves a few times, we devised a lottery-rotation system. We drew numbers for assigned seats around Kissinger's table at the start of every trip and rotated the seats for each briefing. If you drew number one for the first briefing, you sat next to Kissinger. At the second briefing, you moved one seat away, and number fourteen moved into the number one spot. And so on.

Considering the high level of tension and the fatigue-induced testiness on a trip, plus the constant irritation of travel inconveniences, the natural competitiveness of reporters, and the extremely close contact over long periods of time, the degree of equanimity and congeniality among the press corps was probably remarkable.

The corps was rocked by only one major blow-up. In one corner, representing the Washington *Star,* was Jerry O'Leary, a crusty, wisecracking, teetotaling Irishman who had been a newspaperman for thirty-five of his fifty-four years, and who was also an officer in the Marine Corps Reserve. In the other corner, representing the Washington *Post,* was Marilyn Berger, who was fifteen years younger and about eighty-five pounds lighter than O'Leary.

In Washington journalistic society, the *Post* was uptown and the *Star* was downtown, and they regarded each other in about the same way that statues regard pigeons. O'Leary tended to personalize the newspaper rivalry, and he had been baiting *Post* reporters almost since the age of puberty. The feuding intensified after O'Leary accidentally knocked Berger down in a dash to a Kissinger briefing. The two exchanged words that neither of their papers would have printed.

During the Israeli-Syrian shuttle, as the negotiating period lengthened, tempers shortened. After one of the briefing sessions, Berger suggested that O'Leary had violated the rotation rules. Another argument flared. Suddenly, Berger burst into tears, shouted "Fuck off!" and grabbed a serving tray as though to clobber O'Leary, who put up his hands as though he were going to punch her out. Peacemakers Jhabvala and Kalb, seatmates of the combatants, stepped in, and Berger shouted at the rest of us through her sobs, "You're all a bunch of yellow-bellied bastards . . . You let him bully you . . . You're all yellow-bellied cowards." And more. Everyone seemed embarrassed.

Kissinger, the renowned mediator and negotiator, eventually wandered back and asked, "Where's O'Leary? I want to see him hit another woman." O'Leary told him to knock it off, the situation was too explosive.

Jhabvala later negotiated a disengagement agreement between Berger and O'Leary. They exchanged notes and eventually shook hands and almost made up. There were no further exchanges between them, but O'Leary took a certain pleasure in repeating in his gruff voice a line dashed off by Lars-Erik Nelson that "Marilyn had been sent along on the trip to keep our minds off sex." Kissinger, who is as chauvinistic as O'Leary, used to needle Berger a little himself. "I haven't seen what you've written," he said, "but it's ten percent off."

The Secretary clearly had his favorites — and his nonfavorites — among the traveling press, but he betrayed his feelings only rarely and in subtle ways, and as far as I could tell, he never played favorites with information on a trip.

Whatever Kissinger thought about the other reporters who covered him, he did not express on the record. But he did express himself on Darius Jhabvala, under tragic circumstances.

Jhabvala covered a grueling Kissinger trip of seventeen countries in twenty days, then went almost immediately to New York to cover the UN appearance of PLO leader Yasir Arafat. Jhabvala had once worked at the UN and had later covered it for the defunct New York *Herald Tribune.* Shortly after returning to Washington, he died of a heart attack. He was forty-six. Kissinger eulogized Jhabvala in a statement and then in person at a ceremony in the department's briefing room. "He will be missed," the statement said, "not only for the highest professional standards he set for himself, but also for the warmth and gentleness for which he was held in such high esteem by all of us in the department. Darius was a great human being. We have all lost a unique friend." It was a Kissinger statement we all endorsed.

Despite the camaraderie on board and the sense of shared experience, most of us in the rear of the plane made a conscious effort to

maintain our personal distance from the man we were covering.*
Gwertzman put it flatly, "Reporters should not be personal friends
of people they cover." However, the more we traveled, the more we
regulars came to be identified with Kissinger in some personal way
within our profession, as though we were somehow trying to protect
him or glorify him or simply peddle his line. But any good correspondent did as much of his reporting as possible before going on a
trip, so as to have some meaningful measure of the diplomatic
rhythms along the way other than Kissinger's steady beat.

As professionals, we were confident of our ability to remain jour-
nalistically detached despite the close personal contact. So we took
it in stride when we were teased by colleagues, especially anti-Kissinger colleagues, for being too close, and we teased back. Some of
their teasing derived simply from a kind of professional envy.

The resentment felt by some other Washington reporters against
the traveling regulars flared up during the Ford-Sadat meeting in
Salzburg. When the President of the United States travels, the White
House correspondents invariably write the main story. In anticipation of this fact, the diplomatic correspondents who knew they would
be assigned to Salzburg set up a private dinner with the Secretary of
State at a hotel to probe for some diplomatic substance beneath the
surface statements. The White House correspondents screamed
bloody murder — even those correspondents whose organizations
were represented at the dinner.

Since Kissinger held a public news conference after the Ford-Sadat
meeting anyway, the dinner didn't provide much more than good
Wiener schnitzel served with a few nuances on the side. As we came
out of the private dining room, several of the White House correspondents and television anchormen who were eating in the public
dining room of the hotel called out to Kissinger, who started table-

*With one exception, every reporter always called Kissinger "Mr. Secretary" in addressing
him. The one exception was the CBS UN correspondent, Richard Hottelet, who made one trip
and called Kissinger "Henry" throughout.

For his part, Kissinger used first names when he talked to us in private, but in group sessions,
he preferred the military style of calling everybody by his last name, except for the women.

Close aides usually referred to him in private as "HAK." In irreverent moods, they called
him "Fat Heinz."

hopping. When Jim Anderson of UPI came out, he looked around and said in a loud, disdainful voice, "Oh, I didn't realize there would be *press* here."

Only once did the camaraderie impinge directly on the reporting. In Kenya, Kissinger took some time out from the jungle of an UNCTAD Conference to go looking for wild animals in the Masai Mara Game Park. The press planes arrived first, and we were waiting when he arrived, microphones and pencils at the ready for some colorful quote to go with the animals. Whatever he first said on arrival has been lost, as far as is known, in the annals of quippery, but ABC suggested he could do better. He tried again. Still not good enough. ABC urged him on. The third try produced a quotable quote. It came out this way: "Asked if the wildlife reminded him of any recent experiences, Kissinger laughed and said, 'I'm not afraid of wild animals. I've got seventeen on my plane.'" He meant us.

AP filed it. Reuters ignored it as contrived. UPI deplored it and later sent an indignant piece about manufactured quotes. CBS then handed Kissinger a safari hat trimmed with leopardskin, and we had a better picture to go with the quote. To paraphrase Pogo, we had met the manipulator, and it was us.

Kissinger's travel to odd corners of the world presented us with a variety of filing challenges. Telephone service ranged from the excellent instantaneous communications in Europe and Israel to the nonexistent communications in Kabul, Afghanistan (where we amused ourselves by surmising that "Koppel sent Kaplow a cable from Kabul about Kissinger").

The quality of Telex operators varied as widely as that of the telephone service, and reporters were well advised to ride herd on their copy until it was punched by the operators and sent and acknowledged at the other end. On the very first trip, the Telex operation was set up in the headquarters hotel in Rabat, Morocco, where everybody, including all the Telex people, spoke French. No English. AP reporter Barry Schweid, who spoke no French, was not having much luck in explaining what he wanted. John Wallach of the Hearst

Newspapers appeared to go to his rescue. The AP story was duly
sent. But before long, back came a polite message saying, "Received
OK . . . Thank you very much for your report, but why you sending
us this, pls? We London Meat Company."

During a trip to Saudi Arabia before the telephone system improved, Murrey Marder spent hours trying to get through to Washington. He finally succeeded, but the connection was very poor. "Get
me the Foreign Desk," shouted Marder. "What Foreign Desk?"
asked the voice at the other end. "The *Foreign* Desk!" screamed
Marder even louder. "There is no Foreign Desk here," the voice said.
"Is this the Washington *Post*?" shouted Marder. "No," said the
voice, "this is the Colorado Pharmacy on Connecticut Avenue!"
While Marder was looking for choice expletives, one of the other
newsmen cracked, "If they won't take a story, ask if they'll fill a
prescription!"

By the time of the next visit to Riyadh, most of us were already
veterans of the Saudi phone system. But it was a new experience for
the CBS correspondent on the trip, Richard Hottelet, who normally
covers the UN. Hottelet sat for what seemed like hours, explaining
endlessly, "You don't understand, operator. This is *CBS News,* I'm
trying to broadcast to New York . . . Hello, New York. Hello, New
York, do you hear me? . . . OK . . . Let's try it . . . Five, four, three,
two, one — Secretary of State Henry Kissinger . . . Hello, operator,
operator? They don't hear me in New York . . . This is *CBS News*
and . . ."

On the first visit, the Saudis footed the phone bill, but that practice
quickly came to an end — probably after the Saudis saw the size of
the tab, which had been enlarged more than somewhat by the personal calls that were made once we found out about the rates.

But Saudi Arabia was not, of course, the only place with questionable telephone service. Syria also presented problems. While Kissinger fenced for hours with President Hafez Assad at the palace, we
spent hours at the New Omyyad Hotel (quickly dubbed the New
Oh-My-God Hotel) writing, waiting for the telephone, or just waiting. Collect or credit card calls were not available in Syria, so we had
to pay the hotel cashier in Syrian money as soon as we completed

our calls. It occurred to many of us fairly quickly that the rates were rather high; we were obviously being charged for more time than we were actually using. So we began timing our calls more precisely, and when we had finished, we went to the cashier and haggled over the price. It was just like dealing with the merchants in the huge Damascus bazaar.

Officials of the Syrian Press Ministry were always on hand to shepherd us around or to facilitate filing where possible or, during the early trips, to censor copy. I once asked one of them how to say "hurry up" in Arabic. She broke into a big smile and replied, "We don't have those words in this part of the world."

An even more interesting telephone system operated in Zaire. You could place an international call through the hotel switchboard and wait for several hours. Or you could place an international call *sous le système* (under the system), which meant that you got through right away. A man then appeared at your door to collect the bill — at a reduced rate — in cash. The record of the call never appeared on the hotel bill, and the cash disappeared into the pocket of the collector.

Television reporters faced many special problems while chasing Kissinger around the world, apart from the sheer logistical nightmare of moving technicians from place to place for film or video coverage and satellite transmissions. The first problem was simply getting the pictures, a normally routine element of coverage, which was often complicated by the vagaries of host country officials.

Syria almost always insisted on press pools for cameramen, so the networks had to share all their film at the point of satellite origination, usually Amman or Tel Aviv (if Kissinger was flying back to Israel in time). The Egyptians once barred the filming of a Kissinger-Sadat meeting for no apparent reason. The curious and unexpected prohibition came when the Middle East News Agency was reporting that the leader of the PLO, Yasir Arafat, was visiting Cairo, so speculation immediately flourished that Arafat might be present at the meeting. He wasn't, as far as we ever knew; the prohibition apparently had more to do with Third World caprice than third-party talk.

None of the travel was easy, but the shuttle trips were especially difficult for the television correspondents. Since we were operating in the part of the world that is five to seven hours ahead of the United States in time, the almost-daily satellite transmissions to New York or London were always scheduled around midnight. And the television stations were seldom close to the hotels where we were staying.

Most of the shuttle reports originated in Israel, since neither Cairo nor Damascus was able to transmit film. The satellite transmission point was located in the Tel Aviv suburb of Herzliya, which is about an hour-and-fifteen-minute drive from Jerusalem. So when Kissinger's plane landed at Ben-Gurion Airport and he took off for Jerusalem, we TV correspondents rushed to Herzliya with our film, wrote our scripts, made our broadcasts, and then drove to Jerusalem, often arriving after two in the morning, hoping we wouldn't have to get up at seven to go back to Aswan or Cairo or Alexandria or Damascus or Amman.

Kissinger's trip to South Africa in late 1976 seemed like a replay of the Israeli scenario. The action took place in Pretoria, but the television studios were in Johannesburg, more than an hour away. So once again we rode the midnight express, getting back to the hotel around three in the morning.

Herzliya and Johannesburg did have their compensating features. Things worked technically. Elsewhere, a twenty-hour day could easily end in frustration.

During Kissinger's first trip to Africa, NBC and ABC chartered a Lear jet to fly film more than a thousand miles from Lusaka, Zambia, to Kinshasa, Zaire, one of the few potential satellite points in black Africa. Producers and film editors had flown in from London to put together reports about Kissinger's Lusaka declaration of a new African policy for the United States. But it was like tossing a bottle into the ocean. The Zairian technicians never managed to get the signal from Kinshasa to London, and the film was never aired. We spent several frustrating hours in the Kinshasa studios, wondering what Ali-Foreman had that Kissinger didn't.

The frustrations were not confined to the underdeveloped world.

Paris once qualified par excellence. It was the day Kissinger returned to his home town of Fuerth, Germany, to receive an award, with his elderly parents, Louis and Paula, looking on proudly. The story was full of emotion, with the elder Kissinger noting poignantly on camera, "On a day like this, we forget all the past."

After the ceremony, Kissinger flew on to Paris, where plans had been made to transmit the Fuerth film by satellite. We were working on a tight schedule as usual, since all three networks had to have their film processed in the same laboratory before editing and broadcasting. We did manage to get the story packaged in time for the 6:30 P.M. newscast in the United States — so we thought. It turned out that French television technicians were involved in a labor dispute with the national television network, and when the satellite came up, the technicians slowed down. Valuable transmission time was lost. Finally, at 11:40 P.M., Paris time, they began transmitting. But precisely at midnight, when the NBC piece was loaded in the projector, ready to roll, the technicians simply walked off the job, refusing to stay the extra five minutes it would have taken to send the story. They imperviously ignored pleas and then curses. Unfortunately, my supply of French expletives was too quickly exhausted, although the embarrassed local NBC workers didn't think so.

For NBC, the Kissinger-in-Fuerth piece ended up in the film library. What's more, I was so tired and the hour so late that I didn't even eat dinner in Paris. It was just as well. That night, I got sick for the only time on a Kissinger trip. Ironically, it happened in an overdeveloped part of the world. A few others in the party were also sick, and we speculated that it was due to brackish water at Claridge's the previous day.

The usually reliable TV operation at Herzliya also failed us at one critical moment. But it wasn't the fault of anyone in Israel. On the night Kissinger's second Israeli-Egyptian shuttle collapsed, we raced from Jerusalem to the TV studios. But, like the Kissinger mission itself, our trip was ill-fated. All the available satellite time had already been booked — by the European Song Contest finals in Stockholm. We filed our reports the old-fashioned way — by telephone, with a slide appearing on television screens in the United States and our voices over.

Of all the stories I reported throughout the world with Kissinger, from Peking to Kabul to Lusaka, of all the lead items on the *Nightly News,* of all the bulletins from the Middle East or Moscow, the one story that drew the most response was another sightseeing story. And I did it almost as a throwaway.

In October of 1974, Kissinger spent a couple of days in New Delhi. Nancy was going to Agra, to visit the Taj Mahal. For me, the choice was easy. After filing an arrival story on Henry, I went with Nancy.

The Indians closed off the Taj to other tourists — something that did not enhance Kissinger's popularity among those standing in line outside — and we had the grounds to ourselves for almost the whole afternoon.

I made sure the cameraman took some arty shots to capture the splendor of the enormous marble monument to love, and then I wrote a light script about Nancy's touring. I closed by saying, "None of this has much to do with the Secretary of State and the substance of diplomacy, but I've always wanted to be able to sign off: This is Richard Valeriani, NBC News at the Taj Mahal."

I shipped the film to London and was frankly surprised to hear later that *Nightly News* had used the piece for a closer. And when I got back to the States, more people commented on the Taj Mahal piece than on any other travel report I had done. That's how it is when you're a hard-hitting reporter.

Riding the Kissinger coattails on a VIP sightseeing tour was one of the bonuses of traveling with him. Humorist Art Buchwald pointed out other benefits. "There is no greater honor," he wrote,

than to be selected as one of the elite fourteen journalists to fly on Mr. Kissinger's well-appointed Air Force 707 and share the joys and heartbreak of American jet diplomacy.

The advantages of traveling with Mr. Kissinger are enormous. You don't have to go through customs, you don't have to carry your own luggage and you don't have to tip taxi drivers.

The only disadvantage is that you have to stand in hotel lobbies and in front of old castles for five or six hours doing nothing until he is ready to leave for his next stop.

As a new guy, what Buchwald didn't know was how we reporters, or at least some of us, conspired to overcome "the only disadvantage."

One solution was liar's poker, a game played with dollar bills — or more specifically, with the serial numbers on dollar bills, similar to liar's dice. It involves a lot of lying and bluffing and psychology and sometimes guts, and it therefore seemed appropriate as a pastime for reporters who dealt with diplomacy. It began as a form of relief from boredom during the long rides in press buses, during the long stake-outs waiting for Kissinger and some foreign dignitary to emerge from a meeting, and during the long stretches of restlessness aboard the plane.

Since there were lots of press bus rides and stake-outs and plane flights, liar's poker became a permanent adjunct to Kissinger travel. It eventually became a ritual to play at least one hand of liar's poker wherever Kissinger went — in Brezhnev's office, in the Forbidden City, in King Faisal's palace, at the Taj Mahal, at all signing ceremonies. One of the players tape-recorded a memorable game on the Golan Heights, where the bids were punctuated by the sound of artillery fire in the background. The only place we didn't play was the Pope's office in the Vatican. No reporters were allowed in.

We even designated a commissioner to resolve disputes. The job was originally held by Marvin Kalb of CBS, but when he stopped traveling because of a bad back, the position was assumed by Ozzie Johnston of the Los Angeles *Times*. Johnston was known for sage decisions handed down in a pontifical, commissioner-like way, such as, "Play shall be continuous until a round of play is concluded," or "Disputes of a bilateral nature shall be resolved on a bilateral basis."

In writing about liar's poker, I say "we," but I really mean "some of us." Bernie Gwertzman of the New York *Times* split the Kissinger press corps for all time in one of his Reporter's Notebooks by

dividing us into two groups: the liar's poker players and the "philosophers." The "philosophers" discussed matters of substance, such as
Kissinger's afterdinner toast, the weather, the difficulties of filing, the
latest hotel accommodations — whatever, while the players played.

Kissinger himself was undeniably identified with the philosophers,
and he never endangered that classification by playing a single hand
of liar's poker, not even on his final trip, despite the entreaties of the
players. However, his teen-aged son David did accept an invitation
to join the game, although the invitation scandalized Nancy Kissinger. She suggested, albeit not too seriously, that we were contributing to the delinquency of a minor. We didn't see it quite that
way, especially since David even managed to win a few bucks by
conservative play.

It's easy to dismiss liar's poker as a kind of collective silliness, but
Barry Schweid claimed, with some exaggeration, that it helped him
retain his sanity during the long Kissinger days and years. And in
fact, this simple pastime achieved almost metaphysical significance
when Martin Arnold, who wrote for the New York *Times,* apotheo-
sized its importance in a feature story about a Kissinger news conference. Arnold theorized that the "regulars" of the State Department
press corps played liar's poker while waiting for the Secretary to
arrive in order to separate themselves from the fifty or sixty other
reporters who might cover a Kissinger news conference. "Liar's
poker," he pontificated, "is the touch football of the Kissinger State
Department." The Kennedy crowd must have been envious as hell.

What Arnold didn't know was that we did try touch football a
couple of times. A short pick-up game outside the hotel where we
stayed in Peking drew a crowd of a few hundred curiously gawking
Chinese. We also played on the tarmac of a military base during a
refueling stop in Crete, but one of the most athletic types among us,
Barrie Dunsmore of ABC, once a hockey player in Canada, twisted
his ankle on a slope while going long, and he had to be helped aboard
the plane.

Some of the other putative athletes among us established records
for carrying a tennis racket the longest distance on an airplane

without ever using it. There usually wasn't enough time, or no available courts, or we were just too tired.

However, Jerry Schechter of *Time* and Ted Koppel of ABC managed to play an unusual version of the game in Jerusalem one Sunday morning. I had just awakened and thrown open the shutters of the window in my room at the King David Hotel across from the courts at the YMCA. I stood there watching, blinking the sleep from my eyes, envying their energetic determination to play so early. But I sensed something drastically wrong. As the fatigue wore off, it suddenly hit me. It was like a scene out of Fellini. They were playing without a net! The YMCA, hoping to discourage tennis playing on the Christian Sabbath, had taken down the nets on Sunday. It should be pointed out, with no malice, that the absence of the net resulted in a marked improvement in their game.

Most of the games we played were not physical, however. Members of the crew organized a landing pool, which involved betting on the number — one to twelve — in which the nose wheel of the plane locked after it had stopped. On visits to Damascus, some of us bet on the color of the suit in which Zuhair Jannan would appear. He was a short, bespectacled, Foreign Ministry press officer whose wardrobe was as flamboyant as his employer was uninformative. The colors ranged from diarrhetic plum to persimmon puce to mocha chocolate fudge to, simply, bilious bright green.

Another form of entertainment was to pour one's creative or lyrical or cynical talents into a pool report, an account of an event that only a few reporters covered because of logistical restrictions preventing a larger group. The basic pool reports were usually straightforward and informative, but they varied according to circumstances. The pool that covered a Kissinger visit to one of the many residences of President Jomo Kenyatta in Kenya produced a two-part report. Jim Anderson of UPI wrote the basic account of the visit, which ended: "As Kenyatta and Kissinger left the dancing area, they were buttonholed by Lars-Erik Nelson [of Reuters], who will report on that encounter."

Nelson's pool report, "add one," went as follows:

"Mzee," I says to him, "Mzee, could you give us your assessment of
the prospects for peace in Rhodesia now that you have talked to Dr.
Kissinger?"

Blank stare from Mzee.

"Mzee," says I, "other African leaders have given their reactions to the
Rhodesian plan. Could you please tell us your views about the future of
Rhodesia?"

Mzee's rheumy eyes, floating in olive oil, roll sideways.

"Mr. President, could you give us your reaction to the Kissinger plan
for Rhodesia," John Maclean says, approximately.

Mzee speaks: "My reaction? To what?"

"To the Rhodesia peace plan."

"My reaction?"

"Yes please. We would like to know your assessment of what has been
happening about Rhodesia."

"I do not talk to newspaper people about other countries. I only talk
about Kenya," says Mzee and walks off, followed by a nastily chuckling
Kissinger.

P.S. Addendum to Anderson report. Kissinger posed in ranks of warri-
ors and held one of their short, machete-like swords in his right hand
and a painted hide shield in his left hand. There was some nervousness
about all the cutlery in the hands of the natives around him, but they
behaved themselves and showed admirable restraint, considering the
opportunity.

Occasionally, we turned to a pastime commonly practiced by
political reporters on presidential campaigns. We wrote songs, sort
of. As Kissinger extended his December 1973 trip closer and closer
to Christmas (observed by neither Arab nor Jew), we sang, "God rest
you, Henry Kissinger, Please get us home on time . . ." In western
Africa, after Kissinger announced a program to "roll back the desert" to relieve the drought-stricken Sahel region, an eminently forgettable song was composed to the tune of "Roll Out the Bar-
rel." It began, "Roll back the desert, roll back the sands and the
heat . . ."

It was in Africa where our finest lyrical achievement was recorded.
Kissinger was taking a boat ride, and the press was already on board

when he arrived. The stunning results of the Texas primary election had come in overnight. President Ford had been wiped out by Ronald Reagan, and pro-Ford Texas Republicans were muttering about the timing of the Secretary of State's visit to black Africa. As Kissinger stepped onto the boat, he was greeted with a chorus of "The Eyes of Texas Are upon You." For once, he was quipless as he explained the strange behavior of the strange people who traveled with him to his puzzled hosts.

I once amused myself with an original song for a "musical comedy" about a short, fat Secretary of State who spoke with a foreign accent and who flew around the world dispensing foreign policy. It went like this:

They call me Henry the K
And I've come a very long way.
My critics all want to burn me alive
But there's one thing I've learned — and that's how to survive.
That's why Henry will stay.

I've been Ehrlichmanned and Haldemanned, Zieglered and Kleined.
Pay no mind — I've survived.
I've been Nixonized and Simonized, Colson-ated, Mitchell-ated.
It's all for naught. I don't get caught.

I've been Sadat-ized and Rabin-ized, Dayan-ated Faisal-ated.
To no avail. I still prevail.
I've been DeGaulled, but not de-balled
I've been Giscarded, but not discarded.
I've been Husseined, but all in vain. I've been Germained — by Greer.
But never fear — 'cause I'm still here.

I've been Schmidt upon, screwed by Thieu, Kittikatchorned and
    Pompidou'd.
But it's no use. I stand abuse.
I've been Ho Chi Min'd and Vietnamized, zapped by Giap but still
    Peace-Prized.
Despite the war, I'm back for more.

I've been Gromyko'd and Chiang Kai-sheked, Le Duc Tho'd till I'm a
    wreck.
And still it's true — I'm not all through.

I've been spiked by Pike and Churchified, Ronnie Reagan wants
   my hide.
But I'm alive, and I'll survive.

The most expensive game some of us got involved in was known
as "Henry the K." During a Middle East shuttle, I was talking to
Ted Koppel about my desire to own a race horse one day. Koppel
suggested that the traveling correspondents buy a horse and name
him after Kissinger. Six of us did — Barry Schweid, Marvin Kalb,
Bruce van Voorst, Stan Carter of the New York *Daily News,* Koppel,
and I. It seemed like a good idea at the time.

We called ourselves the Off the Record stable, but the Jockey Club
refused to permit us the silks we wanted — a shirt with a typewriter
in a white circle on a field of blue printers' ink. The Jockey Club did
permit the horse to be named "Henry the K" after Kissinger
gave his permission. We told him we were thinking of having
the horse handled by a Maryland trainer who had once been a Foreign Service officer. "That's very interesting," he said. "At last, a
Foreign Service officer is engaged in an activity up to his mental
level." The two Foreign Service officers flanking him smiled
weakly.

Kissinger caught some of our enthusiasm about the horse, whose
grandsire was the classic champion Northern Dancer, and he promised to be on hand when Henry the K was invited to run in the
$150,000 Laurel International at Laurel Race Track in Maryland on
Veterans' Day, which was the owners' hope. But Nancy's skepticism
prevented Kissinger from getting too excited. Our own enthusiasm
began to dwindle when Henry the K made his debut at the age of
three at Timonium, Maryland, and finished far back, with an ABC
network camera recording the embarrassing performance. After
that, the Secretary lost interest in his equine namesake, and we lost
money.

Henry the K finally won his first race at Penn National racetrack
near Harrisburg, Pennsylvania, near the end of 1975. None of us was
there to celebrate. He finished third and second in his next two starts,
and then took off for the winter. But when he returned to action at

Charleston, West Virginia, in early 1976, he suffered a slab fracture of the knee, and he was put out to pasture only several months before the real Henry.

He retired with expenses far in excess of earnings, and our quest for thoroughbred glory ended in a Charleston Chapparal instead of a Seattle Slew. Sic transit Henry (the K) Mundi.

On the road, another costly diversion — for some — was practiced entirely on the ground, especially in a large department store in Peking and in huge Middle East bazaars and in sprawling outdoor markets in Africa. It was loosely called shopping, but some of its devotees threw themselves into it with a passion bordering on obsession. If awards had been given for shopping, the clear-cut winners would have been Jerry Schechter of *Time* and John Wallach of the Hearst papers. Their seats on the return flight to Washington invariably looked like mini-bazaars. When the press buses were loaded at the hotel, Schechter was usually the last one aboard, dragged from the hotel gift shop, where he was buying just one more pair of worry beads or a dried monkey's paw.

Everybody bought something on the trips to exotic places, so the plane always returned loaded down with touristic reminders of travel. After only the first two weeks of the Syrian shuttle, the Secretariat put out a memo to all members of the Secretary's party that read: "Please restrict your personal purchases to small items which you can easily carry and store under your seat. The baggage master states that the baggage compartment is filled to maximum with passenger luggage and equipment." And rugs and copper pots and rusty old rifles, et cetera.

A couple of newsmen wrote that the plane was so laden with gifts it had to make an extra refueling stop in Crete on the way from Nairobi to Paris. The story was wrong. The stop was necessary because the plane could not take off with a full load of fuel in Nairobi's thin air, five thousand feet above sea level.

Kissinger was furious about the reports, which implied that a lot of extra government money was being spent for the stop in Crete because of gifts given to him and the shopping excesses of his party. He was furious not only because the story was wrong, but also because a considerable portion of the carvings, spears, skins, ivory and wooden statues, and ersatz tribal masks on board had been bought by members of the press. In fact, one of our colleagues regularly abused the convenience of Kissinger travel by buying big-ticket items and then selling them at his Georgetown store when he got back. And his wife complained that he listed the rugs he brought back for sale in the want ads, and she had to stay home on weekends in case anybody answered the ads.

Another standard diversion was the custom of giving a fictitious award to the member of the traveling press who had done "the least amount of work under deadline pressure." The award was always at the end of a trip, and it was based on a vague, unscientific, and totally subjective system of collecting impressions throughout the trip. Since the wire service reporters did the most amount of work under deadline pressure, they had the most to say about who got the award.

The most obvious candidates were the reporters from the two weekly news magazines or the *Wall Street Journal* or the *Christian Science Monitor* or even the Los Angeles *Times.* The L.A. *Times* reporter's deadlines were so late, given the time differences, that he was seldom seen typing in public places. Sometimes the magazine guys ostentatiously typed on the plane in the early part of the week, long before their filing deadlines. This was seen as a transparent attempt to avoid the award, and it was discounted. One magazine reporter was "accused" of taping the sound of a typewriter typing and then playing it loudly in his room at night, while he was actually out on the town, so as to lose points for the award. The accusation was never proven. It was also considered bad form to try to win the award openly, and leaving one's typewriter on the plane during an overnight stop usually fell into that category. As Stan Karnow, formerly of the Washington *Post,* once observed, "Journalism is the only profession where you can remain an adolescent all your life."

Our return from yet another trip to the Middle East in the fall of 1974 produced a one-shot diversion on the Kissinger plane. Peter Rodman, note-taker, speech writer, and quipmaker, came into the steerage section and implored us, half-jokingly, to come up with some jokes for the Secretary's speech for the Alfred E. Smith Memorial Dinner in New York. We took him half-seriously, and since we were always looking for new ways to relieve the monotony of the flight, some of us decided to channel our excess creative energies into writing a gag or two — those of us, that is, who had not used up all of our creativity in filling out our expense accounts.

We did it more for our own amusement than Kissinger's, but he was amused as well when we read the product of our efforts during the usual off-the-record session on the homebound flight. It was instructive to see his reaction. He was unable to conceal his preference for the most wicked lines in spite of himself.

To wit: "In a few weeks, I'll be accompanying President Ford to Japan and South Korea. He's told me that he needs me along to chew gum while he negotiates." Kissinger tried not to crack up, but he couldn't hold back his laughter. To more wit: "Incidentally, I'm getting a little tired of being criticized for showing preference to the Arab side in the Middle East. I would point out simply that while I've only kissed the Arabs, my staff will testify to the fact that I'm constantly screwing the Israelis." Kissinger again cracked up.

When we wrote the Arab-Israeli gag, we added parenthetically, "(Yes, we know it will never see the light of day.)" But it did, although in revised form. Proving that great humor runs in the same channels, columnist Art Buchwald closed a travels-with-Henry piece several months later by writing: "The only place there is some question of Kissinger's popularity is among Israelis. At a castle outside of Bonn for the Rabin talks, an embittered Israeli reporter asks me why, if Henry is so happily married to Nancy, does he always screw the Jews?"

For the sake of posterity, here is the rest of the "speech" we wrote for the Smith dinner:

His Eminence, Cardinal Cooke, was understandably apprehensive when he heard that he and I would be eating together this evening. The last time I shared a meal with a distinguished religious leader was when

Archbishop Makarios invited me to lunch in Cyprus — which may explain why His Holiness, the Pope, is not eager to see me when I visit Rome next month.

The Alfred E. Smith dinner, as I understand it, is traditionally an event that brings together some of the outstanding public servants and politicians of our time. It is with some disappointment, therefore, that I note the absence of one of the most far-sighted and perceptive legislators of the twentieth century. I refer, of course, to Congressman Jonathan Bingham, whose amendment to permit foreign-born Americans to run for the presidency is consistently underestimated by the press. I have no illusions about my chances for the nomination, even if the Bingham amendment were passed. There's not the remotest possibility of my receiving the nomination . . . until at least the second ballot.

Which brings up the subject of my alleged megalomania. Cardinal Cooke will bear witness to the fact that I made no scene whatsoever when he refused to kiss my ring.

I am delighted to see the senior senator from New York here. There have been, as you know, a number of articles in the press recently suggesting that I was opposed to the trip that Senator Javits and Senator Pell made to Havana. Nothing could be further from the truth. I had no objections at all to their going. What I objected to was their coming back . . .

But as I was saying about the Javits-Pell trip to Cuba, I was so impressed by the results of that mission, I'm having my staff draw up recommendations for similar trips in the future.

For example, we're thinking of sending Senator Eagleton to Albania — for good. I've proposed to Senator Church that he undertake an extended mission to Outer Mongolia. In fact, I've even offered him the ambassadorship to Ulan Bator, but he insists that we have diplomatic relations first. And we're going to allow Senator Jackson to emigrate anywhere he wants — and we're not going to ask for anything in exchange.

During my latest trip to the Middle East, Mayor Beame saw some pictures of my wearing an Arab headdress, and he suggested that I come here tonight wearing a yarmulke. Except for the fact that my father would have trouble recognizing me, I was tempted by the suggestion — if only to demonstrate an even-headed policy.

But there's already been enough criticism about my wearing too many hats.

Senators Jackson, Javits, and Ribicoff have been worried about stepping up Jewish emigration from the Soviet Union. What they do not realize is that through quiet diplomacy and a predominantly Jewish press corps, I've managed to increase Jewish emigration to Saudi Arabia more than 500 percent over the past year alone.

One small indication of how much conditions have improved in the Middle East since I decided to give it my personal touch can be found in the fact that security is no longer the problem it once was — once I get off my plane.

As you know, my popularity around the world has decreased somewhat during the past few months. In fact, there's scarcely a foreign capital left where I haven't been greeted by pickets carrying signs that say, KISSINGER GO HOME. I can't tell you how profoundly moved I was when I returned to Andrews Air Force Base last night to be greeted by my wife, Nancy, carrying the same sign. I kissed her on both cheeks, and we went straight home where we engaged in a frank and constructive dialogue.

Incidentally, it's absolutely untrue that I insist on being addressed by Nancy as "Mr. Secretary." Around the house, she's perfectly free to call me "Dr. Kissinger," which is more respect than I get from other members of my staff.

Next week at this time, Nancy and I will be in Moscow — visiting our wheat."

The speech itself was off the record, so we never knew whether he used any of the lines. But some of them did crop up, usually with some revision, in future Kissinger speeches and ad-libbed remarks.

The hours of tedium aboard the plane were unavoidable, but the same could not be said of the long periods of time spent on the ground in waiting for Henry, especially at airports. Although we came to expect it, we never stopped grumbling about it. During one of the Middle East shuttles, Bruce van Voorst tried a novel method of waiting at the airport in Tel Aviv. He changed into his bathing suit, then took a blanket, spread it on the tarmac, and sat on it, reading and sun-bathing while sipping a ginger ale. The chief of the Israeli security detachment was not amused. "This is not a circus," he grouched to van Voorst. He then complained to American officials on the plane, who suggested to van Voorst that he'd better confine his sun-bathing to the pool. Before he packed it in, however, an Israeli photographer took his picture, which appeared on the front page of an afternoon newspaper.

Only one correspondent ever missed a flight accidentally. Marilyn Berger achieved that unique distinction in Cyprus. She left the press center in a downtown hotel to have lunch at the beach with a German television correspondent. Kissinger decided to leave early, and when Berger returned to the press center, it was empty. She raced to the airport, but found only her passport waiting for her. The plane was gone. It was not a serious miss, since it was not too difficult to get from Cyprus to Israel, and she quickly caught up with the rest of the party. When Kissinger spotted her at the King David, he jibed, "Ah, I see you've decided to join us." Berger was worried that O'Leary would report in the Washington *Star* that the Washington *Post* reporter had missed the plane. He didn't.

Barry Schweid once overslept in Riyadh and came within thirty seconds of not catching the plane. *That* would have been a serious miss. It was *very* difficult to get from Saudi Arabia to Israel by any means other than a Kissinger plane.

The entire press corps came close to being stranded in Cairo. It was a Friday, and Kissinger was in a hurry to take off so he could get back to Israel and conduct some business before the sun went down, marking the beginning of the Jewish Sabbath. But the press bus, which in Egypt was never fast enough to keep up with the motorcade, got separated from Kissinger's caravan. Without an official escort, the bus was no match for the rest of the Egyptian traffic. A New York *Times* "What's Doing in Cairo" feature once warned tourists about the character of that traffic by pointing out: "Driving a rented automobile would be difficult and perhaps suicidal, given the Egyptians' aggressive driving habits." The bus quickly got bogged down. Really bogged down. At a major crossroads, it was suddenly surrounded by hordes of garbage carts drawn by goats and donkeys. There was no way to get around them, so the bus chugged along at their pace until they turned off.

At the airport, Kissinger's short fuse quickly burned out. "Let's go," he urged. His aides counseled patience, which was in short supply. Finally he announced, "I'm going without them." Aide Jerry Bremer kept telling him we were just a few minutes away and talked him into waiting. We finally rolled up to the plane about half an hour late, and Kissinger fumed all the way to Israel.

After that near-disaster, the Egyptians assigned a motorcycle escort to clear the way for the press bus to rumble to the airport without serious interruption. But this was Egypt. On the way to the airport, the escort got annoyed at a driver who did not move aside quickly enough. The policeman ordered the car to the side of the road, stopped, got off his motorcycle to argue with the driver, and that's the last we saw of him. Luckily, no goats or donkeys converged on the bus this time, and we made it to the plane on time.

Once Kissinger began traveling regularly, John Wallach of the Hearst newspapers sought to establish himself as the class photographer. After we returned from one of the early trips, we walked into the press room at the State Department to find a display of Wallach's pictures in the Hearst newspaper booth at the State Department. The pictures were mounted and numbered for easy selection, and Wallach was offering them for sale at a variety of prices, depending on the combination. One reporter made his selection and asked how much. "That'll be two seventy-five," said Wallach. The reporter gave him $3, but got no change. "What's the extra twenty-five cents for?" the reporter asked. "That's the transportation charge," explained Wallach. His business did not prosper.

Before Kissinger left office, the State Department Correspondents' Association decided to hold a farewell reception for him. Since I was the president of the association that year, I finally had an opportunity to propose the toast myself rather than merely report it, as I had done so often on the road. It came out this way, as transcribed by the State Department stenographers:

MR. VALERIANI: Mr. Secretary, this is the first time in several years that the Correspondents' Association has held a party, and I would like, at the outset, to squelch any speculation that it is being held to celebrate your departure. [Laughter.]

As a matter of fact, quite the contrary. I think the prevalent feeling among most of my colleagues, if I may speak for them, is one of regret that you are leaving. We won't have Henry Kissinger to kick around anymore. [Laughter.]

The fact that your departure is now well established — you, yourself, have acknowledged that you are looking for someone to paint your portrait — and Cyrus Vance will pick the corridor where it should be hung — though I heard some of your colleagues say that they thought it would have been a good idea if you had been hung in any one of the corridors a long time ago. [Laughter.] (They said that.)

But since it is the first time we have had an affair like this in several years, we thought we would do something special tonight.

Bob Funseth suggested that perhaps the members of the press ought to pay tribute to you, so we tried to line up William Shannon, Anthony Lewis [laughter], Lester Kinsolving [laughter], Bill Safire, and Peter Peckarsky — but they weren't available so we thought we would try something else.

Larry Eagleburger thought it would be a nice idea if we had a Foreign Service officer say something about you, but we weren't able to get Ambassador Hillenbrand. [Laughter.]

We also thought, fleetingly — fleetingly, we thought about asking Phil Habib to say something, but he always gets so maudlin at these affairs. [Laughter.]

So we decided to do nothing — and this is it. [Laughter.]

Now this is probably your last appearance among us, or one of your last appearances among us — not counting your next eight or nine final news conferences — and so I would like to allay any fears that exist out there about your financial future. Because Bernie Kalb told me that CBS has offered you fifty thousand dollars for exclusive rights to the first film of you getting on the Eastern shuttle to New York. [Laughter.]

And that you had said for another twenty-five thousand dollars you will sit in the middle seat. [Laughter.]

But if I can be serious for just a minute, those of us, Mr. Secretary, who got stuck with your last trip to Europe, when you went to NATO — I think we were impressed by the words of praise that were lavished upon you by your NATO colleagues, the foreign ministers of Europe. And there was one of them even — I think it was Secretary-General Luns — who said that you were one of the few men in this century to whom the adjective "great" could be legitimately applied. Now, knowing your impatience with that kind of adjectival constraint [laughter] and with the indulgence of my colleagues, I would like to propose a toast to the greatest American Secretary of State . . . since William Rogers. [Laughter.]

SECRETARY KISSINGER: Mr. Valeriani, ladies and gentlemen, I cannot tell you how moved I am [laughter] by this tribute.

And it just confirms my view that the members of this association are "all heart."

I had thought I would give some tips to some of you this evening. I thought I could tell Mr. Peckarsky how to get into the Kurdish rug business [laughter] — but I am so shaken by these remarks that I won't do it now. [Laughter.]

I keep sending out these rather inadequate remarks of the Secretary-General of NATO as my Christmas cards [laughter] so that those of you with whom I am still speaking (which is three or four) will probably receive it.

I commented this morning on the depth to which this department has sunk when I asked the Policy Planning Staff to prepare some remarks for the Harlem Globetrotters and I told one horrible pun that they wanted me to make, for which I couldn't take credit. But there was another one that undoubtedly would have been on every evening news if I had had the courage to put it forward. They had wanted me to say that I feel sympathetic to the Harlem Globetrotters because I get nothing from this department except dribble. [Laughter.]

You will have to give credit to — well, you can see why Winston Lord had to take a few months off in the mountains.

We have had the curious relationship that exists between policymakers and reporters — that mixture of fear on the policymaker's side and superciliousness on the reporter's side. [Laughter.]

A desperate attempt, always doomed to failure of being liked and, on the other hand, the attitude of fraternalism expressed by Chester Gould, the originator of "Dick Tracy," who said: "The way I go at my problem is, I pick myself a repulsive subject — and go on from there." [Laughter.]

Inevitably, policymakers think that what they are doing is right —

odd as it may be for you to believe — and therefore, inevitably they tend to have a somewhat self-righteous attitude.

On the other hand, even the press cannot be right a hundred percent of the time, and so — and the perspective is different — it is the function of the press to find the weaknesses — and sometimes what appears as a credibility gap is genuine confusion. [Laughter.]

It is the intent of most policymakers to try to justify their position. And yet the journalist's role, in the words of Arthur Miller, "is to conduct the nation's dialogue with itself."

Now however this relationship develops — and with all the tensions that sometimes exist — I want to tell the two or three of you that have occasionally written unfavorably about me [laughter] that I may forgive you, but my father won't. [Laughter.]

And since he follows the principles with which I have blackmailed the American correspondents (but I am not sure all the foreign correspondents know it yet) that anybody is given one chance.

The second time he writes an unfavorable article about me, he disappears from the scrapbook. [Laughter.]

My father is now down to half a scrapbook. He was up to about thirty, at one point. [Laughter.]

But this — I have found that this is the time for nostalgia and I am beginning to think, even kindly, of the press conference when O'Leary was pointing a finger at me — and I tried to avoid Peckarsky and a few others — only to be trapped by one more question by Murrey Marder.

I have greatly appreciated the seriousness with which you have tried to do your duties.

America has gone through a difficult eight years, and everybody concerned with national policy has had to attempt to define what role America can play — after so many disappointments, and with so many travails — particularly as we all know how much depends on America in terms of peace and progress.

I know that you set high standards, and when all is said and done — while I will never forgive you — I do appreciate what you have stood for and what you have tried to do.

And I hope you will cover me on the New York–Washington shuttle as you have on the Cairo–Jerusalem shuttle. [Applause and laughter.]
7:38 P.M.

After Kissinger had left office and it was announced that he had joined NBC News as a consultant for a lot of money, I sent him a note welcoming him to the ranks, not only of NBC, but also of journalism, and I invited him to become a member of the State Department Correspondents' Association by paying the $5 dues. I got back a note saying, in part: "I thought that by this time I would be considered to have paid my dues." Indeed he had.

THIRTEEN

Finale

When I told a former Kissinger aide that I planned to write a funny book about Kissinger's travels, he said wryly, "I guess it's going to be a pretty thin book." He then told me a number of funny stories. So did a lot of other people. And the book, like Kissinger himself, just got fatter and fatter. When it came time to cut it, the chapters on Europe, Africa, Latin America, Asia, and Domestic Travel did not survive. It would be inappropriate, however, not to recount his final overseas trip as Secretary of State, when he made his annual December journey to Brussels for the winter meeting of NATO.

Just as the focus of the December 1973 meeting of NATO had been on Kissinger's first appearance there as Secretary of State, so the focus at the December 1976 meeting was on Kissinger's last appearance there as Secretary of State. Most of the foreign ministers embellished their public farewells with lavish praise. Secretary-General Joseph Luns started it off. "I am convinced," he said,

> that you will stand in history as one of the most effective foreign ministers of our century. You have understood the underlying realities of our time.

Your goals have been the goals not only of the free world, but of ordinary men and woman everywhere — peace, security, and prosperity.

And to this task, you have brought your extraordinary energy and outstanding brilliance.

You have had an enormous influence on the shape of international relations of our time. You have been essentially a man of action — a man who has made things happen — a man who has been instrumental in bringing peace and security to many parts of a very troubled world.

We have had our difficult times, but I believe that we have come through them revitalized. The commitment to the Alliance is greater now among our governments and among our peoples than it has been for many years. And this is largely due to the positive and inspiring leadership which you have given us.

I see no harm to your well-known modesty if for a moment I add a contribution to the wave of praise which is showering down on you from all sides . . .

Members of the Council, as we say good-bye to this great Secretary of State, may I summarize our common feeling by quoting Shakespeare: "He was a man, take him for all in all, I shall not look upon his like again."

The waves of praise did indeed "shower down" upon the departing Secretary of State, and although the showering took place, as usual, in a "restricted session," transcripts of Luns's remarks, and the remarks of others, were made available afterward, which was most unusual. For anybody except Kissinger, it might have been embarrassing. He replied extemporaneously in the fashion that had made him so popular with his NATO colleagues:

I want to take this opportunity to thank the Secretary-General and all of my colleagues for some of the friendly things that were said on my behalf.

Some of them had the character of an obituary.

I would like to point out that at the end of the Mondale administration, I will only be sixty-nine years old and that without doubt, Joseph [Luns] will still be in the chair here. And so the future is not entirely closed to me, Joseph.

At any rate, I remember my first meeting here in 1973, and I recall there are only very few of us left. On that occasion, my French colleague was sitting across the table from me ready to spring at me before I even reached the verb in my sentence . . . The Belgian foreign minister insisted despite all of this that there were no differences. Max Van Der Stoel [the Dutch foreign minister] was desperately attempting to move matters to a higher moral plane.

And Gaston Thorn [Prime Minister of Luxembourg] was insisting that if only the small countries were running things, such vulgar displays of bad temper could not occur.

Since then, NATO has greatly strengthened its cohesion.

[Then he turned serious:] Maybe what my European origin has done for me is to help me understand that not all things are possible, and that nations can suffer tragedies if they do not act with wisdom and dedication and foresight. The greatest change that has taken place in America in the last eight years is the realization that we, too, now are inextricably part of a world in which our choices and not simply our resources determine our future.

This is why I feel that this group, which has just now gone through one of its annual exercises, has profound moral responsibilities.

We are responsible for the security of freedom, but we are also responsible for the content of freedom. It is this group of just a few countries of humane institutions that now represents the conscience of free men.

This is why my association with you has meant so much to me, and why I am so grateful for the comments you have all made.

Thank you.

In addition to the encomia, Kissinger also received gifts — a reproduction of a Latin encyclopedia from the year 1120 from the Belgian foreign minister, Renaat van Elslande, and from German Foreign Minister Genscher, a 1642 engraving of Fuerth, Germany, Kissinger's birthplace.

The Secretary of State carried his good humor into his farewell news conference at NATO as well. The first questioner wanted to know, "Don't you think that the purchase by the Libyan government of fifteen percent of the major Italian industry, FIAT, could influence in some ways the foreign policy of Italy, which is still a NATO country?"

Kissinger ducked deftly: "In the waning days of my public career,
I dare not take on both the Italian and Libyan public opinion."
And he kept on ducking.

Q: "Mr. Secretary, do you feel that you can still play any role at all in
helping break the deadlock [over Rhodesia] by meeting Mr. Nkomo in
London, or any of the other participants?"

K: "I have no plan to meet Mr. Nkomo . . . I *will not* meet Mr. Nkomo,
because I know that some of the exegetes here will misinterpret the
words that I have 'no plans.' "

Q: "Mr. Secretary, how do you think your policy regarding the Middle
East, or let us say, American policy regarding the Middle East, will
continue after you and with the new administration? Can you give us
a general assessment about the situation as you see it?"

K: "Well, I am sure you know that I am not the spokesman that has been
chosen for the new administration, so I would not want to make
pronouncements about their policies . . ."

Q: "Mr. Secretary, looking back, what do you consider to be your most
satisfying achievements and your greatest disappointments?"

K: "Well, I have told the NATO Council that it is too early to write
obituaries, and having such a distinguished group of people here that
have been analyzing my drawbacks and achievements, with emphasis
on the former, I would not want to interfere with your work."

Q: "Mr. Secretary, what role do you anticipate playing in the Carter
administration in formulating foreign policy?"

K: "I do not anticipate playing any role in the Carter administration in
formulating foreign policy. On January twenty-first I will achieve in-
fallibility and will join all of you in my capacity to analyze problems . . ."

Q: "There has apparently been a leak from you to the Western delegations at the Conference on International Economic Cooperation in
Paris. Could you give us your assessment of the possible damage that
this leak might incur?"

K: "Well, to tell you the truth, I read an extract of that cable in a
newspaper this morning, and it had the sort of bureaucratic obtuseness
which would make it sound as plausibly having been developed in the
Department of State . . . I have been looking for the cable ever since,
so I cannot vouch for its accuracy. In the present state of our capacity
to guard classified information, it is always possible that documents

appear out of context . . . I would not think this particular document should do any significant damage."

Q: "If Spain joins NATO, have you studied what might be the next response of the Soviet Union to this disequilibrium?"

K: "They might ask Albania to join the Warsaw Pact . . ."

Q: "An easy question for you, sir. What kind of advice, as we sit here at NATO today and you prepare to step down, do you have for Cyrus Vance?"

K: "We will take one more question after this one, but since you will all stampede out to report the monumental news that you have been imparted here, I want to take this opportunity to thank you for the relative courtesy with which I have always been treated here and the fairness that you have shown.

"As far as advice for Cyrus Vance is concerned, I wish him well . . . I do not think it would be appropriate for me, however, to give public advice to my successor before I have had an opportunity for full discussions with him . . ."

Dwane Powell, *The News and Observer*, Raleigh

At the end of the news conference, the foreign newsmen gave Kissinger a standing ovation. Later, on the flight out of Brussels, he chided the traveling newsmen: "I notice none of you guys applauded at that news conference." And he was right.

As usual, Kissinger used the NATO meeting as the occasion for a series of bilateral meetings with European foreign ministers, of which he was almost the senior member by now.

Following a breakfast session with Turkish Foreign Minister Ihsan Caglayangil, a reporter asked, "Is it your last breakfast, or are you going to have more in the near future?" Kissinger could barely keep from laughing out loud as he replied, "Well, I am sure I will continue to have breakfast in the years ahead . . . But whether I will have future breakfasts with the minister depends on whether he has breakfast with private people or whether he is so rank-conscious that he only sees ministers."

CAGLAYANGIL: "I invite His Excellency privately. Very soon he will have a new request."

Q: "You are not going to have a kind of, let us say, shuttle diplomacy between Turks and Greeks when you leave office?"

K: "When I leave office, the only shuttle diplomacy I will carry out is between New York and Washington."

Following another breakfast meeting, with Sir Christopher Soames, commissioner of the European Community, he joked, "You see, they take pictures of me like I'm a corpse." Then he added, "Since we are both retiring from public life, we had a good review — philosophically."

SOAMES: "Speak for yourself."

K: "I mean, retiring from our present positions . . ."

SOAMES: "We have had a talk about how far we have traveled in terms of US-EEC relations in the last four years . . . There is a lot yet to do, but I think that when we look back at what the relationship was in seventy-three and the anxieties that were existing in seventy-three or what it could become, that four years later, we can look back with some satisfaction, realizing that there is, of course, as always, a hell of a lot still to be done."

Kissinger broke in: "This is why I never appear with a graduate of the British educational system. They are so much more eloquent than we are."

SOAMES: "And talk so much longer."
KISSINGER: "But say more."

Following a meeting with German Foreign Minister Hans-Dietrich Genscher:

KISSINGER: "The foreign minister and I had our regular meeting in this period. You know we have been working very closely on all issues of common interest, which means almost all world problems . . . I think we had a review of the whole world situation in the spirit of friendship and cooperation that has characterized our entire relationship. We also discussed a possible political future for me in the Federal Republic."
Q: "In Bavaria, Mr. Secretary?"
K: "Why limit it to one state? . . ."
Q: "If you look back on your term in office, can you tell me what you consider to be your greatest success and your greatest failure?"
K: "I don't quite understand your second point . . . I have never answered this question in America. I believe, now, at the end of my term, that the record is there, and each one has to draw his own conclusions."

On the flight back to Washington, Kissinger remained loose and full of good (inside) humor. Somebody pointed out that on this final overseas trip, the Washington *Post* and *Newsweek,* of the regulars, showed no sentimentality (let alone good news judgment) and did not send a correspondent along.

Bernie Kalb of CBS needled him, "The rest of us are here only because we thought Vance was coming."

Kissinger shot back, "Do you notice how Kalb's interest in me is going down daily now that there's no book in me?" And he added, "I'm going to go with CBS and replace both Kalbs."

Another reporter asked, "Was that really your final news conference [in London]?"

Kissinger replied, "I can't have one in Washington. One of you guys will ask me about Barzani's rug." (A columnist had been harassing Kissinger about a rug he allegedly received from General Mustafa Barzani, the head of the Kurdish rebels.)

"Why don't you just give the rug back and have a news conference?" gibed a reporter.

"I don't know where the damned thing is. It's in the White House somewhere."

"What did Genscher give you?"

Kissinger pulled out an old chestnut. "Whatever it was, it was worth forty-nine ninety-five, one of the great bargains of all time."

A reporter persisted, "Are you going to give it to the government?"

"Not until January twenty-first. And I'm not going to give up this plane at all."

And how about television? "I'm not going to go on television for at least a year — unless they put me in a love story context."

Do you think Vance will travel as much as you did? "That depends on who the NSC adviser is." And he laughed maliciously.

And then, on December 12, 1976, there was a historic last: the last time Henry Kissinger walked off a U.S. Air Force jet at the end of an overseas trip as Secretary of State. In his three years and two months in office, Kissinger had gone on forty-one foreign trips to fifty-nine countries, logging well over half a million miles. That's an average of fifteen thousand miles a month.

During all of that travel, people kept asking me, "What is Henry Kissinger really like?"

I told them he is exceptionally brilliant, especially in his ability to analyze complicated situations. In the last two decades, I have come into personal contact with the last five presidents, their secretaries of state, their national security advisers, and with a host of other top-level officials in Washington, and Kissinger outshines them all in sheer intelligence. He is a genuinely witty man. He is publicly charming. He was as open and outspoken in his way as any public official I've ever dealt with, his reputation for duplicity notwithstanding.

At a birthday luncheon given by the traveling press for Kissinger in May 1976 at Claridge's, Lars-Erik Nelson of Reuters, the vice president of the State Department Correspondents' Association, told a fictitious story about Walter Ulbricht, the hard-nosed former President of East Germany. It went as follows:

When Ulbricht was in office, one East German asked another, "What do you think of him?" The second man motioned to his questioner to follow him. They went around a corner, down a block, through an alley, down another street, through a vacant lot. Finally, the second man ducked into a doorway and whispered, "You know, actually, I like him."

Nelson then raised his glass of wine and whispered, "Mr. Secretary, actually, we like you."

Actually, I liked Henry Kissinger.

"GOOTBYE, EFFERYBODY! DER LONE RANGER ISS LEAVING NOW! NO! NO! DON'T THANK ME! PLEASE — NO APPLAUSE! GOOTBYE NOW..."

Pat Oliphant, *Washington Star*—Los Angeles Times Syndicate